Qadhafi's Libya

Qadhafi's Libya

Jonathan Bearman

with a Foreword by Claudia Wright

Zed Books Ltd.
London and New Jersey

Qadhafi's Libya was first published by Zed Books Ltd.,
57 Caledonian Road, London N1 9BU, UK, and
171 First Avenue, Atlantic Highlands,
New Jersey 07716, USA, in 1986.

Cover designed by Adrian Yeeles/Artworkers.
Maps and diagrams by Del & Co., London.
Printed and bound in the UK
by Biddles Ltd., Guildford and King's Lynn.

British Library Cataloguing in Publication Data

Bearman, Jonathan
    Qadhafi's Libya.
    1. Libya—History
    I. Title
    961'.024   DT236

    ISBN 0-86232-433-5
    ISBN 0-86232-434-3 Pbk

Contents

Tables

Figures

Maps

Foreword

by Claudia Wright

There is a fairy tale that American policymakers used to believe during the Eisenhower administration that has been revived among Reagan administration officials. It is a fairy tale about the Arabs and how the U.S. should deal with them.

Once upon a time, according to this story, there were two kinds of Arabs. Good Arabs and Bad Arabs. The Good Arabs were the ones who would do exactly what the United States wanted if Washington gave them rewards. King Faysal II of Iraq was a Good Arab. He received lavish entertainment and attractive companions when he visted New York. The rewards included such things as pretty blonde women, fast cars, speedboats, and jet aircraft. They also included special bodyguards, Swiss bank accounts, Treasury bills, and safehouses scattered around the world. King Idris of Libya was a Good Arab; so was King Saud of Saudi Arabia; Adib Shishakli, the former President of Syria in the 1950s; Nuri Sa'id, the former prime minister of Iraq; Anwar Sadat and Ja'far Numayri. Those Good Arabs are no longer with us, or in Numayri's case, no longer in power. King Husayn of Jordan and King Hassan of Morocco are also Good Arabs, as Washington has defined them.

Now the Bad Arabs are the ones who refuse to do exactly what Washington wants, no matter what rewards they are offered. Jamal 'Abd al-Nasir was a very Bad Arab indeed, and between 1956 and 1960 he was the target of many attempts by the U.S., along with Britain and Israel, to assassinate him or topple him from power; including, of course, the Suez War of 1956. 'Abd al-Nasir was fortunate that he died in his bed from natural causes. Mehdi Ben Barka, the Moroccan socialist leader, was not nearly so lucky; he was kidnapped and murdered in France in 1965; Ahmad Ben Salah, the Tunisian economic minister and union leader, was also a Bad Arab and he was driven into exile in 1971. Hafiz al-Asad is a very Bad Arab, by Washington standards, and the baddest of them all at the moment is Mu'ammar Qadhafi. As this book demonstrates being a Bad Arab not only causes U.S. rewards to dry up; it invites punishments for the Bad Arab country's economy, encouragements to internal opponents, and assassination plots.

What the Good Arab and the Bad Arab share in common among

American policymakers is that, being Arabs, they have an obligation to take orders from Washington. Over the past 40 years the Americans have offered a variety of justifications for this way of thinking about Arabs. They have spoken about the ideological conflict between East and West; they have identified threats of Soviet and communist expansionism in the Arab world; they have treated Arab resources as strategic requirements for the U.S. and its European allies; they have identified Arab territory as military strongpoints for their global defence plans.

Fundamentally, what this has meant is that the Arab world has been treated as too important to the United States and Western interests to allow the Arabs the self-determination, political and economic independence to conduct their affairs by themselves. The region has therefore been an imperial protectorate – first of the Italians, French and British, and now of the Americans – and the Arabs have been wards of the American state.

No one likes a rebellious or ungrateful ward. And no one respects the ward who always has his hand out for a payoff. Accordingly, it is fair to say that American policymakers have never genuinely respected either the Good Arabs or the Bad Arabs. One of the great differences between the thinking of the Eisenhower administration and that of the Reagan administration is that this lack of respect for the Arabs as a race, that was common 30 years ago, has turned into something much more bitter, contemptuous and vicious. For Reagan administration officials hate, detest, spit blood towards Arabs. They are contemptuous of the Good Arabs; they want to kill the Bad Arabs. Who are the officials who hold these views? The senior ranks of the State Department, the Pentagon, the CIA, and the National Security Council.

Their attitude reflects, in part, the influence of the Israelis, who have served all these years as the strategic instrument by which the U.S. keeps its Good and Bad Arabs in line and the Middle East protectorate under control. The Israelis have served the U.S. interest by helping to punish the Bad Arabs, make war on them, assassinate them; and by threatening to do the same to the Good Arabs if they lose favour with Washington.

In part also, the Reagan administration's belief in the Good and Bad Arab stems from the way the Good Arabs have spoken in private about the Bad Arabs, begging the U.S. to do them the favour of liquidating the Bad Arabs once and for all. And finally, this attitude has been reinforced by the violent failures of the Reagan administration policy in the Middle East that have produced more U.S. casualties in the region than at any time since the North African campaigns of World War II. Out of this experience has developed a *racist* mentality in administration thinking that is much sharper and more confrontational than was true of the Eisenhower administration. In those days, the Bad Arab was called a "nationalist", a "radical", or a "communist". Today he or she is called a "fundamentalist" or a "terrorist", a "Muslim" or a "Palestinian". This shift in terms is worth noting. The Arabs very birthplace and religion have become a stigma. Once that happens, it becomes difficult, if not impossible, for U.S. officials to preserve the distinction between the Good Arabs and the Bad ones. It cannot be long before the Good Arabs will be targeted for liquidation, just like the Bad Arabs have been. In this context, the U.S.–Israeli raid on Tunis on 1 October 1985 was the precursor of the confrontation in the Gulf of Sirte with Libya in January 1986, and the bombing raid on Tripoli and Benghazi on 14 April 1986.

In my view, the Reagan administration adopted a policy of liquidation from the very beginning, and the Israeli invasion of Lebanon was just one of the methods this policy had contemplated from the start. Liquidation of the PLO was as much the objective of the Reagan administration's so-called "peace process" and the Reagan Plan of 1 September 1982, as it was the objective of Israeli operations in Lebanon or the recent Tunis, Tripoli and Benghazi raids. Assistant Secretary of State for Near Eastern Affairs Richard Murphy, the think tank experts and the U.S. media, are no less committed to the goals of the liquidationist policy, however squeamish some of them claim to be in public about the methods. But that squeamishness is limited only to the problem of the PLO, Jordan and Israel. They are just as gungho on liquidating Qadhafi and the pro-Syrian factions in Lebanon as the administration and the Israelis have been.

The *Washington Post* disclosure of 3 November 1985, that two months earlier President Reagan had formally approved a CIA plan for a coup d'etat in Libya should have come as no surprise. Nor was it accurate of the *Post* to suggest that in 1984 the CIA decided not to proceed with a similar plan.

The evidence suggests that the CIA initiated a presidentially approved assassination and coup plan as early as May 1981, that if successful would have involved a call for Egyptian military intervention, supported by U.S. forces. When it failed, it was followed in August of that year by U.S. naval manoeuvers in the Gulf of Sirte and the highly publicized shooting down of two Libyan jets. On that occasion President Reagan hinted broadly to reporters that he would like to see Qadhafi overthrown. Since then there have been many reported coup and assassination attempts. In 1984, to take a few examples, The Libyan ambassador to Rome was shot and killed in January; in March two Libyans were executed in Tunisia; in May, a group of anti-Qadhafi exiles were caught trying to infiltrate across the border from Tunisia and reach a second group already armed and ready in Tripoli. It was only after the May plan went awry and was foiled by the Libyans, that the skepticism the *Post* reported was expressed within the CIA. Memories seem short at the agency, however, and enthusiasm infectious. The presidential approval in autumn 1985 represented the second or possibly third attempt to strike Qadhafi in that year, either through the exile groups or disgruntled Libyan military men inside the country.

Following the hijacking of an Egyptair flight to Malta in November 1985, some administration and Egyptian officials and U.S. reporters attempted briefly (and unsuccessfully) to blame Libya for inspiring the hijackers and providing them with their base of operations. This allegation was repeated, with greater effect though no improvement in the standard of evidence, in the aftermath of the airport killings at Rome and Vienna on 27 December 1985. The allegations linking Qadhafi to Abu Nidal, and the so-called Abu Nidal organization to the Italian and Austrian attacks, then became the basis for U.S. military retaliation against Libya; calls by U.S. officials, by U.S. Senator Howard Metzenbaum, and by the U.S. media for Qadhafi's overthrow and assassination; and finally by the implementation of a further round of economic sanctions against Libya. Libya thus joined Iran (and to a more limited extent Kuwait) in having its financial assets in U.S. banks frozen by presidential fiat.

The question that must be asked in the light of all this evidence is not whether U.S. policy is aimed at overthrowing the Libyan government – of that there can be no doubt. But why do U.S. officials persist, despite their manifest failures to date and counterproductive consequences the campaign has had for a variety of U.S. allies, Arab and European, in the region? Confronted with a string of failures to liquidate 'Abd al-Nassir in the late 1950s, even President Eisenhower began to think better of the CIA plots. Why not President Reagan?

1. The Personal Factor

Personal animus towards Qadhafi has been especially strong among a number of Reagan administration officials who came to power in 1981, and who have by and large remained. General Alexander Haig reportedly believed Qadhafi was behind an almost successful assassination attempt against him in Europe, when Haig was Supreme Allied Commander for Europe. Although he was forced out of the State Department in mid-1982, his anti-Libyan adviser and erstwhile specialist on terrorism, Michael Ledeen, stayed on as a consultant to both the State and Defense departments. During the 1980 presidential election campaign, Ledeen used contacts in the Italian military intelligence service (SISMI) to obtain evidence of Billy Carter's connections with Libya; the objective was to aid the Reagan campaign by making President Carter look pro-Arab among Jewish voters. Ledeen is also closely associated with the network of Israel partisans in the administration, including Richard Perle, the assistant secretary of defense, and with Perle's wife, Leslie Barr, an official of the US Customs Service. Ledeen's wife is employed as an aide in the office of Perle's deputy, Stephen Bryen, and Bryen and Mrs. Perle have used their official positions to press for a total U.S. embargo on oil imports from Libya, as well as U.S. exports to Libya. Another official with a personal grudge against Qadhafi is the Director of Central Intelligence William Casey; Casey is believed to have pursued Qadhafi's demise to restore the damage done to CIA morale and credibility by the Libyan business connections of former CIA agents, Edwin Wilson and Frank Terpil.

2. The Arab Factor

In the past, CIA agents have taken their retirement and gone into business with Arab states without stimulating agency assassination plots and schemes of revenge. The Saudis, Jordanians, Egyptians, and Omanis—to name just a few—have retained former CIA station chiefs and agents to assist them in a variety of ways, including the kind of services Wilson and Terpil provided the Libyans. But the anti-Qadhafi campaign has had *Arab support and encouragement*, and this has been important to the CIA after so many plans have failed. Sadat, who launched a brief border war against Libya in 1977, and Numayri who backed the Chadian comeback of Husayn Habré for a similar reason, were probably the strongest Arab proponents of anti-Qadhafi schemes. So too was King Hassan of Morocco until the Oujda Pact of August 1983, the federation agreement between Morocco and Libya, suited his purposes better. In Tunis, factional conflict over the political succession to President Bourguiba has helped polarize the cabinet along alleged pro-Libyan and anti-Libyan lines, made Qadhafi a scapegoat for domestic economic troubles, and reinforced the Tunisian military's demands for U.S. arms. Both the 1984 and 1985 ruptures in Tunisian-Libyan diplomatic relations were exacerbated by U.S. activity in Tunisia aimed at Qadhafi's overthrow.

But personal animus and Arab encouragement would not, by themselves, have been enough to sustain the liquidation policy.

3. The Bureaucratic Factor

Once prepared and launched, operations like those against Qadhafi develop their own momentum and can be difficult to slow down, stop or reverse. It is this bureaucratic momentum that hinders learning what observers might consider the obvious lessons of failure. The U.S. Navy has long sought to challenge the Libyan claim to exclude the Sixth Fleet from the Gulf of Sirte; but the Navy was restrained by U.S.-Libyan negotiations during the Carter administration. The Reagan administration removed this restraint, leading to the Gulf of Sirte shootdown of August 1981. This in turn seemed to be so popular in domestic U.S. opinion, administration officials were encouraged to develop new displays of force against such an easy target. In Chad, once the CIA had become committed to Habré's return to power, it could not easily abandon him when the battle for Chad swung in Goukkouni Oueddei's favour, nor negotiate with Qadhafi for mutual troop withdrawals, as French President Mitterrand did in 1984. At the State Department, the Office for Combatting Terrorism was a relatively insignificant and impotent bureau until the Reagan administration's anti-terrorism rhetoric gave it greater prominence, and U.S. military intervention in Lebanon became the central foreign policy issue in Washington in 1982-83. This office — renamed the Office for Counter-

Terrorism in 1984 — has steadily expanded its power to wield U.S. economic sanctions — against Greece, for example, during the TWA hijacking crisis of June 1985. It would sooner defend the unsuccessful anti-Qadhafi policy than lose the initiative to proponents of an alternative policy. But as far as Libya is concerned, Qadhafi is the rhetorical constant in the Arabs-equal-terrorism equation and there can be no negotiable alternative to that.

4. The Oil Factor

It now seems so long ago. Inflation in oil prices, the cut in Iranian oil output following the Shah's downfall in late 1978, and the apparent shortage of gasoline supplies in the U.S. market during the summer of 1979 were powerful political forces. They did severe damage to the re-election prospects of the Carter administration. But they also acted as a potent restraint on those within the Carter administration who argued for a campaign to topple Qadhafi.

The Reagan administration has been fortunate that imported oil supplies have increased, OPEC's share of world output and U.S. imports has declined, prices have plummeted, and Arab oil has lost its "strategic" value for the time being. The U.S. economy has thus been cushioned against oil price inflation, and Libya has lost its special significance as the principal supplier of low-sulphur crude to the U.S. East Coast. The international oil glut since 1982 has also induced several of the major U.S. oil companies operating in Libya to reduce their investment, cut their liftings, or withdraw from Libya altogether. At the time the Reagan administration introduced its oil embargo on Libya in March 1982, two of the U.S. majors, Exxon and Mobil, were already seeking to leave Libya for their own commercial reasons; Occidental has followed more recently. That left Libya without a major economic constituent to argue the case for alternative policies in Washington. More recently, a group of independent oil refiners — who have aligned themselves organizationally with the Israel lobby in Congress — has sought protection for their high-priced refined products also. The way they have done this has been to take advantage of the anti-terrorism powers that were legislated in the aftermath of the TWA and "Achille Lauro" hijackings of 1985. The oil factor has allowed U.S. failures in the policy against Libya to be cost-free in U.S. economic terms. And no U.S. economic interest has been threatened by the prospect of that policy succeeding.

Many Arabs believe that Libya is so marginal to the Arab world as a whole or to the main directions of Arab politics, that nothing that happens there is of much consequence. Some resent Qadhafi's claim to an Arab leadership role; others are angered by his alliances and tactics; some are frustrated by his rejectionism.

Notwithstanding, the ease with which U.S. policymakers have been able to pursue a policy of liquidation against Qadhafi has encouraged the

Reagan administration to adopt a liquidation policy in the case of the Lebanese, the Palestinians, and what remains of the front-line resistance to Israeli expansion. The personal factor, the Arab factor, the bureaucratic factor and the oil factor all applied to the Lebanon war between 1982 and 1984 — it is no coincidence that the only other reported case of President Reagan's approval of an assassination plan, reported by the *Washington Post* in May 1985, involved Lebanese Muslim targets. So long as these factors prevail, no Arab who is a target of the Israelis can count on U.S. protection or support.

In these circumstances it is increasingly difficult to sort fact from proaganda, politics from demonology in understanding Libya, its people, and the historical and Arab context in which Qadhafi has pursued his goals. For that understanding Jon Bearman's book is essential.

Washington

Introduction

No contemporary political leader has generated as great a furore as Muammar Qadhafi. In the 17 years since he led the overthrow of the British-backed Sanussi monarchy he has evoked the extremes of passion: supreme adoration from his following, bitter contempt from his opponents. To political leaders in the West, especially the United States, he appears an eccentric bogeyman, a byword for subversion and terrorism. Ronald Reagan has surpassed himself in the language of condemnation, successively calling Qadhafi 'the most dangerous man in the world', 'barbaric', 'flaky', and the 'mad dog of the Middle East'. His Secretary of State George Shultz, architect of current US strategy against Libya, has declared: 'We have to put Qadhafi in his box and close the lid.' Chester Crocker, Assistant-Secretary of State for Africa, has claimed that Qadhafi is 'probably the most potent and disastrous source of destabilisation in Africa.' By his own words Qadhafi is the leader of a world revolutionary movement and has pledged his country's resources to a fight against US designs on Africa and the Middle East.

Libya under Qadhafi has attracted controversy and conflict. The Reagan administration has singled out Qadhafi's Libya, a country of 3.4 million people, to symbolise the threat to the interests of the United States, just as Kennedy focussed on Castro's Cuba or Nixon on Allende's Chile. To bring the current Libyan leadership to its knees, the administration has imposed full diplomatic sanctions and a comprehensive trade embargo, has supported a Contra-style army of exiles and encouraged regional allies to invade, and has itself resorted to a policy of military confrontation. Twice since President Reagan's inauguration in January 1981 the armed forces of Libya and the United states have clashed in the disputed Gulf of Sirte; on many more occasions the two sides have come close to an outbreak of hostilities. The US bombing of Tripoli and Benghazi on 15 April 1986 was only the latest in a long line of actions designed to precipitate Qadhafi's downfall. At the same time, this undoubtedly marks a dramatic escalation of the conflict between the Libyan and American leaderships. The United States' policy towards Libya has entered an aggressive and militaristic phase, bringing back to the streets of several European cities, including London, demonstrations reminiscent of those against the earlier United

States' intervention in Vietnam.

This book is about the society at the centre of the storm. It has been prompted by the dearth of serious literature concerning contemporary Libya, and by the author's disagreement with most conventional analyses of the country's modern development. Overused and misused terms, like 'terrorist state' and 'Muslim fundamentalism', are here given no currency. The book is written from a standpoint antagonistic to the more superficial accounts of Qadhafi's Libya, especially those which sensationalize certain actions of the Libyan state, including the exercise of violence, without offering an explanation of their origins and purposes. By putting events and policies in context, showing they have a material basis, the book tries to provide a fresh perspective on the country's recent history.

A key theme within the following study is the transformation of Libyan society. The book contends that Libya has, in the years of Qadhafi's leadership, undergone a profound social revolution. The various stages of this revolution are traced—through the downfall of the monarchy, the post-colonial and agrarian reforms, the nationalisation of the oil companies, the conflict with merchant capitalism, the overthrow of the traditional religious authorities, the expropriation of private industry, and the state take-over of wholesale and retail distribution. The book seeks to identify the forces of change, put the role of Qadhafi in context, assess the importance and impact of oil in the development of the Libyan state, and explain the relationship between the transformation of the state and the upheavals within Libyan society.

Special attention is paid to the changing function of ideology within Libya. Qadhafi's Third Universal Theory and *Green Book,* frequently dismissed as naive and confused, are shown to have practical relevance within a society riven by tribal allegiances. Qadhafi's hostility to 'representative democracy', expressed at length in the *Green Book*, is linked with the political leadership's drive to create a unified state and prevent tribal and religious affiliations undermining state political institutions. His ideological struggle with the tribal élites is explored in detail; his doctrinal dispute with the Libyan *ulema*, particularly over the questions of private property and wage labour, is similarly dissected. Qadhafi's shift from an anti-communist outlook to an anti-capitalist perspective is not viewed purely as an expedient response to changing foreign alliances; the book stresses the contribution of internal factors to his ideological evolution.

Whilst the book argues that Libya is socially revolutionary, it does not conclude that it is a socialist society. The book pinpoints the weaknesses and contradictions within the process of transformation: the constraints on democracy within political institutions, the lack of democracy and political maturity within the Revolutionary Committee Movement, the limitations on workplace committees and labour organisations, and the pervasive control of the state security apparatus. Through careful analyses of these features of social organisation, the book faults Qadhafi's claim to have instigated a form of popular democracy, namely 'the Authority of the

People'. The book maintains that Libya has moved towards a post-capitalist society, but doubts whether the 'non-capitalist' form of development chosen by the leadership can result in a transition to socialist development.

One criticism that might be levelled at the book is its emphasis on changes and divisions within the leadership. In response, it must be said that tensions and shifts within the highly centralised Libyan political system do acquire a degree of importance not present in political systems with a greater devolution of power. Given the crucial, and all-embracing character of state policy, a study of the Libyan Revolution requires an historical breakdown of developments within the country's political hierarchy. Whilst lack of dependable information has occasionally made it difficult to highpoint the making of decisions, it has been possible to show the influences bearing on the leadership, and reveal the consequences of policy formulation and implementation. Much of the apparent volatility and turbulence within the Libyan state is attributed to the concentration of power in the leadership. Disagreements between the leading personalities can, and have, triggered off conflicts between different social interests and personal followings. The Libyan state has yet to find an adequate method of diffusing and settling political differences.

During the preparation of the manuscript I drew on a huge variety of sources. Four types were particularly important: official Libyan publications; 'technicist' and developmentalist writings on the economy; miscellaneous papers on social anthropology and aspects of Libyan history; and my own personal observations, conversations, and journalistic contributions, which now stretch back a number of years. In my treatment of all the available material, but especially of the pro- and anti-Qadhafi literature, I have of necessity been cautious. It has been my intention to produce an independent and accurate study of contemporary Libya; of course, I alone am responsible for any errors or misrepresentations which may occur.

There is one other disclaimer I feel I have a duty to add. I have not, during the period of work on the manuscript, received any funding from any official or unofficial Libyan source. Nor am I affiliated to any organisation linked with the Libyan state, or to opposition organisations. Whilst I am personally critical of United States policy towards Libya, I do not, by any means, endorse the actions of the Libyan leadership.

Jonathan Bearman
London

Acknowledgements

A number of people have been indispensable to the publication of this book. In particular, I am deeply indebted to Louis Eaks, Managing Director of the Main Event Ltd, former political consultants to the Libyan People's Bureau in London. The book could not have been produced without the knowledge and contacts I gained working as a journalist attached to the Main Event, or the office facilities and archive material I continued to receive free of charge from the company thereafter.

Among the others whom I must thank are: Professor John Davis of Kent University, who gave up his valuable time to answer my questions about tribal structures in Libya; Terisa Turner, Fellow of Columbia University, for stimuating discussions about the nature of the Libyan state; Mr Giuma Said, Director of the Libyan news agency, JANA; Mrs Eleni Cubbitt, wife of the late James Cubitt, architect of Gar Younis University, Benghazi; and Robert Stephens, former Middle East correspondent of *The Observer*. I would also like to thank Robert Molteno and Mike Pallis of Zed Books for their enthusiasm, patience and understanding that the project would take longer than I ever imagined.

The book is dedicated to Sheila Duckenfield, whose love has sustained me throughout.

Jonathan Bearman

POST REVOLUTIONARY ADMINISTRATIVE DIVISIONS OF LIBYA

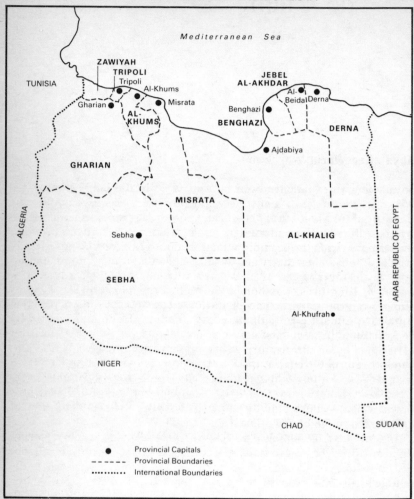

1   The Client State

Libya after World War Two

Libya was granted independence by the United Nations on 24 December 1951, after more than eight years of temporary British and French administration, imposed after the surrender of the Italian colonial governate in 1943. Formally designated the United Kingdom of Libya, the new state was from the beginning an anomalous political configuration. It possessed both an hereditary monarchy and a federal constitution, uniting three distinct provinces of Cyrenaica, Fezzan and Tripolitania. The sovereign, King Idris, was nominally a constitutional monarch, head of state in a representative democracy with limited male suffrage; in practice, he was a spiritual leader with autocratic temporal powers. Patronised by the British and United States governments, his internal authority rested on his leadership of the Sanussi Order, a Sufi offshoot of Sunni Islam, preponderant in Cyrenaica, the Fezzan and parts of Northern Chad. He was at the same time a dynastic ruler, with rights of patronage and decree, and Grand Sanussi, mystical leader, or supreme guide of a religious confraternity, whose family claimed descent from the Prophet Mohammed's daughter, Fatima.

This duality of monarchical power was fundamental to the development of the independent Libyan state. The constitution, approved on 7 October 1951, provided for a system of parliamentary democracy, symbolic of the country's subordination to the democracies of the West. The Sanussi Order, in contrast, was a local institution with pre-capitalist origins, which in Cyrenaica retained its own functioning apparatus of administration, jurisdiction and tax-collection, as well as, most significantly, its own military formation: the Cyrenaican Defence Force, CYDEF. Idris, as *sheikh* of the *Sanussiya*, exercised control over the Order through the institution of the *qaimakaan*, or governate; eight of these, located at al-Bayar, Ajdabiya, Aujela, Jalo, Jughbub, Khulaf, Kufra, Merawa and Takness, existed within Cyrenaica.[1] Whilst there were brethren living outside these areas, Sanussi organisation in 1951 did not extend beyond the borders of the province of Cyrenaica, to Fezzan or Tripolitania. In the period after the Second World War, the Sanussi Order did not have the organisational

1

strength to enforce a unitary state structure on Libya; the compromise solution was federalism.

The federal nature of the constitution accorded with a strong regional diversity, arising historically from an extremely uneven distribution of population. Libya was a vast country of 679,358 square miles, the equivalent of one-third of the United States, but 94.57 per cent of this was desert. No permanent rivers exist, just seasonal watercourses, or *wadis*. With the exception of arid mountain ranges in the far south and south-west along the country's borders, the altitude of the land does not rise above 600 metres. The population was concentrated in only three main areas which had proved capable of sustaining some permanent agriculture. These were the north-western Jefara Plain and Jebel Nafusah, and the north-eastern Jebel Akhdar upland, the only areas of rain-fed cultivation; and, away from the Mediterranean coast, an interrelated group of oases in the Fezzan Depression. Over several hundred years, the population in these areas, separated by large distances, had acquired their own distinct social organisations. Even in antiquity these basic regional variations obtained. The Greek geographer, Strabo, compared Libya to a leopard whose spots were isolated settlements of people.[2]

In his day, the first century A.D., Libya was the Greek term for much of North Africa. Since then the frontiers have shifted on several occasions, usually inwards. At the time of its modern independence, Libya inherited the longest North African coastline of any state and borders with six African countries. The longest, and the most strategically important, were those with Egypt to the east, and Chad to the south. In addition, there were frontiers with Tunisia in the north-west, Algeria in the west, Niger in the south-west, and Sudan in the south-east. As a result the country has always had some strategic significance arising from its propinquity to other areas of more intrinsic value, namely the Mediterranean and Egypt. Throughout its history it was held by a succession of different powers, but their control was invariably impermanent. The various polities which arose on the shores of this part of Africa, including Greek Cyrene and the three Roman towns of Leptis Magna, Oea and Sabrata (from which Tripoli, or *Tripolis*, on the site of Oea, is derived) were linked with the Mediterranean, not the Libyan interior. The hinterland, the preserve of pastoral nomads, was a distinct and separate entity. Not until the 1930s, with the studies of Professor Ardito Desio of Turin University, was the geography of the interior recorded. The contours of modern Libya, therefore, did not emerge from a process of outward expansion, or internal integration, but were constructed as a by-product of European encirclement of the surrounding African territories.

Until the advent of the aeroplane the country's internal communications depended on the uneven distribution of oases. In between were large inhospitable areas of sand-sea, rocky desert, or lava flows which rendered travel difficult. Only three routes intersected the country on an east-west axis: from Ajdabiya on the coast of Cyrenaica, through the oases of Aujela and Jalo, to Jawf in the Kufra oases; from Tripoli, via the Jufra oases, to the Brak oasis, the Sebha oases and the Murzuq oases, and beyond to Bilma in Niger; and lastly from Tripoli via the Yefren oasis in the Jebel Nafusah, the oasis of Ghadamis, to the oasis of Ghat. As for routes from north to south, there were only two: from the Jalo oases to the Jufra oases; and from Kufra via Tazerbu to Murzuq and the Fezzan Depression. In addition, however, both the Jebel Nafusah and the Jebel Akhdar uplands were traversed by tracks joining up several villages, where much of the population was concentrated.

In 1950, the indigenous population of this barren land was estimated at about 1,053,240.[3] The majority consisted of Libyan Arabs, but there were minorities of varying strengths—Berbers (including Tuaregs); Tebu; Turks (including Circassians); and *sephardi*, or oriental, Jews numbering about 8,000. In addition, there was a non-indigenous population of 47,100 Italian settlers and a smaller number of Greek immigrants.[4] Between these ethnic sections of the population inter-marriage was virtually unknown, but the Libyan Arab population did contain a substantial admixture of black Sub-Saharan stock, notably of Sudanese origin in Cyrenaica and West African in Tripolitania. This was the most permanent legacy of the traffic in slaves, which did not altogether cease until the 1920s. Former slaves in fact, through inter-marriage, formed a distinct, though not homogeneous, section of the population.

Despite this ethnic diversity, there were two main mechanisms of integration with Libyan society. The first was the Arabic language; the second, historically associated with Arabic, was Islam. Both had initially come to Libya with the conquests of Amir Ibn al-Aasi, the Arab governor of Egypt. Between 643 and 647 A.D. his Arab armies ousted the Byzantines from control of the Libyan coast, but failed to subjugate the Zenata Berbers of the interior. The Arab and Islamic character of Libya was only fully established with the invasions of the nomadic tribesmen of the Bani Sulayim and the Bani Hilal in the eleventh century. The Bani Sulayim, especially, settled in Libya, subjecting the existing population, including Berbers, to the status of tribal vassals. The very complete assimilation of Arabic and Islam which has since occurred, in comparison with Arab countries with historically more settled populations, remains a distinguishing characteristic of Libyan society.

Another major characteristic, assisting this process of assimilation, was the permanently low density of population. Even in 1950, Libya possessed one of the lowest population densities in Africa: just 1.5 persons a square mile. No census was conducted until 1954, but it is possible to estimate the population distribution in 1951. The urban population, concentrated in the small cities of the northern coast, probably did not exceed 21 per cent.[5] Following the defeat of the Italian colonial authorities in the Second World War, there had been a trend towards urbanisation, but the nomadic and semi-sedentary sections of the population, who migrated constantly on the periphery of the areas of settled agriculture, still constituted a substantial

17 and 12 per cent respectively.[6] And in some areas the nomadic population was actually larger than other sections of the population. In the Jebel Nafusah district of Gharian they substantially outnumbered both the urban and sedentary agricultural populations; in al-Beida in the Jebel Akhdar they were larger than either of these groups; and in Cyrenaica, taken as a whole, they were 45 per cent of the total population, vastly greater than the urban or sedentary populations of the province.[7]

By contrast, when the population distribution of Tripolitania and Fezzan provinces are taken into account, the largest section of the population overall, about 51 per cent, were sedentary agriculturalists, not pastoral nomads or urban dwellers. These agriculturalists were situated predominantly in the Jefara Plain. Table 1.1 shows the distribution of the population in the newly constituted Libyan state at the end of its first decade.

Table 1.1 Distribution of Urban, Rural and Nomadic Populations by District *(muhafadha)* in 1963

Muhafadha	Urban		Rural		Nomadic		Total
	No.	%	No.	%	No.	%	No.
Zawia	5,500	7.1	138,500	21.6	16,000	5.2	160,000
Tripoli	270,000	52	102,500	16.0	18,000	5.0	390,000
Khums	5,000	7	72,000	11.2	57,500	18.6	134,500
Misrata	23,000	4.4	92,400	14.5	30,500	9.9	145,900
Gharian	15,500	0.3	9,200	14.4	51,500	16.7	76,700
Sebha	11,000	2.1	32,000	4.6	4,000	1.3	47,000
Ubari	—	—	26,400	4.1	4,100	1.3	30,000
Benghazi	140,000	27.0	49,700	7.8	65,500	21.2	255,200
Beida	16,200	3.1	24,500	3.8	30,300	9.8	71,000
Derna	33,000	6.3	13,000	2.0	31,000	10.9	77,000
Total	*519,200*	*100.0*	*560,200*	*100.0*	*308,400*	*100.0*	*1,387,800*

Source: M. Alwar, 'Urbanisation in Libya—Present State and Future Prospects', in Joffe & McLachlan (eds.), *Social and Economic Development of Libya,* 1981.

A further aspect of the country's demographic structure, complicating this urban-rural-nomadic breakdown, is the geographic concentration of different ethnic groups. The rural and nomadic inhabitants of the interior consisted primarily of Libyan Arab, Berber and Tebu stock. Their distribution, since they made up the majority of the total population, underlay and accentuated the regional variations. In Cyrenaica the population was predominantly Arab, with some black admixture, but there was a small number of Tebu who migrated between Kufra and the Tebesti mountains. In Tripolitania and Fezzan the Arab population of the interior was less dominant: the Jebel Nafusah was traditionally an area of high Berber concentration, though Berbers had spread out over other parts of Tripolitania, in the direction of Sirte for example. In addition, in the Jebel Nafusah village of Qassabat the majority of the inhabitants were sephardi Jews. Finally, in the Fezzan there were significant minorities of Berber Tuareg, located along the frontier with Algeria and Niger, and of migratory Tebu in the border area with Chad, besides an Arab population in the oases of the Depression. In stark contrast, the urban centres of the Libyan coastline had people not from the interior, but the Mediterranean. These included Greeks, Italians, Turks and (in Tripoli) Jews; but even the majority Arab population tended to have migrated from other Arab lands rather than the rural areas of Libya.

Between the coastal towns and the interior relations were always minimal. The Italian colonial settlement of land in the Jefara Plain, Jebel Nafusah and Jebel Akhdar in the 1920s and '30s did not change this although agricultural enclaves developed around the urban centres in these areas and the local population was forced further out. There were therefore two modes of existence: coastal and interior. The urban centres on the sea retained their character as commercial entities built on trade in the Mediterranean. Whilst no accurate figures for their populations have been produced, it is apparent the largest towns were Tripoli, Benghazi, Derna, Misrata and Ajdabiya, which grew disproportionately with the beginning of urbanisation in the late 1940s. The 1954 census shows the relative size of these towns (see Table 1.2).

Table 1.2   Libya's Urban Population, 1954

	No.	*%*
Tripolitanian towns (exluding Tripoli)	608,610	56.0
Fezzan towns	53,315	4.9
Cyrenaican towns (excluding Benghazi)	221,518	20.4
Tripoli	129,728	11.9
Benghazi	69,728	6.4
Derna	15,891	1.5
Ajdabiya	16,336	1.5
Tobruk	4,995	0.5
Beida	2,500	0.2
Barca	9,992	0.9
Total	*1,088,873*	*100.0*

Source: M. Alwar, 'Urbanisation in Libya—Present State and Future Prospects', in Jaffe and McLachlan (eds.) *Social and Economic Development of Libya,* 1981.

As for the economy, capitalist relations of production were confined to the coastal strip in the north-west and north-east. Furthermore, they were associated with one particular section of the population, the Italian settlers. In 1951 there was a small Libyan working class, consisting of dock and transport workers, hotel and catering staff; but it was only a fraction of the total urban population. The majority of urban-dwellers were merchants, administrators and artisans. Even within the working class minority most full-time wage-earners were of Italian extraction; indeed the first trade unions were founded by Italians. Prior to the Second World War, the Italian authorities had employed numbers of Libyan seasonal workers; for example, during the construction of the coastal road in 1937 a daily average of 12,000 Libyans were employed for every 1,000 Italians.[8] Following the defeat of the Italians in the War, these public works programmes ended and the demand for seasonal, casual labour ceased—with most Libyans reverting to sedentary agriculture or pastoralism. In 1951 the only manufacturing industries of importance were those attached to the estates of the settlers, such as olive pressing and tobacco, but these too had undergone a decline since the War.

With the end of direct Italian control there occurred a major outflow of Italian settlers, particularly from Cyrenaica, which had borne the brunt of the fighting. The provisional British administration stepped in with grants, notably to mitigate the loss of the metropolitan agricultural market, but this policy was curtailed in the late 1940s. Consequently, many agricultural settlers, particularly tenants on the larger estates, were forced to leave the former colony. The agricultural settler population in 1951 was probably no more than three-quarters of its 1940 figure of 38,000. Ironically for an agricultural colony, the majority of settlers were concentrated in the urban areas. Estates on peripheral land, around the Jefara Plain and the Jebel Akhdar, were abandoned. Many began to revert to pre-colonial forms of non-mechanised subsistence farming as the indigenous population, pushed off the land by the colonists in the 1920s and '30s, reclaimed their traditional lands. The Italian colonial period was remarkable in that the social structure of the indigenous population, whilst disrupted by war and colonisation, remained extremely resilient.

Tribal Forms of Association

The predominant form of social organisation in Libya was the tribe. As a structure of related kinship groups united by common lineage, the tribe was an institution of collective responsibility. Relations between individuals were determined by tribal affiliation. Bound by the complex laws of *Amara Dam,* the code of 'bloodwealth', it was incumbent on members of a tribe to avenge collectively the wrongs inflicted on one of their number by another tribe's members. Blood feuding, associated with transgressions of the code, was a familiar feature of Libyan society, perpetuated by the inequalities in status and power that existed between different tribes. Especially in a society with scarce resources, these issues of privilege and rank, both within and between tribes, were of extreme importance. Tribes—and their different kinship groups—were ranked by descent. There were the 'free tribes' and the vassal tribes: nine 'free tribes', tracing their ancestry to the Hilalian Princess Saadi and the rest, Marabtin tribes, reduced to vassal status by the 11th century conquests of the Bani Hilal and Bani Sulayim.

The basis of tribal society was collective ownership of land. Social resources were distributed within the framework of the tribes' corporate ownership of land, through a complex network of patron-client relations secured by marriages arranged by the senior members of a kinship group. For instance, in Tripolitania a male member of one kinship group has the right of access to the resources of his mother's natal group; whilst in Cyrenaica, where there is greater pressure on land, a male member of a particular kinship group can gain similar access to the resources of his mother's kinship unit, but only by grace, not by right. For the male members of a group, the authority to influence and negotiate such marriages constituted an important power—alliances through marriage being one of the few ways wealth in society was transferred. Until independence, there was no individual land ownership among the population of the interior, a kinship group merely had the right to use tribal land.[9]

In the areas of sedentary agriculture a form of share-cropping prevailed on such usufruct lands. A client kin group, whilst owning the basic means of production, would work the land of a patron kin group, which was usually transhumant and which extracted rent in the form of tribute. This tribute varied from place to place: in the oases of Fezzan and Cyrenaica it tended to consist of dates; in the Jefara Plain, where relations of production took the form of *sahab*, they included fixed quotas of wheat, barley, olive oil or wool.[10] In exchange, the patron tribal unit undertook to protect the share-cropping land against competitors. The system, which bound succeeding generations to servitude, could even take a personal form of obligation to deliver certain services. In the elections under Idris the client or vassal group was required to support the candidates of the landowning group.

The division of labour which arose on the basis of share-cropping was not incompatible with tribal organisation. Within the structure of a tribal unit it was possible for many different specialisations to co-exist. Until it died in the 1920s, the trans-Saharan trade was a significant factor promoting differentiation within the tribes' corporate framework. Firstly, the provision of an armed escort, guaranteeing the security of the caravan's cargo, was a vital pre-condition for the growth and prosperity of the trade. Secondly, the traders required food and lodging at the oases along the route. The collection of tolls from merchants was another organisational necessity performed by the tribal leaders. Finally, the most powerful tribal families themselves participated in the trans-Saharan trade. Consequently, the conditions existed for the formation of social classes, including a peasantry tied to serfdom, and a merchant class. Yet, despite these differentiations, it must be emphasised that the main forms of appropriation were collective in character.

Historically, the two most productive forms of collective tribal appropriation were the pillaging and tolling of caravan traders. Tribal leaders—sheikhs—and religious notables—imams—naturally dominated the distribution of the surplus which accrued from these sources. Since the extent of the surplus depended on the domination of territory, local alliances, known as *sufuf*, were formed between the leaders of different tribes, whose land corresponded with the intersection of the caravan routes.[11] Always hostage to the vagaries of the transit trade, the alliances varied in strength and composition. Moreover, as a structure of vested interests, they survived the collapse of the desert traffic. The most important alliances were the Warghamma confederation which dominated the route along the Jefara Plain between Zuwara and Gabes in Tunisia; Tuareg groups operating along the routes in the far west of the country; the Aulad Suleyman tribal confederation, particularly the Saif al-Nasser family, who controlled the road through Central Fezzan to Tripoli; and the Cyrenaican tribes aligned within the Sanussi Order, whose success depended on their superior institutions.

The Sanussi Order was an Islamic Sufi missionary fraternity who taught a doctrine of ascetic existence and renounced later additions to the essential teachings of Islam. The Order prohibited all forms of luxury, including the consumption of alcohol, the practice of smoking and adornment with jewels and gold; it also forbade social intercourse with those not of the Islamic faith, including Jews and Christians. The founder of the Order, Sidi Mohammed Ben Ali as-Sanussi, was born near Mastaghanem in Algeria in 1787, into the Berber family of Awlad Sidi Yusef. Having studied under the theologian Sidi Ahmed Ibn Idris al-Fasi, head of the al-Khadria fraternity, he began the Sanussi Order in Yemen in 1837. The first *zawiya*, a missionary college sometimes called a monastery, was built at Jebel Abu Qubays, many of the brotherhood coming from the former al-Khadria fraternity which had been dissolved on the death of Idris al-Fasi. The first African *zawiya* was constructed at al-Beida in the Jebel Akhdar in 1843. Cyrenaica, like the Arabian Peninsula, was under the nominal authority of the Ottoman Empire, but conditions in this remote part of North Africa were much more conducive to the expansion of an ascetic Sufi order.

The successful spread of the Order in Cyrenaica depended on the conversion of the Zuwaya tribe, specialists in the trans-Saharan trade, whose influence stretched southwards into Ouaddai in Central Chad. Sidi Idris came into contact with their leaders both in al-Beida and in Mecca while on pilgrimage. Following his decision to excommunicate the Ottoman Sultan for religious heresy, he moved his headquarters much closer to Zuwaya territory in the interior. In 1856 he used his following of freed slaves to build a mother house for the Order at the isolated, mosquito-infested oasis of Jughbub on the edge of the Great Libyan sand-sea. There he received a deputation of Zuwaya, headed by Sheikh Abdul Karim Helayig, who paid allegiance to the fraternity. The hostility of other Cyrenaican tribes to the Zuwayas (not a Saadian tribe) proved an initial obstacle to the further growth of the Order's adherents, but the Sanussi, as the anthropologist Evans-Pritchard remarked, aimed for a form of 'externality' from the tribes, which enabled them to consolidate their position in relation to the other tribal forces of the region.[12]

The *zawiya* became an institution which permitted the Sanussi Order to transcend tribal divisions. Whilst ostensibly religious in function, the *zawiya* was also an instrument of conciliation and mediation between the tribes. The location of the *zawiyas* accorded with the distribution of tribal lands, but the staff were brethren, trained at Jughbub, and chosen on the grounds that they were not affiliated to local kinship groups and could, therefore, as religious personalities act as intermediaries. At the peak of Sanussi power, under Mohammed al-Mahdi, who succeeded Sidi Mohammed on his death in 1859, the *zawiyas* had become the key regulatory mechanism within tribal society in Cyrenaica and beyond. The traveller, Rosita Forbes, commented: 'His *zawiyas* were neutral meeting places where difficulties—tribal, commercial, legal or religious—could be settled by an unbiased authority. His *ekhwan* were judges as well as missionaries. They defined tribal areas, settled water and grazing rights, as well as meting out the justice of the Koran to those who infringed the code of Islam.[13]

In the transformation of the Sanussis into a major mercantile force in the Sahara, the role of the *zawiya* was fundamental. Sanussi trading power did not, as has been suggested, develop because of the switch in the trans-Saharan trade from the Fezzan oases to the Kufra oases in Cyrenaica. Rather, using the *zawiyas*, the Sanussi fraternity created the conditions for the diversion of the trade from the medieval Fezzan route so that the Kufra oases became the hub of a regional trading network. The caravanserai took advantage of the relative security and organisation provided by the *zawiyas*, including armed escorts and safe lodgings which extended three days' hospitality free to any traveller. The conversion to Islam of tribes beyond the frontiers of Libya, even as far afield as Senegambia, was another factor underpinning the Sanussi trading empire. Of particular significance was the Sultan of Ouaddai who, following his acceptance of Sanussism, entrusted his northern-bound caravans of slaves and gold to the protection of the Ikhwan.

In return for these services the Order required traders to pay customs dues on entering the territory under the control of Sanussi tribes. On the basis of this tribute they built up an independent mercantile empire. Its frontiers ranged along the southern edges of the Sahara Desert, from the Air massif in Niger to Darfur Province in Sudan, and taking in most of Chad north of the Nigerian border. In 1882, when Mohammed al-Mahdi's minority ended, the brethren of the Order were estimated at between

1,500,000 and 3,000,000 strong.[14] Whilst nominally subjects of the Ottoman Empire, the Order operated independently of the Sultan's local administration. The Order in fact bargained with it on behalf of the tribes of the interior and the Ottomans were forced to reach an accommodation with the Sanussis, in which the Order collected the tithes required by Constantinople, settled tribal disputes and defended the southern borders of the Sultan's provinces from attack. The local Turkish authorities in Benghazi were very dependent on successful collaboration with the fraternity, having little power to enforce their own authority within the province.

Gradually, with the surge of European imperialism towards the end of the nineteenth century, external forces began to impinge on this local autonomy of the Sanussi Order who found it increasingly difficult to resist integration into the world capitalist market. First the British, established in Egypt, set up the Frontier Districts Administration to control the areas bordering on Cyrenaica. Then the French, in the process of colonising much of West Africa, threatened the source of the trade south of the Sahara. Mohammed al-Mahdi, moving his headquarters to Kufra, tried belatedly to rally the tribes of the Sahara against the French advance in Chad, but battles with French expeditionary forces at Zugiba in 1901 and Bir Allahi in 1902 put paid to the Sanussis' mercantile empire, so beginning a rapid process of decline which climaxed in the Italian invasion of Libya in 1911. The Sanussi dynasty was eventually reduced to the position of a client of the British administration in Cairo. In 1918 Mohammed Idris, the second son of Sidi Mohammed, entered a formal, subordinate relationship with the British-Egyptian authorities which was eventually to put him, as a candidate of the British, on the road to the throne of independent Libya in 1951.

The Colonial Period

Until the Italian colonisation in the 20th Century, Libya was constituted of separate *vilayets* of the Ottoman Empire. The Sultanate in Constantinople, as the 'defender of the faith', had assumed sovereignty over the territory in 1551 in response to the threat of attacks against Muslim commercial centres in North Africa by the Sicilian Normans and the Knights of St. John. The main relevance of this sovereignty for the local population, whose leading merchant families supported the move, was the introduction of the Ottoman system of taxation. Political authority, despite Ottoman administrative apparatuses in Tripoli and Benghazi, was nominal. The local leadership enjoyed virtual autonomy from Constantinople. Between 1711 and 1835 power in Tripolitania was retained and exercised independently by the Qaramanlis family of Berber and Janissary descent, who ruled in collaboration with tribal leaders and strongmen, extending their nominal authority into the Fezzan.

In 1835, the Qaramanlis dynasty was overthrown by the Ottoman army on the instructions of the Sultan. Following the French seizure of Algiers and the virtual independence achieved by Mohammed Ali Pasha in Egypt, the Porte decided to pre-empt further loss of Empire, and therefore revenues, by asserting direct control over its Libyan provinces. For the next 40 years, the Ottoman administration struggled to prevent European penetration of the interior trade and to centralise customs, excise and taxation. In 1836, just after the arrival of the first-appointed Pasha, a force of 160 troops was despatched to collect taxes from Aujela in Cyrenaica; in 1842 the Turkish army successfully defeated the Awlad Suleyman tribes, with its major trading interests in the Fezzan; in 1843 they occupied the important border oases of Ghadamis,[15] and thus the Ottomans ensured a monopoly of commerce and trade. Despite the victories of General Ahmed Pasha, however, the costs of maintaining centralised authority proved exorbitant and by the 1870s the Ottoman administration was forced to concede autonomy to the tribes of the interior, relying on collaboration with local strongmen rather than military enforcement to secure tax revenues.

The nature of Ottoman oppression of the Libyan inhabitants was quite different to that resulting from Italian colonisation. The Libyan provinces were denied political independence, but there was no suppression of language or religion. The Ottoman administration encountered resistance from the tribes of the interior, but direct control from Constantinople was supported by leading merchant families resident in the urban centres of the coast. Furthermore, there was active participation within the framework of the Ottoman administration; the Libyan population was not excluded from posts within either the judiciary or the administration. The Committee of Union and Progress, the force behind the 'Young Turk' revolution of 1908, acquired a significant following among the merchant and professional families of Tripolitania. The Italian colonisation gained limited support from some disaffected merchant families who opposed the Young Turk revolution (such as the Muntassers of Misrata) but differed in so far as it was the consequence of European imperialist expansion and involved extreme forms of national and racial oppression.

The Italian decision to colonise the Ottoman's last North African possessions was occasioned by growing domestic and external pressures. Since the turn of the century Italian nationalist circles had waged a jingoistic campaign for settlement of the Libyan North African coast. In 1911, a group of nationalists inaugurated a new weekly entitled *L'Idea Nazionale*, in which the take-over of the Ottoman Libyan provinces was fervently promoted. That same year one Gualtiero Castellini reported in *L'Idea Nazionale* that Cyrenaica was 'a little Eden' where 'almost all the European plants grow, but above all the olive, the date and the vine'.[16] According to the poet, Giovani Pascoli, Libya was uncultivated only because of the 'inertia of the nomadic and slothful population.'[17] Italian enterprise, he argued, would transform Libya into a land 'abundant with water and crops and green with trees'. The journalist Bevione, who carried out his research from a ship, boasted that the indigenous population would welcome the Italians as liberators and sell agricultural land 'for a few lira per hectare'.[18]

Motivating these right-wing groups was Italy's sense of inferiority vis-à-vis the acquisition of colonies by Britain and France. Their confused propaganda, which portrayed a fertile Libya, was largely an attempt to generate support for the idea of relieving Southern Italy of its surplus agricultural population by a programme of settlement in Libya. During the last days of Ottoman control, the numbers of Italian citizens resident in Tripoli had begun to grow. An experimental Italian colony already existed in Tunis; and in 1913, with the Ottoman authorities' permission, the Bank of Rome (which had established a Tripoli branch in the late 19th Century) entered into a series of land-purchase negotiations. From 1907, as the bank's commercial interests grew, local deposits had increased dramatically.

More specifically related to the moment of colonial conquest were strategic considerations. By the beginning of the 20th Century, most of the territory adjoining the provinces of Libya had fallen to Britain or France. If the Italian state failed to secure control of Libya, the signs were that some other European imperialist power would extend hegemony over the last North African possession in Ottoman hands. In July 1911 the German government had despatched a warship, the *Panther*, to the Moroccan port of Agadir with the intention of pressing France to compensate Germany for loss of colonial influence elsewhere in Africa. The German objective was the French Congo, but the Italians feared that the Ottoman provinces in Libya could become vulnerable. Germany, because of its alliance with Constantinople, seemed capable of penetrating North Africa and gaining a foothold with the help of the Sultan. Growing German interest was already indicated by the Rolfs' scientific expedition to Cyrenaica, sponsored by Kaiser Wilhelm in 1879. Conversely, Rome felt that France, having secured former Ottoman territory in Chad and Niger, might try to pre-empt a German move by seizing Tripolitania. The installation of any rival imperialist power on a part of the North African coast in close proximity was deemed a threat to Italy's dominant position in the central Mediterranean.

In September 1911, whilst the Agadir crisis was in progress, the government in Rome delivered an ultimatum to the Ottoman Porte. The Constantinople authorities were informed of the Kingdom of Italy's intention to extend Italian jurisdiction over the Ottoman provinces in North Africa. If the Porte refused to relinquish sovereignty, Italy would apply force. The *casus belli* cited was the hostility of the local administration to Italian commercial interests and land-purchasing activities. The Ottoman authorities protested and announced the Empire's determination to resist; but on 3 October, despite the prospect of conflict, Italy mounted a sea-borne invasion and Italian troops landed at Tripoli, Benghazi, Derna, Tobruk and Khums. Sporadic fighting with Ottoman armed forces broke out almost immediately. The Ottoman garrison in

Tripolitania decided not to capitulate, but to wage a war of resistance. The garrison commanders, including General Ishaq Pasha, withdrew from Tripoli and established a camp south of the capital, at Azzizya, from where they planned a counter-attack, supported by the local people.[19]

The urban-based local leaderships along the coast reacted with confusion. A number of important merchant families, such as the Muntassers of Misrata and the Ben Zikris of Tripoli, favoured conciliation and collaboration with the invaders; other provincial leaders, notably those with strong tribal associations in the hinterland, urged support for the Ottoman garrison. Two important figures sympathetic to the Young Turks, Farhat Bey, a judge from Zawiyah, and Suleyman al-Baruni, a leader of the Ibadi Berbers, both representatives in the Ottoman Parliament, toured the province calling for volunteers to join the Ottoman forces.[20] Thanks largely to these, and similar efforts, the Italians' advance was restricted: but in 1912 the Porte, facing imminent rebellion in the Balkans, decided to extricate itself from Libya. Thus, in November 1912, in Lausanne, Switzerland, the Ottoman authorities reached an agreement conceding sovereignty to the Libyan provinces. The Ottoman forces were pulled out and the local Libyan leadership, left to its own devices, convened in conference at Azzizya. The same positions of conciliation emerged, but deprived of the Ottoman garrison those favouring resistance declared a truce.

The Italians took advantage of the collapse in the armed resistance to proceed with agricultural settlement. Two surveys were prepared under the appointed Italian governor on the particular form land settlement should take. The first of these, the Bertolini Commission report of 1912, proposed a system of private land settlement called *libertist*; the second, the Franchetti Commission of 1913 argued for a state programme of land settlement, called the *statalisti*, in which peasant families were established on small landholdings.[21] The colonial authorities adopted aspects of both approaches, but in the period following the take-over the *libertisti* strategy predominated. In July 1914, the colonial authorities permitted settlement by colonists from Tripoli and Tunis of some 43 landholdings (totalling 1,329 hectares) on some of the 14,070 hectares around Tripoli previously held in tenure by the Ottoman administration. The first landholders were recommended to accept the formula of *colonizazzione associata*, in which local Libyan labour was to be employed. Most evidence, however, indicates that very few of the indigenous people were prepared to accept such terms.

Further agricultural settlement was disrupted by the outbreak of a major revolt coinciding with the duration of the First World War. The rebellion began in April 1915 with the mutiny of Libyan troops under Italian command at Qasr Bu Hadi, and sparked off an uprising throughout Tripolitania. By the time Italy entered into the First World War on the side of Britain and France, colonial control had been whittled down to Tripoli, Benghazi, Khums and a few other locations on the coast. Furthermore, the leader of the Qasr Bu Hadi revolt, Ramadan al-Suwayhili began consolidating his position with the support of Ottoman and German military advisers who had entered the country.[22] Suwayhili's home town, Misrata, became a German submarine base, and the centre of an administration which supervised its own tax collection and military recruitment; it even possessed its own arms factory and printed its own currency. A similar form of local autonomy, though less elaborate, was established under Suleyman al-Baruni in the Jebel al-Gharb, a western outcrop of the Jebel Nafusah. Finally, after the war, with President Woodrow Wilson's declaration of support for the self-determination of nations, a Tripolitanian Republic was founded—the first republic in the Arab world—with its capital of Azzizya. No government recognised the republic, but at Khallet al-Zaytuna, near Tripoli, the Italians agreed to grant the local Libyan administration some independent powers.

In Cyrenaica the circumstances of the colonial occupation were quite different. The Italian authorities had neither inaugurated serious landholding nor brought the interior under control. The Sanussis continued to retain their autonomy despite the coastal administration. After the beginning of the Great War they received overtures from the Ottoman Empire for solidarity action against the British forces in Egypt. Ottoman advisers entered Cyrenaica and, manipulating pan-Islamic sentiments, tried to secure a military alliance with the Sanussi leadership. The Grand Sanussi, Ahmed al-Sherif as-Sanussi, responded by committing his *mujaheddin* forces, estimated at 30,000, to the Ottoman side, a decision which isolated him within the Sanussi leadership. In the face of a military confrontation with the British-Egyptian forces, he was compelled to abdicate, transferring his authority to his cousin, Idris, who had already established contact with the British in Cairo at the outset of the War. In 1916 Idris sent a contingent of *mujaheddin* under another cousin, Safi al-Din, to impose Sanussi authority over the population under the control of the Misrata pro-Ottoman administration, but his forces were defeated by those of Ramadan al-Suwayhili at Bani Walid.[23] Nevertheless, in return for the favourable stance of Idris, the British interceded with the Italians on behalf of the Sanussi, winning them autonomy in Cyrenaica in the Akramah accord of April 1917. The Italians recognised Idris as the hereditary Amir of the interior.

The post-war stand-off between the Italian colonists and the indigenous power was comparatively shortlived. In 1922, the Fascist Premier of Italy, Benito Mussolini, resumed the process of colonial expansion and settlement in Libya. Armed forces, despatched to Libya, embarked on a military campaign to destroy the various local autonomous groups, and secure the country for peasant agricultural production. In July 1922, preceding their advance, the newly-appointed Fascist governor, Count Volpe of Misrata, himself the owner of a large estate, issued a decree confiscating all uncultivated land, the result of which was to deprive nomadic kinship groups of vital grazing land. In April 1923, in a second blow against the livelihood of the local population, Volpe expropriated lands belonging to rebels and their sympathisers. If the sheikh of a particular tribe opposed the Fascist administration's policies, his entire kinship group's traditional corporately-owned land would be seized by the Italian administration.

The Sanussi Order in Cyrenaica, however, proved more difficult to suppress. The Italian army, including units drawn from Eritrea, encountered sustained resistance in the Jebel Akhdar uplands. *Mujaheddin* under the command of Omar al-Mukhtar, an elderly sheikh, conducted a protracted guerrilla war in the uplands for some ten years. Finally, the Italian commander, Field Marshal Rodolfo Graziani, succeeded in eliminating the popular opposition through a policy of 'total war', involving the internment of the desert nomads of Cyrenaica in concentration camps and erecting a 300 km barbed-wire fence and minefield along the frontier with Egypt. The oases of the interior were patrolled by aircraft and armoured columns; the *mujaheddin* carried light carbines and rode into battle on horseback. The outcome of the struggle was inevitable.

According to the current Libyan authorities, about half the indigenous population, or some 750,000 people, died in the Italian conquest. Most evidence suggests this figure is exaggerated. In 1911, according to Ottoman estimates, the indigenous population numbered 826,000; given the country's slow birth rate, it was unlikely to have been 1.5 million when the Italian offensive commenced. What is beyond doubt is that the Libyan population was displaced and decimated. One English source claimed that the Italians executed 12,000 Cyrenaicans annually.[24] Commenting on the representation of the Italian commander in Tripoli, a German visitor, Von Gotberg, observed: 'No army meted out such vile and inhumane treatment as the Italian army in Tripoli. General Kanaiva has shown contempt for every international law, regarding lives as worthless.'[25]

In April 1922, at the start of the Fascist offensive, local resistance leaders in Tripolitania, hard pressed by Italian forces, offered Idris recognition as Amir of all Libya. Fearing that acceptance would provoke the Italians, the Grand Sanussi fled to Cairo, where he nurtured his relationship with the British, leaving Sanussi tribal leaders to defend Cyrenaica. By 1931, nine years after his departure, desert resistance was virtually broken. In March 1930 the Italians had completed the conquest of the Fezzan; in January 1931 Kufra, the Sanussi headquarters, fell to a combined air and ground assault: and finally, in September 1931, Omar al-Mukhtar was captured and summarily executed at Soluq, signalling the demise of the Libyan resistance. In January 1932, Field Marshal Pietro Badoglio, the Fascist governor of a militarily united Libya, officially declared hostilities at an end.

With Libyan resistance eliminated, the programme of Italian colonial settlement was intensified. In 1928, having consolidated control of the coastal areas, Mussolini launched a policy of 'demographic colonisation' with the aim of relocating unemployed Italian agricultural labour on landholdings in Libya. The first phase of the policy consisted of the construction of basic infrastructures to create the general conditions for settlement; the result was a huge, typically Fascist, public works programme of road laying, port construction, housing, public buildings and land reclamation. In June 1932, a parastatal organisation, the *Ente per la Colonizzazione della Cirenaica*, was assigned responsibility for building villages consisting of farms ready for allocation to peasant families. Following the unification of Tripolitania and Cyrenaica in 1934, the organisation became the *Ente per la Colonizzazione della Libya*, empowered to conduct similar development throughout the country.[26] Even small manufacturing companies, related to agricultural production, were established. In 1931 1,000 hectares of land in the Berber area of Gharian, nationalised by the Fascist authorities, were used to create a major tobacco industry in Libya. Land between Misrata and Zliten, and Tripoli and Azzizya, became settlement zones, reserved for land-grants to colonist families. The indigenous population, driven off their historic lands, was reduced to the role of a reserve army of labour; nevertheless available Libyan manpower was considerably under-employed.

It was not until after 1936 that substantial immigration of peasant families began. Previously, settlement was limited to small numbers of families mortgaging state land in the vicinity of Tripoli and Misrata. Many of these were distributed through a semi-governmental organisation, the *Instituto Nazionale Fascista per la Sociale*, financed from funds allocated for the unemployed. The shift towards mass settlement after 1936 is associated with the formation of specific colonisation companies which, acting as agents of the state, assumed control over the settlement of newly developing lands; the state, in contrast, concentrated on the settlement of formerly reclaimed lands.[27] Between the two types of settlement were important differences. Through the companies, tenancies were awarded to peasant families on the basis of three forms of graduated occupation: sharecropping, métayage and mortgage. Through the direct state land grants there were just two forms of tenancy: sharecropping and mortgage. According to the 1937 agricultural census, in Tripolitania 1,606 families (6,665 people) were established on 1,289 state land grants, and 392 families (2,332 people) on colonisation company landholdings. Table 1.3 provides a sectoral breakdown of the agricultural settler population in 1940.

Statehood Without Sovereignty

Libya emerged from the second World War appallingly devastated. During the fighting between the allied and axis powers in North Africa, Cyrenaica was overrun three times and finally occupied by the British Eighth Army in November 1942. Tobruk received a severe pounding; Benghazi endured more than 1,000 air raids. As a consequence of

Table 1.3 Agricultural Settler Population by Sector, 1940

Type of Colonisation by region	Number of Farms	Colonist population	
		Families	No. of people
Tripolitania:			
State land grants and private property	1,322	1,877	8,213
Colonisation Companies*	2,353	1,878	15,308
Total:	*3,675*	*3,755*	*23,521*
Cyrenaica:			
State land grants and private property	264	466	1,524
Colonisation Companies	1,813	1,740	13,490
Total	*2,077*	*2,206*	*15,014*
Total Libya	*5,752*	*5,961*	*38,535*

*Includes the Azienda Tabacchi Italiana (ATI).

Source: G.L. Fowler, 'The Role of Private Estates and Development Companies in the Italian Agricultural Colonisation of Libya', in Joffe and McLachlan (eds.), *Social and Economic Development of Libya,* 1981.

successive military operations, wells were blocked up and buildings razed to the ground. The country was (and still remains) littered with the relics of thousands of landmines and anti-personnel devices, which rendered farming in Cyrenaica a hazardous experience. According to a paper presented by the Institute of Diplomatic Studies to the Geneva-based seminar on 'War Remnants in Libya', in May 1981, 68 per cent of agricultural land was mined.[28] In addition, grazing cattle belonging to nomadic herders were seized in military foraging raids.

At the outbreak of the war between Britain and Germany, the Sanussi leadership, with the encouragement of the British, convened a conference of emigré leaders in Alexandria. Representatives from Tripolitania agreed to concede the leadership of a Libyan resistance to Idris, conditional upon his acceptance of the guidance of a joint advisory committee. Idris agreed with this compromise formula—which increased his bargaining position with the British—but continued to conduct clandestine negotiations with the Cairo-based British administration. These soon became a focus of dissension, particularly after Italy entered the war in June 1940. The Tripolitanian leaders, who believed the axis powers would win, objected to Idris's decision to co-operate with the British without a specific pledge on Libyan independence. The work of the Joint Advisory Committee, intended to smooth out differences, soon broke down under the strain of factional quarrelling between regional representatives. In the event, the

Sanussis accepted wartime collaboration with the British on their own, in the hope that if victorious, the allies would treat them favourably.

The allied victory, completed in January 1943, thus placed Idris in a much stronger diplomatic position than the Tripolitanian leaders. Whilst he signally failed to obtain a clear-cut pledge on Libyan independence, he did succeed in obtaining a British commitment to end Italian rule in Cyrenaica. In answer to a question in parliament on 8th January 1942, the British Foreign Secretary, Sir Anthony Eden, made the following announcement:

I take this opportunity to express the warm appreciation of His Majesty's government for the contribution which Sayyid Idris al Sanusi and his followers have made and are making to the British war effort. We welcome their association with His Majesty's forces in defeating the common enemies. His Majesty's government is determined at the end of the war the Sanussis of Cyrenaica will in no circumstances again fall under Italian domination.[29]

Idris did not hesitate to organise an army to fight alongside the British without having obtained a pledge of Libyan independence. Unlike that of Tripolitania's leaders full independence was not his main objective. In conversations with British officials in Cairo during the war, Idris proposed the formation of a British protectorate, similar to Transjordan and the Amirates in the Gulf, such as Kuwait and the Trucial states. He believed British protection and assistance were indispensable. On 27 August 1940, he wrote to Colonel Bromilow, the British officer assigned responsibility for the Sanussi military force, proposing these minimum conditions.[30]

1. Great Britain to grant Libyans internal independence;
2. Libya to have its own government headed by a Muslim Emir acceptable to the British government.
3. Great Britain to hold the protectorate over Libya and direct the organisation of its financial and military affairs until it reached a higher, social and cultural level.

Idris was evidently making a bid for the political leadership of all Libya. Yet only in Cyrenaica did the basis for a reasonably defined post-war settlement exist. Elsewhere, the prospects were confused and the British were remarkably non-specific. Tripolitania received no clear British pledge, not even a rejection of continued Italian colonialism. In the Fezzan the situation was again different: whilst Cyrenaica and Tripolitania were put under provisional British military administration, Fezzan was occupied by Free French forces commanded by General Leclerc. The French commenced their march on Italian Libya from their base at Fort Lamy in Chad the previous year, and by January 1943 and succeeded in reaching as far north as Ghadamis in Tripolitania—further than was initially intended in an agreement between the Free French and the British General Alexander. The French military administration ruled in collaboration with the local Saif al-Nasser family, but France showed no inclination to grant local independence for the Fezzan, which was regarded as vital for the security of French Algeria and West Africa.

After the cessation of hostilities in Cyrenaica, declared by General Montgomery in December 1942, the emigré Sanussi leaders began to return to their country. Divisions soon appeared between the younger generation of Sanussi exiles and the older tribal sheikhs and confederation officials. The younger emigrés, who had spent years of Italian occupation in Egypt, had been influenced by Arab nationalism. As members of the British Sanussi Force, one group of emigrés, led by Assad Bin Umran, formed the Omar al-Mukhtar Sporting Society. Ostensibly non-political, intended for recreation only, the Society was in fact a forum for discussing post-war solutions for Libya. In April 1943 the society was formally reconstituted in Benghazi as the Omar Mukhtar Club. The Club engaged in cultural activities, but it also became the focus for Arab nationalists, attracting an important following among the sons of tribal families in Benghazi and Derna. Their nationalism neither conflicted with nor superseded, their tribal loyalty, but it did become the source of antagonism with the British military administration established at Ajdabiya. Whilst demanding the immediate recognition of Idris was Amir of Cyrenaica, the group, which underwent a process of radicalisation, called for unification with Egypt. In September 1946 the British chief administrator, E.A.V. de Candole, concerned about the Club's activities, banned its newspaper, *al-Watan*.

The upsurge in nationalism in Tripolitania, whilst more intense than in Cyrenaica, suffered from confusion and factionalism. Lacking the unified structure provided by the apparatus of Sanussism, the various emigré leaders returning from Damascus or Istanbul founded their own parties, or factions, advocating different post-war solutions for Tripolitania among their own tribal supporters. These groups frequently degenerated into vehicles of local interest, vying with rivals for the patronage of the British provisional administration in Tripoli. The failure of a tribal leader to secure a post in the temporary administration was enough to create local opposition to the British. The diverse parties offered alternative solutions to the future status of Tripolitania, whether as a British protectorate or unified with Cyrenaica under Idris. They were united by one major concern: that Tripolitania should not revert to Italy. In 1946, the threat that the British would reimpose Italian rule as part of a post-war settlement was sufficient to bring about an alliance of the most important elements to form the United National Front under the leadership of Selim Muntasser, a member of the region's most eminent merchant family, and the Mufti of Tripoli, Mohammed Abu al-Isad al-Alim. The Front proposed unity and independence for Libya under the Sanussis as the only practical alternative to Italian colonialism.

The prospect of restored Italian rule, in the form of a trusteeship, could not be easily dismissed. Even in Cyrenaica, where the numbers of Italian settlers had fallen dramatically, tribal notables feared that the British might renege on their wartime pledge. In July 1946 Saadi tribal chiefs, anxious about the unresolved deliberations of the British, met in conference at al-Baida and issued a manifesto calling on Whitehall to fulfil its commitment to the Sanussis. Idris himself, in order to strengthen his position, assumed the leadership of a National Front, organised by the leaders of the confraternity in Cyrenaica. On 9 August 1946, the seventh anniversary of the Sanussi Force's inauguration, Idris told a gathering at Municipality Square in Benghazi: 'I have found that the leading tribal chiefs have been thinking of forming a National Front representing all the elements in the country [I have approved of] this organisation, for it will support me in achieving the country's aspirations and lighten the burden of my efforts . . .'[31]

The Front was inaugurated specifically to coincide with the British government's long-delayed decision to send a War Office Working Party, chaired by Lt. Col. Sir Bernard Reilley, to report on the situation in Cyrenaica and make recommendations regarding the province's future. The Party visited the territory towards the end of 1946 and its report, submitted in January 1947, proposed that Cyrenaica receive independence in three consecutive stages:[32]

1. The British military administration to remain for a short time.
2. The establishment of an Arab state under British trusteeship. Adequate financial assistance should be given for not less than ten years, including the rendering of administrative training and promoting educational and technical development.
3. The establishment of a fully independent state. During the second and third stages, Cyrenaica might be connected with Tripolitania in a unified Libya, as the creation of such a state is consistent with the specific recommendations for Cyrenaica. A treaty of alliance with a major power is also recommended.

Despite the recommendations of the Reilly Report, the British government continued to prevaricate, and the question of Libya provoked minor dissension between the foreign ministers of the Big Four. Any British initiative required the unanimous approval of Great Britain, France, the United States and the Soviet Union. The British Foreign Secretary, Ernest Bevin, was pressured by France, which strove to retain control of the Fezzan, and petitioned by Italy for the return of the Libyan colonies. Even after the Italian peace treaty of 1947, in which Rome formally dropped claims to sovereignty, the Italian government sought British support for exercising some sort of trusteeship, in Tripolitania at least. Both the United States and the Soviet Union had objections to any form of European protectorate. The British government, no less frustrated than the Sanussis, by the persistent delay, finally agreed to transfer a decision to the United Nations, where no more than a two-thirds majority was needed.

Shortly before this hand-over to the UN, the British authorities did attempt to set the terms for a favourable settlement. In Cyrenaica, the provisional military administration permitted, if not actively encouraged, the formation by the Sanussi leadership of a National Congress which, meeting at the Manar Palace, Benghazi, on 1 June 1949, proclaimed Idris hereditary Amir. Responding to the decision of the Congress, composed of unelected tribal leaders and notables, de Candole stated: 'The British government recognises the Amir, the freely chosen leader of his people, as the head of the Cyrenaican government.'[33] Furthermore, on 16 September, the Chief Administrator, on behalf of the British government, issued the so-called Transitional Powers Proclamation, which empowered Idris to formulate a constitution for the self-government of Cyrenaica, within the context of a British trusteeship.

In Tripolitania Britain's unilateral action encountered greater resistance. The Foreign Office, influenced by the local dependence of the temporary administration on the Italian settlers, acceded to Rome's demand for a trusteeship over the territory. In May 1949, the British Foreign Secretary concluded an agreement with the Italian Foreign Minister, proposing separate trusteeships for Italy in Tripolitania, for Britain in Cyrenaica and for France in the Fezzan. This proposal, whilst transgressing the clauses of the Italian peace treaty, was referred to the United Nations for approval.

Almost immediately, news of the British-Italian scheme galvanised indigenous public opinion in Tripolitania. On 14 May 1949 the leaders of the major Libyan opposition forces met in Tripoli to co-ordinate their response. They included the United National Front, the Nationalist Party, which claimed a 15,000-strong membership, and an organisation called the Libyan Liberation Committee. The meeting decided on the formation of a Tripolitanian National Congress, under the leadership of Bashir al-Sadawi, a former adviser to King Abdul Azziz Ibn Saud. Having resigned his post in 1946, Sadawi had founded the Libyan Liberation Committee in Cairo in March 1947. Under his leadership (and tacitly backed by the Arab League) the Tripolitanian National Congress inaugurated a campaign of civil disobedience. Tripolitanian towns were swept by strikes and demonstrations against the proposal for Italian trusteeship, and these continued on a near daily basis until 17 May, when the UN voted out the British-Italian agreement.

The protests were but a minor factor in the UN's rejection of the agreement; more important was the role of the United States. The Truman administration objected strongly to the attempt of the European powers to divide Libya into separate spheres of influence. Following the allied victory in the North African campaign, the United States had established a key airbase, its first and most strategic in Africa, at Wheelus Field just outside Tripoli. If the British and French proceeded with their plan for UN-sponsored trusteeships, this facility, central to military domination of the Mediterranean, would become subject to a Soviet veto in the UN Security Council. As Henry Villard, the State Department official then responsible for the former Italian colonies, has explained: 'It may be worth noting that if Libya had passed under any form of United Nations' trusteeship, it would have been impossible for the territory to play a part in the defence arrangements of the Free World.'[34]

The Americans preferred the solution of an independent Libyan state. They calculated that if the country were granted political sovereignty, it would be better placed to serve their interests. In the words of Villard: 'As an independent entity, Libya could freely enter into treaties or arrangements with the Western powers looking towards the defence of the Mediterranean and North Africa.' The British and French, under intense pressure, were reluctantly forced into compliance. In fact, the United States had presented them with a *fait accompli*. When the United Nations' Fourth Session opened in September 1949, the United States, which enjoyed majority support in the General Assembly, backed the formula of an independent Libya. On 12 November, the UN First Committee adopted a draft resolution proposing, 'That Libya, comprising Tripolitania, Cyrenaica and the Fezzan, shall be constituted an independent and sovereign state.'[35] The deadline for independence was set at not later than 1 January 1952, and the responsibility for supervising the transition from the British and French provisional administration was entrusted to a UN Commission, chaired by a Dutch diplomat, Dr Adrian Pelt, deputy General Secretary of the UN.

Commissioner Pelt's task was not easy. Several factors threatened a successful transition to independence. The indigenous population had no experience of unified self-government; Libya lacked the administrative expertise, for the machinery of government was dependent on the British and French. The country, moreover, was bankrupt. Libya was one of the most impoverished countries in the world; *per capita* income, estimated at £35 per annum, was the lowest in the Middle East. Malnutrition was widespread and the majority of the inhabitants were illiterate. As an American economist, who visited Libya during this transition period, reported: 'The standard of housing is extremely low; a large per cent of the population lives in caves, lacking furniture and the simplest conveniences. Clothing is made out of home grown wool. The poor are clad in rags and walk barefoot, even during the fairly cold winters.'[36]

The country's two major exports were esparto grass, originally planted by the Ottomans for its use in paper-making, and the scrap metal retrieved from the battlefields of the Second World War. Neither brought very much income, certainly not enough to offset post-war imports. Pelt linked the future economic viability of Libya with the development of the Italian agricultural sector which he described as Libya's 'greatest asset'. Yet the agricultural sector was sustained only by the intervention of the post-war British administration. Even during the pre-war period, the sector had operated in deficit, dependent on subsidies from Italy; prospects for the sector after independence were bleak. In his *First Annual Report*, Pelt wrote: 'The Arab population of Libya stands in need of as much financial and technical assistance as the United Nations can supply.'

The formulation of a constitution was complicated by the factionalism endemic in Libyan society. According to the terms of the UN General Assembly resolution on independence, one of the UN Commission's objectives was the 'election and convening of the Libyan National Assembly during the fall of 1950'. But the majority of local leaders, especially tribal sheikhs, disapproved of electoral practices which they perceived as threatening their powers of patronage. Through a complex process of consultation, Pelt finally succeeded in establishing a Preparatory Committee which agreed on the formation of an Assembly, in which the provinces were afforded equal representation, with Cyrenaicans chosen by Amir Idris, Fezzanese appointed by the Chief of the Fezzan, Ahmed Saif al-Nasser, and Tripolitanians selected by the Mufti of Tripoli. The designation of Amir Idris and Ahmed Saif al-Nasser aroused little controversy, but in Tripolitania the National Congress Party of Bashir al-Sadawi, unhappy with the Mufti's selection, relinquished its support for the practice of nomination and called for elections on a more or less proportional basis. Invoking the UN resolution, Sadawi demanded the invalidation of the appointed body; however, his position was weakened by the disunity of the Tripolitanian parties. The smaller, rival Istiqlal Party, gambling on Sanussi patronage, came out in support of federalism and the monarchy.

Equal representation of the provinces in the Assembly virtually ensured the creation of a constitution that was both monarchist and federal. Whilst the National Congress Party favoured a unitary state, the Fezzan and Cyrenaican leadership rejected any system bound to reflect Tripolitania's demographic superiority. Both provinces had made it abundantly clear that they would accept unification only if the provinces, whatever their respective populations, were guaranteed equality under the constitution. On the basis of federalism, the Cyrenaicans, supported by the Saif al-Nasser family, could deny Tripolitania its natural tendency to dominate the country politically. The powers exercised by Idris as monarch were seen as another check on the influences, including the growth of nationalist and republican feeling, which emanated from the political organisations in Tripolitania. The Tripolitanians, whose ambition was a unified state, had to accept a merger on Cyrenaican terms. Only the radicals of the Omar al-Mukhtar Club shared the view expressed by the National Congress Party.

Following the proclamation of the monarchical and federal systems on 2 November 1950, the National Assembly formed a committee to draft a formal constitution for the new Libyan kingdom. Fundamental disagreement arose between the representatives of Cyrenaica and Tripolitania over the balance of power. Whilst the National Congress Party sought to minimise the monarch's constitutional privileges, the Sanussis, supported by the Fezzanese Awlad Suleyman, strove to restrict the role of a federal assembly. Again their combined strength ensured that the Congress Party was defeated. Pressed by the British and Americans, as well as the UN, the Sanussi leadership reluctantly conceded limited male suffrage to a lower chamber of a federal assembly in a draft law specifying one deputy for every 20,000 males. This compromise was, however, offset by the formation of a Senate with equal representation for the provinces, and major royal prerogatives which meant that Idris could override the legislature. Under the constitution Idris acquired legislative powers of decree and royal assent, which he could withhold, and retained the right to appoint the federal government and senior officials. When the country attained formal independence in December 1951, its political formation was neither a parliamentary democracy, nor a constitutional monarchy; in fact the designation 'monarchical dictatorship' was more accurate.

Effective power was exercised by the King, via the mechanism of the palace cabinet, namely the royal *diwan*, composed of a *chef de cabinet*, two deputies and senior advisers, including the Head of the Royal Household, the *Nazir al-Khasser*. The *diwan*, whilst working in consultation with the federal government, determined the policies of the Libyan state. Whilst the monarch was formally vested with constitutional powers, his internal authority rested on his power-base among the Sanussi tribes. The most important of these were located in the Jebel Akhdar uplands: the Barassa, al-Awagir, al-Darisa, Abadat, and al-Hassa tribes. The Barassa in particular had extensive and influential connections, linking officials in the provincial government and the Sanussi Force, which later became the Cyrenaican Defence Force. They were also intermarried with the Shalhi family, traditional retainers of the post of *Nazir al-Khasser*. Outside Cyrenaica, the monarch depended on alliances and bargaining with other influential tribal figures, particularly Ahmed Saif al-Nasser in the Fezzan, as well as the leading merchant families of Tripolitania.

The provinces jealously guarded their own local self-government. Whilst the constitution established a uniform judicial system, the provinces retained their separate law enforcement agencies. The federal police, largely a token force, was restricted to inter-state affairs. Nominally, the monarch's control relied on the appointment of a *wali*, or governor, and members of an executive council, but his choice of candidates was invariably constrained by local political factors. The provinces possessed their own legislative assembly which, according to the province, was composed of varying mixtures of elected and non-elected representatives. Only in the Fezzan were they all elected. The *wali*, on behalf of the monarch, had no power to veto legislation, merely to refer or delay it. Given the sectarian nature of Libyan society, obtaining posts within the bureaucracy depended on kinship relations.

Without the aid of the Western powers, it is doubtful if Idris could have established a Libyan state apparatus. He was, from the beginning, dependent on the financial subventions received from the British and Americans, notably the British-backed Libyan Public Development and Stabilisation Agency. At independence, the Agency, besides disbursing £500,000, paid off the budget deficits of Cyrenaica and Tripolitania.[37] The French meanwhile made similar financial provision in the Fezzan.

Supervision of the country's economy lay with western, or international, aid and development agencies which, in the initial post-independence period, operated under the auspices of the country's creditors.[38] The Libyan Public Development and Stabilisation Agency was in fact managed by directors drawn from donor states, chiefly Great Britain: furthermore, in the early period, the agency was entitled to exercise a veto over Libya's annual economic plan. After 1955, projects financed by the United States were overseen by a Libyan-American Reconstruction Committee. In 1951, the British hold was accentuated by Libya's admission to the sterling area.

It was not only the economy which was subject to external control. Much of Libyan infrastructure, including transport and communications, operated with technicians and advisers on loan from Britain or the United States; for example, the RAF initially supervised Idris airport near Tripoli. Labour was organised by a labour bureau, set up and managed by the British following the defeat of the Italian authorities.[39] In addition, sections of the state apparatus were created by the foreign powers. The British helped with the formation of the Cyrenaica Defence Force and the Tripolitanian Police Force. The United States later assisted with the development of a Libyan airforce, and the British loaned instructors and provided training for a national army and navy. The first Libyan trade unions, or labour organisations, formed after the Second World War, were advised, if not founded, by Italians. Libya was in fact an extreme instance of a dependent client state, exogenously formed by imperialist powers for their own strategic advantage.

The heavy dependence on Western aid and technical assistance compelled the regime to sign a number of 'unequal treaties' guaranteeing the country's subordination to Western foreign policy. In 1953, after two years of negotiations, Idris concluded a 20-year treaty with Britain permitting British forces the use of several facilities, including the al-Adem airbase, the naval station at Tobruk, and exercise grounds for the Tenth Armoured Brigade. In return, Libya received an annual subsidy of £3,250,000 and a British pledge to defend the country's territorial integrity from outside attack. This was followed in 1954 by a similar treaty with the United States, which guaranteed US military forces the use of Wheelus Field for 20 years, in exchange for an annual subsidy of $2 million. France, the third most important donor, was permitted air and surface transit rights to pursue insurgents from Algeria. The rentals the government received from these agreements on bases were vital components of the country's national income. Moreover, the levels of foreign aid and assistance were clearly tied to the retention of the bases.

The 1956 Accord with Italy was perhaps the most humiliating of the unequal treaties the regime was obliged to conclude. Under the terms of the agreement, the Italian settler community received special privileges that no other section of the population enjoyed. In particular, the treaty maintained that no claim, even on the part of individuals, can be advanced in respect of properties of Italian citizens in Libya, by reasons of acts by the government or the lapsed Italian administration of Libya, that occurred before the constitution of the Libyan state. The Libyan government consequently guarantees Italian citizens owning property in Libya, in respect of Libyan law, the free and just exercise of their rights.[40]

Despite the fact that most Italian property had been expropriated by the Fascist authorities from collective tribal lands, the regime felt that there was no alternative other than to legitimise the Italian land seizures. The settler agricultural sector remained the key to economic viability, and in the towns, the Italians dominated much of the commercial and business life. The federal government, in order to stem the outflow of settlers from the country after the war, accepted the advice of the aid agencies, which stressed the need to restore the settlers' confidence, or expect the continued decline of the agricultural base.

Notes

1. See Rosita Forbes, *The Secret of the Sahara: Kufara* (Penguin edition, London 1937), which has a useful appendix on the history of the Sanussi. Page 267 outlines the *qaimakaan* apparatus, which included a *qadi*, or judge and the *Mahkama Sharia*, religious court, the *Mudir Amwal*, head of a financial department, a treasurer, clerk, and a *Mamur Tahsil*, or tax-collector. The tax of *onshur*, or tenth part, was levied on palms and livestock.
2. Strabo. *Geographia*, vol. XVII, no. 3. The name Libya is said to derive from a tribe of Berbers who came into contact with Greek traders.
3. Ghanem, Shukri. 'The Libyan Economy Before Independence'. in G. Joffe and K.S. McLachlan (eds.) *Social and Economic Development of Libya* (Menas Socio-Economic Studies, London, 1982).
4. Ibid.
5. Alwar, Mohammed. 'Urbanisation in Libya' in Joffe and McLachlan (eds.) 1982.
6. Author's estimates.
7. Figures based on census returns: breakdowns can be found in Alwar, 'Urbanisation in Libya', and percentage figure for nomadic population in Cyrenaica from Waddam, Frank. *The Libyan Oil Industry* (Croom Helm, London, 1980).
8. Segre, Claudio G. 'Italian Development Policy in Libya: Colonialism as a National Luxury' in Joffe and McLachlan (eds.) 1982.
9. Peters, Emrys. 'Cultural and Social Diversity in Libya', in J.A. Allan (ed.) *Libya Since Independence* (Croom Helm, London, 1982). Forms of land ownership did exist within the coastal enclaves during the period of Ottoman rule and, later, under the Italian colonial authorities.
10. Joffe, G. 'The Jefara Plain in the Late Nineteenth Century' in Joffe and McLachlan (eds.) 1982.
11. Ibid.

12. For details see, Evans-Pritchard, E.E. *The Sanusi of Cyrenaica* (Oxford University Press, 1949). Pritchard's classic study of segmentary formations, remains the key source on the Sanussis.

13. Forbes, R. *The Secret of the Sahara*, p. 261.

14. In ibid.

15. Pennell, C.R. 'Political Loyalty and Central Government in Pre-Colonial Libya' in Joffe and McLachlan (eds.) 1982.

16. Wright, John, 'Libya: Italy's Promised Land' in Joffe and McLachlan (eds.) 1982.

17. Ibid.

18. Ibid.

19. Anderson, Lisa. 'The Tripoli Republic 1918–1922' in Joffe and McLachlan (eds.) 1982.

20. Ibid.

21. Lombardi, P. 'Italian Agrarian Colonisation During the Fascist Period' in Joffe and McLachlan (eds.) 1982.

22. Anderson, L. 'The Tripoli Republic'.

23. Ibid.

24. See Wright, J. 'Libya: Italy's Promised Land'.

25. *Jamahiriya International Report*. Quoted in 'Countries of Italian Colonialism', Vol. 2 No. 14 pp. 6–7.

26. Lombard, P. 'Italian Agrarian Colonisation'.

27. Fowler, G.L. 'The Role of Private Estates and Development Companies in the Italian Agricultural Colonisation of Libya', in Joffe and McLachlan (eds.) 1982.

28. Ghanem, S. 'The Libyan Economy Before Independence.'

29. In Khadduri, Majid. *Modern Libya: A Study in Political Development* (Johns Hopkins, Baltimore, 1963) p. 35.

30. Ibid., p. 33.

31. Ibid., p. 61.

32. Ibid., pp. 66–68.

33. Ibid., p. 73.

34. First, Ruth. *Libya: The Evasive Revolution* (Penguin, London, 1974).

35. Wright, John. *Libya: A Modern History* (Croom Helm, London, 1981), p. 58.

36. Lindberg, John. *General Economic Appraisal of Libya*. United Nations (New York, 1952), p. 32.

37. First, R. op. cit.

38. Ibid.

39. Norman, John. *Labour and Politics in Libya and North Africa*. Bookman Associates (New York, 1965).

40. 'Labour During British Administration', pp. 22–25. *Accordo tra l'Italia et la Libia di Collaborazione Economica*, Article 9.

2 Forces of Change

Rise of the Oil State

The most optimistic economic prognoses in an otherwise gloomy prospectus, were based on the possibility of oil reserves. Traces of methane gas, indicating sources of hydrocarbons, were first discovered in the vicinity of Tripoli during the drilling of a water-well in 1914. Further signs of gas and crude oil, similarly obtained by the Italians, were found in the Jefara Plain in the 1920s, but not until 1937, following the geological surveys of Ardito Desio, did the Italian state oil company, AGIP, commence exploration. Subsequently interrupted by the Second World War, the company's searches were never completed. When, in 1947, the American 'major', Standard Oil of New Jersey despatched a survey team to continue AGIP's initial studies, the British authorities, under pretext of the 1907 Hague Convention on the administration of occupied territories, instructed the mission to leave the country.[1] Only after independence did serious survey work resume.

The 1950s, starting with the Korean War boom in the world economy, were a period of dynamic growth in the oil industry. With the extra demand for supplies of crude, the focus of oil production, particularly in terms of volume, was shifting from the western hemisphere to the Middle East. The change was induced not by exhaustion of reserves in the Americas, but as a deliberate response to local economic conditions by the eight leading companies who dominated the world market: Standard Oil of New Jersey, Royal Dutch-Shell, Texaco, Mobil, British Petroleum, Chevron, Gulf, and Compagnie France des Petroles. These eight, known as the 'majors' of the world oil industry, were at the peak of their power in the post-war period. In transferring the balance of production to the Middle East, their aim was to take advantage of lower royalties and tax exemptions. In Latin America, by contrast, Mexico's oil industry was nationalised, and in Venezuela the government applied a tax on revenue. By forcing down Middle East oil prices in concert, notably in Iran and Saudi Arabia, the 'majors' had, in 1949, achieved complete price equalisation for crudes entering the United States, despite the additional costs of transport from the Persian Gulf.[2] Any bargaining power the Latin American oil-producing countries had hoped to exercise was seriously undermined.

Until 1959, the establishment of oil company operations in Libya remained no more than a possibility. The fact that outside Eastern Europe, the demand for oil was growing at an annual rate of 10 per cent, presented no problem to the companies. In the post-war years, their exploration and drilling activities underwent unparalleled expansion throughout the world. Because of the lower production costs, there was a general trend towards locating development in the Middle East. The specific choice of host state was, however, also influenced by other factors, particularly the policies of the local state; a country wishing to encourage oil company development, had to offer favourable terms and conditions. As observers of the oil industry attest, the regime of King Idris afforded the companies the most generous conditions. Pierre Terzian, in *OPEC: The Inside Story*, describes Idris's Libya as 'a real oil paradise for the companies'.[3]

The first step towards securing oil company development was the formulation of the 1953 Minerals Law. This piece of legislation, drawn up under the auspices of the Ministry of Finance and Economic Affairs, provided for survey work by any company obtaining a permit, but prohibited the actual drilling of exploratory wells. All the 'majors', except Gulf, took advantage of the arrangements; in addition, several independent oil companies, which were to play a vital role in the development of the Libyan oil industry, were awarded survey permits. These were: Amerada, Bunker Hunt, Continental, Marathon and Texas-Gulf. As a result of their various studies, both north-western Tripolitania and northern Cyrenaica were found to possess large anticlinal formations, associated with hydrocarbon deposits. Once the encouraging evidence was produced, the Ministry proceeded to draw up much more complex legislation to provide a framework for potential hydrocarbons development.

In 1954 work began on drafting a petrolum law, to regulate the distribution of oil concessions. According to some sources, an initial draft affording priority to British companies was prepared by a team under the authority of Anis Qassim, a Palestinian lawyer working for the Ministry of Justice. The team also included a former expert employed by Royal-Dutch Shell and two British advisers to the Libyan government.[4] Apparently as a result of intense pressure from American and French interests for the Libyan authorities to operate an open-door policy the scheme for British preferment was subsequently dropped. A final draft, which subsumed the provisions of the previous Minerals Law, dispensed with clauses conferring favoured trading status on the British. Ratified in 1955, the Petroleum Law, containing 25 articles and two schedules, established the practice of granting concessions on a first-come, first-served basis. Inevitably, the system benefited the American companies, which dominated the world oil market.

The Petroleum Law established a grid system for the allocation of concessions. Accordingly, four main zones were created, corresponding to the country's provinces: Zone I, Tripolitania; Zone II, Cyrenaica north of the 38th parallel; Zone III, the Fezzan; and Zone IV, Cyrenaica south of the 38th parallel, an area known locally as al-Khalij. The concession areas, located within these zones, conformed with the grid lines of the map, but there were important differences in the terms available in respect of the northern and the southern zones. With regard to size, the Law specified that the concessions granted to each company in Zones I and II must not exceed 30,000 square kilometres, whilst in Zones III and IV they were permitted territory up to 80,000 square kilometres. Moreover, in Zones III and IV, rents on the concessions were much lower than those set for Zones I and II. Finally, companies were limited to three concessions in the northern Zones and four in the southern Zones. The more generous conditions attached to concessions in the southern Zones arose from the poorer survey findings, but the overall nature of the restrictions imposed on the companies was to have profound consequences for the future development of the Libyan oil industry.

By restricting the number and size of concessions, the Law created conditions which enabled the independent oil companies to make their first crucial breakthrough in Middle Eastern production. In particular, the Oasis consortium, uniting the US independents Amerada, Continental and Marathon with Shell, figured prominently in the bidding. None of the three independent companies had had prior experience of oil production in the Middle East; neither had the independent Bunker Hunt, owned by the Texas oilman Nelson Bunker Hunt, which secured concession number two in 1955. Libya was also the location for the first substantial venture, outside the United States, by the oil company of Armand Hammer. Some oil market commentators, misconstruing Libyan motives, concluded that the policy was deliberately designed to curb the role of the 'majors' in the development of the Libyan oil industry.[5] In fact, the Petroleum Law's specifications were the direct consequence of the 'open-door' policy demanded by the majors themselves, in order to eliminate any British monopoly of oil production. Despite the key role the independents were to play in Libya, out of the 51 concessions granted within a year of the promulgation of the Petroleum Law 31 were awarded to the 'majors'. No evidence has ever been produced to show that the Libyan government intended to curtail the influence of the majors; on the contrary, the law was shaped in co-operation with the big companies.

An important attraction for the companies, majors and independents alike, was a highly flexible price mechanism. As a result, even in comparison with other Middle East oil-producing states, Libya was notoriously prone to company abuse and manipulation. Under the 1955 Petroleum Law, it was not incumbent on the companies to publish a posted price. Instead, the Law tried to establish the royalties due to the state on the basis of income received by the company from the sale of petroleum. Since most of these sales were from subsidiaries, which retained the concessions, to an associated section of the same company, there was ample scope for the parent-organisation to reduce the total amount of royalties due to the

Libyan government by fixing an artificially low price. The sum lost, in transferring shipment from one part of the organisation to another at a depressed price, was recouped externally by price equalisation. The Libyan pricing system, which proved grossly inadequate, bore no relation to what was regarded as a nominal posted-price for Libyan crude, or the posted-prices of competitors in the region. In the absence of any definite criterion, for setting the price of crude, the companies took full advantage of the opportunities this allowed them.

Tax allowances under the Petroleum Law provided a further incentive for the oil companies. According to the provisions of the Libyan legislation, the concessionnaire was required to pay income tax as well as a surtax, which amounted to half the profits accrued from exploration, mining and production. The 50 per cent profit-sharing principle was, in fact, the standard agreement outside North America, but in the case of Libya the companies were entitled to offset against tax the expenses entailed in working the concession, whether or not these were incurred in Libya or abroad. The expenditure on physical assets prior to actual production were amortisable at a rate of 20 per cent; those incurred after production were amortisable at 10 per cent. These expenses, moreover, were deductible in the same financial year they were incurred. In addition, the actual level of the company's income from the concession proved extremely difficult to determine; the internal transfer within the company prevented an accurate calculation of liable income. Not surprisingly, the government suffered a massive loss of revenue, beyond what would have been necessary to sustain a competitive price. Whilst most Middle East oil producers received an average 'take' of 90 cents per barrel, it has been estimated that the Sanussi regime received no more than 30 cents.[6]

A final factor contributing to oil company interest in Libyan concessions arose from the political conditions in the Middle East. The 1956 Suez crisis, following Egyptian nationalisation of the Suez Canal, occasioned an upsurge in the search for oil west of the disputed zone. Libya was a prime beneficiary of the turn of events yet the initial results of exploration drilling, which commenced in 1956, were very discouraging. Hopes were focused on concession no. 1, which was held by Esso, the subsidiary of Standard Oil of New Jersey (later Exxon). The concession was located close to the Algerian border where, the previous year, substantial reserves had been discovered at Ejlele. Despite several drillings, however, the company found only minor deposits, which it adjudged to be commercially unviable. In concessions located in northern Cyrenaica, the Libyan American Company, a subsidiary of Texas Gulf, faired even worse. Three drillings produced only dry holes. In fact, no large reserves were found in any of the areas declared promising. Consequently, after the Suez Canal was reopened in June 1957, oil company interest began to wane, although some drillings continued on the basis of the long-term prospects in the oil market.[7]

The breakthrough came with Esso's discovery of substantial reserves at

Zelten, in the Sirte basin, in June 1959. The field's capacity, estimated at 800,000 barrels per day (b/d) was more than enough to make production commercially viable. Following the discovery, oil company interest was dramatically renewed; a surge of exploration, concentrating on the Sirte desert, was instigated by companies with concessions in proximity to the area. By the end of 1959, oil had been found at Bahi, Dahra, and Waha by the Oasis consortium, at Amal and Hofra by Mobil, and at Beida by the Amoseas consortium. Their strikes revealed an exceptionally high grade crude, with an extremely low sulphur content. The level of proven reserves rose sharply, showing Libya's potential as a major producer. It was not until September 1961, however, when total proven reserves were put at 3,000 million barrels, that Esso commenced output from its Zelten field. Before production could begin, the companies had to install the oil-exporting infrastructure, including pipelines and sea-terminals, requiring a large capital outlay and the creation of a construction labour force. Eventually, five trunk lines, most with shared capacity, were built, connecting the field with five terminals located at Harega, Mersa Brega, Ras Lanuf, Sirte and Zueitina. Mersa Brega, completed by Esso in 1961, carried Libya's first exports from the Zelten field.

In the first half of the 1960s, the boom in Libyan oil development was at a peak. The Libyan oil industry was established at a pace which exceeded that of any other producing state. In 1960, there were 20 companies exploring some 95 concession areas, comprising 60 per cent of the land space. The interval between exploration drilling and well-completion was remarkably short; the number of wells completed reached a high point in the period 1964–65. The following year, Libya became the first country to produce one million b/d within five years of starting production; it had taken Venezuela 40 years, Iran more than 30, and Kuwait 25, to achieve the same level of output. Already by 1967 Libya was supplying one-third of the oil destined for the western European market. Table 2.1 shows the growth in crude, and later, refined oil exports, in the Idrisi period.

Table 2.1   Exports of crude and refined products, 1961–69
('000 b/d)

1961	14.4	1966	1499.6
1962	179.5	1967	1717.3
1963	459.4	1968	2582.4
1964	856.4	1969	3070.9
1965	1212.7		

Source: OPEC.

Note: The export of refined products commenced in 1966, following the completion of a refinery by Esso.

Table 2.2   Total Revenues and Expenditures, 1951–1962 (L£ m).

	Revenue	Expenditure	Surplus	Deficit
1951	4.2	5.9		1.7
1952	6.2	6.6		0.4
1953	9.3	8.2	1.0	
1954	11.2	8.8	2.4	
1955	13.3	13.0	0.3	
1956	18.1	15.4	2.7	
1957	20.4	17.0	3.4	
1958	17.0	20.0		3.0
1959	18.4	20.6		2.2
1960	22.4	28.3		5.9
1961	25.7	34.5		8.8
1962	36.0	44.4		8.4

Source: Bank of Libya, 1967.

Towards the end of the 1950s, the benefits accruing from oil-led development began to take shape. In 1956, the first complete year of exploration drilling, the oil companies spent L£4.5 million on their operations in Libya. By 1959, the year of the first oil strikes, their cumulative expenditure on development in Libya had risen to L£77 million, the equivalent of $216 million. By 1961, with the subsequent costs of oil-field installation and terminal construction, their expenditure had soared to L£210 million. By no means all of this accrued to the government in the form of revenue, but in the period concerned the country's Gross National Income, hitherto dependent on foreign aid and military expenditure, improved substantially. Government revenues increased from L£13,331,000 in the 1955/56 financial year, to L£18,126,000 in 1956/57. Thereafter, the country continued to show a steady growth in gross revenue, although, from 1956, the upturn in the financial position was, undercut by decreases in aid from both the Libyan-American Reconstruction Agency and the Libyan Public Development and Stabilisation Agency. The contribution from these organisations fell from L£4,038,000 and L£1,028,000 respectively in 1956 to L£662,000 and L£477,000 in 1961. Payments ceased completely in 1962, following the beginning of oil production, although the annual subsidies from Britain and the United States, advanced in return for military facilities, continued.[8] Table 2.2 provides the figures for Libyan revenue and expenditure for the period between independence and the beginning of oil exports.

In Table 2.3 a further beakdown of the statistics reveals the comparison between the growth of oil company expenditure on operations in Libya and the decline in allocations of foreign aid:

Table 2.3 Oil Company Expenditures on Libya and aid grants from the Libyan-American Reconstruction Agency and the Libyan Public Development and Stabilisation Agency, 1956–1961 (L£ m).

	Oil Company Expenditure	Agency Aid	
1956	4.5	4.0	1.0
1957	13.5	3.8	1.1
1958	24.0	3.5	0.8
1959	35.0	1.3	0.6
1960	61.0	0.6	0.4
1961	72.0	—	—

Source: Compiled by the author from statistics published by the Libyan Ministry of Petroleum and the Bank of Libya.

Despite a record of abject deference to the oil companies, the Libyan government had an intrinsic interest in maximising income. Once oil production was imminent it moved cautiously towards fiscal parity with other Middle East oil producers. The experience of the early round of concessions, when the government received less than optimal revenues from the companies, resulted in a series of amendments to the Petroleum Law of 1955. Formulated by Dr Nadim Pachachi, an Iraqi oil specialist (subsequently General Secretary of OPEC) these required the publication of a posted-price, and the reduction of allowable pre-production expenses from a rate of 20 per cent amortisation to 10 per cent. The new terms were automatically applied to future concessions, but the government also proposed their adoption by existing concession holders. As the previous oil legislation had guaranteed exemption from changes in the status of concessions, the companies initially refused. The majors, already operating a system of posted-prices elsewhere in the region, finally agreed to the principle of posting a price for Libyan crude, but only on condition that the terms were accepted by all concession holders. The opposition of the independents, notably the vital Oasis consortium, was much more strident; in fact, the Oasis consortium held out long after the legislation was enacted in July 1961. The majors let the independents fight the battle for them, until finally, the government was forced to capitulate. The companies accepted a nominal posted-price, but secured a formula from the government which nullified it. In November the King went through the motions of decreeing Regulation No. 6, which allowed the companies, in calculating their tax liability, to deduct marketing expenses from the posted prices, including real price reductions, in the form of rebates.

Because of the dominant position of the oil companies, the Libyan regime adopted a highly ambivalent attitude towards the Organisation of

Petroleum Exporting Countries (OPEC). Libya formally joined OPEC in 1962, two years after the launch of the organisation in Baghdad, but under the monarchy, remained a deeply conservative force, opposing the more robust measures of other states. When world oil prices started to slide in 1964, Libya raised strong objections to an OPEC scheme for 'pro-rationing' increases in output. In July 1965, when the OPEC conference convened in Tripoli, the Libyan Minister of Petroleum, Fuad al-Qabbazi, told delegates that his country's contractual obligations to the companies prevented participation in the plan.[9] Just one month after the meeting had approved a temporary 'six months trial period' for the plan, Libya withdrew, on the pretext that the increase awarded was insufficient. Although Saudi Arabia made clear its wish to discontinue with pro-rationing, Libya was the only state actually to break ranks. Along with Saudi Arabia, the Libyan state was subsequently rewarded with substantial increases in production. By contrast, those states which had defied the companies, notably Iraq and Kuwait, were penalised with a slowing down in their *rate* of production. Whilst Libya's output rose 6.6 per cent higher than the production plan, Kuwait's fell short of the target by 6.7 per cent.[10] With the elapse of the plan period, countries which had been the staunchest supporters of 'rational increases' lost interest in extending the pro-rationing system.

The companies also circumvented the introduction of the 1962 OPEC formula on the expensing of royalties. Under the provisions of the formula agreed between OPEC and the majors in 1964, the companies were obliged to introduce modifications in their system of tax allowances in every member state. Through the agreement, OPEC hoped to achieve a uniform rate for royalty payments. The companies accepted the expensing of royalties of 12.5 per cent, but insisted on tax allowances, gradually reduced from $8^1/_2$ per cent in 1964 to $6^1/_2$ per cent in 1966. In November 1964, both Esso and the Amoseas consortium, as required by the agreement, informed the Libyan government of the outstanding offer; yet, when presenting the terms of the formula, the companies added a series of unnegotiated conditions. Whilst both companies demanded 'quittance' in regard of their past accounts, which had not even been received by the Libyan government, Amoseas refused to yield on the question of discounts and rebates. In fact, the companies were seeking from the Libyan government a special dispensation which no other producer had afforded them.[11] In response, the Libyan Ministry of Petroleum established a Petroleum Prices Negotiating Committee, consisting of five members, three of them foreign advisers. The Committee was reportedly divided, but recommended adhering to the terms of the OPEC formula. Idris, in pronouncing the final decision, sided with the companies and stressed that, since the success of the oil industry was dependent on the companies, Libya should accept their conditions. These effectively granted them immunity from the key clauses of the OPEC formula.

Following the Six-Day War in June 1967, the Libyan regime assumed a *relatively* more assertive stance. Apart from the social and political impact on the Libyan state, the closure of the Suez Canal as a result of the Israeli occupation of the Sinai strengthened the country's bargaining position. Mediterranean producers' crude (including Saudi Arabia and Iraq who retained pipeline access to terminals in Lebanon and Syria) cost approximately $1.0 to $1.2 less per barrel than oil shipped round the African continent. Consequently, the demand for Mediterranean oil grew, but the companies did not respond by raising the posted-price for supplies from these sources. The Libyan government, the prime beneficiary of the change in fortunes, was itself extremely slow to take advantage of the new conditions. Finally, encouraged by OPEC (which sought to reduce the difference between Gulf and Mediterranean prices) the Libyan authorities submitted a claim for an increase in the posted-price. The companies initially refused but, following a special OPEC conference convened in Rome from 15 to 17 September, they yielded a 14–15 cents increase per barrel. This afforded the government an extra 8–9 cents a barrel, yet so marginal an increase satisfied neither OPEC nor the Libyan authorities. In August 1969, following Palestinian commando operations against oil pipelines from the Gulf in May and June, the Libyan regime demanded a further increase of 10 cents a barrel. Before the companies could reply, however, a radically different leadership had taken power in Libya. Thereafter, Libyan oil policy, and relations with the companies, underwent a profound transformation.

Another indication of Libyan assertiveness was the formation of the Libyan General Petroleum Corporation (Lipetco). Set up in April 1968, by the pro-technocratic government of Prime Minister Abdul Hamid Bakoush, the Corporation had similar objectives to those of the state-owned oil companies already established by other Middle East oil producers, and was intended as a means of increasing state control in the development of the oil industry. According to its charter, the Corporation was empowered to act independently in the exploration and production of oil, but the lack of indigenous skills and local technology effectively ruled out autonomous operations. Initially, its role was limited to joint ventures with other oil companies. In fact, the Corporation was founded for the purposes of a participation agreement signed in April 1968 with the French company Elf/Aquitaine. In May and June 1969, further joint ventures followed between Lipetco and Shell, ENI (Agip), Ashland Oil and Refining, and Chappaqua. Whilst the Corporation undertook a junior part in all these ventures, the government hoped subsequently to expand state involvement. As an incentive for the companies' collaboration, the Corporation undertook most of the investment, whilst owning less than half the equity of the joint venture. The companies took full advantage of an arrangement which defrayed their own costs.

The political weaknesses of the Sanussi state helped the oil companies maintain the subordination of Libyan oil policy. As an exogamous development of British and American strategic co-operation, the Libyan state structure and apparatus were, from the onset of independence, dependent on the leading capitalist powers. Libya derived from the West financial and technological assistance, and skilled manpower. For the formulation of government policy, the regime relied excessively on foreign advisers. With the growth of the oil industry, Libya merely exchanged its economic dependence on disbursements of foreign aid, to revenues from the oil companies. Having developed in collaboration with Britain and the United States, and pursuing policies of political and military alignment with the West, the regime was never in a position to reduce the inequality of the relationship with the oil companies. The oil companies retained sufficient clout to beat off even the timid reforms proposed by OPEC. Frank Waddams, a British oil expert who served on the Petroleum Prices Negotiating Committee, recalls that, when the OPEC formula was under discussion in Libya, a representative of an independent company told the Prime Minister, Dr Hussein Mazegh, that the situation in Libya might become politically precarious if the government aroused opposition to US interests.[12] Indeed, there is no doubt that the companies could bring about changes within the personnel of the regime. Libya remained the junior partner of the oil companies in the development of the economy, just as it remained the client of the West in foreign policy.

The change in the form of dependence from foreign aid to oil revenues is nevertheless important. Through the development of the oil export trade, Libya was integrated within the world economy, obtaining a role, or a specialisation, in the world division of trade as an oil state. Whilst the terms

Table 2.4   Government income and expenditure, 1963/4–1969/70 (L£ m)

| Fiscal year | Actual income | | Actual expenditure (current prices) | | | |
	Oil	Total	Current account	Defence[a]	Dev. Budget	Total[b]
1963/4	23.8	60.3	46.1	—	16.9	63.0
1964/5	54.7	95.9	64.2	—	38.3	102.5
1965/6	83.6	127.8	83.0	—	58.0	141.0
1966/7	141.8	195.2	112.8	—	92.3	215.1
1967/8	191.0	249.4	121.5	15.0	119.7	276.2
1968/9	396.2	475.5	162.1	70.9	193.9	460.0
1969/70[c]	353.0	426.3	190.3	75.0	145.0	415.3

[a] National Defence and Arab aid inclusive.
[b] Includes reserve fund.
[c] Estimated expenditure.

Source: Department of Planning, 1976.

Table 2.5   Gross Domestic and Gross National Product at Current Prices, 1965–70 (L£ m)

	1965	1966	1967	1968	1969	1970
GDP (at factor cost)	508.8	623.4	761.4	1,071.7	1,215.8	1,279.1
Less net factor foreign income transfers	81.6	106.9	128.3	228.3	214.0	216.0
GNP (at factor cost)	423.2	525.5	633.1	843.4	1,001.8	1,063.1
Added indirect taxes	28.1	34.0	35.6	46.3	50.0	49.7
Less subsidies	1.1	2.1	2.8	8.3	8.4	11.0
GNP (market prices)	450.2	557.4	665.9	881.4	1,043.4	1,101.8

Source: National Accounts Department, Ministry of Planning.

of incorporation were fundamentally unequal, in that they allowed the transfer of resources from a backward country to developed capitalist countries, the resultant higher income permitted Libya a form of dependent development. Table 2.4 provides figures for the growth of oil revenues relative to government income and expenditure in the last seven financial years of the Idris period, following the start of crude exports.

Although during the transition from aid dependency to an oil-based economy (from 1958/59 to 1965/66) the Libyan economy was in deficit, these figures indicate that regular surpluses began to accrue after 1966. The non-oil economy remained in deficit, but the income from oil, by relaxing the constraints on foreign exchange, enhanced growth throughout the economy. In real terms, Libya achieved an overall annual growth rate of 15 per cent between 1965 and 1970, but in the non-oil economy the annual growth rate was 9 per cent. *Per capita* income rose by about 61 per cent in real terms. If, however, the net factor income transferred abroad, in the form of worker remittances and profits from the oil sector is excluded, the growth rate in the Gross National Product averaged an annual rate of 14 per cent. The companies, despite breaking even on their investment in 1967, were absorbing 1 per cent of the annual growth rate of the Gross Domestic Product. Table 2.5 shows this outflow from the economy.

Libya was characteristically a *rentier* state. Typically, the country received large external payments, best classified as rents, in return for the use of land under the control of the Libyan state.[13] Indeed, the two most important forms of income, base rentals and, particularly, oil revenues, come within the classification of rents. Distinct from the costs of fixed capital, both are sums paid to the Libyan state for natural conditions which cannot be generalised. The growing proportion of such rents as a share of Libya's GNP arose from the predominance of the extractive over the industrial sector in the country's economic development. In short, the

Libyan state accrued most of its income in the form of rents from the provision of land, which could provide a natural basis for production. Whereas in 1959/60 oil revenues constituted just L£0.1 million, compared with other revenues of L£13 million, in 1969/70 oil revenues amounted to L£353 million, and revenues from other sources totalled L£73 million. As a proportion of the state's overall income, aid and internal taxes steadily declined.

Input into the economy from external rents had major implications for the development of the Libyan state. Neither the military bases nor the oil industry, the prime sources of income, established significant linkages with the rest of the economy.[14] Economic development, including the growth of other economic sectors, hinged on the role of the Libyan state. Through control of the largest share of the GNP, acquired independently of the local economy, the state achieved a position of pervasive dominance in the economy. The huge surpluses available for redistribution created conditions for the development of Libyan *étatisme*.[15] Inevitably, the class and sectarian interests of the Sanussi leadership were reflected in the pattern of distribution, but the impact of the state's spending policies, more than the direct economic penetration of the oil companies, had far-reaching social and political consequences for Libya.

Social Antagonisms

Urbanisation was the major feature in the transition from an aid dependency to an oil state. The drift from the interior to the towns, which had begun after the defeat of Italian colonialism, accelerated rapidly with the period of oil exploration and development. Between 1954 and 1964, the urban population grew from 21.6 to 24.6 per cent of the total population, rising from 235,000 to 385,000.[16] In the main urban centres along the northern coast, the growth rate was even higher; Ajdabiya, Barce, Beida, Benghazi, Derna, Tobruk and Tripoli, population increased at a rate of 6.5 per cent, from 22.3 per cent in 1954 to 27.4 per cent in 1964.[17] The level of influx to the two major cities, Benghazi and Tripoli, was higher again than in second rank urban centres. Estimates for 1966 reveal that Tripoli and Benghazi jointly absorbed some 80 per cent of migrants from the interior.[18] Derna, the city with the third largest concentration, accounted for just 24,000 persons; Benghazi, by comparison, had a population of 150,000, and Tripoli, with a clear lead over other cities, some 234,000.[19] According to the 1964 census, 56 per cent of the total population migrated from the interior to the urban centres, although initially only 36 per cent settled permanently. Significantly, the rate of growth in the urban concentrations outstripped the country's birth rate, which itself achieved much higher levels in the period between 1954 and 1964; after years in which population growth had been virtually static, the country's birth rate rose concurrently by 3.6 per cent.[20]

Table 2.6   Population increase, Benghazi and Tripoli, 1954, 1964 and 1973

	Population			*Per cent of total population*		
	1954	*1964*	*1973*	*1954*	*1964*	*1973*
Tripoli	129,728	231,506	234,000	11.9	13.6	13.9
Benghazi	69,718	137,295	150,000	6.4	8.8	8.9

Source: Population Census, 1954, 1964 and 1973.

By any standards, the shift in Libya's demographic balance was dramatic. The previous stability in the rural and urban populations was lost. The trend towards urbanisation had become a constant, if not permanent, fixture of Libyan society. Although no census was completed between 1964 and 1973, following the overthrow of the monarchy, the influx from the interior continued, maintaining linear rates of growth in the last years of the Idrisi period. Table 2.6 shows the increase in the urban populations of Benghazi and Tripoli, as indicated by the census returns of 1954, 1964 and 1973.

These figures cannot reflect the effects of urbanisation. The migration from the rural areas had painful social consequences for the country. The build-up of population in the urban centres produced conditions of appalling congestion and overcrowding. The strains imposed on the existing social infrastructure were immense: housing construction failed to keep pace with the inflow from the interior; the migrant population was compelled to settle in tent-cities and shanty-towns which began to envelop the urban centres, particularly Benghazi and Tripoli. In 1967, it was estimated that the shanty-town population of Tripoli was at least 40,000 strong.[21] Hadi Bulugma, author of *Benghazi Through the Ages,* has described the squalor of Sabri, a bidonville on the edge of Benghazi, in these following terms:

> The shantytown of Sabri . . . gives a clear picture of a primitive and miserable society living on the lowest margins of human subsistence. In winter, the people suffer from dirt, mud and rain. Summer conditions were better than those of winter, but millions of flies live on the dirt and sewage found all over the place. In brief, it is undoubtedly the poorest living area in the whole of Libya. Neither modern dwellings nor medical services, sanitation, hygiene, piped water or electricity are yet known, despite the fact that the eastern part of the area lies along the main northern entrance to the city.'[22]

Sabri alone is said to have housed one-quarter, or about 35,000 of Benghazi's population. It was perhaps the worst single instance of overcrowding owing to migration, but similar conditions existed in other encampments around Libya's urban centres.

The pattern of urban settlement had a particular social significance. The migrations from the interior were largely collective; nomadic or semi-nomadic kinship groups moved in units from the interior to the periphery of the urban centres, where land was settled corporately in the name of the relevant tribe. The process of re-location did not destroy tribal society, but replicated kinship relations in an urban, or semi-urban, context. Professor John Davis, who conducted anthropological field work in Cyrenaica between 1977 and 1978, concluded that:

> Urbanisation, therefore, does not seem to have entailed a process of uprooting, of dislocation of traditional relationships. Rather, groups of herders arrived more or less as they were, and sedentarized themselves by, so to speak, sitting down as they found themselves to be.[23]

Indeed, the migrants transferred their collective tribal affiliations and solidarity from rural Libya to the urban concentrations. Whole streets, or specific areas of encampments, became reserved for members of a certain kin group. Only rarely did a member of one group settle in 'the territory' of another. Davis, in a case study of Sidi Hassan, a southern quarter of Ajdabiya, has described the process in these terms:

> Sidi Hassan is surprisingly geneological in its residential distribution: a terrace of houses for Awadl section next to a terrace of Ali section, both from the major of section of Jlulat; across the road, the villas of the Mannai, a major segment—and so on. In fact these spatial relations among representatives of sections and segments are more or less replicated in the peripheral oases of Kufra, in Tazerbu, in Ajkarra.[24]

What factors prompted a tribal decision to migrate? Much the most important reason was the infusion of revenues into the local economy, following the allocation of the first oil concessions. The expansion of the money supply, from L£9.8 million in 1955, to L£26.0 million in 1961, generated a commercial boom,[25] which, concentrated in the urban areas, engendered a strong demand for goods and services. Wages in the urban centres offered a higher standard of living than could be obtained from subsistence farming: the price of sheep and camels rose by over 500 per cent in the period from independence to oil production.[26] The nomadic and semi-nomadic peoples, having long sustained a static economic existence, were drawn to dependence on the expanding urban markets. Whole kinship groups moved in the hope of benefiting from the increased level of economic activity. Although only a minority of their male members gained wage work, many more pursued collective ventures. In particular, the growing urban markets encouraged the formation of the *sharika*, or partnership, consisting of semi-urbanised kinship trading groups, which practised commercial herding on the semi-desert periphery.[27] Migrating between rural and urban Libya, they took advantage of the urban markets in livestock without completely abandoning their former pastoral livelihood. An increasing proportion of other migrants became no more than surplus to the requirements of the commercial boom, but could rely on the economic support of their kin group. The conditions of the shanty-towns proved no deterrent to urbanisation. Whole areas of agricultural land were rapidly stripped of labour.

The problems were aggravated by the regime's agrarian policy. In 1961, the state decided to provide agricultural credit, in the form of long-term loans, for the purchase of land by Libyan nationals. The measure, prompted by the publication of World Bank recommendations in 1960, was specifically designed to help buy out Italian settlers.[28] Demand for land had risen steadily with the commercial boom, but initially only the most wealthy urban traders were successful in acquiring Italian settlements. Under the impact of the commercial upturn, the prices of Italian agricultural land soared. The Italian community, estimated at just 20,000 in 1964, experienced a period of revived economic fortunes—notably in the commercial sector. If Libyan land acquisition was not to remain a rare event, state intervention was required to effect a general transfer of ownership. Pressed by the urban merchants (though not tribal sheikhs) the state hoped—incorrectly—that the policy could revitalise the country's deteriorating agricultural base. In the event, it contributed to the flow of population from the countryside.

Previously lacking the funds for major agrarian reforms, the growth of oil revenues gave the state the means to initiate the process. Through the offer of long-term loans, increased from 50 to 100 per cent of the sale price in 1962, the state sponsored a transition to landownership, promoting a trend towards *latifundism* within Libyan society.[29] The main beneficiaries were urban merchants, who treated the land as commercial property, but in the break up of estates, some peasants, former tenant smallholders on the Italian lands, gained minor landholdings. The chief casualty was the system of tribal collective landownership, which underpinned tribal society. The state did not carry through a reform of traditional tribal lands, as proposed by the World Bank: a direct attack on the interests of the tribal sheikhs would have undermined the regime's power base. But corporate lands were, nevertheless, disrupted by the changing patterns of land ownership within Libyan society. In fact, the rise of private ownership spelled the dissolution of corporate landownership. The Italian lands, instead of reverting to *usufruct* use, began to develop along capitalist lines. Formal class divisions arose between large landowners and peasant smallholders. Subsistence farmers made landless by the sale of Italian lands joined the mass migrations to the urban centres.

The formation of social classes was brought about by Libya's integration within the world market. Commercial capital, stimulated by the injection of money into the economy, expanded into landownership and service industries. Beginning with oil company exploration and development, the working class, just a small section of the urban population, increased in size and social importance. The growth in the workforce was most pronounced in the service sector, but the core section of the emerging working class

Table 2.7 Oil company employees in Libya, 1956–61

	1956	1957	1958	1959	1960	1961
Libyans	1,150	2,900	4,600	5,000	7,600	7,950
Non-Libyan	850	850	1,300	1,800	2,650	2,700

Source: Ministry of Petroleum, Tripoli, quoted in F. Waddams, *The Libyan Oil Industry* (Croom Helm, London, 1980).

crystallised around the oil industry. Table 2.7 shows the growth in the labour force employed by the oil companies in the period prior to production.

Besides revealing the dependency of the rising oil industry on non-Libyan labour, owing to sectoral labour shortages within the indigenous population, these statistics indicate the small scale of the workforce in the oil industry. They, nevertheless, conceal an extremely high turnover rate within both the oil industry and its ancillary services, such as transport and construction. According to F.C. Thomas, writing in the *Middle East Journal* in 1963: 'Because of the nature of these operations and the high labour turnover, probably twice the number presently employed have at some time worked in petroleum exploration.' In fact, the widespread conditions of job insecurity, compounded by generally low wages in the period of commercial boom, precipitated an extraordinary upsurge in trade union organisation.

Trade union structures made their first appearance in Libya during the urban protests against the trusteeship proposals. Concentrated in the province of Tripolitania, notably Tripoli, they were modelled on their Italian counterparts; indeed, the first union to organise Libyan workers, the Tripolitanian Workers' Union, was founded by Dr Enrico Cibelli after the defeat of the colonial administration. A former Fascist official, Cibelli's intention was to increase the bargaining strength of Italian workers with the British military administration. The first Libyan trade unions attempted to emulate his example in respect of Libyan workers. However, the majority were poor imitations, extremely sectionalised in their development. Perhaps the most important were the Transport Workers' Union, founded by Hajj Ibrahim Arabi in 1947, and the Libyan Bakers' Union, inaugurated in Tripoli the following year. By 1949–50, rival trade union federations, uniting several sectoral unions, had begun to coalesce. In January 1949, Arabi joined forces with other local trade unionists, especially Mohammed Bashir Sherif, Mohammed Ben Zaid Ibrahim Hafed and Mohammed Talman, to create the Union of Libyan Labour. The next year, Mohammed Buras, the founder of the dock workers' union, formed an organisation called Trade Unions of Tripoli, which claimed the affiliation of 16 unions, ranging from the port, tourism, hotel, gas and fire service workers, to street cleaners and taxi drivers. Most of their affiliated unions were, in fact, extremely small (in 1951, trade union membership was estimated at 2,000).[30] Yet some proved surprisingly effective in pressing their demands. In February 1949, the Bakers' Union won shorter working hours after depriving the local market of bread for a whole month; in 1952, workers at a soft drinks factory also won shorter hours, and workers at Idris airport, in Tripoli, forced the RAF to concede better pay and working conditions.[31]

Following these birth pangs, no further spasms of growth occurred in the trade union movement until oil development began to recast the Libyan economy. The pause in activity came to án end with the formation of the Petroleum Workers' Union in 1957. Founded by Abdul Latif Kekhia, an avowed Marxist, the infant union strove to organise oil company workers, agitating around issues of pay and conditions. The union's potential bargaining power soon prompted the companies, in co-operation with the government, to clamp down heavily on the self-organising of workers in the industry. Cases of victimisation were widespread. Kekhia himself was dismissed by his employer, Esso in 1958 in a witch-hunt for militants in the industry. Thereafter, the passivity of the workforce was temporarily assured, but the agitation and organisation of the oil workers' union inspired the service sector of the economy and service industry workers, newly inducted into the labour force, began to demand their share of profits from the country's commercial boom. The first reported unrest was a strike by hotel workers in Tripoli in July 1959. The hotel workers, who saw huge increases in the owners' profits, demanded shorter hours and an equal distribution of tips among staff. In November, their example was repeated, on a much broader scale, by 350 airport workers—porters, firemen, radio operators and refuellers. During the same period, the country's largest press, the Italian-owned Poligrafico Maggi, was brought to a standstill by a printers' union strike for better pay.

Within merchant capitalist circles pressures for the suppression of the reinvigorated trade union movement began to build up. The Sanussi leadership, fearing the disruption of oil development, tended to concur, but the federal state itself played only a minor part in the decision to clamp down on union activities. At the urging of local traders, the lead was taken by the provinical authorities in Tripolitania. The provincial governor Ali Dhili put together a plan to halt the generalised spread of trade union militancy by smashing the Libyan General Labour Union (LGLU). Under its General Secretary Selim Shita, the LGLU was one of two rival trade union federations formed during the commercial upturn, the other being the Libyan Federation of Labour and Professional Unions; but the LGLU had proved to be the more militant.[32]

In 1961, the LGLU had compelled the provincial authorities to concede a review of wages. A commission was formed to conduct an inquiry, but when it reported, Dhili rejected all its recommendations, except the proposal for a minimum wage. In reply to his *volte-face,* the LGLU called a general strike. Dhili was, however, more than adequately prepared for a showdown. His administration systematically had recourse to black-legs—who were in abundant supply due to the large numbers of urban unemployed possessed of no real conception of solidarity. Striking workers at Idris airport were quickly replaced. A new labour law, imposing restrictions on union membership, was immediately decreed. The LGLU offices were occupied by police, and Shita, along with other trade union leaders, detained. Subsequently tried on state security charges, all were aquitted in November 1961. The LGLU, however, had been destroyed and the development of trade unionism undermined.

The suppression of trade unionism became a precondition for the growth of merchant capitalist power. Following the defeat of the LGLU, there occurred a partial shift in the basis of state power, from pre-capitalist institutions to capitalist state forms. The state entered a period of crucial self-transformation. Between 1961 and 1963, political power was massively centralised and concentrated in the hands of the state. Through a number of internal reforms eroding the tribal and regional basis of the state, the way was opened up for commercial expansion. The agricultural credit policy was characteristic of these reforms, but the agrarian changes occurred in context with general moves towards centralised economic planning. Also, in 1961, just prior to the beginning of oil production, the Libyan Petroleum Commission, the state agency nominally supervising the oil industry, was replaced by a Ministry of Petroleum. Previously a federal structure with provincial representatives, the Commission was unified under federal government control with a minister of state appointed by the monarch!

The following year, the King began to dismantle the federal structure of the country. This was completed in April 1963, when Libya became a unitary state and the designation 'Unified' was removed from its title. Henceforth, the provinces were divided into ten governates, or *muhafadha*, sub-divided into municipalities, or *baladiyat*. The Sanussi leadership, having achieved a monopoly in the control of oil rents, completed the process of unification they had been unable to impose at independence. In the same year, the new unitary government commenced central economic planning, when the country's First Five-Year Development Plan was launched. Table 2.8 provides a sectoral breakdown of this plan.

Despite the strong emphasis on agriculture, these figures indicate that the state's most important social priority, taking precedence over health and housing, was education. Indeed, the need to expand education and training facilities had become apparent during the commercial boom. Efficient sectoral growth in the economy, particularly in agriculture, was hindered by acute shortages of skilled manpower and technically qualified personnel. Through substantial investment in education (23 per cent in 1967) the state hoped to raise the technical capabilities of the indigenous workforce, but was naturally obliged to begin at an extremely low level of development. In 1950, there were only 138 schools in Libya; the United

Table 2.8   First Five-Year Development Plan, 1963–68 (L£ '000)

Sector	Allocation	Per Cent
Agriculture	29,275	17.3
Industry	6,900	4.1
Economy	2,870	1.7
Communications	27,460	16.2
Public Works	38,662	22.9
Education	22,365	13.2
Health	12,500	7.4
Labour and Social Affairs	8,690	5.1
News and Guidance	2,550	1.5
Public Administration	6,425	3.8
Planning and Development	11,400	6.7

Source: Ministry of Planning, 1963.

Nations estimated that only 2 per cent of those eligible for schooling received tuition of any sort.[33] Until 1956, there was no facility for university education in Libya: the first university, at Benghazi, initially consisted of no more than an Arts and Education College of six lecturers and 31 students. A College of Commerce and Economics was added in the following year in response to the growing social significance of the urban trading class; not until after large oil revenues had accrued did both primary and higher education undergo a major expansion. In 1962, a College of Law was established at Benghazi, but following the inauguration of centralised planning, the growth in education was increasingly orientated towards the provision of technical knowledge, notably in Tripolitania, rather than Cyrenaica, the more backward of the two regions. In 1966, a College of Agriculture was created in Tripoli and engineering and education colleges were opened in 1967. By the 1968–69 academic year, there were 809 students in science faculties, and 2,601 in classical faculties: one in five of the school-age population, or 310,000 pupils were receiving education. Typically, the majority of those gaining admission to higher education were the sons of the urban merchant families. Nevertheless, faced with severe shortages of skilled manpower, especially in agriculture, the state encouraged much wider social access to primary and elementary education.

Despite the negligible number of students within society, the majority became very vocal in their support for the process of modernisation, embarked on in 1961. Indeed, not only did they agree with the reform of the state, most wanted to carry forward the transformation, despite strenuous opposition from entrenched tribal and religious interests. As their model, many looked to the development of Nasser's Egypt.[36] For the whole generation admitted to education in the late 1950s and early 1960s, Cairo's Voice of the Arab World radio exerted the strongest, most pervasive, influence. Barred from joining political organisations, since the banning of parties in 1952, students nevertheless found other channels through which to express their opinions. In Benghazi, on 16 January 1964, several hundred boycotted classes in a show of solidarity with the Arab Nations' Conference in Cairo, called by Nasser to rally Arab states against an Israeli plan to divert the waters of the Jordan river. The more militant used the occasion to demonstrate for a student union. Against this unique act of defiance, the Cyrenaican Defence Force responded with particular ruthlessness. The Force not only violently broke up the demonstration, but killed two students and injured dozens of others. As news of the bloodshed spread, protests erupted in schools throughout the country. On 22 January, over 1,000 students in Tripoli met to discuss their reaction. Prime Minister Mohieddine Fekini went to the King to demand the dismissal and punishment of the Cydef commander, Mohammed Bukuwaytin. Idris not only refused, but, blaming Fekini's policies for student agitation, sacked his Prime Minister on the spot. More protests followed on 24 and 25 January, this time against the dismissal of Fekini, but the unrest eventually subsided under a heavy-handed crackdown by an ultra-conservative Premier, Mahmoud Muntasser, who succeeded Fekini. A student union was belatedly permitted in 1966.

Fekini's dismissal was not without political significance. The sacked Prime Minister was a comparatively young moderniser, whose appointment, on the creation of the unitary state, proved popular with the commercial sector. The tempo of his domestic reforms nevertheless angered the Sanussi hierarchy, who urged his removal. Idris finally succumbed to these elements when it became clear Fekini was emerging as a focus of modernising sentiment, particularly among the students. His replacement by the conservative, former Prime Minister Mahmoud Muntasser indicated just how partial the process of capitalist transition was. Muntasser came from, perhaps, the most pre-eminent merchant family of Libya, and represented much older trading interests, not the new commercial forces. The Muntassers customarily occupied an anomalous position, collaborating first with the Ottoman Sultan Abdul Hamid against the Young Turks, then with the Italians and British, before they emerged as a vital pillar of support for the Sanussis. Mahmoud Muntasser himself sought co-operation with the Sanussis in order to deny other commercial interests political power. Under his government, the Sanussi leadership aimed to restore the equilibrium lost with the commercial expansion. Through the dominant economic position the state derived from oil rents the traditional forces planned to preserve and strengthen the basis of their rule. Eventually, through the co-option of key merchant families, in the fashion of Saudi Arabia, they may have succeeded. However, the fragile structure of monarchical power cracked under the impact of a dramatic external event: the June 1967 War.

The fighting in Sinai, following the Israeli attack on 5 June, stirred powerful Arab nationalist feeling, which found a resonance in both the Libyan student movement and the trade unions – the two sections of society most susceptible to Arab nationalism. When Cairo radio broadcast news of the Israeli attack, students led the urban poor in a rampage against foreign-owned property. Not only was the Jewish part of Tripoli devastated, but several of the inhabitants were killed. Once the initial frenzy was over, however, popular outrage began to coalesce into a more organised form of opposition to the invidious role of the Libyan state, focusing in particular on the regime's hosting of American and British military bases. The trade union movement, dormant since 1961, formed a higher committee which decided to proceed with an oil boycott ahead of a formal decision by a scheduled meeting of the Arab oil producers in Baghdad. On 7 June, the oil workers struck; workers at the terminals refused to load tankers and dockers in the Port of Tripoli refused to handle other oil company vessels. Government appeals to reopen the terminals to tankers from 'friendly countries' were flatly rejected. The companies, fearing the government could lose control, ordered the tankers to remain outside territorial waters. A confidential oil company memorandum, issued on 14 June, warned that Libya was 'on the verge of revolt'.[37] Much of the government was already paralysed and some leading families had fled abroad. Sanussi Libya was saved only by the absence of an organised opposition capable of articulating a political challenge to the regime. Once the scale of the catastrophic Arab military defeat became apparent, the upsurge of student and trade union activity inevitably gave way to demoralisation.

The Sanussi leadership tried to solve the crisis confronting the state with determined repression. A new premier, Abdul Khader Badri, began a campaign to weed out the trade union and student militants who had played prominent roles in the rebellion.[38] Eventually, seven workers' leaders were arraigned and, later, sentenced to terms of imprisonment. Among them was the then General Secretary of the Oil Workers' Union, Dr Suleyman Mughrabi – a Palestinian-born, American-trained lawyer. By August, much to the satisfaction of the Sanussi leadership, Badri had effectively stamped out the opposition. The immediate danger to the ruling faction had passed, but mere repression, of the kind deployed by Badri, failed to restore social stability. The weaknesses of the monarchical state, still largely based on pre-capitalist structures, had been exposed by its impotence during the oil workers' strike. If the ruling group were to consolidate their position, they had to reach an accommodation with sections of commercial capital. Thus, in October 1967, Badri yielded the Premiership to Abdul Hamid Bakkoush, another moderniser, popular with the commercial sector. Aged just 35, Bakkoush planned more reforms in the structure of the state and, in 1968, launched a Second Five Year Plan, with a pronounced emphasis on the development of manufacturing industry. His tenure of office, like that of Fekini before him, lasted until pressures built up among the tribal sheikhs for his removal.[39] Manoeuvred into resignation in September 1968, he was succeeded by Wannis Qadhafi, a bureaucrat of a notably cautious and subaltern type. The transition from a pre-capitalist to a capitalist state, which had seemed possible under Bakkoush, was halted. The deadlock was only broken by the intervention of an outside force, which maintained independence of action from either social stratum.

Notes

1. See Waddams, Frank. *The Libyan Oil Industry* Croom Helm, London, 1980), p. 28.
2. For details of the various basing points and pricing mechanisms, see chapter 1, 'The International Petroleum Industry', in Ghanem, Shukri. *The Pricing of Libyan Crude* (Adams Publishing House, Malta, 1975).
3. Terzian, Pierre. *OPEC: The Inside Story* (Zed Books, London, 1985), p. 113.
4. Eiches, D.B. 'Trek of the Oil Finders – A History of Exploration for Petroleum', article published for the American Association of Geologists, 1975, quoted in Waddams, *The Libyan Oil Industry.*
5. See Ruth First, *Libya: The Elusive Revolution,* Penguin, 1974, p. 187.
6. Terzian *OPEC,* p. 114.
7. Waddams stresses: 'The decisions of oil companies to embark on costly and risky investment in an unproved area were based, not on prospective short-run profitability, but on long-term considerations of a fast-expanding market for a primary energy source.' *The Libyan Oil Industry,* p. 49.
8. The formal decision to wind up these agencies was taken by the Libyan government as a result of their declining contribution to the country's income. See Allan, J.A., McLachlan, K., and E. Penrose (eds.) *Libya: Agriculture and Economic Development* (F. Cass, London, 1973).
9. Waddams, *The Libyan Oil Industry*, p. 139.
10. Terzian, *OPEC,* p. 104. See table 5.1.
11. The independents did not regard themselves as bound by the terms of the formula agreed between OPEC and the Majors.
12. Waddams, *The Libyan Oil Industry*, p. 144, says: 'Dr Mazegh listened with sympathy and interest to the representation of the delegation to the point of toleration without rebuke of a suggestion by one independent that Libya's geographical position between two stronger countries might become politically precarious if it aroused the opposition of American interests.'
13. For an interesting discussion of the oil *rentier* state, see Massarat, Mohsen. 'The Energy Crisis', in Nore, P. & Turner, T. *Oil and Class Struggle,* Zed Press, London, 1980.
14. The main linkages created by the oil industry are forward, capital-intensive rather than labour-intensive.
15. First, R. 'Libya: Class and State in an Oil Economy', in P. Nore and T. Turner (eds.), *Oil and Class Struggle,* Zed Press, 1980.
16. In 1954, the census did not provide a rural-urban breakdown of population; the urban population was determined by occupation criteria. See Alwar,

Mohammed, 'Urbanisation in Libya—Present State and Future Prospects', in Joffe and McLachlan (eds.) pp. 332 and 338.

17. Ibid., p. 338.

18. See Kezeiri, Saad Khalil. 'Restructuring the Urban System in Libya', in Joffe and McLachlan (eds.), p. 355.

19. Ibid., p. 342.

20. The total population of Libya rose from 1,088,000 in 1955 to 1,564,000 in 1964.

21. Harrison, R.F., 'Migrants in the City of Tripoli, Libya' in *Geographical Review*, Vol. LVII, 1967.

22. Bulugma, Hadi M., *Benghazi through the Ages,* 1972.

23. Davis, J.H. 'Quaddafi's Theory and Practice of Non-Representative Government', in *Government and Opposition* (London School of Economics and Political Science, London, 1981), p. 75.

24. Ibid., pp. 74–5.

25. See Allan, McLachlan and Penrose.

26. Peters, E. p. 118.

27. Ibid., p. 118.

28. The World Bank recommendations are quoted in Allan, McLachlan and Penrose; Allan, J.A. *Libya: The Experience of Oil* (Croom Helm, London, 1981) p. 101 is misleading when he claims that 'the interests of Libyan farmers with small holdings as well as those of some of the business community were consistent with that of the government, namely to have Libyan farms run by Libyans.' Whilst there was general support for a transfer of ownership, there were also important tensions between the regime, as a nexus of Sanussi tribal relationships, and the business sector. Tribal sheikhs wanted to reclaim traditional corporate land seized by the Italians.

29. The main implication of this trend was the penetration of capitalist commodity relationships into agricultural production.

30. Norman, John. 'Government and Labour' pp. 125–37, 'Labour in Cyrenaica', pp. 138–144 and 'Labour in Fezzan', pp. 145–56 in *Labour and Politics,* Bookman Associates' (New York 1965).

31. Ibid.

32. Shita was previously associated with the Tripolitanian Congress Party of Sadawi. Following the banning of the party in 1952, he went into trade union organisation. An Arab nationalist, despite his links with the ALF-CIO, he was awarded by Nasser with the Order of the Nile.

33. Ghanem, Shukri, 'The Subsistence Economy; Libya without Oil', Paper presented at Conference on Economic and Social Development of Libya, SOAS, July 1981.

34. Ibid.

35. Department of Information, *Horizons and Prospects* (Tripoli, 1981).

36. Reportedly, there were also groups of Arab Baath Party supporters and Communists, but these were never more than handfuls of individuals.

37. Wright, John. *Libya: A Modern History,* p. 103.

38. Badri replaced another conservative Premier, Dr Hussein Mazegh, who succeeded Mahmoud Muntasser in 1965.

39. Bakkoush threatened the Sanussis with a situation of dual power in Libya. Like Fekini, he was extremely popular with students and graduates, and nationalist sentiment had begun to crystallise around him. According to Saladin Hassan Sury,

'The Political Development of Libya 1952–1969: Institutions, Policies and Ideology', in ed. J.A. Allan. *Libya Since Independence* (Croom Helm, London, 1981), p. 134: 'The Bakkoush Reform Programme gained widespread publicity and he was able to mobilise a large section of graduates for its implementation. The Sanussi hierarchy had him ousted to prevent the process of capitalist transformation from intensifying.'

3 The Emergence of Qadhafi

'Operation Jerusalem'

After months of repeated delay the clandestine Free Unionist Officer movement fixed the date for a military *coup d'état* against the Sanussi state as the early hours of Monday, 1 September 1969. This date had been finalised at a series of meetings, convened the week before, in the office of Signals Captain Muammar al-Qadhafi, at Gar Younis Barracks, just outside Benghazi. The *coup*, code named 'Operation Jerusalem', depended on a simultaneous takeover of key military and governmental installations in Benghazi and Tripoli. Neither could be achieved without an adequate number of Free Officers in barracks close to both cities. Transfers constantly affected the numbers in each barracks, but in late August, Qadhafi and an 'inner circle' of junior officers concluded that there was sufficient manpower to seize control of both urban centres.[1] Postponement was likely to induce further complications, as on 2 September several important members of the movement were detailed to depart for training courses in Britain connected with Libya's purchase of *Thunderbird* and *Rapier* missile systems, and months would elapse before another opportunity would arise.[2]

Qadhafi, who was Chairman of the Free Unionist Officers' Central Committee, personally commanded and supervised details of the operation in Benghazi. Final arrangements for a take-over of the city were completed during a meeting at 1 am in his room at Gar Younis, where there was a final assessment of the plan for the uprising. The meeting heard reports from units in the vicinity of Benghazi, most of which were favourable, but there were many unresolved logistical problems. The officers were short of ammunition, which could not be appropriated from heavily guarded depots without alerting senior officers' suspicion. If the Free Officers had the misfortune to tangle with Cydef units, the whole operation would be imperilled. But, it was agreed, there could be no turning back. That evening Qadhafi sent Lieutenant Omar al-Meheshi with a message to the movement in Tripoli confirming that 'Operation Jerusalem' would proceed as scheduled for zero hour – 2.30 am. Any retreat by the leadership in Benghazi would dangerously expose the officers in Tripoli and elsewhere.

Preparations for the operation in Tripoli had begun during the weekend of 30–31 August, under the command of four junior officers, namely Khweildi Hamidi, Abdul Munim al-Houni, Abu Bakr Younis Jaber and Abdessalam Jalloud. Joining them on the eve of the coup attempt was Omar al-Meheshi, who flew in from Benghazi. Although all were members of the movement's Central Committee, none appear to have been party to the actual decision to mount the coup. The general principle was agreed at a meeting of the Central Committee earlier in August, but the timing, for reasons of security, was left to Qadhafi and his inner circle in Benghazi, comprising Mustafa al-Kharoubi and Mohammed al-Migharief, both members of the Central Committee, and two other junior officers, Abdallah al-Unn and Abdul Fatah Younis. The officers in Tripoli received news of the decision on Friday, 29 August. Travelling from Benghazi, Qadhafi met with his colleagues from Tripoli at a farmhouse off the Tarhouna-Tripoli road. The officers, who informed him they were doubtful of the strength of their position, were persuaded by the arguments in favour, including the good fortune that Jalloud was commanding units on night-time exercises on the outskirts of Tripoli.

A blueprint for the operations in Benghazi and Tripoli had existed for many months. In past discussions, the Free Officers' Central Committee had formulated a plan which began in Benghazi with an uprising in Gar Younis Barracks, from where a motorised column would advance on the city, seizing the radio stations, the police station, the post office, as well as several high-ranking military and government officials. That the King was in Turkey was an additional bonus, but the arrest and detention of the monarch's relatives and advisers remained a top priority. In Tripoli, the operation was intended to begin with the capture of the Crown Prince, who lived in a luxury apartment on the Suni Road, before troops from Tarhouna Barracks advanced on the town centre in armoured cars, occupying installations similar to those in Benghazi.

A series of vital secondary actions for securing and consolidating the coup coincided with the double strike on Benghazi and Tripoli. The most important of these was the seizure of the Cydef headquarters at Qarnadah, near al-Beida. According to the plan, Free Officers belonging to the Army's Fifth Battalion, based at Derna, would assume control of their barracks and set off in a mobile column towards Qarnadah. Having captured the base, they would then move on to al-Beida itself, occupy the Army High Command and detain senior officers from the General Staff, along with prominent political figures, like the Prime Minister, Wannis Qadhafi.[3] In command of the mission was Lieutenant Musa Ahmed, who was not a Free Officer, but was considered trustworthy because of his affiliation to the Hassa tribe which had a traditional blood feud with the Barassa, the politically dominant Sanussi tribe. Ahmed's rank and links with officers inside Cydef were viewed as important assets by Qadhafi. The outcome of the coup depended on Ahmed's success in incapacitating Cydef.

Further consolidation of the coup required seizure of the major means of communications. To prevent hostile movement between the key cities, roadblocks had to be erected and control established at Idris airport in Tripoli and Benina airport in Benghazi. Vital military facilities, including the signals system and the arsenal at al-Abjar, had to be captured. Trouble was not anticipated from either the US base at Wheelus Field or the British base at al-Adem, but the officers took the precaution of assigning detachments to block traffic going in and out of their premises. The least of the Free Officers' problems seemed to be the Fezzan. The leading Free Officers in Sebha, Bashir Hawwadi and Ahmed Hamza, had no knowledge of the coup but Qadhafi evidently believed they would have no difficulty in asserting control if the operations in Benghazi and Tripoli were successful. The Free Officers had been strongly entrenched in Sebha for many years.

In the event, the coup passed off remarkably smoothly. At 2.30 am the Free Officers raised their barracks and mounted an armoured column, which set off in the directions of Benghazi and Tripoli. By 4 am they had secured most of the key installations in both cities. Bloodshed was kept to a minimum; in Tripoli, the Crown Prince was taken without a struggle by troops from Tarhouna under the command of First Lieutenant Omar Hariri. The Chief of Staff, Abdul Aziz Shalhi, having initially eluded his captors, was found by mid-morning after spending the night in his swimming pool. In both Benghazi and Tripoli limited gun-fights with the local police forces occurred, but the stiffest resistance, as expected, was outside the urban centres. At Qarnada, in the Sanussi's Jebel Akhar heartland, a clash with Cydef delayed the advanced on al-Beida, but had no effect on the ultimate course of the coup. At most, Qadhafi suffered some minor delay at the hands of the Benghazi police, but in Tripoli the operation was ahead of schedule. The presence of armour convinced the local police to desist from defending the radio station. Soon after, Lieutenant Khweildi Hamidi broadcast a message, telling the people of Libya to await an historic announcement.

The announcement finally came at 6.30 am, from the radio station in Benghazi. In what has become celebrated as 'Communiqué No.1', Qadhafi declared:

> People of Libya! In response to your own will, fulfilling your most heartfelt wishes, answering your most incessant demands for change and regeneration, and your longing to strive towards these ends: listening to your incitement to rebel, your armed forces have undertaken the overthrow of the corrupt regime, the stench of which has sickened and horrified us all. At a single blow your gallant army has toppled these idols and has destroyed their images. By a single stroke it has lightened the long dark night in which the Turkish domination was followed first by Italian rule, then by this reactionary and decadent regime, which was no more than a hotbed of extortion, faction, treachery and treason.[4]

Regarding the future, he continued:

> From this day forward Libya is a free self-governing republic. She will adopt

the name of The Libyan Arab Republic and will, by grace of God, begin her task. She will advance on the road to freedom, the path of unity and social justice, guaranteeing equality to all her citizens and throwing wide in front of them the gate of honest employment, where injustice and exploitation are banished, where no one will count himself master and servant, and where all will be free, brothers within a society in which, with God's help, prosperity and equality will be seen to rule us all.[5]

Beyond the abolition of the monarchy, the statement contained no references to concrete change. Foreign states received reassurances that the coup implied no alteration in the status of their nationals or property, as Qadhafi was careful to remove any pretext for external intervention, saying:

On this occasion I have the pleasure of assuring all foreign friends that they have no fear for their property or for their safety; they are under protection of our armed forces. And I would add, moreover, that our enterprise is in no sense directed against any state whatever, nor against international agreement or recognised international law. This is purely an internal affair concerning Libya and her problems alone. Forward then and peace be with you.[6]

Few of those listening knew the identity of those who had carried out the coup, even less that of the author of Communiqué No.1. Among the country's ruling families, the main reaction was confusion and resignation, brought about by the speed of the collapse. By the afternoon, the Crown Prince, aware that the military take-over had been decisive, broadcast a message renouncing his claim to the throne and urging co-operation with the new Army authorities. The local commanders of the country's 12,000-strong police force gradually accepted subordination to representatives of those responsible for the coup. Remnants of Cydef continued to operate in the east of the country, but the arrest of their Commander, Brigadier Sanussi al-Fezzani, on the morning of the coup, along with other senior officers, undermined their capacity to launch a counter-attack. Three days after the coup, the last Cydef unit was compelled to surrender, having failed to gain sanctuary in the British base at Tobruk.

Paradoxically, it was King Idris who, despite long-standing rumours of his impending abdication, proved to be the most determined not to give in. From the Turkish holiday resort of Bursa where he was convalescing, the ailing monarch despatched to London the Head of the Royal Household, Omar Shalhi. His mission was to obtain the British government's assistance to reinstate the monarchy. The two countries remained bound by the 1953 Anglo-Libyan Treaty, pledging Britain to protect the Libyan state from external aggression, but Harold Wilson's Labour government refused to invoke the pact in relation to an internal political struggle. According to Whitehall sources, Foreign Secretary, Michael Stewart, granted Shalhi no more than a 20 minute interview.[7] Iraq, Egypt, Syria and Sudan had already formally recognised the new republic, and rather than jeopardize British interests, Stewart preferred to wait and develop a relationship with the government which emerged in Tripoli. Britain abandoned its Sanussi clients after a partnership of 50 years.

Shalhi flew on to the United States in an attempt to enlist the help of the Nixon administration. But his reception there was even cooler than in London. American private investment in Libya, chiefly oil assets worth $1,500 million, was the highest in Africa, and State Department officials believed these interests were best protected through contacts and agreements with the officers responsible for the coup.[8] Accordingly, Shalhi was neither invited to official interviews in Washington nor granted the protocol normally afforded the diplomatic emissaries of foreign governments. Snubbed, Shalhi was obliged to leave empty-handed. Idris had no alternative but to bow to the inevitable and, in a *Daily Express* interview on 5 September, he publicly disassociated himself from Shalhi's mission and acknowledged the take-over as a *fait accompli*. He claimed that he had not enjoyed being King 'very much', and had tried to abdicate in August. Subsequently, he accepted Nasser's offer of exile in Egypt, where he lived out his retirement in the Cairo residential area of Dokki, dying on 25 May 1983, aged 93 years.

The Free Unionist Officers

The overthrow of the monarchy proved popular with most sections of Libyan society. The major exceptions were Sanussi tribal sheikhs, and the bigger merchant families who had benefited from collaboration with the monarchy. Support for the take-over was manifest even among certain 'client' tribes adhering to the Sanussi Order. In fact, traditional tribal animosities accounted for much of the coup's popularity but were not the sole reason for such support; social responses were also influenced by the formation of a class-based opposition to the pre-capitalist state. Welcomed by the commercial sector and the intelligentsia, support for the deposition of the monarchy was strongest among the lower social strata, including the working class and urban poor. At rallies in Tripoli, Benghazi and Sebha, in the aftermath of the coup, Qadhafi was greeted euphorically by crowds drawn from the urbanised and semi-urbanised masses; Qadhafi himself chose to identify the Free Officers with the interests of the lower strata of the population.

Associating the military movement with the aspirations of the working class and urban poor, Qadhafi always insisted that the take-over was a revolution and not a coup. Delivering a speech in Benghazi on 16 September, he said: 'What took place on 1 September was something quite different from a military *coup*: it was at once the logical consequence and the faithful reflection of the turning-point in history, which our people are attaining at the present time.'[9]

This distinction was more than a trivial propaganda point. The Free Officers' seizure of power was more than just a change of personnel within the Libyan state, or as Qadhafi put it in a Libyan newspaper, 'a casual event occurring at the pleasure of senior officers'.[10] Predominantly, the movement consisted of NCOs with different tribal and class interests from those of the top commanders. There was even a distinction in the composition of the Free Officer movement and the middle-ranking officers, despite greater social compatibility. Whilst the movement acquired a degree of autonomy from the institutionalised structure of the Army, its members were not immune from wider social trends and shifts. On the contrary, the Free Officers were largely conscious participants in the developing conflict with the monarchy. 'Operation Jerusalem' may have been a classic textbook military coup, but it also overturned the political power of the ruling families and provided the preconditions for social transformation. Accordingly, Qadhafi designated the takeover 'the *Al Fateh* Revolution, meaning 'an opening' or a beginning to a period of radical change.

The origins of most Free Officers lay within the lower strata of society. The exceptions included Meheshi, born to a Circassian family in Misrata, the son of a provincial administrator; and Houni, from Zanzour to the west of Tripoli, came from a similar civic town-based background. But the participation of a few individuals with roots among the traditional provincial families of the coast did not alter the overall character of the Free Officer movement, which was located among the nomadic and semi-nomadic tribes of the interior, many of whose families had become urbanised since the Second World War. Qadhafi and Jalloud both had semi-nomadic backgrounds; Migharief was a member of the Sanussi Magarba tribe; Abu Bakr Younis Jaber was from a nomadic tribe which had migrated to the Aujela oasis in Chad when he was born; Kharoubi came from a low-status client tribe which had settled in Zawiah.

Because of the their social links with the lower strata of Libyan society, Qadhafi has maintained that the Free Officers more faithfully represented the broad masses of the population than the various political factions based on the intelligentsia and the professions. Justifying the Free Officers' assumption of state power, in an interview with *Le Figaro* he said:

> Frankly speaking, the officers have the conscience to recognise the people's claims better than others. This depends on our origin, which is characterised by humbleness. We are not rich people; the parents of the majority of us are living in huts. My parents are still living in a tent near Sirte. The interests we represent are genuinely those of the Libyan people.[11]

The Free Unionist Officer movement grew out of the sense of disillusionment with the existing political opposition experienced by students and youth from the same underprivileged sections of the population. Three main currents, all Arab nationalist, already had a presence in Libya before the movement was founded: pro-Iraqi Baathism, Nasserism, and the Arab Nationalist Movement, led by the Palestinian Dr George Habash. In addition, there were occasional smaller circles, often no more than discussion groups, of socialists and communists. Many in the Free Officer leadership had flirted with one or more of these factions: Meheshi reputedly had contacts with the communists; Abu Bakr Younis Jaber briefly joined the Baathists; Quadhafi toyed with the idea of participating in the Arab Nationalist Movement. Eventually, they turned to the Army because their social background precluded their advancement by the way of the civilian political milieu. For the post-independence generation, the only real example of change came from Egypt and thus, Qadhafi turned to Nasser's methods while still a student in the desert city of Sebha.

Qadhafi is, indeed, a remarkable figure. Born somewhere in the Sirte desert in 1942, his father was Mohammed Abdul Salem Ben Hamid Ben Mohammed, known as 'Abu Meniar' and his mother was Ayesha, both nomads from a Berber tribe, the Qadhadfah.[12] Named after Sidi Muammar, a revered saint of the Tarhouna region, he was brought up as a Beduoin, his home for much of his childhood was a tent. His first politics were learnt from listening to Nasser's speeches, broadcast by Cairo's 'Voice of the Arabs'. Sent to a primary school in Sirte, he was one of only four children from Beduoin, Berber families, and was the victim of much prejudice. An old school friend, Mufta Ali, recalls: 'There were three or four of us Beduoin at school and we were held in utter contempt.'[13]

Between 1956 and 1961, Qadhafi was at secondary school in Sebha. Here he took the initiative in founding a pro-Nasserist political study group with friends from a similar background to his own, notably Abdessalam Jalloud, a native of the Fezzan. Qadhafi obtained Nasserist and nationalist literature and distributed it to his trusted circle. Nationalist protests were organised at the death of the Congolese leader Patrice Lumumba; the French explosion of an atomic device in the Sahara, and the Algerian civil war and, most importantly, Syria's decision to secede from the United Arab Republic with Egypt. The latter protest, carried out in defiance of the local authorities, led to Qadhafi's prompt expulsion from school.

At Misrata, where he finished his schooling, Qadhafi's views developed. He endeavoured to expand the nationalist group he had started in Sebha, but his exchanges with other nationalists convinced him that civilian politics were doomed to impotency. In his own words: 'The opposition parties and groups were weak. They didn't have the strength for confrontation and didn't have definite ideas. As for the people they continued in opposition without organisation.'[14]

In 1961, after graduating from school in Misrata, Qadhafi called the first general meeting of the organisation he had secretly founded in Sebha in 1959. This meeting, which brought together cells from Sebha, Misrata and Tripoli, adopted a proposal to form separate civilian and military sections. Three members, including Qadhafi, agreed to infiltrate the Libyan Army and create a nucleus of pro-Nasserist officers, in the mould of the Egyptian Free Unionist Officers. Initially, the civilian wing of the organisation, The Popular Formation, was the larger of the two, but the initiative lay with

Qadhafi and those who followed him into the Military Academy. Contact between the two wings broke down and The Popular Formation eventually became moribund, playing no significant part in the preparations for the take-over on 1 September 1969.

By 1964, Qadhafi had gained enough support among members of the seventh (1963) batch of graduates from the Military Academy in Benghazi formally to launch the Free Unionist Officers. The first meetings of its Central Committee, convened on the beach at Tolemaide, coincided with the holidays of lesser and greater Bairum, respectively 9 August and 24 December. From the outset, strict rules were applied to guarantee the movement's security. The process of recruitment took place with care and discrimination. According to Suleyman Mahmoud, a military graduate among the first to join Qadhafi: 'It was decided that each member of the Central Committee of the Free Officers should present a monthly report on officers not belonging to the movement, especially on officers of a high rank, so as to avoid injustice when the moment came.'[15]

The recruits came almost exclusively from the seventh and eighth batch of graduates. The inner nucleus comprised Qadhafi, Younis Jaber, Jalloud, Kharoubi and Migharief, but Meheshi and Houni were brought in because of localised family and kinship relations in Tripolitania. Only Meheshi and Migharief, within the leadership, emerged from the eighth batch.

When the June 1967 War erupted, Free Officer cells had been established in barracks where graduates from these batches were posted. With the growth of popular antipathy towards the regime, the Central Committee decided to launch an operation against the Sanussi state. But the circumstances were premature. Hastily drawn up plans for sabotage attacks on military installations, including the foreign bases, had to be dropped when Qadhafi was transferred to Tripoli and put in charge of constructing a wireless station. His posting indicated that military intelligence may have got wind of their plans. But, nevertheless, in Tripoli, Qadhafi associated himself with the protests building up against the monarchy. Contacting people from the Arab Party, he tried to win support for an operation against Wheelus Field. Refused, ostensibly on the grounds that he was not a Party member, his single contribution to the revolt of 1967 appears to have been the distribution of leaflets prepared on behalf of the oil workers' strike committee.

A year later the conditions seemed more favourable. Evidence of growing disaffection within the ranks of Army NCOs awakened the movement from a dormant period and put the organisation of a coup d'état back on the agenda. At a meeting in Sirte on 10 August 1968, the Central Committee agreed to begin the detailed preparations required for a viable operation.[16] Whilst Kharoubi was charged with planning the actual mechanics of the take-over, Qadhafi assumed responsibility for circulating instructions to the various cells of the movement and sounding out those officers who, though not members of the movement, appeared ready to collaborate in the overthrow of the monarchic state. When a survey of the movement's strength was conducted in January 1969, considerable progress had been achieved in both areas of organisation. At Abdessalam Jalloud's house in Zawit Dahmani in Tripoli, and Mohammed al-Migharief's house in Benghazi, groups of Free Officers held regular sessions to exchange information and co-ordinate activity. In addition, Qadhafi had ensured the collusion of several senior officers with access to military intelligence and the Army's vital communications system.

Following the positive results of the January survey, the Central Committee set 'Zero Hour' for 12 March 1969. A date was chosen because it coincided with the King's birthday, but as the day drew closer, it began to appear a highly inauspicious date. The night before, the famous, popular Egyptian singer, Um Kalthoum, was due to give a performance at the sports stadium in Benghazi. Thousands were expected to attend, including a number of senior officers, many of them Cydef commanders. Seizing and detaining these officers and other officials would be hazardous in conditions of crowded city streets. The Central Committee decided to postpone the operation and reschedule 'Zero Hour' for 24 March.

This attempt was aborted within days of the deadline. In deciding to cancel the operation, the Central Committee was evidently concerned that military intelligence was aware of unusual activity within the Army. Just a week before the operation was due to start, there were signs of irregular military movements.[17] Colonel Abdul Aziz Shalhi, the Chief of Staff, had personally ordered the armoured regiments in Tripoli to gather at one base – the Bab al-Azizya barracks south of the capital. All the military vehicles assigned to units in proximity to Tripoli were withdrawn. Furthermore, two top security officials, Lt. Colonel Ali Fagih and Major Ali Shabaan, were making lightning tours of inspection. Troops were being redeployed with only a moment's prior notification. The King, who had been staying at his residence in Tripoli, had abruptly moved to the relative security of Tobruk. Lastly, military intelligence had issued a warrant for the arrest of Qadhafi himself. The warrant, it transpired, was no more than a precautionary measure – no charges were brought against the Free Officer leader – but the movement was clearly under suspicion and in no position to stage the take-over.

The movement was reactivated in August 1969 after a temporary hiatus intended to preserve the secrecy of operations. On 13 August, a conference of Army officers in the Military Academy in Benghazi, called to hear the Chief of Staff present the country's air defence strategy, following the purchase of missile systems from Britain, provided the Free Officers with a unique opportunity. Except those on duty that day, all the officers would be gathered in one place at the same time. Accordingly, Qadhafi's 'inner circle' met at Migharief's house and decided to prepare plans at once for an uprising. Mohammed al-Najm, one of the inner circle from Benghazi, was assigned responsibility for the take-over of the Academy; the Free Officers present would then be released and given instructions for their role in the coup. In comparison with the other attempts, the plan seemed relatively simple, but the situation in Tripoli proved radically different from that in Benghazi. That evening, those meeting at Migharief's house received a phone call from Houni informing them that the officers in Tripoli were not strong enough to carry out the operation. It was, said Houni, 'suicide'.[18] Once again, though for the last time, the operation was postponed.

The Egyptian Model

Following the success of 'Operation Jerusalem', Qadhafi's first public statement on the take-over's political objectives was in Benghazi on 16 September 1969. Speaking to a mass rally, Qadhafi, the Chairman of the recently instituted Revolutionary Command Council (RCC), declared:

> The revolution does not claim that its leadership is the monopoly of the Revolutionary Command Council. Government must revert to the people, just as sovereignty and final decisions. I hand over to the people responsibility for the philosophy of the Revolution. They must make it part of themselves, with its foundations and objectives; it is for the man in the street, the small official and merchant to work for the Revolution. For should we announce that all has already been achieved we should be liars; should we ask you to stay at home and promise you to realise our aims on our own, we should be deceiving you. On the contrary, what we do say is this: nothing can be achieved except by you, by your labour, your sweat and your struggle. The Revolution imposes a very heavy responsibility on you, the responsibility for its protection, its continuation and its consolidation. These things can be achieved only by a day-to-day struggle; otherwise the Revolution will remain a *coup d'état*.[19]

Despite the disclaimer of military dictatorship, these comments did not imply the imminent dissolution of military control. Qadhafi was casting the RCC, constituted of the former Free Officers' Central Committee, in the role of a political vanguard, which had to establish support among those strata of the population recognisably sympathetic to nationalist transform-ation. In his words, these were epitomised by the 'small official and merchant' – representatives of the strata that largely comprised the Free Officers' movement. Not until the RCC had consolidated its position and determined the character of post-Sanussi Libya did Qadhafi plan broadly-based mass political institutions.

The centralisation of power in the hands of the RCC remained the immediate priority in the post-coup period. Accordingly, eight days after the coup, the Council issued the following communiqué:

> The Council of the Revolution is the only body entitled to administer the affairs of the Libyan Arab Republic. This being so, all government departments, officials and armed forces of law are henceforward at the disposal of the Council of the Revolution. Any contravention will come before the Courts.[20]

Guiding the actions of the RCC was the particular example of Egyptian *étatisme.* Members of the Council had gleaned their limited knowledge of state transformation from accounts of the 1952 Egyptian Revolution, and the various speeches and tracts of Nasser, especially, *The Philosophy of the Revolution.* Their methods of political organisation emulated the Egyptian Revolutionary Command Council under Nasser, which had achieved a massive concentration of state power. The Nasserist concept of 'hegemony of the military', in which the armed forces' vanguard dominate state and society, provided them with their model. Just as Nasser had built up a Free Unionist Officers' movement in the Army, so had Qadhafi; just as the Egyptian Free Officers had formed a Revolutionary Command Council, so too had their Libyan counterparts. The institutions of the Egyptian nationalist revolution were thus transposed into a Libyan context.

Belief in Nasserism was an essential credential for membership of the Free Unionist Officers. When Qadhafi arrived in Misrata, after his expulsion from school in Sebha, he is reported to have told his friend, Mohammed Khalil: 'It is to Nasser that all of us must look, for his personality and the magnetism he exercises over young Arabs offer the only hope of recovering independence for our people.[21] According to Omar al-Meheshi, with whom he joined up in Misrata: 'Right from the beginning we had decided to follow Nasser and Nasser alone; our aim was to support Arab nationalism through Nasser and the action the Rais was taking in support of Arabism.'[22] Before officers were admitted to the movement, they underwent a probationary period in which their attitude to Nasserism wa gauged. As Khweildi Hamidi revealed: 'We would lend our candidate a few books and try to discover whether he approved of Nasser, whether he thought of himself as Nasser's man.'[23]

At meetings of Free Officers, Qadhafi would take the lead in discussions about Nasserism and developments in the Arab world. Captain Suleyman Mahmoud remembers:

> Really, you know, we were surprised by the strength of his feeling. All the same, little by little, we too began to think along similar lines, and we began to give more and more consideration to the subjects Qadhafi kept raising: the future of the Arabs, the work and deeds of Gamal Abdel Nasser, the necessity of ridding our country of the British presence, just as Nasser had freed Egypt and the canal. Qadhafi cited Nasser's example as the only hope of acquiring our own independence.[24]

Despite initial confusion among some Western observers, the Free Officers had, in fact, broadcast their political affiliations in Communiqué No.1. The slogan, 'Freedom, Socialism and Unity', invoked by Qadhafi, was code language signalling a Nasserist brand of Arab nationalism. Had the coup proved pro-Baath Party, influenced by the Iraqi form of Arab nationalism, the key words would have been spoken in reverse order: 'Unity, Socialism and Freedom'. In principle, the sequence indicated the priorities of the different creeds of Nasserism, but in practice it was no more than a symbol of political identity.

When the political orientation of the Libyan RCC had become clearer, there was a tendency among Western observers, including intelligence officials, to assume that Nasser had masterminded the take-over in an attempt to restore his political fortunes after the catastrophe of the 1967 War. In fact, there has never been any real doubt that the operation was organised completely independently. In the first week, no one was more in the dark about the origins of the sudden development in Libya than the Egyptian intelligence service, which had failed badly. Evidence points to a series of contacts between Egyptian intelligence and some senior or middle-ranking officers in the Libyan armed forces, but not with NCOs and members of the Free Unionist Officers.

Nasser became appraised of the situation prevailing in Libya only after his political confidant, Mohammed Heikal, editor of the Egyptian daily, *al-Ahram*, had visited the country, at the request of the RCC through the Egyptian consulate in Benghazi. Nasser had quickly agreed and, after some 36 hours of discussions with Libyan Free Officers, Heikal returned to Cairo jubilant, with this message from Qadhafi: 'Tell President Nasser we made this revolution for him. He can take everything of ours and add it to the rest of the Arab world's resources to be used for the battle.'[25] Writing days later in *al-Ahram*, Heikal declared: 'What I saw in Libya affected me more deeply than anything else. This is a new type of youth . . . the post setback generation of young people, whose upbringing and schooling were dominated by the setback.'[26]

Heikal's talks indicated that members of the Libyan RCC regarded their coup as a precondition for unity with Egypt. Preoccupied with their country's location within the politics of the wider Arab world, they had not formulated a long-term domestic programme. In his speeches and interviews of the period, Qadhafi limits the role of the RCC to a transitionary period, in which Libya would be prepared for a merger with Egypt. In a keynote speech in Tripoli on 16 October 1969, he declared:

> These are the banners we shall raise and behind which we shall march to ensure the realisation of all that they represent: total evacuation [of foreign forces], positive neutrality, and non-alignment, conflict with all those who would fight us, the open hand of friendship to those who hold out their own. And we shall hold high the flag of national unity, the first step on the path of unity with all Arab countries.[27]

From Qadhafi's standpoint the fundamental goal was Arab unity, which could be achieved only by raising Libyan society from the conditions of neo-colonialism and traditional, pre-nationalist leadership. In his 16 October speech, he stressed:

> The Arab citizen of Libya must complete his political and social liberation. He must eliminate all causes of backwardness. He must rid himself of poverty, of fear, of the presence of foreigners, of reaction and exploitation. But he must not

forget that liberty consists in setting free the Arab people, be it politically economically or socially, not only in Libya but in all parts of the Arab world.[28]

Perhaps Qadhafi's most explicit statement of his intentions came in a discussion with students at Tripoli University on 2 January 1970, in which he said:

From the very first day it was evident that the revolutionary government proposed to follow the path of unity. And it is not only recently that we have done so; we have been supporters of unity since 1959, that is, from the very beginnings of our movement. Unity is our aim, our destiny, an ineluctable necessity.[29]

The previous month, the RCC had embarked on its first Pan-Arab initiative. In mid-December, Qadhafi had attended the Islamic Conference Organisation summit in Rabat, Morocco, and met heads of state from several Muslim countries, including Nasser and President Jaafar Numeiri of Sudan, who had come to power in a military coup in May and, like Qadhafi himself, favoured closer political links with Egypt. These two leaders were invited to stop off in Tripoli, on their return from Rabat, for talks concerning the co-ordination of policy between the three states. On 27 December, their consultations resulted in a document: the 'Tripoli Charter', which committed the three countries to the formation of an Arab Revolutionary Front.

The Front was specifically formed in response to criticism of Nasser's policies, which had gained ground at the Islamic summit. The Tripoli Charter contained no reference to the unification of the three states. When Qadhafi pressed for a commitment binding the three countries to a merger, Nasser advised caution, urging practical steps first. These included the integration of economic planning and the formulation of joint development schemes; the Egyptian President proposed an airline merger and the inauguration of a joint development bank. To supervise the process, the Charter established the principle of joint ministerial commissions and quarterly meetings between the three leaders.

The RCCs second Pan-Arab initiative also centred on strengthening Nasser's foreign policy. In May 1970, Qadhafi and Saleh Busair, Foreign Minister in the first post-revolutionary government, toured Arab capitals, aiming to win support for a military offensive against Israel, which would swing the balance of forces back towards Egypt after the 1967 defeat. Besides Egypt, together they visited Jordan, Syria and Lebanon. Thereafter Busair, who was a known Nasserist, independently visited Kuwait, Qatar and the Yemens. In their talks, the Libyan delegation called on the Arab front-line states to increase support for Palestinian guerrilla operations, through the mechanism of a mutual defence pact linking the Arab states and the PLO.

Even in their relations with the PLO the Libyan leadership adopted the same basic stance as Nasser. Following the example set by Egypt, the RCC started to supply material and military aid to the Palestinian resistance, particularly Yasser Arafat's movement, *al-Fateh*, but remained sharply critical of the more radical Palestinian groupings, such as the Popular Front for the Liberation of Palestine (PFLP) and the Popular Democratic Front for the Liberation of Palestine (PDFLP), which had manifested Marxist tendencies. When PFLP supporters put up posters and distributed literature, following the 1 September coup, their actions were condemned by Free Officers. In March, Qadhafi publicly complained about the factional differences dividing Palestinian resistance organisations. Failing to secure a merger between the PFLP and al-Fateh, which expounded a broader, non-Marxist nationalism, he expelled the Front's members from Libya in 1970. Regarding the Palestinian resistance as the subordinate partner in a Pan-Arab confrontation, Qadhafi was concerned to ensure that the presence of radical Palestinian organisations had no ideological repercussions for Libyan society.

Qadhafi's approach varied from Nasser's in tempo, not in content. This was demonstrated most clearly during the events of 'Black' September 1970. In that month, when King Hussein of Jordan began a crackdown on Palestinian *fedayeen* organisations, plunging his country into a savage civil war, Qadhafi's reaction was much less restrained than Nasser's. The Libyans backed Nasser's mediation in the internecine conflict, but broke off diplomatic relations with Amman, and the aid, allocated to Jordan after the 1967 war, was transferred to the guerrilla organisations. At summit negotiations conducted in Cairo, Qadhafi is reported to have objected to the presence of King Hussein, saying: 'What's the use of getting him? He's crazy. He's mad.'[30] Despite a ceasefire arranged by Nasser on 27 September, Libyan relations with the Jordanian monarch remained strained.

Qadhafi was also less cautious in his stance towards the Soviet Union. While circumstances compelled Nasser to develop a form of strategic co-operation with the Soviet Union (if only for arms and aid he could not otherwise obtain) Qadhafi vigorously decried ties of dependency with either superpower. Free of the constraints imposed by a Western arms embargo and shortages of foreign aid, Qadhafi was able, at least temporarily, to employ rhetoric much more hostile to the Soviet Union, in particular and to communism in general, than was Nasser.

Nasser himself appears to have believed that with experience and responsibility Qadhafi would mature as an Arab leader. Despite the impetuosity of the younger man, aged just 28 in 1970, Nasser recognised in Qadhafi a kind of protégé who broadly shared his concepts of Arab unity and nationalism. Speaking at a rally in Benghazi in June 1970, the Egyptian leader declared:

> I am leaving you, I say to you: My brother Muamer Qadhafi is the representative of Arab nationalism, of the Arab revolution and Arab unity. My dear brothers, may God watch over you for the well-being of the Arab people.

May you go from victory to victory, for your victories are the victories of the Arab people.[31]

Nasser's death on 28 September, the day after the summit negotiations in Cairo, moved Qadhafi to grief. He played a prominent part in the funeral on 1 October. Standing alongside President Jaafar Numeiri of Sudan and Chairman Yasser Arafat of the PLO, he received messages of condolences from foreign diplomats, presenting himself to those present and to the world as heir to Nasser's legacy.

Notes

1. The decision was made despite a distribution which favoured Tripoli rather than Benghazi. See Muscat, Frederick. *My President, My Son* (Adam Publishers, Malta, 1974) p. 99. 'At that time most of the Free Unitary Officers were assigned on duties in Tripoli. They were not scattered in convenient proportions all over the country as Mu'Ammar would have wished. However, that presented no hurdle which could not be overcome. The revolution could still be planned and executed. Admittedly, the uneven distribution of Free Officers would make the last minute preparations a more difficult task, but not an impossible one to surmount.'

2. First, R. *Libya: The Elusive Revolution.* p. 109.

3. Although drawn from the same tribe, Wannis Quadhafi was no immediate relative of Muamar Qadhafi.

4. The text of Communique No. 1 can be found in Bianco, Mirella. *Gadhafi: Voice from the Desert.* (Langmans, London, 1975) p. 67.

5. Ibid., pp. 67–8.

6. Ibid., p. 68.

7. John Wright. *Libya: A Modern History*, p. 121. Quotes an unnamed Foreign Office source. The Libyan authorities reacted strongly to Shalhi's visit to London; the British, more than the Americans were seen as the main threat in Libya.

8. Ibid., p. 122.

9. Mirella Bianco. p. 69.

10. *Al-Yawm,* 5 September 1969. He adds: 'A revolution is a vital necessity which grows naturally in the consciousness of the society as a whole.'

11. *Le Figaro,* 30 September 1969.

12. The Qadhadfah belonged to the Arabs of the West (*Arab al-Gharb*) and had a historical blood feud with the pro-Sanussi tribes of the Barassa and Magharba. Their tribal lands extended south and south-west of Sirte, and they had commercial ties with the oasis of Hon. Formerly, during the Ottoman and Italian colonial periods, the tribe was affiliated to the Awlad Suleyman confederation, led by the Saif al-Nassers, and retained strong bonds with Chad. Following Graziani's conquest of the Sirte desert, several hundred Qadhadfah sought refuge in Chad. See 'Muammer El Kadhafi', *Maghreb,* no. 48 (1971).

13. Bianco, Mirella. p. 7.

14. See First, R. (1974), p. 102.

15. Ibid., p. 34.

16. Muscat, Frederick. p. 63. The meeting seems to have been attended by Qadhafi, Jalloud, Hamidi, Kharoubi, Abu Bakr Younis Jaber, Houni, Nejm and Qirwi.

17. Ibid., p. 84. According to Muscat: 'The decision to postpone the date had been ill met by some, and received with certain reservations by others.'

18. Ibid., p. 94.

19. Bianco, Mirella. (1974), p. 69.

20. Ibid., p. 67.

21. Ibid., p. 28.

22. Ibid., pp. 48–49.

23. Ibid., p. 50.

24. Ibid., p. 35.

25. Heikal, Mohammed. *The Road to Ramadan* (Collins, London, 1975) p. 70.

26. See First, Ruth (1974) p. 113.

27. Bianco, Mirella (1974), p. 68.

28. Ibid., pp. 68–9.

29. Ibid., pp. 69–70.

30. Heikal, Mohammed. *Nasser: The Cairo Documents* (Mentor, London, 1973) p. 17. Heikal relates an interesting encounter between Nasser and Qadhafi showing the former's personal influence over the latter.

31. Nasser, Gamal Abdul. Speech in Benghazi, June 1970; quoted in frontispiece of Bianco, Mirella. (1974).

4 Beginning of the Revolution

An Enigmatic Leadership

In the first few weeks after the coup period, members of the RCC made a tactical decision to preserve their anonymity. The secrecy, in order to conceal the identity of the junior ranks of the Free Officers, was maintained while the Council established control within the armed forces. The Council made its first diplomatic and political contacts through sympathetic senior officers, particularly the Colonels Ahmed and Hawwaz, as well as a retired pro-Nasserist officer, Colonel Saad al-Din Bushweir Abu Shwerib, although he was not in Libya on the day of the take-over. The initial communication with the Egyptian government, a cable sent via the Egyptian consulate in Benghazi, was signed by Colonel Abu Shwerib.[1] Qadhafi's identity was revealed only eight days after the coup when the Council announced his appointment as Supreme Commander-in-Chief of the Libyan Armed Forces. Even four days later, when he was publicly declared President of the Republic and Chairman of the RCC, Qadhafi withheld permission to publish his photograph and biographical data. The names of the other 11 members of the RCC were not revealed.

This practice of working through intermediaries was reflected in the country's administration. The RCC appointed a government composed largely of civilian politicians with an established record of opposition to the monarchy. The Premier was Dr. Suleyman Maghrabi, the former leader of the oil workers' revolt in 1967, and the Foreign Minister was Saleh Busair, a journalist who had previously gone into exile in Egypt. The only military presence in the cabinet was that of Colonel Musa Ahmed, the Interior Minister, and Colonel Adem al-Hawwaz, the Defence Minister.

From the beginning, relations between the RCC and the government remained ambiguous and undefined. By setting up a separate tier of administration, whilst retaining anonymity, the RCC was in grave danger of creating a situation of dual power in the country. Despite its self-proclaimed authority, the RCC encountered some difficulty in imposing its 'will' on the government, which developed a tendency towards autonomy, particularly in the formulation of policy. The threat came not from the civilian politicians, such as Maghrabi and Busair, but rather from the military members of the cabinet, Ahmed and Hawwaz, who as respectively ministers of the Interior and Defence were in a position to exercise some control both over the armed forces and the internal security services. On 10 December 1969, Egyptian security officials, seconded to the RCC rather than to the Interior Ministry, discovered that both men were engaged in a conspiracy to oust the RCC and establish their own leadership.

The motives for the Ahmed-Hawwaz plot were never fully ascertained. In an interview on 11 December, the day after the conspiracy was exposed, Qadhafi claimed that 'the plotters wanted imperialism to stay in Libya. They wanted the bases to stay in Libya. They wanted to obstruct negotiations. They enjoyed support from the bases.'[2] As the attempted coup was foiled just before the RCC planned to open talks on the future of the bases, there may have been some truth in these words; alternatively, Qadhafi may simply have made the link in order to discredit officers activated mainly by personal ambition. The trial of the two ringleaders and 15 accessories, in August 1970, failed to shed much light on their specific intentions.

Following the attempted coup, the RCC decided to abandon the policy of working through intermediaries and proceeded to assert direct control over the government. On 11 December, the RCC issued a provisional 'constitutional proclamation', which redefined its powers; Article 18 stated: 'It exercises the functions of supreme authority and legislation and draws up the general policy of the state on behalf of the people'.[3]

Also in December 1969, the RCC decreed a law entitled 'Decision on the Protection of the Revolution', which made it a criminal offence to engage in political propaganda against the state, arouse 'class hatred', disseminate misinformation about the country's economic and political circumstances, and participate in strikes and demonstrations. It warned that: 'Anyone who takes up arms against the republican regime of the Revolution of 1st September, or takes part in armed bands for this purpose. shall be sentenced to death.'[4]

That same month the 12 names and ranks of RCC members were published for the first time. They were:

Colonel Muammar al-Qadhafi
Staff Major Abdessalam Jalloud
Major Bashir Saghir Hawwadi
Captain Khweildi al-Hamidi
Captain Ali Awad Hamza
Captain Abdul Mounim al-Houni
Captain Abu Bakr Younis Jaber
Captain Mustafa Kharoubi
Captain Omar Abdallah al-Meheshi
Captain Mohammed Nejm
Captain Mukhtar Abdallah al-Qirwi
Lieutenant Mohammed Abu Bakr al-Migharief

Their agreement to end anonymity was in response to a specific request from President Nasser who, following the Ahmed-Hawwaz conspiracy, advised them to personally identify themselves with the Revolution, lest they encourage challenges from other forces within society and the armed forces.[5]

Accepting the general line of the Egyptian leader's advice, the RCC resolved to assume direct control of the administration. On 16 January, having received the resignation of Premier Maghrabi, the RCC appointed a new government containing five of its own members. Qadhafi himself became Premier and Defence Minister; Jalloud became Interior Minister and Local Government Minister; and Hawwadi, Meheshi and Migharief received other portfolios. The one surviving member of the previous administration was Saleh Busair, who retained his post as Foreign Minister. Maghrabi himself, though dropped from the cabinet, was retained as adviser.

Post-colonial Reform

Although almost 20 years of formal independence separated Libya from the era of foreign political control, the first stage of the Libyan revolution, following the deposition of the monarchy, was characterised by post-colonial reform and consolidation. Four initial themes in the programme of the Free Officer leadership amply denote this orientation: firstly, the promotion of Arabism, including the commitment to pursue the conflict with Israel; secondly, a determination to revoke the 1954 Italo-Libyan Treaty and appropriate the property of Italian settlers; thirdly, the dissolution of the military relationship with Britain and the United States and the removal of their bases from Libyan soil; and fourthly, the desire to bring under domestic control the principal source of the country's productive wealth, namely the oil industry. The failure of the monarchy to achieve results in any of these areas was a sufficient indicator of the country's continued semi-colonial status.

As with other Third World countries where pre-capitalist monarchies and dynasties have been overthrown, the process of reform and consolidation began in the state apparatus with the replacement of elements belonging to the old order by personnel associated with the new forces. Most importantly, the armed forces, the guarantor of the RCC's control, underwent a period of reorganisation designed to cement new loyalties and prevent malcontented officers from regrouping. Thus, following Qadhafi's appointment to the position of Supreme Commander-in-Chief of the armed forces, the RCC froze the bank accounts of senior officers, some of whom had fled the country; retired or posted abroad all officers above the rank of major; integrated Cydef, the King's praetorian guard, into the regular army; made a two-fold increase in pay for the ranks; honoured those who had taken part in 'Operation Jerusalem' with promotion and a medal of bravery; and counterbalanced regionally based recruitment – favouring Cyrenaica – with the introduction of comprehensive national conscription. In addition, in the absence of sufficient Libyan military instructors and technicians, the RCC concluded a military co-operation agreement with Egypt, which enabled the armed forces to replace British and American advisers and training courses, and second staff from Egyptian military intelligence to supervise the military reorganisation.

Once the RCC had secured its position within the armed forces, reforms in the constitution and apparatus of royal power began. The *zawiyas*, the independent tier of Sanussi political control, were dissolved; the administrative capital was moved from al-Beida to Tripoli and, in November 1970, the Islamic University at al-Beida was closed; crown lands were expropriated by the state and held for redistribution; and the development projects commissioned under the monarchy were either cancelled, or suspended pending review. The trials of the main personalities of the monarchist state followed: first, the King was tried *in absentia* and sentenced to death by a special court presiding under the authority of the RCC; his wife, also *in absentia*, was sentenced to four years imprisonment; by contrast, Omar al-Shalhi, the Head of the Royal Household, received a life sentence *in absentia*; the Crown Prince, having recognised and co-operated with the new authorities, was dealt the more lenient sentence of three years imprisonment; four former Prime Ministers also received sentences, one *in absentia*; and finally, leading officials and propagandists of the monarchist state were sentenced. All the trials were televised at peak viewing hours in order that the lengthy indictments of corruption and betrayal could generate maximum opprobrium.

Evidence that monarchist forces could still pose a threat to the new regime came in May 1970. The discovery of an arms cache in Sebha revealed proof of a monarchist plot centred on the Fezzan, in which former Sanussi officers planned to invade Libya from Chad with an army of 200 brotherhood members and tribesmen, seize Sebha itself, and mount a campaign to take back Benghazi and Tripoli.[6] Whilst Qadhafi attributed the conspiracy to 'reactionary retired police officers and contractors who had profited from the defunct regime', several leading figures of the Idrisi period were implicated. They incuded Omar al-Shalhi, Prince Abdallah al-Sanussi, a cousin of the ex-King, the Saif al-Nasser family, and two former Prime Ministers, Abdul Hamid Bakkoush and Hussein Mazegh. Eventually, about 20 individuals, some of them policemen, were detained in connection with the plot and sentenced to various terms of imprisonment.

The first anti-colonial reforms followed the dissolution of monarchical power. Initially, in a country still characterised by many semi-colonial features, these were directed against the two most important social forms of national oppression: religion and language. The RCC, in an assertion of

Islam and Arabism, reinstated the precedence of the Arabic alphabet over the Latin; Italian place and street names were changed to Arabic; Christian churches were closed and the Roman Catholic cathedral, consecrated in 1928, was converted into a mosque; finally, bringing the country into line with the customs of Islam, the sale of alcohol, mainly from Italian restaurants and hotels, was prohibited. In addition, intensifying the process of economic 'Libyanisation' inaugurated under the monarchy, the RCC imposed various restrictions on foreign commercial firms, banned their representatives from work in Libya and limited the transfer of funds by foreign residents (in contrast with contract migrants) to 60 per cent of their income.[7]

Principally, the target for these measures was the Italian settler community. From the beginning of the revolution, the RCC had refused to accept the legality of Italian-owned property in Libya, or to endorse the provisions of the 1956 Italo-Libyan Treaty, guaranteeing the property rights of Italian immigrants in Libya. The restrictions placed on the transfer of funds by foreign residents were a pre-emptive move implemented before the general expropriation of Italian property. Following a year of internal consolidation, this was eventually initiated in autumn 1970 and intended to be completed by the first anniversary of 'Operation Jerusalem'. Speaking on 21 July 1970, thereafter known as 'Vengeance Day', Qadhafi announced that the property of foreign residents – including the small Jewish community – was to be 'restored' to the Libyan people. 'The people want back the property which the Italian citizens usurped when their invading armies were in control or when terror of unjust Italian rule prevailed in the country,' he declared.[8]

The expropriations were effected in three stages. In August, Italian commercial property was confiscated; shops and workshops, night clubs and restaurants were closed. In September, the assets of the Banco di Roma and the Banco di Napoli were nationalised. Finally, between the middle of September and the middle of October, the landholdings and private residences of the Italian settlers were taken over. Dispossessed of their property and denied the exercise of their property rights, the vast majority of settlers were induced to leave Libya. Within three months of Qadhafi's 'Vengeance Day' proclamation, 12,770 settlers had departed, relinquishing to the Libyan state: 21,000 hectares of farming land, 687 apartments, 467 villas and 548 other dwellings; 1,207 vehicles, including tractors and lorries; and about LD9 million in frozen funds.[9] On 17 October 1970, Qadhafi pronounced what he described as 'the end of the hated fascist colonisation'.[10]

The Italian government accused Tripoli of flagrant violations of the terms of the 1950 UN resolution on Libyan independence, and the 1956 treaty. Despite this outcry and the calls for compensation, there was no support for sanctions, diplomatic or economic, against Libya. The settler community was a factor of declining importance in Italian politics, and major sections of Italian capital, such as the state-owned hydrocarbons company AGIP, did not want to disrupt their trading relations. Realising the strength of their position, the Libyan authorities refused to recognise any outstanding claims from Italy. Replying to President Guiseppe Saragat in August 1970, Qadhafi stated: 'No provisions or treaties will stand in our way because treaties and agreements which do not recognise our rights will not be treated as such.'[11]

This appropriation of Italian property took place in the ideological context of national rectification. The major components of this ideology were nationalism and modernisation; what was put forward as a process of 'restoration' was, in reality, a process of nation-building and social modernisation. The specifically anti-colonial reforms were implemented in conjunction with a programme of post-colonial reforms designed to eradicate social backwardness as it was maintained and reproduced under the monarchy. The measure of such backwardness was the comparative absence of social infrastructures: notably, when the Free Officers assumed power, Libya possessed inadequate, and inegalitarian systems of housing, health and education. Despite increased social spending in the 1963–68 First Five Year Plan, the monarchy proved incapable of effecting the combined economic *and* social reforms required by the upheavals in society caused by the infusion of oil income – especially the pattern of internal migration and mass urbanisation.

By 1969, urbanisation had reached crisis proportions. Between 1966 and 1973, the urban population was increasing at an average rate of 16 per cent; over 50 per cent of the total population were living in settlements of 20,000 or more people.[12] With the concentration of population, rents and food prices had begun to soar beyond the range of large sections of the newly-urbanised populations The supply of public and private rented accommodation was limited; according to the post-monarchist Ministry of Information in 1970, there were about 300,000 shanties in Libya, 'most of which were about to fall down or in urgent need of rehabilitation'.[13]

For immediate relief from the social stresses produced by these conditions, the RCC promptly doubled the minimum wage, ended the system of contract labour, introduced statutory price controls and compulsorily reduced rents by between 30 to 40 per cent. Subsequently, the Ministry of Housing launched a campaign to increase the rate of house construction in order to eradicate homelessness and demolish the shanty towns. The text of the 1972–75 Three Year Intermediary Plan, which treated housing construction as the major social priority, stated: 'As for housing, the ultimate goal is to provide one housing unit per family in the next ten years, by 1982'. Accordingly, to realise such an objective, the annual housing budget rose from LD32 million in 1970 to LD185 million in 1978. In 1974, the peak building year, Libya was producing housing units at a rate of 13 per 1,000 head of population; in the Western world, only Sweden and Denmark had higher rates of construction.[14] In a celebration of the revolution's achievements, the last shanty was bulldozed in 1976, by

Qadhafi; by 1978, 148,626 housing units had been completed – half as many again as the total housing stock of 1969.

Table 4.1   Completed Housing Units, 1964–1978

	Private Sector	Public Sector	Per cent	Total
1964/70				
average	2,305	2,912	(55.8)	5,217
1970/71	2,957	3,012	(50.5)	5,969
1971/72	5,634	3,891	(40.9)	9,525
1972/73	8,173	6,651	(44.9)	14,824
1973	12,754	4,650	(26.7)	17,404
1974	18,480	12,633	(40.6)	31,113
1975	17,682	10,595	(37.5)	28,277
1976	13,800	12,744	(48.0)	26,544
1977	6,401	5,924	(48.1)	12,325
1978	3,400	3,855	(53.1)	7,255

Source: Secretariat of Information, 1979.

Despite the exaggerations of official reports, the country's health sector also experienced an intense period of expansion and development. In 1968, there were 41 hospitals with a total 5,646 beds; by 1978, the number of hospitals had risen by 50 per cent and the number of beds was 13,347. The growth in the country's hospital capacity was outstripping the growth in the population; whereas, in 1968, there existed only 3.1 beds per 1,000, by 1978 there were 5.0 beds per 1,000; in 1968, there were 700 doctors in Libya; in 1978 there were more than 3,000. Within five years of the military take-over, the ratio of nurses to population had been reduced from 1 to 2,040 patients to 1 to 240 patients.[15] In addition, following medical campaigns to immunise and treat the population against specific illnesses, the early years of the post-revolutionary period witnessed the effective eradication of malaria, and a decline in the outbreaks of trachoma and tuberculosis. Patients in the remoter parts of the interior received treatment from a flying doctor service. Life expectancy rose from 45 years in 1960 to 53 years in 1974.

Education was the third major priority area of social reform and development. Following comparatively high sectoral expenditure in the 1963–68 first five-year plan of the Idrisi period, the RCC enacted a gradual transition from the monarchist system of education, suitable to the needs of the country's merchant class, to a system of universal education. Ranging from 5.7 per cent of the annual development budget in 1970, to 9.5 per cent in 1975, the total outlay on education was proportionally less than in the

Table 4.2   Libya Nationals: Levels of educational attainment, 1973

Educational Status	Total population		Males	
	Number	Per cent	Number	Per Cent
Illiterate	616,900	60.8	204,630	38.6
Literate (reading only)	8,500	0.8	6,930	1.3
Literate (reading & writing)	207,900	20.6	167,740	31.8
Primary certificate attained	97,600	9.6	79,530	15.1
Preparatory certificate	41,400	4.1	34,210	6.5
Secondary certificate	33,500	3.3	28,040	5.3
University degree	5,800	0.6	6,370	1.2
Not stated	1,700	0.2	840	0.2
Totals	*1,013,300*	*100.0*	*526,290*	*100.0*

Source: Ministry of Planning and Scientific Research, Census and Statistical Department, *Some Preliminary Results of the 1973 Population Census* (Benghazi, 1975).

plan period 1963–68. Nevertheless, whilst education was not accorded the same priority in the initial stage of post-monarchist reform, the previously excluded lower strata of the Libyan population were successively integrated into the education process.

The two basic indicators of educational progress are levels of literacy, and primary education. Between 1952 and 1973, the illiteracy rate among the Libyan population fell from 90 per cent to 61 per cent. Correspondingly, between 1964 and 1973, the rate of primary school enrolment for boys aged 6 to 14 rose from 51 per cent to 81 per cent.[16] Admittedly, there were some advances in literacy rates and primary school enrolment in the 1963–68 period, but most evidence indicates the attainment of higher levels following the overthrow of the monarchy. In other sections of the education system, the achievements were less dramatic. Student places at Tripoli University increased from 1,374 in 1969–70 to 5,702 in 1978–79, and those at Gar Younis in Benghazi rose from 3,360 in 1969–70 to 7,481 in 1978–79, but considered in terms of the population growth, and a rising foreign student intake, the increase was not substantial.[17]

Two reasons have conventionally been given for this rapid growth of social infrastructure. First, that social reforms were concessions necessary to help establish popular allegiance to the new regime; and second, that the increase in social development proceeded from the growth of oil income. Clearly, both were major contributory factors. There remains, however, a key third factor of overriding importance; in essence, this is the social role undertaken by the state. In Libya, under Qadhafi's leadership, the role of the state was not limited to planning and preparing the conditions for the reproduction of services and skills. After the September Al Fateh Revolution, the state machinery was not only applied to these objectives, but actively and increasingly supervised the social *and* economic organisation of the population.

The Expulsion of the Bases

For Libya's strategic patrons, Britain and the United States, the anti-colonial course embarked on by the new authorities had its most immediate and devastating impact in the elimination of their military bases. These were of no minor significance. The British and American military facilities in Libya added an extra dimension to the Western, NATO alliance, particularly regarding possible intervention in the region. The ranges around Wheelus Field and al-Adem were unrivalled in the scope they offered for military exercises. Whilst the RAF and the USAF benefited from near perfect conditions for low-level flying runs with live ammunition, in Cyrenaica the British retained access to terrain ideal for large-scale practice manoeuvres. British and American resistance to the new regime's stated intention of expelling the foreign military presence was expected. For the United States in particular, the closure of Wheelus Field would be a strategic loss, affecting their military capacity in the region at a time when the Soviet presence in Egypt was growing.

The threat to the bases was the main concern in London and Washington after the sudden deposition of the monarchy. Indeed, the British and Americans, in eschewing precipitous action in support of the Idris regime, had hoped to safeguard the future of their facilities in a fresh agreement with the new authorities. There was no guarantee, once the RCC's official position had become clear, that either country would comply without the exercise of force. Despite the *pro forma* denials of the British Foreign Office, it was common knowledge in the Arab world that the British had a contingency plan for intervention in Libya. As part of the 1953 Anglo-Libya treaty, a secret protocol was attached providing for the invasion of Libya in case of an emergency. Details of the plan, code-named 'Operation Radford', were obtained by the Egyptians in 1965 from an archivist at the British Ministry of Defence.[18] Published in full in *al-Ahram*, the plan called for the movement of British troops from Germany, Malta and Cyprus in order to defend the King and restore order. According to Mohammed Heikal, *al-Ahram's* editor, the contingency scheme was intended precisely for the situation which had occurred in Libya. What deterred the British was the speed and decisiveness with which the Free Officers acted. Had a prolonged struggle ensued, Britain and the United States would have been handed a pretext for intervention.

In Qadhafi, the British and Americans were faced with a new leader who would brook no compromise. In his keynote speech in Tripoli on 16

October, Qadhafi boldly pledged that he would turn the country into a 'battlefield' if the British and Americans failed to withdraw by 'reasonable means'.[19] Two weeks later, on 29 October, the RCC made its first formal approach to Britain on the subject, demanded the prompt evacuation of British forces from Libyan territory. The British, under Defence Minister Denis Healey, assessed the situation carefully. Loss of the training grounds in Cyrenaica was considered damaging, but there seemed no alternative to acquiescence.[20] The experience of Suez and the Algerian civil war, warned against further colonial adventures. The Wilson government responded with a call for talks; these lasted for two sessions – a total of six hours. At the first meeting on 8 December, the British Ambassador Donald Maitland, was instructed to concede the principle of withdrawal. After that, it was simply a question of working out the details. At the second session, a week later, Maitland announced a departure deadline of 31 March 1970. Even before the talks had commenced, the British had reduced their presence at al-Adem and Tobruk from 2,000 in October to 1,000 in December.

In forcing the issue, the Libyans had adeptly deployed a number of powerful bargaining counters. The most important was their ability – particularly injurious in a rising oil power – to threaten the withdrawal of their sterling balances, standing at £384 million. If that proved insufficient, they could also initiate the revision of the dispensable contracts, and nationalise BP and other British interests in Libya. The British, on the other hand, were in a relatively weak position; they could only counter Libya with a threat to suspend the contract for the supply of 200 Chieftain tanks, ordered by the previous regime to boost the Libyan armed forces' ground capacity. It was a defiant gesture unlikely to be effective. At the time, British overseas military commitments were under general review as the Labour government began Britain's retreat from east of Suez. The British were simply disinclined for an entanglement with another nationalist government. Maitland's mission, as far as Whitehall was concerned, was to urge on the Libyans a joint communiqué emphasising the mutual benefits of further Anglo-Libyan co-operation. For London it was a question of damage-control, chiefly to protect extensive British economic interests.

Flushed with success, the RCC turned its attention to the evacuation of the American airbase at Wheelus Field. Talks commenced in December, soon after the British had conceded, but not without much disquiet at the prospect of handling over the sophisticated base — the regional head-quarters, of the USAF — to a 'radical Arab regime'. Indeed, had it seemed probable that the Libyans would hand over the facilities to the Soviet Union, the Nixon administration may have baulked at withdrawal. But Qadhafi was insistent that Libya would not open the facilities to other foreign powers. 'Revolutionary Libya will never substitute a foreigner for another foreigner or an intruder for another intruder', he was quoted as saying in the *Libyan Mail* in May 1970. In any event, Britain's decision to withdraw had already pulled the rug from under the feet of the Americans, so Washington submitted. On 24 December, the day after the British announced their withdrawal, a joint Libyan-American statement tersely announced that the United States would follow suit by 30 June. In fact, the American evacuation, like the British, was carried out before the deadline, and with a minimum of fuss. The British finally left Libya on 28 March, and the Americans completed their withdrawal on 11 June. It was a historic achievement. Celebrating a 'victory over imperialism', the revolutionary authorities renamed al-Adem Airbase, Gamal Abdul Nasser Airbase, and Wheelus Field, Okba bin Nafi Airbase, after one of the original Arab conquerors of Libya.

Any hope that either country had of maintaining some military influence in Libya, through supply and training arrangements, was soon dissipated. On 29 December, following up their initial success, the RCC cancelled the former regime's contract with the British Aircraft Corporation for the *Thunderbird* and *Rapier* missile systems – which were of no use to the country except in a Western-backed conflict with its Arab neighbours. In retaliation, the British held up the delivery of the Chieftains. The RCC, not to be blackmailed, demanded back various down-payments and began a major review of arms supply policy. In November, the first tentative approaches were made to the French government as an alternative arms supplier.[21] The Libyans asked to purchase Dassault Mirage planes earmarked for Israel embargoed because of the 1967 War. The prospect of such a sale, to an Arab country not actually covered by the embargo, was too attractive to be ignored. The French saw in it a means to extend their influence in North Africa at the expense of the British and Americans. On 9 January 1970, the conclusion of the deal was announced: France agreed to sell Libya an initial 50 *Mirage* V aircraft, 15 to be delivered by 1971.

The Libyans wanted these highly-coveted French warplanes to rebuild the Arab arsenal in the confrontation with Israel. Nasser viewed Libya as a conduit for arms that were otherwise blocked by the Western arms embargo. While the negotiation was still taking place he told Qadhafi: 'If you can get *Phantoms* or *Mirages*, this will be a colossal addition to Arab strength.'[22]

The performance of the Israeli *Mirages* in the June 1967 War had been outstanding. The surprise attacks, which wiped out most of the Egyptian airforce while still on the ground, were led by squadrons of *Mirage* fighters. Thanks to France, the Arabs would now have access to the same level of technology as the Zionists, instead of the usual disparity in the air. Vigorous protest naturally followed. The British and Americans were enraged at the blatant opportunism of the French. Both countries had decided to pass up lavish arms contracts with the new Libyan regime precisely because they did not want to shift the balance of forces in favour of the Arabs; they were in favour of Israel's military superiority.

The French, ambitious to become the leading arms supplier in the Arab world, ignored this hypocrisy on the part of the British and Americans. On

22 January, the French Minister of Defence, Michel Debré, announced that the arms deal was expanded to include the supply of 30 *Mirage* 111E interceptors and 20 *Mirage* 111B and 111R trainers.[23] The planes would come armed with *Matra 530* air-to-air missiles. In addition, France agreed to start training Libyan pilots at Wheelus Field – then still in the process of being evacuated. It was to be the largest-ever single arms agreement yet secured by the French. With the final addition of team *Mirage* 111E interceptors on 31 January, the package totalled 110 warplanes. It was astronomically expensive, and the cost of operational maintenance would be much higher, but in the Libya of 1970, funds for the defence of Libyan interests were ample. No conditions were attached to their use in the Middle East conflict, other than that they must be 'based' and 'maintained' in Libya. The only real restrictions applied to their use in a clash with French client states in Africa.

The deal was another triumph for the revolutionary authorities. Not only had the RCC expelled the foreign bases, it had dramatically ended its military dependence on Britain and the United States; Britain had lost its place as the leading supplier of the Libyan Army and Navy, and the United States had been ousted from its role as the main contractor for the Libyan air force. The switch in arms purchase to France permitted the RCC greater room to manoeuvre in pursuit of its nationalist objectives. The British attempt to hold the new Libyan political leadership to ransom with the suspension of the Chieftain tank contract rebounded on Whitehall. The revolutionary authorities succeeded in their most important goal: the British and American military stranglehold on Libya was broken.

Victory over the Oil Companies

The world outside Libya felt the impact of the political transformation chiefly through the changes instituted in oil policy. Within weeks of the Free Officer take-over, the companies could discern a more searching and assertive government stance, belying official attempts to calm oil market fears. Speaking on 17 September, Prime Minister Dr Suleyman Maghrabi linked co-operation with the concession-holders to greater exploration. 'I can confirm,' said Maghrabi, 'that we shall endeavour to co-operate with the oil companies provided that the interests of the Libyan people – which were neglected by the former regime – are taken into account.'[24] He went on to claim that these interests could, if the government deemed necessary, be safeguarded 'by means of a more effective control over oil operations'. On 7 October, the first republican Petroleum Minister Anis Shtawi added: 'We demand a fair price for our oil. The Revolution will not hesitate to be firm with the oil companies.'[25] The years of obsequiousness had clearly gone. From these, and similar statements, the companies' executives even speculated that nationalisation measures were imminent.

In reality, the Libyan authorities were immediately preoccupied with the eradication of the abuse and privilege endemic to the oil industry. Beyond an early anti-corruption drive, they had no coherent oil policy. The first act of government intervention, undertaken by Shtawi on 27 October, was to cancel a dubious joint venture between Lipetco and Chappaqua, which, in the words of the Under-Secretary at the Petroleum Ministry Isa al-Ghiblawi, 'was the result of pressure from one of the most notorious personalities of our time' – Colonel Shalhi.[26] In fact, Chappaqua had acquired the partnership without any previous record of oil production. Two days later, Ghiblawi stressed that the decision did not infer the repudiation of signed agreements. 'We have no intention of nationalising oil. We consider ourselves bound by the agreements concluded with all the oil companies in Libya.'[27] The exposure of corruption at the heart of the old regime nevertheless provided the revolutionary government with a useful rallying point, around which to mobilise opinion for further reform in the oil industry. Previously, according to US State Department adviser, oilman Walter Levy, 'Idris's regime was thought to be sound because it was corrupt.'[28]

A consistent oil policy was formulated only following a review of the Libyan oil industry. The review was launched by Shtawi on 7 October, but with the fall of the Maghrabi government in January 1970, oil policy came under the joint supervision of Abdessalam Jalloud and Ezzedine Mabrouk, a barrister and court of appeal judge, who took over the portfolio of Petroleum Minister. Together, both men, despite their different backgrounds, began to devise a strategy for modifying the terms of the dependent relationship between the Libyan state and oil capital. Lacking the indigenous expertise to conduct a technical survey, they turned to other producing countries, notably Algeria and Venezuela, for advice. As Libyan crude was being used to undercut and depress world oil prices, both states responded positively. Venezuela, among the most experienced of oil producing countries, despatched its leading technician, Arevalo Guzman Reyes. He rapidly produced a report showing instances of oil-field malpractice, including the failure by numerous companies to observe proper standards of conservation. Following this report, and the instructive lessons of other producers, the Libyan duo emerged with a twin-track strategy: simultaneously, though separately, they would try to secure both the transfer of technology and higher oil rents. Along the one track, they would expand state involvement in downstream ventures, prior to longer-term participation in upstream operations. Along the other, they would seek a higher rate of income, by pushing up posted-prices.

Armed with this strategy, the Libyans started to square up to the challenge of renegotiating with the companies. Their first priority was an increase in posted-prices. On 20 January 1970, Mabrouk summoned the representatives of the 21 oil companies operating in the country, and insisted that they begin talks with a Pricing Committee, set up in December 1969. Nine days later, the companies met the Committee for the first time, but resisted further changes in the terms of their contracts. Qadhafi, who attended the meeting, warned the companies of their intransigence, stressing that 'the Libyan people, who have lived for five thousand years without petroleum, are able to live again without it.'[29] The companies were clearly disturbed by the remark, but two rounds of meetings with individual companies, convened over the next few weeks, failed to bring the required shift in position. Nevertheless, the tactic of dealing with the companies on a one-by-one basis revealed sufficient disunity to encourage further efforts by the revolutionary government. Qadhafi decided it was worth escalating the power struggle. In early April, he declared: 'The battle with the oil companies is becoming ineluctable and we must be prepared to face up to it.'[30]

In the confrontation ahead, the Libyans were fortunate in having a number of factors in their favour. One of which was the growth in oil production: by 1969, Libya had begun exporting, on a monthly basis, 3.1 million b/d, which put the country in the same rank as other leading oil exporters, such as Iran, Saudi Arabia and Venezuela. In the same year, the country's share of OPEC production rose to a peak of 15.5 per cent, or 7.5 per cent of global oil production. The following year, production *per annum* reached a highpoint of 1,211 million barrels. Table 4.3 provides a break-down of production by company.

The Libyans also benefited from changes within the oil market. The continued closure of the Suez Canal raised the demand for 'short-haul' Mediterranean oil, especially the higher graded Libyan crudes, which satisfied new American anti-pollution legislation. The number of wells completed in 1969 was greater than in any previous year since the peak year – 1964 – when the total passed 400. By the beginning of the Libyan negotiations, this demand was again strengthened by generally firmer conditions within the market caused, in part, by a succession of events in the Middle East. Following the June 1967 War, the Popular Front for the Liberation of Palestine had declared war on Western economic targets in the region. The oil pipelines from the Gulf to the Mediterranean were prime targets. In May 1969, a commando unit from the Front blew up a section of the key Tapline in the area of the Golan Heights, which had recently come under Israeli occupation. Pumping came to an abrupt halt. In October, after the line was repaired, they attacked again; once more, pumping was halted. Then, on 3 May 1970, just as the Libyans commenced negotiations, the Tapline, repaired for a second time, was 'accidently' damaged by a bulldozer from the Syrian Ministry of Public Works. This time the Syrian authorities delayed repairs for nearly nine months. Eastern Mediterranean supplies were reduced by 475,000 b/d. No evidence of collusion between the two governments has ever come to light, but the sudden elimination of Tapline supplies put the Libyans in an immeasurably stronger bargaining position.

Finally, the Libyan government was assisted by the intense competition between majors and independents for the European market. Since gaining

Table 4.3 Growth in Libyan Crude Production by Operating Company, 1961–70 ('000 b/d)

Company	1961	1962	1963	1964	1965	1966	1967	1968	1969	1970
Esso Standard	18.2	126.2	250.0	408.9	471.7	488.1	495.9	615.4	618.3	570.6
Esso Sirte	—	—	43.6	73.1	95.4	95.8	107.2	128.0	127.9	121.4
Oasis	—	57.7	167.2	324.0	505.8	650.5	630.0	687.9	789.0	946.1
Mobil	—	—	2.8	45.6	100.7	170.5	204.2	237.7	264.2	252.9
Amoseas	—	—	—	13.1	43.7	81.9	128.9	244.5	369.1	322.9
BP/NB Hunt	—	—	—	—	—	4.0	168.5	304.9	321.3	412.9
Phillips[a]	—	—	—	—	2.9	8.2	4.8	7.5	6.0	4.2
Amoco	—	—	—	—	—	8.3	4.4	1.1	0.4	7.7
Occidental	—	—	—	—	—	—	—	382.1	607.8	659.4
Aquitaine	—	—	—	—	—	—	—	—	5.1	19.9
Total	18.2	183.9	463.6	864.7	1220.2	1507.3	1743.9	2609.1	3109.1	3318.0

Note: a. Concession surrendered to the Libyan National Oil Corporation in November 1970.

Source: Ministry of Petroleum Affairs, *Libyan Oil, 1954–67*; Ministry of Petroleum, *Libyan Oil, 1954–1971*.

a substantial foothold in Middle Eastern production, through their concessions in Libya, the independents had used the relatively less costly Libyan crude to break into the European market. The expenses they had incurred in establishing marketing operations were largely borne by the Libyan government in the form of discounts. Whilst the practice was subsequently stopped after pressure from the majors and OPEC, both Continental and Marathon had already eroded the majors' distribution monopoly. Neither Occidental nor Bunker Hunt, when they later entered into European marketing, faced serious impediments. The majors, compelled to equalise their prices for crude from several sources, suffered an on-going decline in their market share. Any action on the part of the producing state to bring the independents' prices closer to parity with the equalised rate was tacitly welcomed by the majors. Their diversity of supply ensured that, in the long run, they would be in a stronger negotiating position. The independents, which had no large interests outside North America, were in a much more vulnerable position.

The main weaknesses on the Libyan side arose from the companies' control of technology. Despite their various rivalries, majors and independents shared a common interest in preventing the transfer of technology to the host state. The Libyan government, nevertheless, made its own contingency plans, designed to reduce technological dependence on the companies. On 24 January 1970, a delegation arrived from Algeria, then engaged in its own conflict with the oil companies, for a series of consultations with the Petroleum Ministry; a subsequent communiqué expressed mutual solidarity. Soon after, the government began to receive the support of other signatories to the January 1970 Baghdad hydrocarbons co-operation agreement, namely Egypt and Iraq. Then, on 3 March, Lipetco, the Libyan partner in joint ventures, was reorganised in the form of a national oil company, under the name of the Libyan National Oil Corporation, or Linoco, by which the Libyans hoped, eventually, to increase their own technical capacity. Finally, and most importantly, Mabrouk travelled to Moscow on 8 March and concluded a crucial co-operation agreement, in which Libya secured Soviet technological assistance. One of the companies' key bargaining tools, their monopoly of technical manpower, was greatly weakened. If the Libyans decided to withdraw concessions, the means to continue production, independent of the companies, were now available to them.

By April, the revolutionary government felt confident enough for the trial of strength. On 14 April, the former Prime Minister, Dr Suleyman Maghrabi, was appointed President of the Pricing Committee. A former lawyer, who had worked for Exxon, he astutely commenced negotiations with the company most vulnerable to pressure: Occidental. Occidental representatives were accused of damaging oil-field practices and instructed to cut back their production at the Intissar field from 320,000 b/d to 219,000 b/d. Justifying their action, the Libyans invoked a 1968 conservation regulation, circulated, but never endorsed by the companies.[31] When the tactic failed to secure compliance on pricing, the Ministry's Technical Department, which implemented the regulation, ordered the company to cut back its total Libyan production from 800,000 b/d to 485,000 b/d. Rather than yield, the President of Occidental Armand Hammer turned to Exxon, known as 'the majors' major', for support. Hammer asked the company, as a temporary measure, to supply Occidental with crude just above the cost of production. In reply, Exxon's President Kenneth Jamieson would only offer crude at the market rate.[32] Moreover, having been turned down by Exxon, Occidental was subsequently abandoned by the State Department. Hammer, realising the game was not worth a candle, decided to abandon his intransigent position and start talking in earnest.

Meanwhile, the Petroleum Ministry had started to apply the strategy of cut-backs more generally. Libyan exports were reduced from a peak of 3.7 million b/d in April, to about 3 million b/d in August and September. The total volume of lost production equalled nearly 900,000 b/d. In the circumstances of the Tapline shutdown and firmer conditions in the oil market, the effects were devastating, as the figures in Table 4.4 show.

Whilst these restrictions were implemented, the authorities also piled on the pressure in other ways. For example, Esso was barred from inaugurating exports of Liquid Natural Gas (LNG) from Mersa Brega until the dispute over posted-prices was resolved. In addition, port dues of 1 cent per barrel were imposed on tankers loading crude oil. Furthermore, staying with their two-track policy, the Petroleum Ministry expanded state ownership in downstream oil operations. By a decree issued on 4 July, the government nationalised the internal oil marketing operations of the companies, bringing the companies' distributive installation and service stations under state ownership. These had belonged to just three companies: ENI (Asseil), Esso and Shell. Finally, in another decree issued in August, the government banned *overseas* payments to employees and contractors in Libya.

As expected, Occidental was the first to succumb to the Libyan pressures. In September, the company signed an agreement – later called the 1 September Agreement – accepting increases in the posted-price of 30 cents per barrel by 2 cents per barrel on 1 January for each of the next five years. The deal, which according to Occidental was concluded 'under duress',[33] also provided for a rise from 50 to 58 per cent in the rate of tax, although five per cent of the increase was paid in lieu of expenditure on an agricultural scheme at Kufra, to which the company was required to contribute under the terms of its concessions obtained in 1968. Lastly, the agreement with Occidental recognised the principle of price differentials for different grades of crude. The base gravity was increased from 39 degrees to 40 degrees, and the price reductions for each degree below were set at 1.5 instead of 2 cents.

Within the next six weeks, with one exception, all the other concession-

Table 4.4   Ministry of Petroleum Cutbacks in Crude Oil Production, 1970

Company	Field	Cutback Date	Daily Production From	To	Cutbacks
Occidental	103A	1/5/1970	359,342	219,246	140,096
	103C	25/5/1970	37,578	34,000	3,578
	103D	25/5/1970	380,664	165,000	215,664
	102	25/8/1970	67,863	46,319	21,544
Total			*845,447*	*464,565*	*380,882*
Amoseas	Dour	15/6/1970	9,339	4,361	4,978
	Beida	15/6/1970	16,284	8,733	7,551
	Kutla	15/6/1970	14,112	13,162	950
	Nafura	15/6/1970	332,796	247,839	84,957
Total			*372,531*	*274,095*	*98,436*
Oasis	Daffa	30/7/1970	192,472	161,358	31,114
	Waha	30/7/1970	155,168	130,633	24,535
	Jalo	30/7/1970	420,292	371,508	48,784
	Zasat	30/7/1970	3,323	2,921	402
	Samah	30/7/1970	84,312	75,883	8,429
	Bu Hezan	30/7/1970	7,989	7,883	642
	Bahi	30/7/1970	130,730	109,119	21,611
	Zahra	30/7/1970	82,303	36,131	46,172
Total			*1,076,589*	*894,900*	*181,689*
Mobil Oil	Abu Meras	15/8/1970	489	345	144
	Deeb	15/8/1970	2,506	2,447	59
	Aura	15/8/1970	16,270	11,149	5,121
	Dor-Mrada	15/8/1970	13,569	4,774	8,795
	Amal	15/8/1970	219,501	183,389	36,112
	Rakb D	15/8/1970	12,999	10,771	2,228
	Raeub Z	15/8/1970	4,041	2,559	2,482
	Hofra	15/8/1970	11,185	1,836	9,349
	Frood	15/8/1970	4,761	3,684	1,077
Total			*286,804*	*222,146*	*64,658*
Esso	Zelten	20/8/1970	587,106	486,069	101,037
	Raguba	20/8/1970	134,214	105,104	29,110
	Caheeb	20/8/1970	12,095	10,080	2,080
	Jabal	20/8/1970	28,082	21,122	6,960
	Arshad	20/8/1970	21,122	4,386	868
	Ralah	20/8/1970	30,613	30,595	18
Total			*770,364*	*630,316*	*140,048*

Source: Ministry of Petroleum, Technical Department Publication, October 1970.

holders had submitted along lines similar to this 'model' agreement with Occidental. The exception, Phillips, surrendered its small and higher cost field, which subsequently was taken over by Linoco.

Coming just after the nationalisation of the Algerian oil industry in June 1970, these changes precipitated a dramatic shift in the relations between the producing countries and the oil companies. The ghost of the former Iranian Premier Mohammed Mossadegh, whose nationalisation of the Anglo-Iranian Oil Company was defeated by an oil boycott in 1951, was exorcised. Ironically, the Shah of Iran, who contributed to Mossadegh's downfall, was the first beneficiary. In November, after demands from the Iranian authorities, taxes were raised from 50 to 55 per cent, prompting the companies to introduce price adjustments to stabilise the market. The majors offered the Gulf states and Nigeria the additional five per cent tax increase for their heavier crudes, but the concession was rapidly overshadowed by developments at the OPEC summit meeting at Caracas between 9–12 December. A resolution passed at this meeting stressed that the 55 per cent rate of taxation was simply the 'minimum', and insisted that 'the reference price for the purpose of determining the tax liability of the concessionnaire companies should be determined by the governments of the member countries'.[34] Indeed Venezuela, acting on the resolution, legislated a 60 per cent liability in late December and demanded the right to control the reference price. Libya, encouraged by the Venezuelan example, soon followed suit.

On 3 January 1971, the Libyan authorities relaunched their drive for higher levels of tax income, with Staff Major Jalloud summoning representatives of the 21 companies to his office in Tripoli. His initiative coincided with negotiations between the majors and an inter-ministerial commission acting on behalf of Gulf producers; but Jalloud told the companies that whatever the result of the talks in the Gulf, Libya insisted on a favoured nation status. More specifically, he laid out a list of demands, which included a rise of 69 cents per barrel – an increase of 27 per cent – and an agreement to backdate 39 cents to 5 June 1967 (when the Suez Canal was closed) and the remaining 30 cents to May 1970, when the Tapline was severed. The increases would be permanent in the case of the 'Suez surcharge' and temporary in the case of the Tapline supplement. Finally, Jalloud said that in future the Libyan government would require the companies to invest 25 per cent of their local profits within Libya itself.

The wily Armand Hammer, President of Occidental, decided that his company's best defence lay in the formation of a united front. Bracing himself for a further confrontation with the Libyan authorities, he proposed a surplus oil-sharing agreement between the majors and independents. Exxon, which had disappointed Hammer in the 1971 negotiations, remained unimpressed, but Occidental found a powerful ally in Sir David Barran, the President of Shell. Under the influence of Shell, the only major to have tried to resist the government in the first round, a conference of 23 oil companies met in New York on 11 January 1971. After four days of discussion an agreement — kept secret for four years — emerged, binding the majors to equal-out oil supplies if the Libyan authorities should contrive a shortage of production.[35] Normally, such an agreement would have violated United States anti-trust legislation, but the companies applied – and received – a special dispensation. In fact, there is strong evidence that the Nixon administration tacitly encouraged the development of a cartel agreement to thwart the Libyan leadership. According to Pierre Terzian, 'the US government decided to intervene by calling on its friends within OPEC to facilitate the companies' risk.'

Although Jalloud and Mabrouk remained in the dark about the precise terms of the New York agreement, they were well aware of increased coordination between the oil companies. This had become apparent after a second round of oil company talks in London in late January, when the companies had decided they would be represented by a single negotiator in 'separate but linked' negotiations with the Gulf and Mediterranean producers.[36] In the case of the Gulf, they chose Lord Strathalmond; in the case of the Mediterranean, Charles Piercy, an experienced negotiator from Exxon. He was duly despatched to Tripoli for talks with Libya, the key Mediterranean producer, but Jalloud refused to meet him, regarding him simply as the representative of Exxon. Refusing to accept joint negotiations, he demanded one-to-one talks with the companies.[37] Consequently, Strathalmond's mission in the Gulf soon became untenable because the companies' joint strategy required the establishment of recognised and balanced price differentials between Mediterranean crudes. The Libyan authorities' resistance to the companies' negotiating strategy, made this impossible.

Reluctantly, the companies were compelled to settle in separate and disunited negotiations. Following the 22nd extraordinary OPEC conference in Teheran on 3 February, the producer states' organisation issued an ultimatum, backed by the Shah of Iran, giving the companies until 15 February to accept the 'minimum demands' of the six Gulf countries, which included a 35 cents a barrel rise for this 'long-haul' crude. On 14 February, an agreement, subsequently signed in Teheran, was finally reached in negotiations in Paris between Strathalmond and Jamshid Amouzegar, the chief Iranian negotiator. According to the terms of the settlement, the Gulf producers were awarded a 33 per cent increase in posted-prices. Saudi Arabian light crude thereafter rose from $1.80 per barrel to $2.18 and soon oil was again flowing down the Tapline. In the meantime, on 28 January, with the prospect of agreement in sight, the Syrian government had granted permission for Tapline repairs to begin.

Under the terms of the Teheran agreement Libya would have received an estimated 56.6 cents a barrel for crude. Jalloud, however, held out for $1.20 barrel. Despite the resumption of Tapline supplies, he refused to accept a lower differential between Mediterranean and Gulf crude. In addition, the Libyan Vice-Premier reiterated his call for the companies to invest in oil exploration in Libya. Reacting to the slow-down in exploration surveying and drilling, he declared: 'For each barrel of oil produced, a new barrel must be discovered.'[38] Moreover, he stressed that the Teheran agreement did not, in his opinion, 'fulfil the aspirations of the Gulf peoples.' He commented: 'We shall not be satisfied with what was obtained in the agreement.'[39]

In pressing their claims, the Libyan authorities benefited from the formation of a 'united front' of Mediterranean oil producers, initiated by the Algerian Minister of Industry and Energy, Belaid Abdessalam. In January 1971, he visited Tripoli for consultations with Staff Major Jalloud, resulting in a communiqué affirming a 'common front' between both North African countries. The following month, a conference of all OPEC Mediterranean producers – Algeria, Iraq, Libya and Saudi Arabia – was convened in Tripoli. As an indication of the dominant position Libya retained among 'short-haul' Mediterranean crude production, the conference granted the Libyan government a mandate to negotiate on behalf of the four states. The day after the conference, 24 February, Jalloud began summoning the companies to his office in Tripoli. He told company representatives that negotiations must be completed in two weeks, otherwise the ministers from the four states would reconvene in the Libyan capital and 'decide on the appropriate measures to take, including a stoppage of all oil exports to the Mediterranean.'[40]

On 2 March the companies presented their response to the Libyan government. They proposed posted-prices of $2.985 per barrel – just over half the asking price. In fact, the offer may have been a 'starter' in what the companies believed could develop into an oil-price auction. Jalloud, however, was in no mood to haggle. He not only dismissed this first offer, but the second offer of $3.15 per barrel, too. On 10 March, impatient with the companies' dissembling, he issued an ultimatum affording them three days grace in which to come up with a final, satisfactory offer. When the companies replied with a mere four cents extra, he immediately took steps to reconvene the Mediterranean producing countries, warning the companies of both an embargo and nationalisation. Resuming in session on 15 March, the conference of ministers produced a statement unilaterally fixing posted-prices. For the purposes of negotiation, the actual rate was kept a closely-guarded secret, but the companies were warned of an embargo if the levels were not applied. Meeting in London, the companies responded with an offer of $3.31 per barrel, which was sufficient to induce serious negotiations. These were concluded on 25 March, when, at the last moment, Jalloud successfully extracted a further 2 cents from the companies. Libyan obstinacy, compounded by the country's 'swing' capacity in short-haul exports, had triumphed again.

The fruits of success were, however, short-lived. Movements within the international economy robbed the producers' victory of any kind of permanency. The oil companies, because of their integrated relationships, were able to pass on the increased costs to the consumers; in turn, the higher costs of production in the industrialised countries were transferred to the Third World, including the expanding economies of the oil producers, in the form of manufactured goods, notably arms and weapons systems, which absorbed a growing share of the producers' increased 'rents'. In effect, the surpluses of the oil producing countries were recycled in such a way as to benefit key sections of Western capital. Before long, as the exchange value of producers' surpluses suffered major deterioration, their improved trade terms began to decline.

Changes in the international financial system also dealt a severe blow to the producing countries. Like other exporters of primary products, the oil producers' income steadily declined following the decision of the US administration, under President Nixon, to abandon a fixed rate of exchange, whereby the dollar was pegged at $35 an ounce of gold. The depreciation of the dollar, allowed to float from 15 August 1971, drastically reduced the earnings of the oil producers, which were fixed in dollars. The 25th OPEC conference, in Beirut in September 1971, demanded price adjustments, but the companies, who were buying in dollars and selling in Europe in appreciating currencies, prevaricated for several months. In fact, not until December after an OPEC ultimatum, did the companies agree to discuss a compensatory price increase. Finally, in January 1972, the companies met with OPEC in Geneva and agreed to raise the price of crude by 8.4 per cent, but a further devaluation in the dollar, announced in December 1971, meant that the producers were far from satisfied. It was not until a second Geneva agreement was concluded in March 1972 that the companies accepted the principle of compensatory increases for the devaluation of the dollar.

Libya was not party to either of the Geneva agreements, which included only the signatories of the Teheran agreement, not the Mediterranean suppliers. Libya, which insisted on oil company payments in the local currency, was compelled to introduce its own exchange adjustments. Consequently, in September 1971, the Libyan pound was converted to the dinar and revalued from the middle rate of LD1 to $2.80–$2.90.[41] A subsequent adjustment in February 1972, corresponding with the depreciation of the US dollar, fixed the rate of exchange at LD1=$3.04 and, following the signing of the second Geneva agreement, an almost identical arrangement was concluded with the companies, affording Libya the necessary built-in mechanism for raising the level of posted-prices.

Confronted with a depreciating dollar, the oil exporters in general concluded that it was desirable, if not necessary, to have more direct control of prices and production. Ultimatums from OPEC, or the host government, were blunt and disruptive, but an alternative mechanism remained a matter of dispute. Two positions began to emerge: the most nationalistic states, such as Algeria, Iraq and Libya, were increasingly moving towards the option of majority share-holding: the conservative Gulf states, largely as a response, proposed 'participation'. At the OPEC conference in Beirut in 1971, the Saudi Arabian Oil Minister, Sheikh Yamani, proposed a scheme for 20 per cent nationalisation, gradually increased to 50 per cent after 12 years. Libya, attracted by the model of Algerian control, favoured immediate 51 per cent share-holding. It soon became clear, however, that the Libyan authorities also leant towards outright nationalisation, not so much as an instrument of oil policy, but as a method of penalising a company, or its national government, for actions which violated domestic interests.

On 7 December 1971, the RCC announced the unilateral nationalisation of BP in Libya. This action, which was selective and politically motivated, did not indicate the start of a nationalisation policy. BP was taken over in reprisal for the British government's decision to transfer sovereignty of the Tumbs islands, then a British protectorate, to Iran. Libya, like other Arab states, claimed that these islands, strategically positioned in the Straits of Hormuz, were the legitimate territory of the Arab Trucial States, subsequently federated in the United Arab Emirates. The management of BP fields and assets was duly assumed by the Arab Gulf Exploration Company (INJAZ), a subsidiary of Linoco specifically formed for the purpose. The British government, which refused to recognise the nationalisation, asked other OECD countries for help in boycotting oil from the former BP fields. Despite provisions for compensation under the nationalisation decree, BP itself initiated several judicial proceedings to prevent the movement of oil from the Sarir field it had previously operated jointly with Bunker Hunt. In particular, in January 1972, BP tried to block the shipment of crude to Sincat in Syracuse, for processing.[42]

For Britain in particular, and the Western countries in general, these measures proved not only unsuccessful, but even counter-productive. The Libyans encountered some difficulty in finding buyers for Sarir crude, but BP's attempt to impose an embargo failed miserably. The decision of the British government to expel Libya from the Sterling Area on 14 December had a merely marginal effect; in fact, pulling out of the Area was a threat the RCC had considered using against the British! Meanwhile, the confrontation the British government sought with the RCC served only to encourage closer ties with the Soviet Union. Awakened to the dangers of a boycott, the Libyan authorities began to diversify their sources of hydrocarbons technology. Most importantly, in March 1972, Staff Major Jalloud visited Moscow for talks with the Soviet leadership. In a wide-ranging treaty, signed on 4 March, the Soviet Union undertook to provide Libya with assistance in the development of oil production and refining. Furthermore, until a settlement was concluded with BP in 1974, crude from the INJAZ was traded with a number of East European countries, including Bulgaria, Romania, the Soviet Union and Yugoslavia.

There were no further instances of nationalisation until the following year. When the RCC next used this method, it remained the exception rather than the rule. In general, their oil industry policy was based on securing a transfer of technology through majority participation in joint ventures. After the establishment of an OPEC ministerial committee on participation, the Libyan authorities had announced their intention to 'pursue negotiations for participation with their concessionaires on an individual basis.' The first of these agreements was concluded with the Italian state-owned oil company ENI, whose subsidiary, Agip, had begun to develop the extensive Bu Ateiffel field, in concession No. 100. In September 1972, ENI belatedly agreed to 50 per cent participation, in concession No. 100, and in concession No. 82, where exploration was being conducted by another ENI subsidiary, following an order from the Petroleum Ministry shutting down production in the Bu Ateiffel field.

Next, the Ministry made a similar demand to the American independent, Bunker Hunt. The company was also instructed to yield 50 per cent of all income from the jointly-operated Sarir field since the nationalisation of BP's share. When the Texas oilman refused to comply, his company suffered a temporary export embargo, which the government hoped would soften his stance, but Bunker Hunt continued to resist. The embargo was lifted in January 1973, and reimposed in June. When this failed to secure compliance, the Libyan authorities, albeit reluctantly, decided that nationalisation was their only available option. Speaking on the third anniversary of the American forces' evacuation on 11 June, Qadhafi announced the immediate takeover of Bunker Hunt, saying the action was undertaken to deliver the United States 'a big, hard slap . . . on its cold, insolent face'.[43]

Negotiations on participation with the other companies continued. The companies maintained their offer of 25 per cent participation, but, in August 1973, Jalloud demanded a 51 per cent government holding and indicated that he was prepared to use force to achieve his objective. Occidental, whose allowable production had been cut to 360,000 b/d in December, was partially nationalised on 11 August and, in an agreement accepting the change, was obliged to settle for compensation on the basis of net assets. Next, the independents in the Oasis group – Amerada, Continental and Marathon – conceded on the same terms: Shell, with a 16 per cent share in the consortium, decided to hold out, fearing a precedent which could have repercussions for its other concessions in the region. In response, the government intensified pressure on all the majors. The Petroleum Ministry ordered a complete halt in Shell's production, and Texaco and Socal, the majors within the Amoseas group, received instructions to cut production by 50 per cent to 100,000 b/d.

Days later the government went ahead and risked imposing a comprehensive settlement of its own choosing. On 1 September 1973, the fourth anniversary of the al-Fateh Revolution, a unilateral decree was issued which nationalised 51 per cent of all the majors and the independent partners, Grace, Gelsenberg and Liamco. Furthermore, in February 1974, in response to President Nixon's decision to convene the Washington Energy Conference, the Libyan leadership completely nationalised the Amoseas consortium, and took over the Liamco share of Esso Sirte. The following month, as no unified strategy had emerged among the companies, Mobil settled on the government's terms, followed, in April, by Esso. BP also acted to resolve its outstanding dispute with the Libyan authorities, accepting the government's compensation offer. Shell, the one company which showed no sign of accommodation, lost its 16-per-cent stake in the Oasis group to complete state ownership, declared in April.

The outbreak of the fourth Arab-Israeli war on 6 October 1973 undoubtedly contributed to the speed of the Libyan's settlement. The phased cutbacks in production, supplemented by the embargo of 'unfriendly' countries, declared in Kuwait on 17 October by the Conference of Arab Oil Ministers (from the Organisation of Arab Petroleum Exporting Countries (OAPEC)), posed the oil companies a number of severe problems. By January, shipments from Arab countries to the United States and the Netherlands, both regarded as hostile, had begun to dry up, as the sanctions were to remain in force until an agreement or disengagement was secured. No serious shortage had faced any country, when the embargo was lifted on 18 March, but the cutbacks in production, by preventing the build-up of a surplus in the market, created conditions for further price increases. In fact, the Gulf members of OPEC, meeting on the day prior to the Conference of Arab Oil Ministers, had unilaterally decided to raise prices by 70 per cent. Much more important, however, was the decision of the OPEC conference in Teheran in December 1973 to set posted-prices on the basis of $7 per barrel for each member state. Furthermore, the circumstances of the October war set the scene for a massive extension of state ownership by the Gulf states.

When the war broke out, Libya was already conducting its embargoes on the majors, who had yet to agree participation terms. Following the meeting of Arab oil ministers in Kuwait, these were supplemented by OAPEC's sanctions. Libya's own performance as the pace-setter within the Arab world had to some extent declined, as the special conditions of 1971 no longer obtained, but the RCC was, nevertheless, a leading proponent of the oil embargo. Along with Iraq and Syria, Libya maintained the sanctions until July 1974. In the meantime, the companies' ability to hold down prices depended on increasing the flow of production, which in turn required coming to terms with partial nationalisation, both in Libya and, since the war, in the Gulf states.

By the following year, Libya's position had begun to fall from the dizzy heights attained in 1974. Having resolved the issue of participation, the oil companies were able to generate a larger surplus within the oil market. Accordingly, the demand for Libyan crude declined and the country was temporarily compelled to cut projected expenditure in its development plans. At the beginning of 1975, several companies, including the independent Continental and Occidental, complained that Libyan prices were uncompetitive; in May, Occidental, which was selling crude at 55 cents below cost, asked for 100 per cent nationalisation, with the right to purchase oil on a per barrel basis. Exports, which had slumped to 800,000 barrels a day in December 1974, did not pick up again until June 1975, when they passed the psychological marker of 1.5 million barrels a day. Even so, it was not until the second oil 'price shock' of 1979 that events began to swing back in Libya's favour. But by then, Libya no longer possessed the market strength it had enjoyed in the early 1970s.

The subsequent deterioration in the terms of trade do not obscure the fact that the RCC fundamentally changed the nature of the relationship between the producer state and the oil companies. Whilst Libya, more than most exporters, remained acutely sensitive to the vagaries of the international oil market, the domestic state had succeeded in gaining direct control of prices and production. Most importantly, the RCC had established state ownership of the country's oil industry and, in so doing, had stimulated changes in the pattern of ownership in other producer states. Although the country would continue to remain dependent on external oil expertise, Libya had begun to make headway in securing a limited transfer of technology. Within five years, Libya had gone from trailing OPEC to setting the pace among producing countries. In real terms, when the rising cost of living is taken into account, *per capita* income had risen from LD673 in 1971, to LD1,278 in 1976. Yet oil, the basis of the country's economy, remained a finite resource. The future economic development of Libya hinged on equal success in diversifying the economy away from the oil sector.

Notes

1. For the brief role of Colonel Schwerib, see R. First, 1974, *Libya: The Elusive Revolution,* pp. 111–12; also, John Wright. 1982. *Libya: A Modern History,* p. 124. Following this mediation Schwerib went back into retirement and took no further part in the takeover.

2. The evidence of possible collusion between the conspirators and the British and United States governments, or their intelligence services, has only ever been circumstantial. According to the *Libyan Mail* (14 December 1969) Qadhafi dismissed the coup attempt as 'a matter of a grudge by senior officers against the unitary and free officers who are mainly junior officers.'

3. The full text of the 'constitutional proclamation' is published in Meredith O. Ansell and Ibrahim Massoud al-Arif. *The Libyan Revolution: A Sourcebook of Legal and Historical Documents. Vol. 1. 1 September 1969–30 August 1970* (Oleander Press, Wis., and London, 1972) pp. 108–113.

4. Ibid., pp. 113–4.

5. Nasser apparently decided to build up Qadhafi as an individual leader, rather than the head of a collective, because of the latter's pro-Egyptian stance and willingness to accept Egyptian leadership in the Arab world. Nasser was aware that other members of the RCC had reservations about close links, and subordination to his own leadership. See R. First, 1974, p. 113.

6. This was known as the 'Black Prince' conspiracy, due to the dark complexion of Abdullah al-Sanussi. The origins of the plot went back to a secret meeting of royalists in Rome in February 1970, attended by Omar al-Shalhi, Abdullah al-Sanussi and members of the Saif al-Nasser family. In practice, it relied on the residue of loyalties to the Sanussis in Chad and the Saif al-Nasser family in the Fezzan. According to John Cooley: 'Arms were smuggled, perhaps with Israeli help, from Chad into southern Fezzan' *Libyan Sandstorm* Sidgwick & Jackson, London, 1982) p. 99.

7. Some details provided in Mirella Bianco, 1974 *Gadafi: Voice from the Desert* (Longmans, London, 1975) p. 70.

8. BBC Summary of World Broadcasts, ME/3427/A/2–6. (In an excess of Arab nationalism, the small Jewish community was referred to as 'Israeli' in official statements.)

9. BBC SWB, ME3512/A/1–3.

10. Ibid.

11. BBC SWB ME/3445/A/6. Aldo Moro, the acting foreign minister, ruled out the use of force.

12. Saad Khalil Kezeiri. 'Restructuring the Urban System in Libya', paper presented to the conference *Economic and Social Development of Libya,* School of Oriental and African Studies, London, 1981.

13. *Facts and Figures* (Secretariat of Information, 1979) p. 76.

14. J.A. Allan 1981 *Libya: The Experience of Oil* p. 223.

15. These statistics, showing the expansion in the country's health service and hospital capacity, come from *JIR* vol. 1 no. 9 (3 September 1982); see also *The Al-Fateh Revolution Ten Years On,* Secretariat of Information, 1979; and *Facts and Figures* (Secretariat of Information, 1979).

16. S. Birks and C. Sinclair *Arab Manpower: The Crisis of Development* (Croom Helm, London, 1980) p. 121.

17. J.A. Allan 1981, p. 229.

18. *Arab Report and Record,* no. 17 (1–15 September 1969) p. 364. According to Mohammed Heikal, the Radford Plan was created to deal with just such a situation as had arisen in Libya, but 'the lightning success of the revolution' had prevented the British from putting it into operation.

19. John Wright 1980 *Libya: A Modern History* p. 140.

20. In March 1970, Healey told the House of Commons that, whist the training grounds in Cyrenaica were irreplaceable, 'the effect of the loss of our other facilities in Libya on our military capability will be negligible.' *Hansard*, vol. 795 131 (March 1970).

21. Reported in the *Jerusalem Post* and the *New York Times* on 19 November 1976.

22. BBC SWB ME/4119/A/1970.

23. Edward A. Klodziej 'French Mediterranean Policy: The Politics of Weakness', *International Affairs,* vol. 47. no. 3 (July 1970).

24. *Middle East Economic Survey* (19 September 1969). Shtawi, a former employee of Oasis, combined the Oil portfolio with that of Labour and Social Affairs: he introduced labour legislation increasing the minimum wage.

25. Pierre Terzian *OPEC: The Inside Story* (ZED Books, London 1985) p. 115.

26. Frank Waddams, *The Libyan Oil Industry,* (1980), p. 230.

27. Ibid., p. 229.

28. Pierre Terzian *OPEC,* p. 113. Levy was a German-born economist and oil

adviser to the US government; in 1951, he was recruited to the 'task force' set up by Washington to deal with Mossadegh's nationalisation of oil in Iran.

29. See Frank Waddams 1980, p. 230.

30. See Pierre Terzian 1985, p. 117.

31. Whilst the companies claimed the cutbacks were technically a violation of the Petroleum Law, oil legislation did permit restrictions 'in cases of absolute necessity connected with the high interests of the state.' For conservation regulations, see P. Barker and K.S. McLachlan 'Development of the Libyan Oil Industry', in J.A. Allan (ed.) 1982 *Libya, Development Since Independence*, p. 39.

32. Pierre Terzian 1985, p. 119.

33. Frank Waddams 1980, p. 232.

34. Frank Waddams 1980, p. 237. In addition, the resolution called for the elimination of disparities in posted or tax reference prices between countries; 'a uniform general increase in the posted or tax reference prices'; a new system of differentials for gravity; and the elimination of allowances.

35. According to Pierre Terzian: 'The decision taken at New York was to negotiate *en bloc,* and with OPEC as such. The intention was thereby to neutralise the troublemakers such as Algeria and Libya.' *OPEC,* p. 125.

36. Ibid., p. 136.

37. Ibid.

38. Ibid., p. 139.

39. Ibid.

40. Ibid., p. 140.

41. By revaluing the currency at this rate, and insisting that it was used in company accounts, the Libyan authorities ensured that the Central Bank of Libya, the sole seller of Libyan currency, would receive $3\frac{1}{2}$ per cent more in dollars than would have been paid previously.

42. Frank Waddams 1980, p. 251. BP appears to have taken these counter-measures, not because they were likely to prove successful in themselves, but in order to deter potential buyers of Libyan crude.

43. John Wright 1982, p. 247. Qadhafi also warned the United States 'to end its recklessness and hostility to the Arab nation'.

5   The Revolution Abroad

Arab Unity: Libya's Prussian Role

The Free Officers credited Libya with what can be described as a Prussian role in the unification of the Arab world. Just as Prussia had welded together German and Piedmont-Sardinia Italian unity, so the RCC saw Libya as the driving force behind Arab unity. They were encouraged in this view by the possession of enormous oil wealth, which served to spur their ambitions. But Libya neither had, nor in the foreseeable future was likely to have, the superiority in population and military power necessary to establish undisputed political hegemony over the Arab nation. The unification process in Germany and Italy required the use of military power, not only to ensure the submission of the weaker states, but in order that the rulers of these states would sue for the protection of the more powerful state. If Nasser's Egypt, the political centre of gravity in the region, had failed to achieve this historical goal, how much less likely that Qadhafi would succeed? Palestinian liberation might have provided a symbolic cause around which Qadhafi hoped Arab unity could coalesce, but the loss of Palestine was itself symptomatic of Arab disunity. The Arab world had accumulated centuries of regional and sectarian tensions, whose pattern of development was accentuated by colonialism, and cold war confrontation. The Free Officers' answer to this dilemma was a number of attempts to conclude agreements with prospective partners, many of which were no more than makeshift tactical alliances, in which financial incentive became a substitute for political supremacy.

The first Libyan-backed unification agreement was concluded with Egypt and Sudan just after Nasser's death. At Qadhafi's exhortation, the three signatories of the Tripoli declaration responded to the vacuum caused by Nasser's death by bringing forward their plans for eventual unification. On 9 November 1970, it was announced that they had agreed to form a federation in order 'to hasten and develop integration and co-operation'.[1] Following General Hafez al-Assad's takeover in Damascus on 16 November, they were joined at the end of the month by Baathist Syria, about which Qadhafi had a number of political doubts, dating back to the collapse of the United Arab Republic. The unification scheme was, nevertheless, endorsed in Egypt, Libya and Syria by plebiscites organised on the second anniversary of the al-Fateh Revolution. Sudan, omitted because of a power struggle within the Khartoum regime, was expected similarly to ratify the treaty if Numeiri triumphed over the radical members of his coalition government. In the meantime, Egypt, Libya and Syria proceeded to declare the Union of Arab Republics in April 1971. Thus, the creation of a united block of Arab states, nationalist in character, seemed imminent.

That this failed to come about can be explained by the rise of one man: Anwar al-Sadat. Sadat, whose struggle with Qadhafi became a feature of the Arab world in the 1970s, was a master of opportunism. Whilst others within the Egyptian hierarchy deserted Nasser after the 1967 defeat, he closed ranks and ostensibly defended Nasser's policies. These tactics were rewarded with his appointment as Vice-President, a largely ceremonial post. Aware that Sadat lacked political perspective, nevertheless Nasser was apparently unconcerned that he had put Sadat in line for the succession. With something of an ambiguous record as a Free Officer, Sadat was intended as a figurehead President only. Real power and political control in Egypt were to lie with 'the centres of power' within the Arab Socialist Union and the armed forces. Nasser's rationale, according to Mohammed Heikal, intimated to him personally, was that 'Sadat would be all right for an interim period. People in the socialist union and the army would look after the real business, and Sadat's job would be largely ceremonial.[2]

Sadat supported unification with Libya as long as it was expedient for him to do so. The proposed merger required a new set of institutions and elections which would enable Sadat to assert himself over the 'centres of power'. Consequently, the 'centres power', for reasons unknown to Qadhafi, decided to resist the scheme. At a meeting of the Higher Executive Committee of the ASU on 21 April, Sadat quarrelled bitterly with the spokesman of the centres of power, Ali Sabri, who demanded that the proposed union be vetoed. On 4 May, the two sides clashed again, this time over the conciliatory proposals put by Sadat to the American Secretary of State, William Rodgers, when he arrived in Cairo that week. Sadat, they felt, had to be stopped. Armed Forces Commander-in-Chief General Mohammed Fawzi, summoned to Sadat's office, informed the President that his position in talks with the United States was unacceptable to the army.[3] The issue finally came to a head on 13 May, when Sadat dismissed the Interior Minister Sharamy Gomaa, on grounds that his phone was tapped; this action provoked the resignation of other senior government officials. The same day, General Fawzi called together the service chiefs and told them that the time had come to act because Sadat was planning to sell out to the Americans. Sadat survived only because of the continued loyalty of many of these commanders, most notably General Sadiq. The conspirators, betrayed from within their own ranks, were subsequently arrested on 15 May in what has since been called the 'Corrective Revolution'.

Sadat's victory in this power struggle was to have important repercussions for Libyan relations with Egypt. Now that he was substantive rather than nominal President, Sadat began to contemplate foreign policy developments that would militate against unification with Libya and Syria. In the summer of 1971, he entered into covert negotiations with Saudi Arabia, and a secret hotline was set-up between his house in Giza and the Cairo residence of Kamel Adhem, the Director of the CIA-trained Saudi intelligence service. Whilst fostering such contacts, through which he eventually established links with the Nixon administration, he was content to go along with the proposed unification without over-committing himself. The union strengthened his prestige and bargaining power. On 4 October, the three Arab leaders had met in Egypt, as guests of Sadat, and had decided that he should be the new head of state of the UAR, with Cairo as its capital. When formally inaugurated on 1 January 1972, neither Qadhafi nor Assad had reason to believe that Sadat would not continue the nationalist policies of his predecessor. In the words of Heikal: 'Whatever Sadat's real thoughts and intentions may have been, this was a time when he managed to conceal them from more or less everyone.'[4]

The outside world surmised what it could from developments in Egypt. In general, the Libyans were encouraged by Sadat's positive support for the union. Qadhafi was, in fact, optimistic that the process could be taken further. In February 1972 he proposed to Sadat a total union of Egypt and Libya, but stressed that Egypt must first loosen its links with the Soviet Union and evacuate Soviet advisers from its territory. In particular, the Libyans objected to the Friendship Treaty Sadat had signed with the Soviet Union in May 1971. Sadat asked for six months to reflect. Meantime, on 8 July, he ordered the expulsion of the Soviet forces stationed in Egypt; this dramatic move satisfied Libya's precondition but astounded most observers. Praising Sadat's action, on 23 July Qadhafi renewed his call for a total union. Sadat, calculating that such a union could strengthen his internal position, responded favourably and flew to Benghazi for talks with Qadhafi. On 2 August, the two leaders agreed to 'create a unified state and establish a unified political command to bring about, in stages, the merger of the two countries by 1 September 1973.'[5] Qadhafi's relations with Sadat had reached their apogee. The Libyan RCC, oblivious to or unconcerned about Sadat's ulterior motives for his decision, nominated the Egyptian leader for the presidency of the new unitary state.

The advent of the Libyan cultural revolution was the undoing of this union agreement. Sadat had hoped that Egypt could contain Qadhafi's political influence, but the cultural revolution forced him to reconsider. What finally caused him to baulk was the Popular March that Qadhafi launched from Libya to Egypt to consummate the union of the two countries. The objective of the march, which was intended to arrive in Cairo in time for the inauguration of the new union on 1 September, was to mobilise the Egyptian people for confrontation with Zionism. Sadat, who was averse to creating conditions for such popular mobilisation, was anxious that the 20,000-strong march should be halted. The marchers set off from Ras Jedir on the Tunisian frontier, reached the Egyptian border on 18 July 1973, and started to dismantle the barriers, but Sadat sent a message to Qadhafi asking him to halt the procession. The following day, having received no reply, he despatched Hafez Ghanem, Secretary of the Egyptian ASU, to confront Qadhafi. But when Ghanem arrived he was told that Qadhafi had resigned and that, in effect, Sadat was the leader of the two countries. Sadat, having failed to secure Libyan co-operation in halting the march, therefore ordered the Egyptian authorities to turn the march back. Refused access through the town of Fouka on 21 July, the march turned and headed for Libya, where it became transformed into a popular demonstration of support for Qadhafi.

On 21 July also Qadhafi withdrew his resignation and declared that he would persist in his efforts to establish unification with Egypt. 'Amalgamation with Egypt is inevitable, even if it means civil war,' he declared. When, days later, Sadat sent Deputy Prime Minister Abdul Khader Hakim to confer with Qadhafi, he was told that the total unification of the two countries must go ahead according to schedule. Both Qadhafi and Jalloud flew to Cairo unannounced in order to seek out Sadat and obtain from him a reaffirmation of the unification agreement. On arrival, however, they were informed that Sadat was not available, but was in Saudi Arabia for talks with King Feisal. On 27 August, when they did eventually meet, Sadat declared that Egypt was not ready for 'total union'.[6] The referendum set for 1 September was postponed and no future date fixed. When Qadhafi was invited to address students at Alexandria University on 28 September – the anniversary of Nasser's death – Sadat withheld his permission, expecting the occasion would become a political attack on the now indefinitely postponed unification of the two countries.

Compared with the humiliation that was to come, this snub was trivial. Throughout the period Qadhafi was pressing for the unification with Egypt, Sadat was engaged in intensive preparations for war with Israel. Qadhafi, unlike King Feisal of Saudi Arabia, was not informed of the detailed aspects of strategy because of sharp differences over objectives. Qadhafi wanted Egypt – and the Arab powers in general – to commit themselves to a war of liberation against Zionism. But what Sadat had in mind was, in conjunction with Saudi Arabia and Syria, a limited war of recovery. As Samir Amin has pointed out in *The Arab Nation*:

The aims of the war were thus clearly defined: to re-establish Arab dignity, to obtain the restitution of Sinai and the Golan Heights through negotiations, to establish a little Arab Palestine independent of King Hussein, to definitely recognise, in exchange, the state of Israel reduced to its just proportions, and thus to impose the Arab bourgeoisie as the main voice in the dialogue with the United

States and to put an end to Israel and Iran's ambitions to become the main sub-imperialisms. Military strategy was geared to these aims.[8]

For this conflict Libya was deemed superfluous. On a tour of North Africa in 1973, during the period of Egyptian re-armament, Sadat ignored Libya, visiting only Morocco and Algeria, countries he believed capable of more substantial assistance. From a military standpoint, Egyptian interest in Libya was confined to the supply of one Mirage squadron, volunteered by Qadhafi in talks with the Egyptian Chief-of-Staff, General Saad al-Shazly. When the fighting broke out on 7 October, the Libyan RCC was placed in the invidious position of supporting a war, the objectives of which they strongly opposed. Nevertheless, the Libyans were better than their word: they sent two, not one Mirage squadron (the second piloted by the Egyptians) as well as an auxiliary armoured brigade. Yet the Libyan observers Qadhafi despatched to Egypt, Omar Meheshi and Abdul Munim al-Houni, were not extended the same preferential treatment as that accorded to Saudi officials. The breach between the two countries was further widened when Sadat accepted a ceasefire on 25 October. Qadhafi exhorted Sadat by telephone to push on into Sinai. He then flew to Cairo himself to remonstrate with the Egyptian leadership. When Sadat began disengagement talks in November, Qadhafi boycotted the Arab League summit in Algiers and soon afterwards extended the protest by withdrawing the Libyan diplomatic mission from Cairo. Sadat, furious at such treatment, responded in kind.

Libya's first experience of Arab unity had not been an auspicious one. Qadhafi, however, persisted with his nationalist mission. Rejected by Sadat, he focused on unification with Tunisia. On 11 January 1974, Qadhafi and President Bourguiba signed a document committing their countries to the formation of a single unified state, called the Arab Islamic Republic, immediately following joint referendums on 18 January. Known as the Jerba Declaration, this agreement appeared to arise spontaneously out of a 45-minute tête-à-tête between the two leaders on the Mediterranean island of the same name. Inasmuch as Bourguiba had always counselled caution and gradualism in respect of Arab unity, the declaration was an unexpected *volte-face*. When Qadhafi had paid his first official visit to the country, Bourguiba was not available to meet him. On a second visit to Tunisia in December 1972, Qadhafi's overtures for unity received a bizarre rebuttal from the veteran '*combattant supérieur*'. Addressing an audience in Tunisia's Palmarian cinema on 16 December, Qadhafi publicly proposed unification. Bourguiba, who saw the performance live on his own television set, decided that Qadhafi could not go unchallenged. Jumping into his Mercedes he proceeded to the debate, seized the microphone, stressed that the Arab nation had never been united, made a point of Libya's backwardness and disunity, and dismissed Qadhafi's case for unity. Now he had apparently thrown caution to the wind, acquiescing in a hurried scheme that would give both countries a single constitution, a single president and a single army.

Bourguiba's change of heart undoubtedly had something to do with the promise of Libyan largesse. As things were, some 30,000 Tunisian workers were employed across the border in Libya and their wages provided a significant contribution to the Tunisian economy. In addition, Tunisia's Foreign Minister, Mohammed Masmoudi, who favoured unity with Libya, is believed to have persuaded Bourguiba that closer political collaboration would increase the prospect of direct financial benefits. Under Masmoudi's influence, a series of protocols and agreements embracing trade, customs duties, transfer of investments, regulations affecting migrant workers, education, the creation of a joint shipping company and social security, were concluded in 1973. On 1 September 1973, Tunisia was the only country in the Arab world to celebrate the anniversary of the al-Fateh Revolution. Indeed, as long as there seemed a prospect of accruing revenues from Libyan oil production, Bourguiba's ruling Socialist Destour Party was prepared to pay such political tributes. What the party was not prepared to counternance was the loss of political control over the Tunisian state. In pledging Tunisia to unification with Libya Bourguiba exceeded that mandate. Leaders of the Socialist Destour Party rebelled against an agreement which contained no blueprint on political institutions, and after crisis talks with Hedi Noura, a former governor of the Central Bank and future Prime Minister, Bourguiba was forced to abandon the Jerba Declaration. On 12 January Tunisian state radio announced that the referendum would be postponed and the agreement introduced in stages. The next day Foreign Minister Masmoudi, the scheme's promoter, was dismissed and relieved of all his posts within the Destour Party, of which he was joint Secretary General. Hedi Noura and his faction within the party were triumphant in an internal coup, which effectively ousted those sympathetic to union with Libya. Bourguiba himself flew to Switzerland for convalescence.

Libya's unity overtures to another Maghreb state, Algeria, fared even worse. Superficially, there seemed ground for unification. Algeria under President Houari Boumedienne espoused a form of Arab nationalism, had praised the Libyan decision to expel the foreign bases, and had provided expertise to keep the Libyan oil industry running during Libya's confrontation with the oil companies. But behind an edifice of anti-colonial co-operation, there were strong differences over inter-Arab policy and the concept of Arab unity; in addition relations were aggravated by a border dispute, in which the Libyans claimed sections of Algerian territory adjacent to the Fezzan.[9] The Algerian FLN, like Tunisia's SDP, had strong reservations about political unions, feeling that they compromised the Algerian state's independence. Determined to keep intact the FLN's monopoly of power, Boumedienne had refused an invitation to join the union with Egypt, Libya and Syria. Qadhafi had responded by publicly criticising Algerian inflexibility in a speech delivered at Sabratha in

October 1971: 'We think that it is high time that Algeria took the trouble to make her position clear. Her attitude to Arab unity and the future is ambiguous. Let her reassure us and tell us openly what she intends to do.'[10] On 11 October Boumedienne did, in fact, meet Qadhafi at Hassi Massaoud, and agreed that Arab unity remained the ultimate goal. He rejected participation in a Nasserist-inspired union, however, fearing the constraints this would place on the FLN. Algeria's predominant foreign policy interests were regional, predicated on maintaining a balance of power in North Africa. When the Jerba Declaration was announced, Boumedienne put pressure on the SDP to revoke the agreement because, like the UAR, it threatened to create a strong state on Algeria's eastern border.

Yet the formation of a strong Arab union to the east of Algeria, focused on Egypt, was the precise and overriding objective of Libyan policy. Sadat had become an impediment to that goal, but it remained Qadhafi's key concern. He argued that the interests of Arab unity were greater than those of any individual. When, on 18 January 1974, Sadat suspended military aid and recalled advisers, Qadhafi went to Cairo the following day in an attempt to pacify the Egyptian leader. He stepped into a barrage of official criticism which his conciliatory remarks about the 'friendship' and 'bond' between the Egyptian and Libyan peoples did little to counter. Indeed, the propaganda attacks escalated. When a Muslim group launched an operation against Cairo's military academy on 18 April, Libya was blamed. In a further effort at reconciliation, RCC member Kweildi Hamidi was despatched to Cairo to broach the question of improved relations. But none of Libya's diplomatic activity bore fruit. As Sadat commenced further disengagement talks with Israel and the United States, Qadhafi was becoming the butt of his campaign to discredit Arab nationalism. In May, Sadat accused the Libyans of economic blackmail, using financial pressure to make him change course; an allegation that ensured the United States provided Egypt with increased economic aid. Then in June he prohibited Egyptian civil servants from travelling to Libya. The RCC reacted by banning all Egyptian propaganda connected with the 1973 war, and closing the Egyptian cultural centre in Benghazi. Relations between both countries were set on a prolonged downward course.

Throughout the summer of 1974 the propaganda war between Qadhafi and Sadat intensified. On 26 July, the Egyptian press accused Libyan agents of blowing up an Alexandria nightclub. The Libyan authorities then claimed that the Egyptian regime was stirring up unrest among border tribes; Tripoli in particular cited the activities of Sadat's brother-in-law and member of parliament, Mohammed Abu Waft. Next, Cairo alleged that Qadhafi had tried to have the Egyptian leadership assassinated. In August Sadat attempted to undermine Libyan links with France with a statement officially confirming that Libyan Mirage jets were in Egyptian bases during the 1973 conflict, in direct contravention of the sales agreement with the French government. A ceasefire in the rhetorical war was finally arranged by Sheikh Zayed, the Federal President of the United Arab Emirates; following his mediation, both Sadat and Qadhafi met briefly in Alexandria and agreed to 'avoid futile quarrels in the future'. Further Arab mediation in December 1974, initiated by President Numeiri of Sudan, resulted in the establishment of a joint Egyptian-Libyan Committee, to lead an inquiry into the dispute between the two regimes. At last it seemed that it might be possible at least to stabilise relations on the basis of normal diplomacy.

The truce was, however, only temporary. On 12 April 1975, Sadat, who was poised to sign the second Sinai disengagement agreement, expressed the view, in an interview published in the Kuwaiti newspaper, *al-Siyasah*, that Qadhafi was 'one-hundred per cent mad' and claimed that Libya was trying to drive a wedge between the Arab Gulf and Egypt. Sadat, it seemed, was intent on provoking a new storm in Egypt's fragile relations with Libya. His subsequent claim that the Libyans were trying to annex the Siwa Oases in Egypt's western desert indicated that he was hoping to rally Egyptian support for his regime by deflecting the growing internal opposition, and generating an alternative centre of conflict to the war with Israel. Libya's expulsion of 265 Egyptian workers, in retaliation for these accusations about the Siwa Oases, triggered the kind of internal public reaction against Libya which Sadat aimed to achieve. The death of an Egyptian in Libyan police custody became a pretext for the Egyptian parliament, which Sadat controlled, to demand the withdrawal of the entire workforce in Libya. In addition, there followed a series of allegations in the Egyptian press that Qadhafi was out to assassinate journalists hostile to him. So inflamed did the situation become that, on 10 May 1975, the building that housed the Libyan diplomatic mission in Cairo was ransacked by a crowd protesting over the treatment of Egyptian workers in Libya. Qadhafi, lodging a complaint with the Arab League, forbade entry to Libya all Egyptians who did not possess a work permit in advance. As the day approached for Sadat to sign the second Sinai disengagement agreement, demonstrations were organised in Libyan towns against 'the capitulationist Egyptian regime'.

Prospects for a reconciliation with Sadat were now bleak indeed. The changes in Egyptian foreign policy, the most immediate source of friction, were underlined by important developments within the structure of society. After he succeeded Nasser, Sadat had proposed to resolve the economic depression in Egypt with an influx of foreign capital. The 1973 war, whose limited objectives Qadhafi rejected, was fought to instil confidence in Egypt as a base of capitalist expansion. Once Egypt had been made secure for international investment, Sadat expected that funds would pour in. Within two years of the October War, the governments of Dr Abdul Aziz Hegazi and Mamdouh Saleh had deregulated much of the economy in the hope that this would attract foreign capital: laws introduced in 1974 and 1975 exempted foreign investment from taxation for five years; foreign merchant banks were authorised to operate currency exchange at market rates; the Suez Canal area became a Free Trade Zone; the private sector was encouraged and the public sector dismantled. Known as the *'infittah'* or 'opening up' policy, the liberalisation of the economy, ending a period economic autarky, resulted in the creation of a stratum of speculative capitalists, called euphemistically 'the Sadat class'. Unlike the old landlord class prior to the advent of Nasser, this new class had no nationalist ties; the first loyalty of the 'Sadat class' was to international capitalism, of which it was the junior partner in Egypt. As it proliferated throughout the 1970s, chances of a Nasserist restoration became increasingly remote.

The turning point came in 1975. So wide did the political cleavage become that the unification of Egypt and Libya was inconceivable without a major revision of Sadat's policies, domestic and foreign. Nasser's achievements had been steadily eroded from the time Sadat took office, but in this year his total departure from Nasserism was clearly demonstrated. In putting his signature to the second Sinai disengagement agreement, he signalled his abandonment of Nasser's anti-imperialist stance, and collusion with the opponents of Arab nationalism. Symbolic of the breach was Sadat's own personal break with Mohammed Heikal, in whom he had confided since succeeding to the presidency. Beyond Egypt the consequences of Sadat's policies were already beginning to have their impact. The Cairo-Riyadh axis tipped the balance of forces in the Arab world against Arab nationalism. Pan-Arabism, already on the wane since the 1967 defeat, yielded to the regionalism that Qadhafi feared. The failure of Libya's unity initiatives merely served to confirm that Libya did not have the political power to ensure that unification, once initiated, could be sustained. If an honest assessment is to be made, the Libyan Revolution came too late, and was too weak to reverse the decline.

The Islamic Context

During the early stages of the Libyan Revolution, foreign policy was conceived and conducted principally in Islamic terms, and, as a result, Libyan strategy frequently converged with, or worked to the advantage of United States' objectives. A prime example of this was Libya's action in helping President Numeiri of Sudan regain power in 1971, when a *coup d'état* was launched against him by the Communist Party and their sympathisers in his coalition government. Numeiri had, in fact, already been ousted on 19 July when the Libyan authorities assisted in a counter-coup to restore him to office. A BOAC plane, on a flight from London to Khartoum on 22 July, carrying two of the coup leaders, was ordered down by the Libyans when it entered Libyan airspace. Both men were arrested and subsequently handed over to Numeiri for execution. This unsolicited intervention, which had little bearing on the final outcome of the power struggle, was inspired by Qadhafi's staunch opposition to Marxism. Politically, he perceived a threat to the *umma*, or Islamic family of nations, from the intrusion of so-called alien creeds whose origins lay outside the Arab and Muslim world. Whether it was Zionism, which he linked with the

United States, or communism, which he linked with the Soviet Union, Qadhafi believed that political systems which had developed exogenously had no place in the Muslim world.

So dogmatic was Qadhafi's anti-Communism that he was positively affronted when, in 1971, the Soviet Union, in a conciliatory gesture, awarded him the Order of Lenin in recognition of his contribution 'to world peace'. Qadhafi was unimpressed and did not attend the presentation in Moscow. His views on Communism were summarised in an official publication on the 4th anniversary of the Revolution which, under the title 'Holy War Against Communism', declared:

> Perhaps the biggest threat facing man nowadays is the communist theory. Arab revolutionary thought did not miss the blatant contradictions between communism and Islamic thought. The leader of the September revolution says in this regard: "Communism starts with man by saying: curse God and do this and that. On this basis, then, there is no way in which the atheist and the Moslem believer can see eye to eye. For the Moslem, religion is everything and he cannot be cordial to a communist at the expense of religion . . . Since Moslems believe that the utmost reason is the law of God and the communist slogan is atheism, then it is the duty of every Moslem to combat this threat and he should always be on the look-out for the poison that is spilled out by atheists through books and pamphlets."[11]

Although Qadhafi was instrumental in expelling American bases from Libya, it seemed to the Nixon administration that, on balance, his anti-Communism was a beneficial influence in the Arab world. Instances of Libyan anti-Communism, in addition to the support afforded to Numeiri, added conviction to this opinion. Qadhafi, had persistently criticised the Soviet military presence in Egypt and had condemned the Friendship Treaty Sadat signed with the Soviet Union in 1971. He had been similarly critical of a friendship agreement signed by Iraq with the Soviet Union in April 1972, and had recalled the Libyan ambassador from Baghdad in protest. In the Yemen, he had encouraged unification between the conservative north and the radical south, but argued that unity could proceed only if the Aden government abandoned its pro-Moscow orientation and adopted a non-aligned stance. Once again his views accorded with the interests of the Nixon administration, which saw in unification the means of prising Soviet influence out of South Yemen.

Qadhafi's role in the 1971 war between India and Pakistan also pleased the Nixon administration. During this conflict, which saw India decisively established as the supreme power of the sub-continent, Qadhafi had supported Pakistan on the grounds that it was a Muslim state. His offer of a token force of Libyan Northrop F-5s in solidarity with the General Yahya Khan's regime was welcomed by the US State Department, which saw Pakistan as an important component of its Asian strategy. Indeed, in the initial years of the Free Officer leadership the frequent coincidence between the policies of Washington and Tripoli were such that, in the more radical circles of Beirut, it was not unusual to hear Qadhafi referred to as an American agent, or a party to a 'devil's pact' with the United States. Whilst there were a number of indications that the United States had blocked monarchist attempts to overthrow Qadhafi, on the specific question of the new Libyan leader's complicity with Washington, there has never been any shred of documented confirmation.

A more serious assessment of Libyan foreign policy discredits allegations that Qadhafi was some sort of US proxy. From a survey of Libyan commitments during this period, it can be seen that Libya was equally supportive of Muslim conflicts with pro-Western governments and interests and of Muslim struggles with Soviet-orientated states. In the Far East, for example, Libya aligned with the Bangsa Moro secessionist movement in the southern Philippines, the Pattani movement in southern Thailand and the Muslim minority in Burma. Libya extended support to all three minorities irrespective of whether the governments were neutral, as in the case of Burma, or pro-Western, as in Thailand and the Philippines. After its foundation in 1976, the Pattani United Liberation Movement in the southern provinces of Thailand received a limited degree of Libyan financial and military aid.[12] The organisation's General Secretary, Hisham Abdullah, retained an office in Tripoli and delegations from the organisation have attended various seminars and conferences in Libya. When, in 1978, there was a series of outrages against Muslims in Burma, Libya protested to the Burmese government.[13] In Thailand, in 1983, the Libyans financed the construction of a mosque in Bangkok.[14]

The Islamic emphasis in Libyan foreign policy was evidenced by the support given to the Moro United Liberation Front (MULF) in the southern Philippines. The secession of the 6.5 million Bangsa Moro people was a political objective with which the Libyans became associated some time in 1971, shortly after the formation of the MULF. Libya was one of several Muslim states approached by MULF for support, and subsequently the state most conspicuously identified with the Bangsa Moro struggle. Whilst Saudi Arabia and a number of other Arab states are known to have donated funds to the MULF, only Libya responded with substantial financial aid and arms for the secessionist movement. The MULF was also provided with a diplomatic office in Tripoli, and support extended to the Front until 1976, when Imelda, wife of President Ferdinand Marcos, visited Libya and pledged, or so the Libyan authorities claim, to introduce some form of autonomy for the southern provinces.[15] The Libyans then sought to apply pressure on the Moro movement to accept the formula, but once it became clear that the Philippines government did not intend to proceed with autonomy, support for the secessionist movement was renewed.

The vehicle whereby Libya aspired to a leadership role was the Islamic Call Society, an organisation founded in 1970, during the same period that the Council for National Guidance, under the direction of Sheikh

Mahmoud Subhi, was formed.[16] The Society's task was to consolidate the faith outside Libya's frontiers, while the Council's duties were confined to Libya itself. The first conference of the Society in 1970, attended by Muslim scholars from Africa, Asia, Europe and the Americas, decided to establish a Permanent General Committee for the Conference of the Islamic World, with a secretariat and headquarters based in Libya. Within this forum the Libyan leadership hoped to crystallise Muslim solidarity, drawing the support of Muslim countries toward Libyan objectives such as the liberation of Palestine. Qadhafi's persistently emphatic theme was the need for Islamic unity, especially in the face of Communism and imperialism. During this period, speaking of the dangers confronting Muslim peoples, he commented: 'It is, therefore, our duty now to draw up a Pan-Islamic strategy with which to return to the spirit of Islam and shoulder our burden in *jihad* for the sake of God and the unity of the Muslims.'[17]

Libya also became self-appointed protector of the black Muslim minority within the United States. When New York police clashed with black Muslims in Harlem Street, the Libyan Arab Republic lodged an official complaint with the federal government, and demanded an explanation.[18] In the early 1970s, black Muslim leader Mohammed Elijah and the boxer Mohammed Ali were received in Libya as honoured guests. As in the case of the Moro movement in the southern Philippines, this commitment to distant causes was intended to exemplify the leading role of the al-Fateh Revolution in the defence of Muslim peoples, regardless of their location.

The main theatre of operations was Africa. Shortly after the formation of the Islamic Call Society in 1970, it sent a delegation to Niger (one of the six countries bordering Libya) to improve Islamic and cultural links. As a result of talks in Niamey, the Nigerien capital, agreements were concluded pertaining to the rights of pilgrimage to Mecca (enabling Nigeriens to travel via Libya) and the construction of an Islamic centre in Niamey, financed by the society. A similar agreement, to contribute to an Islamic institute in Dakar, Senegal, preceded negotiations with the government of President Leopold Senghor. The society also participated in a Libyan delegation from the Ministries of Information and Housing to the Camerouns in October 1972. According to a press release, the purpose of this visit was 'to explore the possibilities of close co-operation between the LAR and Cameroun, and to review the conditions of the Muslim population.'[19] The Camerouns' President al-Hajj Ahmadou Ahidjo was an official state guest at the 1972 anniversary celebrations of the September 1st Revolution, indicating the development of close links between both states.

Combined with the programme of Islamic promotion a campaign to drive out Zionist influence from Africa, was launched concurrently with the Islamic Call Society. The aim of this campaign was the overriding strategic priority of Libyan foreign policy in the African continent. In 1968 Israel had 32 diplomatic missions in the 35 non-Arab states, several of them predominantly Muslim. The Israelis were heavily involved in a military capacity in a number of African states: these included Zaïre, where bodyguards and training were provided for President Mobuto; Chad, where Israel trained President Tombalbaye's bodyguard; and Uganda, where the Israelis had had similar military arrangements with ex-President Milton Obote; in addition, they were providing some logistical support for the secessionist movement in southern Sudan. In Tripoli, these instances of Israeli penetration, encircling Arab-Africa, were seen as a threat. The reinvigoration of Islam, whilst not exclusively orientated towards expunging the Zionist influence from Africa, was nevertheless intended to ensure that the Israelis could not exploit the divisions between Arab Muslim and non-Arab Muslim Africa. An official statement in 1972 reported that Libyan policy was based on: 'Helping muslims in Africa where Libya aims at spreading the Arab culture and language and uniting all Muslims' efforts to fight back against the widescale missionary activities backed by the Zionists and imperialism.'[20]

The campaign developed into the most fruitful ever mounted under Qadhafi's political leadership. Even prior to the outbreak of the October 1973 war, several African states, namely, Chad, Uganda, Niger, Mali, Congo, Togo and Zaïre, had severed their relations with Israel under the impetus of the Libyan campaign; some formally signing treaties which banned an Israeli presence on their territory. The Arab oil embargo, called by the Organisation of Arab Petroleum Exporting Countries (OAPEC) in Kuwait on 16 October 1973, brought the majority of the other states into line. By the end of the year, as the embargo and price rises had their effect on the economies of African states, a total of 29 non-Arab African states had broken their ties with Israel. Libya, which had long argued for the deployment of the oil weapon, a strategy previously unable to generate wide support, found that it possessed much greater political leverage in Africa. The assertion of Arab oil power in fact created conditions for an alliance between Arab Africa and sub-Saharan Africa, most obviously on the question of mutual solidarity on the issues of Israel and South Africa. The most obvious manifestation of the collaboration between these two groups of states was the decision of the OAU Foreign Ministers, meeting on 21 November, to call on African countries not to resume diplomatic relations with Israel until it had withdrawn from occupied Arab territory. The following year, in another example of such cooperation, the UN General Assembly voted to condemn Zionism as racism. The subsequent decisions of many African states to recognise the PLO had their genesis in the same Libyan-led, anti-Zionist offensive.

The Muslim or part-Muslim states of Africa provided Libya with an obvious constituency for solidarity initiatives. In May 1971, the Mauretanian President Ould Daddah was invited to Tripoli for exploratory talks, following which a communiqué was issued declaring 'the need for solidarity to serve the cause of African liberation and unity of its forces against colonialism.'[21] What this meant was revealed in February

1972 when Qadhafi paid a return visit to Nouakchott, and stressed Libyan backing for Mauretanian claims to the colony of Spanish Sahara, whilst Daddah agreed to a statement reaffirming the 'rights of the Palestinian people to their homeland'. A similar relationship based on mutual support was forged with Somalia, whose population, like that of Mauretania, was virtually 100 per cent Muslim. In 1971, a delegation from Somalia participated in the second anniversary celebration of the Free Officers assumption of power and, in January 1972, the Somali President General Mohammed Siad Barre arrived on a state visit and attended an OAU liberation committee meeting hosted in Benghazi. A second official Somali visit to Libya was undertaken by Somali Vice-President Colonel Ismail Ali Bakr, who was a guest at the 1975 1 September celebrations. During 1973 and 1974, Libya consecutively sponsored the initiation of Mauretania and Somalia into the Arab League. Although a deliberate move to strengthen Arab bargaining power, Somalia's credentials for membership were nevertheless dubious since the majority of the population were non-Arabic speakers.

As part of the campaign against Zionist penetration of Africa, the Libyan authorities invited the leaders of those African states with Zionist connections to Libya for talks. The Nigerien President Hamami Diori was the first African leader invited to Libya and he explained the inconsistency of his government's position. Received in Libya on the first anniversary of the al-Fateh Revolution, on 19 October 1970, he signed a series of co-operation agreements with Libya, relating to trade, finance and communications. It was under these treaties that Libya gained an interest in the mining of uranium yellowcake in northern Niger.

Diori, persuaded of the benefits that could accrue from solidarity with Libyan political objectives, renounced Niger's ties with Israel. Through Diori's mediation in 1972, Libya secured better relations with another leader of a part-Muslim state, President Tombalbaye of Chad. The following year, during the Sahel drought, Libya repaid Diori's assistance with relief for the afflicted Nigerien population. Under Diori's successor, Lieutenant General Seyni Kountche, continued strengthening of links seemed likely; Kountche's take-over was backed by Libya and, under his leadership, Libya's economic interest in uranium mining in the country reached its peak. But as the decade wore on, the Niamey regime began to resist the growing Libyan political and economic interests. Relations deteriorated sharply after Kountche, worried by the Libyan involvement in Chad, accepted French military advisers.

Sekou Toure's Guinea was another part-Muslim country Libya tried to influence towards a pro-Arab orientation. When, in 1971, Portuguese and Guinean oppositionists launched a joint attack on Guinea, which was providing limited facilities, including bases, for the PAIGC liberation movement in the Portuguese colony of Guinea-Bissau, Tripoli reacted by despatching plane-loads of military assistance to bolster Guinea's armed forces.[22] The unusually bold gesture served temporarily to ingratiate the

Libyans with the regime in Conakry. The Libyan role in the provision of military assistance to the Guinean government was recognised by the conclusion of a mutual defence pact between the two states in November 1974. Similarly, ambitious pledges of military assistance were made to Zambia and Madagascar; Tripoli went on record stating that Libya would reinforce those front-line states in southern Africa which faced military aggression from Pretoria. The intention was to demonstrate Libyan commitment to Arab-African solidarity. Indeed, the Libyans subscribed financially, and in some cases militarily, to SWAPO, the ANC, Frelimo, the MPLA and especially PAIGC. Ironically, it was among the front-line states of southern Africa rather than the part-Muslim states of northern Africa that Libya found the most dependable allies of the Arab nationalist cause.

Outside South Africa, the Libyans believed that the main African-based threat to solidarity came from Ethiopia. From the beginning, the Israeli and American high profile in Ethiopia determined confrontation with the regime of Emperor Haile Selassie. In 1973, an official review of Libyan achievements published by the Ministry of Information and Culture commented:

> Ever since the establishment of the Zionist state on the land of Palestine, Haile Selassie and his regime never concealed their hatred of the Arabs, their hopes, and their rights. Addis Ababa has become the springboard for Zionist agents for the penetration of the African continent . . . At a time when Egypt's lands are under occupation by the Zionist Army, Ethiopia has bolstered its military, political and economic ties with the Zionist state. In this way, Ethiopia has proved that it has no interest whatsoever in the future of this continent and does not share the suffering and pain of its people . . . The whole world knows that the most dangerous American bases in this part of the world are in Ethiopia.'[23]

The Libyan RCC called for the OAU headquarters to be moved from Addis Ababa to a more neutral African capital representative of the new relationship. At the same time, the Libyans extended backing to both the Eritrean liberation movement and the Western Somali Liberation Front. Although the Eritrean people are by no means exclusively Muslim, the Libyan policy was to concentrate resources on that part of the Eritrean movement which had an Islamic orientation, namely, the Eritrean Liberation Front (ELF). The Eritrean Peoples' Liberation Front, which broke away in 1972, was less favoured because it was based among the Christian highlanders and had more of a Marxist political complexion. As early as November 1970, the presence of an ELF delegation at the conference of Afro-Asian Solidarity indicated Libyan involvement in the Eritrean question. The Ethiopian government's decision to break ties with Israel in response to the October War did little to improve relations. Libya maintained its opposition to the Emperor, and, therefore, its support for the Eritrean Liberation Front and the Western Somali Liberation Front, on the grounds that the character of the regime had not fundamentally changed – as instanced by the retention of the US listening station at Kagnew near Asmara.

The Islamic emphasis in Libyan policy also caused a minor conflict with Tanzania. This arose from a dispute over the mainly Muslim island of Zanzibar, that in 1964 was merged with Tanganyika to form Tanzania. In order to gain Libyan political and financial backing for their troubled administration of the island, the Zanzibaran Afro-Shirazi Party persuaded the Libyan authorities that the mainland government of President Julius Nyerere was bent on the repression of the Muslim islanders, in order to achieve the integration of the island and mainland administrations. The assassination of the Afro-Shirazi leader, Sheikh Abeid Kasame, was said to attest to the anti-Muslim nature of Nyerere's government. The Libyans responded by assisting Zanzibari opponents of Nyerere; much later, however, as it became clear that the various groups receiving such support enjoyed no political popularity it was withdrawn.[24]

The Libyan practice was to cultivate those African countries which showed the greatest tendency towards Islam and Arabism. For this reason Tripoli extended its patronage to Idi Amin of Uganda. Pre-empting his own removal from command within the Ugandan army, Amin had seized power in January 1971, evidently, with the backing of both Britain and Israel whose governments had become alarmed by Milton Obote's flirtation with China and Eastern Europe. Amin's anti-Communism, however, did not necessarily bind him closer to the objectives of the British and Israeli governments. He soon discovered that his Muslim faith paid better dividends if used in another direction. The state which he inherited was deeply in debt, and within weeks he had embarked on a fund-raising tour which took him to West Germany and Libya. It is not known who suggested the visit, but once in Tripoli Amin met Qadhafi and signed a communiqué supporting the 'Arab peoples' rights to Palestine'. The Libyans, as with Jean Bodel Bokassa of Central Africa, promised to do what they could financially, but explained that the Zionist presence in Uganda was not conducive to friendly relations. On his return to Uganda Amin demanded that Israel reschedule its debts. When this was refused, he severed diplomatic ties and repudiated his debts. In a theatrical show of solidarity with the Arab cause, Amin expelled the Israelis and turned over their embassy in Kampala to the Palestine Liberation Organisation.

His action was highly praised by the Libyans. According to one official Ministry of Information Publication in 1972, Amin was 'a symbol of resurgent Africa fighting to liberate the continent from the pockets of imperialism and its agents'.[25] So that he could solicit Arab economic support, in mid-1972 the Libyan Foreign Ministry arranged for Amin to tour nine Arab capitals, and a plane for this purpose was provided by Qadhafi. In addition, in June 1972, at Qadhafi's behest, he attended the summit meeting of the UAR in Mersa Metruh, Egypt, and in the same month a Libyan delegation arrived in Kampala to begin preparations for the establishment of a joint commercial bank. (Morocco, in response to Amin's tour, had offered to build a mosque at the headquarters of the Uganda Supreme Council.) When Ugandan exile groups initiated armed attacks from neighbouring Tanzania in September 1972, Libya met Amin's appeals for assistance with supplies of military equipment and contingents of troops. For several days, in fact, Libya teetered on the brink of military hostilities with Tanzania, until that prospect was averted by the mediation of the Somali leader, Siad Barre.

The Libyans treated Amin as an important protégé. Their patronage extended not merely to one military intervention, but to two. The second occasion was precipitated by the events which followed Amin's invasion of Tanzania in October 1978. Having launched an operation to crack down on opposition groups operating along the border, Amin's threat to occupy the Kagera salient, into which his forces had entered, became a pretext for the Tanzanian government to mount a counter-attack in conjunction with rebel Ugandan forces, organised under the leadership of the Tanzanian-based Uganda National Liberation Front. Undercut by purges and low morale, Amin's armed forces failed to withstand their assault. When the Tanzanian forces routed them from the Kagera salient and continued towards Kampala, Amin turned to his Libyan patrons for help. Tripoli responded by raising an expeditionary force of volunteers. Equipped with tanks and armoured cars, this force was deployed in Uganda during February and March 1979. According to sources in Nairobi in March 1979,[26] there were some 2,500 Libyan troops in Uganda. Their main role was to organise the defence of Kampala on Amin's behalf. The desertions from Amin's army were such, however, that the Libyans decided not to take on the burden of the fight. Libyan units were involved in some rearguard actions, in the north of the country, but by the end of April 1979 the expeditionary force had pulled out.

Based on opportunism, Libya's association with Amin gathered few long-term political benefits. The heyday of the relationship was the first part of the decade, when Amin paid his state visit to Tripoli in September 1975, joining Qadhafi and Luis Cabral of Guinea-Bissau on the platform for the 1 September military parade. Libyan support for him continued after it had become politically counter-productive because until the end he remained a client of Tripoli. The Libyans pursued a similar but less successful policy in regard to Jean Bodel Bokassa of Central Africa. By coincidence, he was overthrown in the same year as Amin, whilst on a visit to Libya. Libya, however, was only interested in the two leaders as long as they held power; after the overthrow of Amin and Bokassa in 1979, Tripoli exerted itself to improve relations with the new regimes. Qadhafi has since admitted that to have backed Amin against Tanzania was an error, stating:

> It appeared that the Uganda which Idi Amin took over was full of Israelis during the time of Obote and Idi Amin had thrown out the Israelis. But he pretended that he was a Muslim and that he was trying to save Muslims about to

be liquidated in Uganda. It is a fact that they actually faced liquidation. However, under the circumstances, Idi Amin should never have been supported against Obote. In the last analysis he was a fascist, he had no plan to lead Uganda to recovery, to make it a progressive country. He is simply a show-off.[27]

Amin's fall from power marked the effective demise of Libya's pan-Islamic foreign policy. By 1979, Qadhafi's commitment to Islamic unity had become increasingly abstract. The policy had achieved its greatest successes during the particular conditions of the assertion of Arab oil power. The ousting of Zionist influence in Africa was Libya's most important victory, but the emergence of the Saudi-Egyptian alliance following the 1973 War undermined the strength of the Libyan position. Thanks to the Libyan initiative, the Zionists had become an unacceptable third party for American aims in Africa, bu ultimately that did not prevent that third-party role being assumed by the Egyptians and Saudis. The Egyptian government's involvement in support for Holden Roberto's National Front for the Liberation of Angola in the 1976 civil war showed the developing trend. For those African states wishing to retain their pro-Western orientation, Saudi Arabia, rather than Libya, became a preferred source of aid. Consequently, Libyan influence within the part-Muslim states such as Niger, the Camerouns and Somalia waned. The ramifications for Libyan policy, including the shift away from pan-Islam, will be explored in later chapters.

Anti-Imperialism

The foreign policy objectives of the new regime differed from those of its predecessor, but the pro-islamic orientation, notably the strident anti-Communism, indicated an element of continuity. A distinguishing feature was the new leadership's use of terrorism to carry out certain policies. Libya has been correctly linked with many terrorist actions, either carried out by foreign groups such as the IRA and Black September, or by personnel acting on behalf of the Libyan state. Libya and terrorism have become associated to the extent that the Libyan state has been imputed with responsibility for operations in which it played no part. There is a crucial need to explain the causes of Qadhafi's sponsorship of terrorism, but an analysis is complicated by two factors. First is the question of what, in fact, constitutes terrorism? Briefly defined, it is the covert use of violence against selective political targets. As such, it is a tactic, but those groups which employ this tactic do not necessarily constitute terrorist organisations *per se*. The military wings of both the PLO and the ANC have used the terrorist mode of action, but as mass-based liberation movements they should not be categorised as 'terrorist organisations'. So it is with Libya; the authorities have carried out terrorist operations, but it is incorrect to describe Libya as a 'terrorist state', that is, to say that the state consists of terrorists. The second factor relates to the motives of those who have been most vociferous in condemning Libyan support for terrorism. Those states engaged in a political conflict with Qadhafi have sought to mobilise opposition to the regime for reasons not specifically connected with acts of terrorism.

Charges of Libyan terrorism can be traced back to the Israeli intelligence service, MOSSAD. Alarmed by the Nixon administration's positive disposition towards the Free Officer regime in the early 1970s, MOSSAD was anxious to undermine Libya's credibility, particularly within the United States. The Black September operation against Israeli athletes participating in the 1972 Olympic Games in Munich supplied them with an appropriate pretext. On the morning of 5 September that year, eight members of Black September siezed the Israeli pavilion in the Olympic village. Several athletes were killed and others taken hostage. When the Israelis refused to negotiate, let alone consider the demands for the release of some 200 Palestinians prisoners, a shoot-out took place at Furstenfeldbruck military airport, in which five Black September fighters where killed and three captured. Their bodies, proudly claimed by the Tripoli authorities, were flown to Tripoli and honoured with a heroes' funeral, described by the Libyan news agency as 'a majestic spectacle'. Libya was consequently branded as a haven for terrorists and accused of complicity in the operation, which was in no way mounted or directed from Libya.

The indictments of Libyan terrorism that began after the Munich massacre tended to overlook certain obvious facts. The Black September operation had taken place in the context of a war between Israel and the Arab nation, of which Libya was an integral part. The violent aspect, which inevitably caught the headlines, could not be construed as being independent of this conflict. For Qadhafi, violence in the Middle East was partisan; there was the violence of the oppressed and there was the violence of the oppressor. Arab violence was, in his terms, an act of resistance against aggression from outside. The actions of Black September were those of an oppressed people fighting against the colonisation of their homeland. Just as partisans in Nazi-occupied Europe had resorted to sabotage and assassination, even to operations involving civilian casualties, so did the Arab resistance have no option bu to use terror in its struggle. Such fighters as those of Black September were perceived as heroes who deserved their countrymen's highest commendation. Libya, through its association with them, demonstrated that it was in the vanguard of this national struggle. The nations of the West, responsible for assisting Israel politically and financially, could not expect immunity from its ramifications.

Terrorism in the Middle East has never been the prerogative of the Arab side. Events were soon to demonstrate that in relation to Libya. On 21 February 1973, a Libyan passenger airliner carrying 113 Arabs to Cairo, was attacked by Israeli Phantoms and blown out of the sky.[28] Nothing like it had ever happened before: 106 passengers, including former Foreign Minister Saleh Busair, were killed. The plane, a Boeing 727 piloted by a crew on loan from Air France, had lost its bearings and was over occupied Sinai when it was intercepted and fired on. Subsequent Israeli attempts to mitigate their action by claiming that the Boeing could have been on a suicide mission to an Israeli city, were discredited by evidence that it had corrected its course and was heading for Cairo when hit by rockets from the Phantoms. Initially, the Israelis had issued a terse disclaimer which assigned responsibility to Egyptian MIGs. Eventually, at a press conference the following day, the Israeli Minister of Defence Moshe Dyan admitted Israel's responsibility. Nevertheless, he claimed that he was 'completely satisfied' by the action of the Air Force, ordered by General Mordecai Hod, and announced that there would be no court of inquiry.[29] Compared with the outcry that was to greet the shooting down of a South Korean airliner by the Soviet Union a decade later, the reaction from the White House was muted. Suspicions that the atrocity was Israeli's revenge on Libya for praising the Black September operation in Munich have never been allayed. As *The Times* commented on 23 February 1973: 'A suspicion remains that the Israelis were lured into such an intemperate act by their over-obsession with Libya and the general but ill-concealed desire to strike a blow at President Gaddafi.'

The incident brought home to the Libyan people in a real and direct way the full meaning of Israeli aggression, something they had not previously experienced. Few events could have had the mass radicalising effect on public opinion as the shooting down of a civilian airliner. Throughout the country, popular support for the struggle against Zionism surged. Qadhafi, under immediate pressure to avenge the atrocity, decided on reprisals. As part of the UAR, he consulted Sadat on a plan to launch an air raid aimed at Haifa. Sadat convinced Qadhafi that this would jeopardise his war preparations. But when the bodies of the dead were returned via the Egyptians, protests erupted in Libya over Sadat's timidity. Saleh Busair's some printed and distributed tracts accusing Sadat of betrayal, but fearing potential damage to the strategy of unification, Qadhafi had him arrested. Nevertheless, the demonstrations continued, culminating on 23 February in the siege of the Egyptian consulate in Benghazi. Compelled once again to seek retaliation, Qadhafi ordered an Egyptian submarine, berthed at Tripoli, and supposedly under his joint command, to ambush and sink the British cruise liner, the *Queen Elizabeth II*, as it carried Jewish supporters of Israel from Southampton to Ashdod, to attend celebrations to mark the 25th anniversary of Israel. Once outside Libyan waters, however, the submarine surfaced and radioed Cairo for confirmation. The query was referred up the chain of command, and Sadat himself promptly countermanded the captain's orders. Humiliated, Qadhafi sank into depression.

It is often the perception in the West that Qadhafi has hoodwinked the Libyan people into confrontation with Israel against their better interests. The episode of the Libyan Boeing showed that Qadhafi was, in fact, reacting to popular demands for action against Israel, rather than manipulating the situation to his own advantage. In the aftermath of the QE II incident, Qadhafi did, in fact, tender his resignation and, together with his family, left to live in Cairo. Such was his popularity at this stage that the other RCC members, however individually ambitious, failed to obtain sufficient support to succeed him. The RCC refused to accept his resignation, then submitted its own *en bloc*. The crisis was resolved only when Qadhafi decided to return from Cairo and resume the presidency, responding, or appearing to respond, to the mass demonstrations in Libyan towns and cities urging him to stay on. The incident, perhaps intentionally, recalled Nasser's resignation, tendered but rejected as demonstrators clamoured for him to continue after defeat in the 1967 War.

A feature of the Libyan Revolution was that the nationalist struggle against Zionism enjoyed popular support. The political constraints placed on the provision of assistance to those organisations fighting Zionism, Palestinians or otherwise, were considerably fewer in Libya than in other Arab countries. Palestinian organisations, regarded in general as patriotic Arab organisations, could receive arms and money from Libya without public disquiet or opposition to their activities. Much of the money and equipment the Palestinian resistance required to establish itself in southern Lebanon after the expulsion from Jordan in 1970 came from this source. The main string apparently attached to this aid was that the groups should remain committed to the armed struggle with Israel. Previous to Yasser Arafat's address to the United Nations on 13 November 1974, Libya had primarily supported al-Fateh, the largest Palestinian organisation, but following Arafat's evident move towards diplomacy, the Libyan authorities began to diversify their support. The recipients included the Popular Front for the Liberation of Palestine, the Popular Front for the Liberation of Palestine-General Command, the Democratic Front for the Liberation of Palestine and the Palestinian Popular Struggle Front, in addition to al-Fateh, which continued to receive a large portion of funds throughout the 1970s, whilst Qadhafi voiced criticism of Arafat's tactics.

The logical extension of this policy was support for those peoples and movements fighting states which collaborated with Israel, or which were otherwise deemed oppressors of the Arab nation. Qadhafi believed that, just as the imperialist powers which supported Zionism were organised on a world scale, so the struggle for the liberation of the Arab people had to be conducted on a global basis. The British, who had surrendered Palestine to the Zionists and imposed Sanussi rule on Libya were an obvious target. The IRA, perceived as a legitimate movement for Irish emancipation, received support on the basis that it was opposed to British colonialism.

Justification for such intervention was provided by Qadhafi in an interview with the Italian journalist Mirella Bianco. He told her:

> If we assist the Irish people it is simply because we see a small people still under the yoke of Great Britain and fighting to free themselves from it. And it must also be remembered the revolutionaries are striking, and striking hard, at a power that has humiliated the Arabs for centuries.[30]

Consignments of Libyan-supplied arms probably began to reach the IRA some time in 1971, but the discovery of a Libyan arms cache on the *Claudia* in 1973 brought the shipments into the open. After that disclosure, the supply was interrupted, but shipments are believed to have continued on an intermittent basis until the election of the Labour government in 1974. Libya then shifted to what was officially described as 'moral and political support'.

Bitter blows were struck against British imperial interests in the Mediterranean. Although Malta was granted independence in 1965, the British had retained military facilities on the island as a contribution to NATO. These facilities were located approximately 200 miles off the Libyan coastline. Exposure of the Radford plan had drawn attention to the possibility that they could be used as a staging post for the invasion of Libya, in the same way that the sovereign bases in Cyprus had served as launching-pads for the intervention in Suez in 1956. Despite the loss of the military bases in Libya in 1970, the facilities in Malta continued to provide the Western Alliance with the military capability to dominate the central Mediterranean area. As these facilities posed a threat to Libyan security in the region, the Libyan leadership had an obvious interest in obtaining the closure of Malta to Western military forces. The first chance to act came in 1971 with the election of the ebullient and nationalist Labour Party leader Dom Mintoff.

Like Qadhafi, Mintoff was committed to a policy of 'positive non-alignment'. The British, nevertheless, believed he could be persuaded to accept the bases' transfer to NATO supervision. The belief rested on the island's dependency on rentals from the bases, but the British failed to take into account the intervention of the Libyan authorities. When Mintoff commenced talks with the British over the future of the facilities, the Libyans supported him by making up the shortfall the island would lose in the way of rentals. When the lease expired in 1980, the bases could, therefore, be closed without loss to the Maltese government.

Libyan assistance enabled the Maltese government to reduce its dependence on Britain in others ways too.[31] At Luqa, the main airport near the capital, Valetta, Libyan air-control technicians took over from the RAF and British personnel. A school for technical and vocational training, financed and to some extent staffed by Libya, was set-up to enable the Maltese to replace Western expertise. The Libyans added helicopters to the West German-supplied Maltese helicopter force, which played a vital life-saving role in the floods which swept the Masa area of the island in October 1979. Libyan technicians, some 40 of whom were stationed at Luqa, aided the helicopter squadron in a maintenance and communications capacity. Both political and economic co-operation with the Mintoff government expanded rapidly throughout the 1970s. Malta became an important location for the production of Libyan English-language publications, including the regular newspaper, the *Jamahiriya Mail*. Mintoff himself was a frequent visitor to Libya, where he signed numerous trade and economic agreements with the Tripoli authorities. The Libyans were not, of course, acting for altruistic reasons, but the result was a significant contribution to Maltese independence from the West that otherwise could not have been achieved.

Based on the same principles of non-alignment was a much broader Libyan policy towards the whole Mediterranean area. At the European-Arab Youth Conference, hosted in Tripoli in May 1973, Qadhafi promoted an initiative to turn the Mediterranean Basin area into a 'zone of peace', declaring: 'Nothing is currently more urgent than an appeal by this meeting for peace and justice, the removal of foreign fleets and a return of the Mediterranean to its former vocation as a zone of peace and security.'

In December that year President Makarios of Cyprus was invited on a state visit to Libya, during which the Libyan side raised the question of the British sovereign bases. There was to be no Libyan role in Cyprus, however as there was in Malta. Qadhafi, nevertheless, persisted with the policy in the belief that support could be won. The political liberalisation in southern Europe, following the fall of the Colonels in Greece and the fascist regimes in Spain and Portugal, convinced him that the new conditions in southern Europe, particularly with the growth of social democratic parties in the region, were conductive to the 'zone of peace' initiative. In 1976, the Libyans sponsored the first conference of Socialist Organisations of the Mediterranean, in Barcelona; and parties attended from Portugal, Spain, Malta, Greece and Cyprus, as well as their counterparts on the Arab side of the sea. A declaration, further elaborated at a second conference, in Athens, in 1977, called for the evacuation of all foreign bases from the Mediterranean area. As the Mediterranean was largely regarded as a NATO lake, this Libyan challenge to the presence of the Western Alliance was seen in Brussels and Washington as a minor political threat.

The challenge was specifically directed at Italy. As the most strategically important NATO state in the Mediterranean, Italy was the host for the Sixth Fleet and a cluster of American bases. The Libyan authorities indicated that this presence was a threat to their security, not least because it was the headquarters of the Sixth Fleet. The Libyans also regarded it of political importance to maintain stable relations with Rome and even made political overtures to the Vatican, ostensibly to establish diplomatic ties, but in reality because they believed a dialogue with the Papal State would help counter adverse Italian propaganda. In February 1974, Jalloud received an audience with Pope Paul XI, and in February 1976, Cardinal Sergio Pignedoli returned the visit on behalf of the Vatican.[32] The United States, greeting these manoeuvres with growing concern, tried to manipulate opposition to Libyan contacts with Italy. But American influence was limited by extensive Libyan economic interests in Italy and major Italian interests in trade with Libya. The 10 per cent share the Libyans purchased in Fiat in 1973 was greeted with alarm by the United States, but was probably no more of a strategic constraint than was Italy's dependence on Libya as supplier of one-third of its oil imports. The Italian state was in the unenviable position of balancing competing political and economic interests.

Through the Non-Aligned Movement Qadhafi sought to continue similar policies on a global level. At the 1973 Non-Aligned summit in Algiers, the fourth largest ever held at that date, Qadhafi gave some guidelines as to what should, in his opinion, constitute a truly non-aligned state.[33] He argued that the essential criterion was that each state must exclude, both in principle and in fact, foreign military bases from its territory. Calling for the Third World to assert independence and solidarity, he claimed that many of those states attending the summit were neither neutral nor non-aligned, since they maintained strong links with either the Soviet Union or the United States. In addition, he stressed that no state should be permitted to qualify for membership whilst it recognised Israel or South Africa. Days after he had spoken, Cuba responded by severing links with Israel. Thereafter, relations with Cuba improved, although the country was still treated with suspicion because of its orientation towards the Soviet Union. Through the Non-Aligned Movement, Libya also established supportive relationships with the governments of Salvador Allende in Chile, and Omar Torrijos of Panama, whose efforts to restore sovereignty over the Panama Canal zone, occupied by the United States, were praised as exemplary action for a non-aligned state.

Qadhafi saw the issue of foreign bases as a key test of Third World solidarity. He rejected in principle the existence of all foreign bases in the Third World, but was particularly sensitive on the question of foreign bases in the Arab world. He was outraged by King Hassan's decision to provide facilities for the United States in Morocco. At the Islamic summit in Rabat in December 1969, Qadhafi took exception to the pro-Western sentiments of Hassan–the only Arab head of state overtly to accept the presence of American military forces. Within weeks of the Rabat summit, Qadhafi had responded to what he perceived as Hassan's infraction of Arab sovereignty by supporting opposition forces trying to overthrow the Moroccan monarch. When, in July 1971, sections of the Moroccan armed forces tried to depose Hassan, and succeeded as far as broadcasting a message claiming victory, Libyan radio responded by welcoming their action and promising reinforcements to consolidate their position. Hassan, who defeated the rebellion, blamed Libya for instigating the attempted coup. He also implicated Libya in a conspiracy against him in 1972, when Moroccan fighter aircraft attacked his plane as it returned from France. In fact, the evidence of Libyan involvement in either attempt was slight. There was, however, substantial evidence to show that Libya was backing and funding opposition groups. The Istiqlal Party, the social democratic *Union Nationale des Forces Populaires*, and the radical-leftist *Frontiste* movement, all at one time or another received financial contributions from Libya. The *Frontiste's* attempt to mount an insurrection in March 1973, when police stations and government buildings in Rabat, Casablanca and the Middle Atlas were bombed, apparently had Qadhafi's blessing.[34]

Notes

1. J. Wright, Libya: *A Modern History* (Croom Helm, London, 1981)
2. Mohammed Hussein Heikal, *Autumn of Fury: The Assassination of Sadat* (Corgi, London, 1984) p. 43.
3. Ibid., p. 50.
4. Ibid., p. 54.
5. John K. Cooley, *Libyan Sandstorm: The Complete Account of Qaddafi's Revolution* (Sidgwick and Jackson, London, 1982) p. 105.
6. See chronology in M. Bianco, *Ghadhafi: Voice from the Desert* p. 185, and Wright (1981) p. 163.
7. J. Cooley (1982) pp. 112-13.
8. Samir Amin, *The Arab Nation* (Zed Press, London, 1980).
9. These were territories historically deemed Libyan, which France had ceded to Algeria during the period of French colonial rule.
10. M. Bianco (1974) p. 181.
11. *The Revolution of the First September: The Fourth Anniversary* (Ministry of Information and Culture, Benghazi, 1973).
12. See 'The Struggle for Libya', *Arabia: World Islamic Review* (June, 1984).
13. *Arab Dawn* (August 1978).
14. *Jamahiriya Review* (December 1983).
15. The Tripoli Agreement, in which Qadhafi mediated between Imelda Marcos and Musairi Nur.
16. For origins, *see Arab Dawn* (September 1975).
17. Muammar Qadhafi, *The Battle of Destiny: Speeches and Interviews* (Kalahari Publications, London, 1976).
18. *The Revolution of First September: Third Anniversary* (ministry of Information and Culture, Benghazi, 1972).
19. Ibid.
20. Ibid.
21. Ibid.
22. Qadhafi (1976) and Henry Habib, *Libya: Past and Present* (Adams Publishers, Malta, 1979).
23. *1973 Yearbook* (Ministry of Information and Culture, Benghazi, 1973).
24. Account in R. First, 1974.
25. *1972 Yearbook* (Ministry of Information and Culture, Benghazi, 1972).
26. *Nairobi Times,* (5 March, 1979).
27. Enahoro, Heart to Heart with Qadhafi, *Africa Now*, February 1983, pp. 37-46 (1983).
28. Full Libyan-sided account in *Slaughter in the Skies*, The Last Flight of LN114 (Libyan Embassy, London, 1973).
29. Ibid.
30. M. Bianco, p. 154.
31. Account in J. Cooley (1982).
32. See *Arab Dawn* (March 1976).
33. Habib, H., p. 295.
34. Amnesty International Briefing, *Morocco* (London, October 1977).

6 The Transformation of Society

The Promotion of State-Capitalism

When the monarchist state was overthrown in 1969, Libya possessed only a marginal industrial base. The official 'industrial survey', produced in collaboration with the Egyptian Organisation for Industrialisation, reported visits to 13,310 so-called 'industrial plants' between November 1971 and the following year; however, the data reveals that the vast majority consisted of workplaces employing either under 19 or under 5 workers. Despite the growth in the commercial sector in the 1960s, the underlying structure of the productive sector of the economy had not significantly changed since the years prior to oil production. According to the 1956 census, there were 3,121 'industrial plants', but 87 per cent employed fewer than 10 workers.[1] Typically, what were described as 'industrial plants' were artisan craft workshops. Especially in Cyrenaica, the domestic economy was characterised by petty-commodity production.[2]

Manufacturing capacity was extremely limited. Just a handful of agricultural processing plants, two tanneries and two shoe factories constituted the basis of the country's manufacturing industry. The majority, established by Italian companies and settlers in the colonial period, were small-scale and concentrated in the key urban centres of Benghazi, Derna, Misrata and Tripoli. The only major exception was a cigarette factory founded by Anglo-American Tobacco, which, on independence, was the biggest industrial venture, producing in 1950 380.6 million cigarettes and 120 tonnes of tobacco.[3] Apart from this single enterprise, industry was essentially geared to producing goods for domestic consumption, and foreign export earnings from the sector were extremely low. Despite the formation of the Ministry of Industry in 1961 and the inauguration of the first Five-Year Development Plan in 1963, industry contributed just a fraction of the Libyan GDP. The figures in Table 5.1 show the proportion of earnings in relation to other sectors.

Under the monarchy, the salient feature of government policy was non-intervention. Successive administrations appointed by the king made no attempt to transform the state into a vehicle of capital accumulation. Instances of state-sponsored industrialisation were minimal and erratic: in

Table 6.1   Gross Domestic Product as percentage of economic sectors, 1965–72

	1965	*1966*	*1967*	*1968*	*1969*	*1970*	*1971*	*1972*
GDP	*100*	*100*	*100*	*100*	*100*	*100*	*100*	*100*
Agriculture and fishing	5.0	4.3	4.0	3.1	3.1	2.5	2.0	2.4
Petroleum, mining and quarrying	54.1	54.4	53.5	60.7	62.2	57.2	51.4	50.6
Manufacturing industries	2.5	2.3	2.2	1.9	1.7	1.7	1.5	2.1
Construction Electricity	7.0	7.4	8.7	8.3	7.1	6.6	7.2	10.2
and gas	0.3	0.3	0.2	0.3	0.3	0.5	0.5	0.5
Trade, restaurants and hotels	6.6	6.7	6.4	4.2	4.0	3.5	4.7	5.3
Transport, storage and communications	3.7	3.9	4.1	3.7	3.3	3.2	5.3	5.6
Other	20.8	20.7	20.9	17.8	18.3	20.8	21.6	22.5
	100	*100*	*100*	*100*	*100*	*100*	*100*	*100*

Source: Ministry of Planning, National Accounts, Tripoli, Libya.

the First Five-Year Plan from 1963–68, just three per cent of the development budget was allocated to industry, whilst in the whole of the Idrisi period, investment was concentrated on less than 10 projects. In the demanding conditions of mass urbanisation and the private housing boom, most of these were bound to cement production, but the pace of development was slow and plants commissioned by the state came on stream late. The two main industrial projects, the cement factories at Benghazi and al-Khums, were finished in 1969, just prior to the Free Officer coup, and provided only 10 per cent of the quantity in demand from contractors. The rest was made up from imports.

Industrial policy in pre-revolutionary Libya emphasised private enterprise, not state investment. Through the Real Estate Industrial Bank, formed by the modernising Fekini government in 1965, the state made loan facilities available to putative entrepreneurs, but the preferred goal was the 'Libyanisation' of the existing industrial base, rather than the creation of new industrial capacity. Beyond the limited provision of banking funds, the state did not become involved in the process of capital formation. The commercial bourgeoisie was left largely to its own devices. In consequence, industrial growth occurred only in those areas requiring small-scale investment and low-level technology, mainly in the form of workshops dependent on the construction business; otherwise, during the pre-revolutionary period, Libya experienced no trend towards investment in manufacturing industry. In 1969, textiles were still being produced by the traditional handicraft methods, in small shops or homes, rather than in mechanised factories.

Initially, in the post-coup period there were important elements of continuity and discontinuity between the policy of the monarchical state and its successor. The post-revolutionary authorities favoured capitalist development, but unlike governments in the Idrisi years, actively promoted the development of the urban bourgeoisie through systematic state intervention. Despite later misconceptions, there is no evidence that, at this stage, the military leadership adopted a negative stance towards private ownership of capital. In 1973, the official publication of the General Administration for Information, *The Revolution of 1st September: The Fourth Anniversary,* defined policy in these terms:

> Since the liberation of the national economy from dependence and foreign influence was one of the most important goals of the revolution, a new industrial policy consistent with the general outlook of the state policy was drawn up.
>
> This new policy may be summed up as clear and frank definition of the role of each of the private and public sector in the execution of projects and helping the former [private sector] to overcome the difficulties, by providing financial and technical encouragement.[4]

To assist with the development of localised capitalism, two new state institutions were created. The first was the Industrial Research Centre, founded on 1 November 1970 with the objective of

> providing technical and economic services to industrialists from both the private and public sector, undertaking applied industrial researches and industrial experiments related to industrial production and development, in addition to carrying out geological researches and mineral rock prospecting to define their positions, recommend means of reaching them, and the economies of extraction, transportation and exploitation.[5]

The second was the General National Organisation for Industrialisation. Launched on 3 August 1970, in accordance with the RCC's Law No. 26, this was the principal body responsible for supervising state industrial investment and commissioning industrial projects from foreign companies. Among the 32 initial schemes contracted by the Organisation between 1971 and 1973 were a glass factory in Azzizya, begun in March 1971 with *Société Mécanique Frères* of France; three textile mills located separately at al-Marj, Derna and Janzour; an electrical cable and wire plant in Benghazi with the West German company Franzkershweild, and four pipe-producing and fitting factories, involving the West German companies Startzkoff and Lantra West and the Spanish group Arasta. By 1977, the Organisation had prepared and commissioned a total of 91 projects.

Thirdly, the role of the Real Estate Industrial Bank was expanded, specifically with the intention of encouraging Libyan entrepreneurs.

Between September 1969 and September 1972, the Bank had participated in private-sector projects by providing 291 loans, the majority linked with small investments in the food-processing industries. In the larger schemes, those demanding more than LD60,000, the Bank required 51 per cent ownership. Initially, no limit was set on the level of credit, but in September 1972, following evidence that merchants were abusing the system of 100 per cent funding, an amendment was introduced restricting loans to 60 per cent of the total investment.

Governing this shift towards state-sponsored capitalist development was the prospective decline in the country's oil resources which, in the early 1970s, provided over 90 per cent of foreign exchange and over 50 per cent of the GDP. Estimates of reserves, made in the initial post-coup period, indicated that the oil export trade had a life span of about 40 years. When production began to dry up, some time between 2010 and 2020, Libya would have no option but to rely on other sources of foreign earnings. Agricultural expansion could, at most, offset growing food consumption, but offered no real possibility of generating export earnings. The only possible source, therefore, was industry. Despite much higher comparative costs than the developed capitalist countries, and acute shortages of manpower, industrialisation appeared the most viable route to self-sustained growth, independent of the hydrocarbons sector.

Until the deposition of the monarchy, no social agent existed for the transition from mercantile to industrial capitalism. Libya was integrated into the world economy by the production and exchange of oil: faced with a negligible local market, foreign capital exhibited no interest in the development of industry. The commercial bourgeoisie, lacking the necessary concentrations of capital, preferred expansion into landowning. The state, the body with the capacity to diversify the economy, encouraged this trend. Controlled by elements socially and ideologically antipathetic to the growth of industrial capitalism, the state diverted the financial surpluses derived from oil into largely non-productive ends, including the luxury consumption of the ruling families, or the purchase of arms, which posed no danger to the social stability of the monarchical dictatorship.[6] Not until the overthrow of the monarchist regime were the preconditions set for the transition from merchant capitalism to productive capitalism.

Under the RCC, the state pursued a policy of state capitalism. Acting as a *collective capitalist*, the Libyan state intervened in the economy, by investing in plant and machinery and organising production. The shift in priorities can be observed from the growing allocations to the industrial development budgets after 1969: from an average of 3 per cent in the period between 1961–69 expenditure on industry jumped to 10.3 per cent in 1970 and 10.7 per cent in 1971, in consecutive annual development plans, and rose again in the RCC's first integrated development plan, the 1972–75 Intermediate Development Plan. In addition, the sectoral increases took place in the context of a much higher total outlay on development.

Throughout the period of these plans, Libyan state capitalism was not

Table 6.2 Allocations of National Development Plans, 1969–75 (LD)

	Annual Plans			1972–75 Development Plan			
	1969	1970	1971	1972	1973	1974	1975
Agriculture	16.4	50.0	50.4	61.1	92.8	70.5	100.1
Integrated Development						100.4	131.0
Industry and mineral resources	7.9	20.5	32.0	48.0	56.1	90.2	138.7
Oil and gas	—	—	21.6	22.9	23.2	64.7	83.8
Public Works (1972–Electricity)	24.9	18.4	21.5	62.3	71.7	81.4	114.3
Transport & communications	22.6	27.1	39.8	39.2	35.5	67.1	72.4
Education	14.6	11.4	27.2	32.7	36.8	60.2	110.2
Health	7.4	5.9	17.0	14.0	9.3	16.5	25.2
Labour force	2.0	1.3	4.9	—	—	7.4	9.1
Social security	—	—	—	—	—	8.5	6.9
Housing	22.2	32.8	40.0	68.6	61.8	100.0	130.0
Economy	0.3	0.1	5.6	& Trade		3.5	3.4
Tourism & sport				Inform & Culture			
Information	8.4	2.9	5.3			8.5	8.1
Municipalities	13.0	25.5	29.2	4.9	9.7	55.0	95.9
Planning	0.7	0.4	1.6	(other)	(other)	2.1	8.5
Reserve	1.5	2.4	2.0			3.9	5.3
Nutrition	—	—				0	3.9
Marine transport		1				0	63.4
Interior	1.5	1.0	2.7	Security services		0	0
Total	*145.0*	*200.0*	*300.0*	*353.7*	*396.9*	*740.0*	*1110.0*

Source: Ministry of Planning, 1976.

untypical of the experience of other modernising states at a similar early stage of industrialisation. Turkey, Iran, Egypt and Algeria had all, before Libya, transformed the state into an instrument designed to organise and promote industrial capitalism.[7] Especially important in the case of Libya was the pattern of industrialisation in neighbouring Algeria, where the state-based diversification of revenues derived from the hydrocarbons sector of the economy. Whilst Algeria accrued a smaller financial surplus and possessed a larger population than Libya (17.6 million to 2.7 million respectively in 1978) there were some notable parallels between their methods of centralised planning and redistribution of hydrocarbons income.

The huge financial surpluses acquired from oil production removed many of the impediments from the accumulation of capital in Libya. The chief constraints on development derived from acute manpower shortages. In 1973, just 432,700 members of the indigenous Libyan population of over 2 million were economically active; the Libyan workforce, concentrated in the tertiary sector and government services, was characterised by extreme immobility and low rates of labour productivity. Due to the absence of both skilled and non-skilled workers, the productive sectors of the economy, other than oil, were unable to absorb the large sums allocated for investment. Whilst the non-oil productive sectors of the economy exceeded their targeted growth rate of 17.5 per cent by two per cent in the 1973–75 Three-Year Intermediate Development Plan, much of the investment was ineffectually placed. In 1973, the manufacturing sector accounted for 13,300 Libyan workers, the equivalent of 3.1 per cent of the indigenous workforce; by 1975, despite the growth rate of over 19 per cent in the non-oil productive sectors, the numbers employed had risen to just 19,100 from a national workforce of 454,000 a rise of no more than 1.1 per cent. In relative terms the contribution of the manufacturing sector declined.

Table 6.3   Workforce by units employing over 500 people, 1975

	Workforce
Food processing	2,037
Cement and related	1,651
Beverages	1,328
Tobacco manufacturing	1,267
Wood production	886
Rubber and plastics	859
Chemical industries	736
Total	*8,764*

Source: Ministry of Labour, 'Labour Statistics' (1975)

Table 6.4 Libyan and migrant labour by sector, 1975

Economic Activity	Per cent	
	Libyan	Migrant
Agriculture	86.8	13.2
Petroleum & gas	74.8	25.2
Mining & quarrying	59.5	40.57
Manufacturing	58.1	41.9
Electricity, gas & water	72.4	27.6
Construction	22.7	77.3
Trade, restaurants & hotels	84.2	15.87
Transport, storage & communications	88.4	11.6
Finance, insurance & real estate	79.3	20.7
Administration	92.8	77.2
Educational services	75.7	24.3
Health services	67.9	32.1
Other	66.6	33.3
Total	*67.2*	*32.8*

Source: Author, compiled from figures in Birks and Sinclair, *Arab Manpower* (Croom Helm, London, 1980).

The proportion of the indigenous workforce retained by manufacturing units of significant industrial size was even smaller than the total for the sector. Table 6.3 provides a breakdown for the total manufacturing labour force distributed in workplaces of major importance.

As the demand for labour could not be satisfied from local sources, the Libyan authorities responded by importing manpower. From 1974 the Libyan economy required increasing inputs of foreign labour. Between 1970 and 1975, the migrant workforce in Libya grew from 50,000 to 323,000.[8] The country's former dependency on foreign labour in the oil sector was massively reinforced by reliance on migrant workers, skilled and non-skilled, in the other productive sectors of the economy. By 1975, migrant workers constituted more than 15 per cent of the workforce in every sector of the economy except government services (which were specifically reserved for Libyans), agriculture, transport and storage. Not only was 58 per cent of the country's professional and managerial manpower expatriate, but 41 per cent of non-skilled labour derived from foreign sources.[9] In the construction industry, where dependence on non-skilled foreign migrants was most acute, expatriate labour accounted for 77.3 per cent of the total labour force.

For the structure of the Libyan economy and society, there were major implications from the growing size of the foreign workforce. The outflow of foreign exchange, in the form of migrant workers' remittances, reached substantial proportions under the 1972–75 Three-Year Intermediate Development Plan. The bill from the import of foreign services rose from LD1,059 in 1970 to LD1,553 in 1975, and continued to soar until the 1980s. Despite temporary dips in the country's balance of payments, Libya never lacked the means to finance these transfers. The country's reserves of gold and foreign exchange increased from LD576 million in 1970 to LD1,110 million in 1974 and, whilst they slumped briefly to LD696 in 1975, they rose again to LD1,026 in 1976. Much more debilitating was the effect on the indigenous workforce of the long-term dependence on imported labour. Despite the RCC's objective of internal labour self-sufficiency, throughout the period of the 1970s the entry of foreign workers into the economy enabled Libyan workers to withdraw from the productive sectors of industry and agriculture.[10]

The Green Revolution

The most pressing economic problem facing the new revolutionary leadership was the stagnation of agriculture. Despite interest-free credit and subsidies for machinery, fertilisers, well-drilling, feed and seeds, made available in the period from 1963 to 1969, the rate of agricultural growth averaged just 4.5 per cent annually. The revenues allocated to the sector, 17.7 per cent of the 1963–68 First Five-Year Development Plan, failed to offset the decline of the sector in relative terms; much of the agricultural budget, strengthened from L£29.3 to L£49.9 after 1965, was absorbed in price support for locally produced cereals, olive oil, almonds and groundnuts. Whilst agriculture continued to retain the largest sectoral workforce, domestic production could not keep pace with the rise in food consumption stimulated by higher *per capita* income and natural population growth. As food imports increased by 22 per cent per annum in the years between 1962–67, reaching a level of L£19.2 million, the proportion of food consumed from local production fell to just 35 per cent of the total requirement. The country's agricultural exports declined from L£1.8 million to L£0.8 million in the period 1962–67 and the deficit in food increased from L£16.6 million to L£18.6 million.

Raising the level of agricultural productivity was an immediate priority. Thus, within days of the Free Officer takeover, Qadhafi launched the well-publicised 'Green Revolution'. Speaking at Sebha on 22 September 1969, he claimed:

the Jefara Plain, the great Jebel al-Akhdar . . . the Fezzan valleys are witnessing the great agricultural revolution that will enable the Libyan people to earn their living, to eat freely . . . the food that was normally imported from overseas . . . this is freedom, this is independence and this is revolution.[11]

The initial phase of the Green Revolution was agrarian reform in the lands under indigenous ownership. The new leadership introduced two measures designed to curb land speculation and accumulation. First, it was decreed that all lands not in use would automatically be taken into state ownership for redistribution. Second, in order to prevent tribal *sheikhs* increasing their own landholdings during the annual redivision of usufructs, strict quotas were placed on the level of subsidised fodder.[12] In effect, the incentives the previous regime had provided for tribal leaders to accumulate land, encouraging the acquisition of smaller landholdings and thereby the migration of subsistence farmers to the urban centres, were removed. The traditional cultivators and herders, although declining in numbers gained a limited form of protection, by which the state hoped to retain the labour, particularly of the younger generation of males, in agricultural production. By 1970, if not before, the drain in manpower from the land had become a principal factor eroding agricultural productivity.

In the next phase of the Green Revolution agrarian reform was applied to the lands held by Italian settlers. The properties, confiscated under the decree of 21 July 1970, were placed in the authority of a newly-created agricultural administrative body called the Department of Land Reclamation and Agrarian Reform. Divided into 16 project areas, the lands were reorganised by the Department into model farms under the management of graduates from the Libyan College of Agriculture. When reconstituted they were reallocated to smallholders who would become entitled to purchase the land following a production period of 15 years.

In 1973, the third phase of the Green Revolution began with the inauguration of a long-term state plan for agriculture, the 1973–83 Ten-Year Integrated Agricultural Development Plan, comprising 27 agrarian projects. Running concurrently with the 1972–75 Three-Year Intermediate Development Plan, and the subsequent 1976–80 Five-Year Transformation Plan, the initiative marked a decisive break with established agricultural policy. Previously, there had been a strong element of continuity between the policies of the pre-revolutionary and post-revolutionary governments. Under the RCC, the administration had continued with the practice of assisting capitalist production in agriculture with the incentives of interest-free credit and other subsidies. In 1972, a newly constituted Agricultural Bank provided interest-free credit worth LD514 million to landowners. In response, the output of various crops, notably fruit and vegetables, increased, but the landowners failed significantly to expand the acreage under cultivation. The expansion of agricultural production required the application of state capitalism in agriculture. This occurred principally through the medium of the Integrated Plan; the state, being the only body with sufficient concentration of capital, began the direct development and organisation of agricultural production, building farming settlements for distribution on the basis of farmer proprietorship. Accordingly, with the introduction of the plan, capital outlays rose from 11.3 per cent in 1969, to 23.4 per cent in 1973, of which the larger portion was allocated to integrated projects.

The schemes with the greatest potential were located in the areas of rain-fed cultivation along the north-east and north-west coasts. The Jefara Plain in the north-west was consistently the most productive zone. Excluded from the Integrated Agricultural Development Plan, agricultural development in the Plain required the least subsidy per hectare. Already in 1972, ahead of the Integrated Plan, the Ministry of Agriculture and Agrarian Reform launched the Great Jefara Wheat Project here, aiming to turn the zone into the country's 'bread-basket'. Elsewhere, agricultural production was largely predicated on capital intensive land reclamation, sponsored by the Ministry of Agriculture and Agrarian Reform's Department of Land Reclamation. Even the Jebal al-Akhdar, where rainfall was the highest in the country – an average of 350mm per year – required major redevelopment, having fallen into substantial and widespread dereliction since the devastation of the Second World War.

Inland from the coast, cultivation was constrained by the lack of water. At some oases, such as Jufra and Aujelo and Jalo, limited crop production was possible, but there were three particular oases where the Ministry aimed to induce agricultural development by irrigation from underground water sources, namely Maknoussa in the Fezzan, and Kufra and Sarir in the Khalij area of Cyrenaica. According to hydrogeological analyses, aquifers in these isolated parts were capable of supporting wheat and cereal production. The key lay with massive state investment in agro-technology, especially in irrigation systems, such as rotating centre-pivot sprinklers and drip-feed equipment, which conserve 90 per cent of the water supply. At Maknoussa, the efficient distribution of water and chemical inputs, including insecticides and fertilisers, was – initially – regulated under controlled conditions by a computer based in the United States.[13]

The Kufra scheme was the most ambitious conceived.[14] The oases of Kufra are situated in one of the driest places on earth. With temperatures of up to 45°C in summer, and average rainfall of 0.7mm per year, the only natural flora is the date-palm. Yet the Libyan Ministry of Agriculture and Land Reform decided to persist with a pre-revolutionary proposal to develop the Kufra oases as a centre of agricultural production. Following the discovery, during exploratory drilling by the Occidental Company in 1967, of artesian water near Tazerbu in the Kufra basin, plans were formulated for the reclamation of land from the desert, along the lines of similar schemes in Arizona and California. Tests conducted by hydrogeologists, mainly American, indicated that the underground water reserves existed in sufficient, if unquantifiable, measure to develop 50,000 acres of arable land. Given the right technological and manpower inputs, it was estimated that the consevative use of artesian water could sustain a variety of high-yielding crops and pasture for an indefinite period.

Expanding the cultivable acreage was a central feature of the drive for increased productivity. During the period of the 1973–83 Integrated Plan,

the Ministry of Agriculture's Department of Agrarian Reform and Land
Reclamation, and its construction and engineering subsidiary, the General
Land Reclamation Company, planned to bring an additional 1,500,000
acres into production. In the adverse climatic conditions of Libya, this

Table 6.5   Integrated Agricultural Development Projects, 1973-83

	Area (ha)	Total estimated cost (LDm)	Cost per farm (LD'000)	Cost per hectare (LD'000)	Farm size (ha)	Type
Tawurgha	3,000	8.0	2.7	—	—	I
Al-Hadaba al-Khadra	1,115	—	—	—	6	I
Qarahbulli Tar-houna al-Qasabat	25,000	62.2	2.5	62.2	25	D
Al-Ramla Valley	24,000	35.2	1.5	—	—	D
Megenin Project	41,000	75.4	1.8	46.0	25	D
Bir al-Ghanem (Azzizya)	21,100	53.0	2.5	—	—	I/D
Al-Mayet-al-Athel	35,000	34.2	1.0	24.4	25	D/G
Nalut and Sian	39,000	104.3	2.7	—	—	D
Jebel al-Akhdar	115,650	83.4	0.7	—	—	G
Benghazi Plain	58,200	8.1	0.1	—	—	G
Tobruk and Derna	1,300+	37.5	—	—	—	I
As-Shatti	1,000	8.1	0.1	81.1	10	I
Sebha	2,100	15.0	7.1	71.4	10	I
Wadi al-Ajal	3,200	19.6	6.1	61.3	10	I
Murzuq	3,200	19.6	6.1	61.3	10	I
Ghat al-Uweinat	1,500	11.6	7.7	77.3	10	I
Jufra	3,000	17.9	6.0	59.7	—	I
Kufra Production	10,000	30.0	3.0	—	na	I
Kufra Settlement	5,400	—	—	—	6.5	I
Sarir	50,000	36.9	0.7	—	—	I
Jalu and Aujelo	10,000	20.3	2.0	20.3	10.0	I
Wadi Ki'am	1,200	17.3	14.4	—	—	I/D
Misrata Project	22,100	17.3	0.8	—	—	I/D
Wadi Talal	7,000	12.0	1.7	—	—	—
Al-Qatara Valley	5,000	26.0	5.2	—	—	—
Al-Qawarsa Valley	385	3.9	10.1	66.9	6.6	—
Samlus and Zuba	583	0.5	0.9	—	—	—

Note: — = not available; na = not applicable; I = irrigated; D = dry land;
G = grazing land.
Source: Ministry of Information and Culture, Tripoli, 1974, quoted in J.A. Allan,
Libya: The Experience of Oil (Croom Helm, London 1981).

required capital-intensive development, including building windbreaks, dams, water reservoirs, pumping stations and, to prevent wind damage and soil erosion, afforestation of tracts of land adjoining areas of crop production.[15]

Land reclamation was most extensive in the coastal regions of the north-west and north-east. At Wadi Ramil, in the Jefara Plain, a project commenced to restore 57,600 hectares of land, by fixing the soil and constructing windbreaks. At Wadi Athel and Wadi Mait, also in the Jefara Plain, new dams were built to provide irrigation over 24,000 and 60,000 acres respectively. Between Tahouna and al-Kasbet a project was launched to reclaim 48,000 acres, involving terracing on the slopes of the Jebel Nafusah. In the area of Bir Tarfas the goal was the recovery of 14,400 acres, through piping water from deep wells. Altogether the objective was the reclamation of 1.2 million acres on the rangelands of the Jefara Plain, and 139,680 acres in the Jebel al-Akhdar uplands.[16]

Linked with the process of land reclamation was the establishment of farming settlements. This began after the Free Officer takeover in 1969, when migration from the land was accelerating and the urban population growing at a rate of 16 per cent annually, farming settlements were designed to attract Libyan labour back to the land. Work on the first settlement started at Kufra in 1969, and thereafter similar farming projects started elsewhere in the country. To the extent that the programme was successful, the best results were achieved along the northern coast; at Wadi Talal, on 25 October 1974, 380 farms, started in 1971, were distributed to farmer-proprietors in the Sirte area. On 30 October, Qadhafi personally handed over a further 500 farming units on the Jebel al-Akhdar.[17] By contrast, there were few takers for the settlements located in the isolated interior. When the Kufra scheme was completed in 1973, it failed to secure sufficient indigenous labour. Despite plans to construct 4,600 farming settlements, the authorities were unable to halt the migratory pull of the urban centres.

With the exception of some produce from privately-owned farms in the Jefara Plain, Libyan agricultural production remained in deficit. Even the best farms depended heavily on government subsidies; on the remoter and relatively capital-intensive schemes, the running costs could even outstrip the value of production. In a study of the Kufra Production Project, the economist J. A. Allan has observed: 'Even if the scheme were producing 20,000 tonnes of wheat and the highly subsidised price of LD150 realised, the LD3 million per year would not cover the running costs of the scheme, never mind the capital outlays already made and those which continue.'[18]

The constant demand for inputs of agro-technology enforced a relationship of dependence on foreign sources. For example, by the mid-1970s, Libya was importing 80 per cent of its cattle feed, 50 per cent of its sheep feed and almost 100 per cent of its poultry feed. Irrigation equipment and machinery also came from foreign sources, principally the United States. The projects financed under the Integrated Plan, especially the schemes of Kufra, Maknoussa and Sarir, were slices of Western technology transplanted and inserted into the Libyan economy. Furthermore, to overcome indigenous shortages of technical know-how and agricultural labour, the Ministry of Agriculture had, in the short term, no option other than to compensate by importing foreign manpower. Farming in the west of the country gradually came to depend on migrants from Tunisia, and production in the east relied on Egyptian workers from villages along the Nile, many from the Giza governorate.[19] In 1975 13.2 per cent of the sectoral workforce was expatriate, but among technicians and skilled workers the range of expatriate dependency was from 80 to 90 per cent. The workforce at Kufra, according to J. A. Allan, 'was a disparate polyglot assemblage of people from all corners of the world'.[20] In fact, 80 per cent of the workforce at Kufra was non-Libyan. Until 1976 even the shepherds were Sudanese.

Irrespective of the huge inputs of foreign labour and technology, Libyan agriculture experienced a decline in the production of certain major crops. Whilst yields obviously varied with seasonal rainfall, by the mid-1970s the production of cereals was on a clear downward curve. In 1977 wheat production was 65 per cent lower than it was in 1970; in the same period, the acreage under wheat production was 45 per cent less. Yields were, in other words, diminishing even more sharply than the acreage. Farms in the Jefara Plain expected to achieve outputs of at least 500 kilograms per hectare were returning an average of 200 per hectare. Even in the peak 1967–77 season, when rainfall was above average, the levels of wheat production in the Jefara Plain were around 230 kilograms per hectare. In the meantime, the Ministry failed to fulfil its targets for the total area of cereal production. By 1979 the goal was cereal production on 374,895 hectares; in the event, production was achieved on just 206,872 hectares.

The slump in cereal production was brought about by the misuse of water resources. In the Jefara Plain extensive over-irrigation by privately-owned farms caused the groundwater reserves to drop to dangerously low levels. What was previously natural grazing land, receiving less than 50mm of rainfall annually, was ploughed up and irrigated in the Great Wheat Project.[21] In 1976, the Ministry of Agriculture responded by placing restrictions on the production of crops with a high water consumption, such as citrus fruits and tomatoes, but by the 1977–78 harvesting season, the area under cultivation in the Jefara Plain had fallen to 20,330 hectares, and the country faced the ruin of its most productive agricultural asset. Evidently, there was no prospect of agriculture providing Libya with the foreign exchange earnings required once oil exports began to wind down. Efficiently managed production could at most offset a rising food import bill.

Table 6.6 Output of selected agricultural items, 1970–77

Year	Area Harvested		Quantity Produced (in Kilograms)												
	Barley	Wheat	Barley	Wheat	Potatoes	Onions	Groundnuts	Tomatoes	Apples	Figs	Olives	Poultry	Cattle	Goats	Sheep
1970	100	100	100	100	100	100	100	100	100	100	100	100	100	100	100
1971	31	34	6	23	230	75	104	91	162	122	7	84	95	92	106
1972	76	70	220	41	495	118	128	119	123	130	136	95	99	90	105
1973	133	95	387	86	791	166	104	122	177	161	212	366	113	81	143
1974	155	85	274	49	657	117	85	72	77	183	33	273	142	93	132
1975	171	92	363	58	898	199	118	134	123	13	215	360	178	137	193
1976	181	107	348	81	806	239	120	150	154	204	220	390	184	150	208
1977	66	65	110	35	999	252	122	122	200	270	60	362	169	123	177

Source: S. Birks and C. Sinclair 'Libya: Problems of a Rentier State', in A. Findlay and R. Lawless (eds.) *North Africa: Contemporary Politics and Economic Development* (Croom Helm, London, 1984). Statistics based on figures from Ministry and Secretariat of Planning, Tripoli.

DIAGRAM 6.1: STRUCTURE OF THE ASU

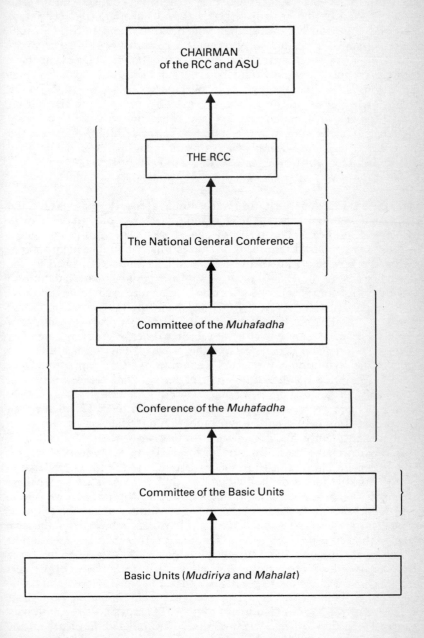

The Arab Socialist Union

The application of state capitalism in industry and agriculture was complemented by the growth of political and social *étatisme*. The state machinery, previously subordinate to the monarchy and an élite of tribal notables, gained a position of enormous ascendancy within society. No specific class exercised control over the state apparatus. Whilst members of the RCC retained their individual social ties, they achieved autonomy from the various class forces through their collective control of the state. As the largest owner of capital in Libya, the state did not have to depend on sharing power with the commercial capitalists or the stratum of petty capitalists. On the contrary, the state was in the position to *exclude* the bourgeoisie and petty-bourgeoisie from the administration of political power. In other words, the state in Libya did not govern on behalf of a ruling class; it was the *embodiment* of the ruling class.

Despite this vast superiority in the economic arena, the state lacked the same degree of dominance in politics and society; it could call on no mass ideological following. To fill the vacuum the RCC decided to convene a series of seminars to determine those forces which should be incorporated within the framework of institutions established and controlled by the state. The first of these, in May 1970, was called to formulate 'a definition of the working forces of the peoples who have an interest in the revolution', and the participants included RCC members, the Mufti of Tripoli, the Rector of the Islamic University, a number of so-called 'revolutionary intellectuals' and 'representatives of Libyan women'.[22] Actively guided by Qadhafi, the seminar concluded that the 'crushed' classes constituted the basis of the revolution, yet rejected the notion of class domination. On 1 June 1970, following the completion of the seminar series, an official statement was issued to the effect that there would be a single mass political institution comprising elements of the 'crushed' classes.[23] To enhance the prospect of unification with Egypt, this was modelled on the Egyptian Arab Socialist Union and named the Libyan Arab Socialist Union (ASU).

Qadhafi declared the formation of the ASU on 11 June 1971. In his announcement, the new institution was described as the mass organisation of 'the working forces of the revolution'. Under the ASU's Charter these were specified as intellectuals, farmers, soldiers, workers, and what were called 'non-exploitative' capitalists. What constituted a 'non-exploitative' capitalist was never adequately clarified, but practice showed that the term 'exploitation' was interpreted in a nationalist rather than class sense. The commercial bourgeoisie and the petty-bourgeoisie were not banned *per se* from membership; merely those elements which were the agents or partners of foreign-owned capital. Explicitly barred from admission were those who had held posts in any of the pre-revolutionary administrations and those convicted of various crimes under the judicial system of post-revolutionary Libya. The general rules of the organisation stipulated that workers and farmers between them comprise 50 per cent of the representation on the various bodies in the superstructure of the ASU. Otherwise, anyone over 18 years of age, including women, was eligible for membership, as long as they paid the fees set by the RCC.[24]

Formed in order to provide the military leadership with an institutional support base, the ASU was constricted in what it could and could not do. Excluded from the formulation of policy and the exercise of power, the organisation was confined to implementing the decisions, and popularising the message, of Qadhafi and his colleagues. Under the ASU'S Charter, members were ascribed eight duties: the first, and most significant, was that a member 'must live the problems of the masses and teach them their responsibilities'. Stressed the Charter: 'Citizens must be convinced by the ASU to perform the best they can; they are warned against laziness and neglect of duties'. A member was urged 'to get to know his milieu and awaken and educate those around him in ASU principles'.[25]

The ASU was organised in a pyramid structure in which decisions were communicated downwards. At the summit was the RCC, the sole repository of political power, which supervised the organisation's apparatus with the assistance of a secretariat. Below this level, in order of authority, was the biennial National General Conference which, although restricted to policy recommendations, provided the leadership with information about trends within the membership. Whilst containing a large number of representatives from the armed forces, police, labour, women's and youth organisations, the majority of delegates were elected by the conferences of each ASU district unit, or *muhafadha*. Meeting regularly every six months, the members of the *muhafadha* elected their own committee and monitored the work of the organisation's branches. These consisted of two types: a sub-district basic unit, the *mudiriya*, and the workplace unit, namely the *mahalat*.

The pro-capitalist orientation of the ASU became evident at the proceedings of its first National General Conference. The Conference, convened in Tripoli from 28 March to 8 April 1972, under Secretary General Bashir Hawwadi and Deputy General Secretary Omar al-Meheshi, heard Qadhafi spell out the division between the political and economic organisation of the Libyan population. Denying workers' organisations the right to raise political demands and express their class interests, he declared:

> The ASU is political work, a popular political organisation. The trade unions have nothing to do with politics – at no time and at no place. Trade unions and federations are professional organisations, which tackle the problems of their members. Politics must be confined to the ASU. It is impermissible to conduct politics outside the ASU in any union or profession. Otherwise, federations and trade unions would turn into parties. Consequently, there would not be a single organisation for the regime's working forces. There would be a group of political parties.[26]

The RCC regulated the workforce under a programme of labour legislation. Having banned independent trade unions in 1969, the Ministry of Labour began to establish a series of official unions and professional organisations. Such bodies were restricted to what Qadhafi called 'ordinary administrative duties':[27] the government, on the recommendation of the Ministry of Labour's Advisory Council on Wages, determined levels of pay and the conditions of workers' contracts. Inspectors appointed by the Labour Ministry were empowered to enforce levels of pay on employers and unions alike. In a new labour code, introduced in May 1970, trade unions were required by statute to accept the mediation of a Conciliation Council before resorting to stoppages. Strike action against employers was permitted only after the relevant organisation had given the Director General of Labour, appointed by the Ministry of Labour, two weeks' official notification.[28]

Working-class militancy was not immediately dissipated by these measures. In early 1972 dockworkers went on strike over levels of pay set by the Ministry of Labour.[29] Not until after the suppression of this two-week long dispute was labour policy elaborated in more effective ways. The RCC, aware that the restrictions on independent organisation had failed, began to combine two interrelated themes in its approach to the labour force: on the one hand, the repressive measures were increased, with a complete ban on strikes and forms of workplace disruption; on the other, the RCC introduced three important social and welfare provisions. First, in March 1973, the authorities introduced profit-sharing schemes into many workplaces; secondly, in August 1973, the Ministry of Labour inaugurated a policy of joint workers-management councils in the larger enterprises; and thirdly, in September 1973, the RCC set up a Central Labour Fund Office to provide workers with housing.[30] In addition, the authorities maintained and strengthened the system of social insurance initiated by the monarchy in 1961. Given the appallingly low productivity of the Libyan workforce, these measures were designed to elicit the workers' assent in the industrialisation of the country, whilst stringently preventing the working class from independent economic and political organisation.

The emphasis on the inclusion of workers and farmers did not contradict the pro-capitalist bias of the ASU. The stress on their involvement was merely symptomatic of the regime's *desire* to incorporate the workforce in the productive sectors of the society into the political apparatus. In reality, despite the stipulation concerning 50 per cent representation, workers and farmers never dominated the ASU, either locally or centrally. A total of 300,000 people joined the organisation, but this did not reflect the level of popular participation. The ASU was steered and controlled by officials who, frequently in collusion with local capitalists, sought to acquire power and wealth by controlling different sectors of the state machinery and political apparatus. Inevitably, the organisation remained an ossified bureaucratic shell incapable of mobilising mass support behind the RCC.

The lack of ideological purity exhibited by officials of the ASU was a constant source of concern to Qadhafi. Just two weeks after the First National General Conference of the organisation, he threatened resignation over the internal corruption and power-broking which ensued in the scramble to gain posts. At Sabrata in late April 1972, he delivered a speech in which he claimed to have stepped down from the leadership of the revolution because of the 'pecuniary lust' of officials.[31] In the event, his withdrawal from the political arena did not take place, but his frustration with the kind of persons who infested the state apparatus–bureaucrats motivated by self-enrichment rather than by their commitment to Arab nationalism and modernisation, persisted. He continued to occupy the Presidency and Command of the Armed Forces, but in July he handed over the Premiership to his closest ally, Abdessalam Jalloud.

Popular Cultural Revolution

The incorporation of merchant capitalists and tribal leaders into the ASU resulted in its bureaucratisation. By seeking to co-opt these traditional élites into the state apparatus the RCC merely enhanced their position in society, and reproduced the prevailing sectarian and tribal affiliations within the context of the ASU. The mass of the population, the urban working class and petty-bourgeoisie, were compelled to rely on the patronage of individuals who, because of their different class aspirations and social status, did not necessarily identify with the same social interests. Based on the collaboration of military officers and this traditional leadership, the ASU worked to the exclusion of the majority of the Libyan population. Whilst, in theory, intended to synthesise the interests of different social classes, the ASU in practice was controlled by the merchant and business class in partnership with officials defending bureaucratic privilege.

Qadhafi's objections to this bureaucratic alliance are complex. Essentially, he realised that the form of collaboration with this layer of society was jeopardising the successful transition from the pre-capitalist, semi-colonial society: by penetrating the ASU and the institutions of government, sectarian and kinship affiliations were militating against the development of his own mass political support and the popularity of nationalist ideology. Having, for reasons of expediency, favoured rule in co-operation with traditional social leaders in the absence of an independent political following of his own, Qadhafi became convinced that the ASU and state apparatus required urgent transformation. Accordingly, in 1973 he abandoned the policy of relying on existing social and political leaders and, to break the control they exercised over the ASU and state institutions, he initiated a 'popular and cultural revolution'.

Qadhafi embarked on this course with a speech in the coastal town of Zuwara on 15 April 1973. Calling for the overthrow of those elements in society who interposed their authority between the RCC and the population in general, and thereby preventing the evolution of allegiance to his leadership. Qadhafi declared that 'the revolutionary accomplishments you want to achieve are threatened, in my opinion, if you continue your present course'. To rejuvenate the revolution, he put forward a five-point programme:

1. All existing laws must be repealed and replaced by revolutionary enactments designed to produce the necessary revolutionary change.
2. The weeding out of all weak minds from society by taking appropriate measures towards perverts and deviationists.
3. The staging of an administrative revolution in order to eliminate all forms of bourgeoisie and bureaucracy.
4. The setting up of popular committees whereby the people might begin to seize power. This was meant to ensure freedom for the people with regard to bureaucrats and opportunists.
5. The staging of a cultural revolution to eliminate all poisonous imported ideas, and fuse together the people's genuine moral and material potentialities.[31]

In search of cadres to carry out this programme Qadhafi turned to the student movement. Soon after his Zuwara speech, the first popular committee was set up at the Faculty of Law of Benghazi University. Qadhafi, meeting the committee there on 28 April, praised the students' action. Describing them as the 'vanguard of the revolution', he pronounced that the students had become 'an instrument to implement popular wishes'. Visiting the Faculty of Engineering on 3 May, where another committee had been formed, he encouraged students to spread the cultural revolution. Within days popular committees had proliferated throughout schools and colleges, following the lead of those at Benghazi University. These committees vetted the political correctness of the staff and the courses; they even revised curricula and censored politically dubious textbooks. They were also active outside the campus. In Benghazi, students invaded the congested harbour and instituted a system to shift the back-log of traffic. In Tripoli, agricultural students left their class-rooms and marched on the countryside to lead peasants and farmers in campaigns to increase production. In local government they deposed the local, factional-orientated administrations and formed popular committees in their place. In the factories, managers and foremen deemed corrupt and inefficient were dismissed.

The phenomenon bore hallmarks similar to those of the Chinese cultural revolution. Indeed, the Libyan cultural revolution replicated, on a smaller scale, all the important features of the Chinese cultural revolution. Through the intervention of the popular committees, the leadership imposed a series of structural changes it was unable to accomplish through the state apparatus. Even the justification for the mobilisation in Libya was similar to that in China. In the 1966 Chinese Red Guards' phase, the target was a layer of so-called 'bourgeois-bureaucrats'. According to Qadhafi's

Zuwara speech, the objective of the popular committee movement was also the elimination of 'this bourgeois class, this bureaucratic class, which rouses itself only through fear'. Qadhafi himself has denied that he was influenced by Mao, but in an interview with Italian journalist Mirella Bianco in 1973 he said:

> Concerning content, the present events in Libya go much further than the [Chinese] cultural revolution, which incidentally was also, I think, much more a popular than a cultural revolution. This is exactly what is happening here: a cultural revolution that cuts its way through the red tape and the self-interested groups.[32]

Perhaps the main achievement of the popular and cultural revolution was the suppression of factions and individuals with followings in Libyan society. Foremost among these were the Muslim Brotherhood, the Islamic Liberation Movement, the Arab Baath Socialist Party, and Marxists of various denominations. During the period of the popular revolution, members of these factions and their sympathisers were systematically arrested by the Libyan security services and, following denunciations, some 1,000 were apparently detained. Towards the end of the year some were released after televised confessions, but senior opponents were held indefinitely. In August, Qadhafi issued an ultimatum in which 'anyone who still belongs to any organisation can come forward and surrender' within 30 days. Thereafter, he declared, anyone 'who seeks to dominate the people or society through a class or party will be considered a traitor subject to the death penalty'.

Although the popular cultural revolution apparently alienated some of Qadhafi's more bureaucratically-bound colleagues within the RCC, he nevertheless emerged with the nucleus of his own ideological following. Through the purge of the bureaucracy and the creation of the people's committees, he became less dependent on the collaboration of locally-based sheikhs and businessmen. The traditional élites continued to operate their systems of patronage and clientage, but their capacity to diminish the impact of post-revolutionary changes was reduced. In effect, the process of popular revolution tightened Qadhafi's grip on the state machine and the administrative apparatus. Whilst the committees remained open to some forms of manipulation by élite figures, they also provided Tripoli with a structure of authority, and acted as an antidote to traditional patron-figures who utilised local government as a power base and a means of self-enrichment. For a country of strong provincial loyalties, where the concept of Libyan identity was modern and abstract, the committees became a key mechanism of centralisation and national integration.

Instigated from the centre by Qadhafi, the people's committees never became a spontaneous and independent popular movement. The direction and parameters of the revolution were set by a sector of the state apparatus. Beyond the takeover of local government services, the work of the committees was rigorously circumscribed: the establishment of people's committees in the ministries of central government was explicitly denied. After August 1973, the final deadline for the overthrow of the former system of local administration, the committees were institutionalised within the framework of national government. Lastly, on 16 October 1973, in Law No. 78, formalising the responsibilities in local administration, the committees became legally constituted bodies charged with the supervision of local services and state-run companies. Elected from the population of each administrative district, or the staff of each company, the committees elected their own secretariat and convened their own local meetings to decide upon the distribution of resources.

Even within the limits devised by Qadhafi, the committees had many defects. The level of participation was low and there were persistent shortages of skilled administrators. Because of the passivity with which the population greeted the initiative, the traditional leaderships were frequently able to reassert their influence within the committees; indeed, as the most experienced administrators, local notables found it easy to gain support for election to senior posts within the committees.[33] Disappointment with election results appears to have been a principal factor that prompted Qadhafi eventually to call a halt to the popular revolution, albeit claiming that 'most areas are being governed by the people'. The absence of cadres ideologically wedded to his brand of nationalism inevitably determined the outcome. Although the number of committees grew from about 400 in April to around 2,000 in August, much of the programme was never fulfilled.

It is important to bear in mind the historical conjuncture within Libya on the inauguration of the popular cultural revolution. With the development of capitalism, Libyan society was in the process of transition from pre-capitalist to class relationships. The 1967 oil workers' strike and the 1972 dockworkers' strike were the most obvious indications of this social transformation. The goal of the popular cultural revolution was the eradication of all forms of political allegiance, except that functioning between the mass of the population and the leadership. Different forms of loyalty, based on sections of the population, were counterposed by the articulation of a state capitalist, nationalist ideology, which legitimised the incorporation of various strata into the institutions of the state.

Notes

1. M. El Mehdawi, 'The Industrialisation of Libya', in *Change and Economic Development in the Middle East* (Methuen, London, 1981); also quoted by P. Barker, 'The Development of Libyan Industry', in J.A. Allan (ed.) *Libya since Independence* (Croom Helm, London, 1982).

2. Cyrenaica reverted to a handicraft economy following the destruction of several Italian-owned factories in the Second World War. See Pandeli Glavanis, 'State and Labour in Libya', in R. Lawless and A. Findlay (eds.) *North Africa:*

Contemporary Politics and Economic Development (Croom Helm/St Martins, London, 1984) p. 128.

3. Ibid., p. 128.

4. *The Revolution of 1st September: The Fourth Anniversary,* Annual Yearbook 1973. (General Administration for Information, Benghazi) p. 52. In the passage quoted there is some confusion in the translation; this has been amended in this text.

5. Ibid., p. 53.

6. This resembles the current policy of the conservative Gulf states, who seek to preserve their existing social structures by diverting funds abroad, often into foreign property investments and bank deposits.

7. Turkey under Ataturk provided the prototype of this form of state-controlled industrialisation; for an interesting account see Turgut Taylan, 'Capital and State in Contemporary Turkey', in *Modern Turkey: Development and Crisis, Khamsin,* no. 11.

8. S. Birks and C. Sinclair, 'Libya: Problems of a *Rentier* State', in Lawless and Findlay (eds.) *North Africa: Contemporary Politics and Economic Development,* p. 268. Sources include official data, ILO and author's estimates.

9. J.S. Birks and C.A. Sinclair, *Arab Manpower: The Crisis of Development* (Croom Helm, London, 1980) p. 134.

10. This problem is discussed by Birks and Sinclair, ibid., pp. 136–137.

11. Qadhafi's address at Sebha on 22 September 1969 is quoted in M.O. Ansell and I.M. Arif, *The Libyan Revolution* (Oleander Press, Cambridge) p. 75.

12. See R. First, 'Libya: Class and State in an Oil Economy', in Peter Nore and Terisa Turner (eds.) *Oil and Class Struggle* (Zed Press, London, 1980) p. 135.

13. S. Birks and C. Sinclair, 'Libya: Problems of a *Rentier* State', in Lawless and Findlay, *North Africa* p.262. The cost of $1,350 per tonne of wheat from these three schemes compared with a world market price of $241.

14. Kufra is the most extensively analysed of the three oases' agricultural project schemes: for a detailed account, written from an essentially 'technicist' point of view, see J.A. Allan, *Libya: The Experience of Oil* (1981) pp. 202-215.

15. 'Agriculture: The Desert Comes Alive', *Arab Dawn* (September 1976) provides a semi-official account of the programme and methods of the Department of Agrarian Reform and Land Reclamation during this period.

16. For details of these land reclamation schemes in the Jefara Plain and elsewhere, see 'LAR's Four Major Agricultural Projects', *Arab Dawn* (December 1974).

17. '1.5m Acres of Land Reclaimed and Self-sufficiency in Food by 1983', *Arab Dawn* (December 1974).

18. J.A. Allan, 'Managing Agricultural Reosurces in Libya: Recent Experience', *Libyan Studies: Tenth Annual Report of the Society for Libyan Studies* 1978–79 (London 1979).

19. See Elizabeth Taylor, 'Egyptian Migration and Peasant Wives', MERIP *Reports* (June 1984).

20. J.A. Allan, 1981 p. 204.

21. Ibid., p. 208.

22. R. First, 1974, p. 125.

23. The Arabic word is *mashruta*; the usual translation is 'powder'.

24. The rules and regulations of the ASU can be found in Henry Habib, *Politics and Government of Revolutionary Libya* (Le Cercle du Livre, Montreal, 1975) pp. 189-200.

25. Ibid.

26. BBC SWB ME/3954, 4 April 1972.

27. Qadhafi, address in Tripoli, October 1969.

28. H. Habib *Politics and Government,* contains further details of labour legislation.

29. R. First, *Libya: Class and State,* 1980, p. 137.

30. H. Habib, 1974.

31. These are encapsulations of Qadhafi's five points. In the actual text of the speech, Qadhafi develops his criticism of the bureaucracy. Quoted verbatim, point 4 says: 'There must be a revolution within the bureaucracy against those who, by staying at home, interpose between the revolution and the masses; against those who stop working as soon as the overseer turns his back; against those who shut their offices in the face of the people or allow their interests to be neglected. This bourgeois class, this bureaucratic class, which rouses itself only through fear, must be made an object of administrative revolution launched by the people.'

32. M. Bianco, *Gadafy: Voice from the Desert*, 1974, p 92.

33. Two particular works deal with the relationship between the local elites and the central political authority in some detail: Richard Chackerian, Omar Fathaly and Monte Palmer, *Political Development and Bureaucracy in Libya* (Lexington Books, Lexington, Mass. 1977); and Omar Fathaly and Monte Palmer, *Political Development and Social Change in Libya* (Lexington Books, Lexington, Mass, 1980).

7   Rise of the Jamahiriya

The Turning Point

1975 was a watershed year in Libya. Qadhafi faced rising discontent from two distinct but interrelated sources. The first was the student movement: a backlash against the political purges of the cultural revolution appeared to have taken hold in the universities and other institutes. The second, and more important, was the commercial sector, whose position within the economy was, in 1975, eroded by the first of several reforms bringing foreign trade within the sphere of state control. The convergence of these two sources of opposition precipitated a serious internal crisis and, subsequently, an important change in the political direction of the Revolution.

These social upheavals developed against the backdrop of a temporary balance of payments crisis. The slackening of world oil demand in 1975 produced an excess of expenditure over revenues. Owing to the lower unit prices brought about by market conditions, the value of the country's exports fell below the 1974 level, when their appreciation had doubled, despite the decreases in production experienced since 1970.[1] The effects of this brief reversal in the country's terms of trade are shown in Table 7.1.

In May 1975, the drop in projected revenues prompted a government review of expenditure priorities. Planning Minister and RCC member Omar al-Meheshi proposed major cutbacks in military spending which, he insisted, were necessary to maintain investment in the country's development programme. In making this proposal, he placed Qadhafi, as President, and Jalloud, as Prime Minister, in an awkward position. By implication, although not perhaps by intention, he was questioning both the role of the Army as the 'revolutionary vanguard' in society, and the policy of confrontation with Israel, which absorbed an enormous, but unspecified, amount of the country's resources. Being wedded to the aim of a Libyan Pan-Arab role, as well as to a military-orientated government, Jalloud, supported by Qadhafi, dismissed Meheshi's proposal. Instead, to save foreign exchange earnings, he favoured measures designed to curb domestic consumption, including a state monopoly of foreign trade, although this would inevitably delay the country's development programme.

Table 7.1   Libya's Balance of Payments 1970–76 (LD millions)

	1970	1971	1972	1973	1974	1975	1976
Exports	+856	+962	+812	+1,053	+2,135	+1,847	+2,547
Imports	–241	–330	–424	–600	–1,109	–1,310	–1,369
Invisibles (net)	–345	–322	–276	–387	–464	–509	–648
Current Account Balance	+270	+310	+112	+66	562	+28	+530
Gov. grants	–40	–32	–34	–47	–20	–49	–28
Long-term capital	+50	+46	–14	–152	–125	–461	–379
Short-term capital	–35	–15	+72	–183	+93	+22	+187
Total balance	*+245*	*+309*	*+136*	*–316*	*+510*	*–460*	*+310*
Gold and for. exchange assets	576	875	977	666	1,110	696	1,026

Sources: Central Bank of Libya. *Economic Bulletin* (March/April 1977); IMF, Balance of Payments Yearbooks.

The decision to establish a state monopoly of foreign trade, taken in principle by the summer of 1975, provoked simmering unrest among the country's merchant class. Meheshi, the emergent critic of government policy, became the focus for this opposition. His disagreement with the nature of spending cuts developed into general dissatisfaction with the direction of policy. Whilst not explicitly articulating the interests of the commercial sector capitalists, he nevertheless wished to avert a conflict with the merchants– a situation that threatened to become a trend under Qadhafi's leadership. Other RCC members, namely Hamza, Hawwadi, Houni, Nejm and Qirwi, appeared to share at least some of his reservations. By July, believing he had substantive support, Meheshi had begun preparations for an attempt to oust Qadhafi.[2]

Meheshi began to organise underground cells within the armed forces and the state apparatus, relying extensively on networks of personal and kinship ties, which centred on his home-town of Misrata; but these relations proved neither effective nor dependable. Evidence that Meheshi's relatives and staff were engaged in secret activity soon came to the attention of the secret police, the *mukhabarrat*. Meheshi doubtless hoped he was covered by the collaboration of Houni, who was entrusted with intelligence work, but indications of his involvement in a conspiracy nevertheless reached Qadhafi's office at Bab al-Azzizya barracks. Tipped off in advance, perhaps by Houni, or another member of the RCC, in August Meheshi and members of his staff fled to neighbouring Tunisia. Five months later, following official attempts to secure his extradition, he moved to Egypt, where he was granted asylum by President Sadat. Quoted in *al-Ahram* on 12 March 1976, he explained that his only aim was 'correcting Qadhafi's errors'.

The most mysterious aspect of the whole affair is the role played by Houni. According to the American journalist John K. Cooley, by no means a friendly witness of the Libyan Revolution:

> Houny, who toured eye clinics throughout Western Europe and the United States in desperate attempts to restore his failing vision, also during his travels contacted the CIA sometime between 1972 and 1975. He may have been feeding information to Tripoli station chief John Stein, or to Stein's superiors in Washington.[3]

Be that as it may, Houni evaded detection for a much longer period than his other RCC colleagues who were in evident collusion with Meheshi, most notably Ahmed Hamza. At meetings within the RCC Houni apparently expressed little disagreement with Qadhafi. His rupture with the Libyan leader became apparent only when, towards the end of 1975, he boarded a plane bound for Rome and never returned, finally joining Meheshi in Cairo early in 1976.

By the end of 1975, the original twelve-strong RCC had contracted to five members. The same August of Meheshi's flight, Mukhtar al-Qirwi took off for the United States and requested asylum there; back in Libya, Hawwadi and Hamza were placed under house arrest and Nejm had been put in detention. The RCC comprised Qadhafi and four loyalists: Khweildi al-Hamidi, Abu Bakr Younis Jaber, Abdessalam Jalloud and Mustafa Kharoubi. Of the original twelve the remaining member, Mohammed al-Migharief, had been killed during a motoring accident in 1972. Following the crisis, the institution of the RCC became rapidly defunct and meetings of the five highly irregular. Power had become concentrated in the hands of Qadhafi himself.

The evident volatility of Qadhafi's leadership prior to this important centralisation of power owed much to the nature of the RCC. This institution, like its predecessor, the Free Officer Central Committee, tried to bring together divergent social and personal interests. Against the single enemy of the monarchy it had been possible to maintain a united front, but following the initial post-coup period the basis of solidarity began to disintegrate, and failure to achieve unity with Egypt had accelerated the process. From the episode of the 'Cultural Revolution' onwards, Qadhafi was frequently at odds with his more bureaucratic RCC colleagues. Even before that, he appears to have become periodically frustrated. On three occasions he impulsively withdrew from political activity: on 28 September 1971 he vanished to re-emerge on 4 October in Cairo for talks with the Presidents Assad and Sadat; in the summer of 1972, after the founding of the ASU, he disappeared for three weeks, surfacing again on 10 July, to hand over the Premiership to Jalloud; finally, on 11 July 1973, he temporarily resigned after the aborted Green March on Egypt. Only when his personal control was decisively established, following the ousting of the pro-Meheshi faction, did Qadhafi's leadership seem permanent and dominant. The rout of his opponents became a turning point in the country's political development.

Despite Meheshi's objections to Qadhafi's foreign policy preoccupations, the core of the dispute between the two men was a different set of economic and political perspectives. Meheshi stood for a form of Nasserite state-controlled capitalist development; in short, he believed it was necessary for the state to intervene in the economy to assist the transformation from merchant capital to productive capital. As Planning Minister, he was the architect of Libya's bold industrial development schemes: the iron and steel complex at Misrata was the centrepiece of his economic strategy. Initially, Qadhafi and all the members of the RCC had shared this Nasserite concept of assisting the development of indigenous capitalism, but following the cultural revolution, and the *infitah* – or opendoor – policy in Egypt, a process of differentiation began within the ranks of the RCC. The loss of confidence by key sections of the commercial sector, demonstrated by their negative attitude to the popular committees, caused Qadhafi to question the role of the capitalist class in the Revolution. After 1975, having initially supported the involvement of 'non-exploitative capitalists' in the forces comprising the Revolution, he gradually started to adopt and form models of socialist economic development.

Following the removal of Meheshi, Libyan society experienced a period of polarisation. The development was most manifest within the universities: students divided into supporters and opponents of Qadhafi's leadership. In fact, the first protests against the authorities were organised by students. At Benghazi University in January 1976 a group of students tried to resist the election of ASU candidates to the Student Council; fighting subsequently broke out between pro- and anti-Qadhafi factions. The security services intervened and ten anti-Qadhafi students were killed. Their deaths sparked off further anti-Qadhafi protests at Tripoli University and by foreign-based Libyan students outside the embassies in Bonn, London and Washington.[4]

In the face of this spasm of opposition, Qadhafi exhorted his own substantial student following to drive out 'the reactionary elements'. By April 1976, they were formed into 'revolutionary student committees', which then seized control of the student councils. All private Islamic institutions were taken over; the Islamic *Awqaf* Library in Tripoli had its books and archives removed, and the building was pulled down. Those aspects off curricula conflicting with the goals of the Revolution were changed. Several students at Tripoli University were detained and, according to later reports, executed.[5] This transformation was called 'the students revolution' and Tripoli University was renamed 'al-Fateh University' – an allusion to the al-Fateh Revolution.

The activity in the universities was linked with developments that occurred before and during the Third Congress of the ASU. Convened in

January 1976, this Congress endorsed the measures favoured by Qadhafi and Jalloud for dealing with the temporary balance of payments problems of 1975. Military expenditure was exempt from cutbacks, but the Congress approved an administrative budget that provided approximately half the amount required by government departments; in short, the Congress accepted the Council of Ministers' recommendation of LD 679 million, from a budget request of LD 1.1 billion.[6] Jalloud, addressing delegates, revealed that his government had decided to reschedule plans for the construction of refineries at Misrata and Zueitina. Lastly, but most significantly, the Congress resolved to establish a state monopoly of foreign trade and to introduce statutory rent controls – an especially strong demand from the layers of society which formed Qadhafi's popular base of support.

Further controversy was stimulated by a major political reform effected by the Congress, which, in the absence of Meheshi and Hawwadi, was closely guided by Qadhafi and Jalloud. Following Qadhafi's growing criticism of the ASU, which implied that under Meheshi and Hawwadi it had become a bureaucratic apparatus, operating in collaboration with leading merchants and tribal sheikhs, the Congress reconstituted itself as 'the General People's Congress'. In a reference to the ASU's original intentions, the move was described as an attempt 'to reflect the democratic principles which had brought about the creation of the assembly'. During the election of Congress delegates by ASU Basic Units in November and December, Qadhafi, having taken over control from his purged opponents, used the secretariat of the organisation to ensure that representatives of the commercial sector, and their allies, would not be selected. Jalloud, with Qadhafi's backing, became the ASU's new General Secretary.

Despite official claims, notably from Staff Major Jalloud himself, that there were no classes in Libya, the society had, in fact, entered into a period of heightened class conflict between two rising social forces: the merchant capitalists and the working class,[7] which, in 1976, was estimated to comprise 300,000 from a total population of 2.6 million. The transformation of the ASU, following the flight of Meheshi, tipped the balance of class forces towards the working class and the lower strata of the society. The merchant capitalists remained an extremely powerful section of society, but as a result of the internal changes within the state, they had been deprived of an important vehicle for their political interests.

The Green Book

The Third Congress of the ASU consummated an important shift in domestic policy. Until the transformation of the institution in January 1976, the revolutionary authorities had tried to build a base of support by collaboration with traditional leaderships, namely urban merchants, rural tribal sheikhs and holy men. In 1973, the RCC even commissioned a study from the academics, Richard Chickerian, Omar al-Fathaly and Monte Palmer on the question of whether or not the traditional leaderships could become agents of change.[8] Following the Congress, having decided they could not, Qadhafi switched from co-opting these established social leaders to minimising their social and political influence. The tribal sheikhs, like the merchants of the commercial sector, became the revolutionary state's competitors, rather than 'conductors'

Developing Nasser's twin themes of nationalism and religion, Qadhafi began to expound an ideology that emphasised the factors underpinning the unity and indivisibility of Libya. This ideology, known as the Third Universal Theory, was tentatively outlined at the Conference of European and Arab Youth, in Tripoli in May 1973, but was never adequately elaborated until 1975. By intention the theory was not static. Drawing initially on the general concept of a 'third way' between capitalism and Communism, Qadhafi has given the theory specific application to Libyan society. By 1975, in a country fragmented by local tribal allegiances and social polarisation, the theory became a statement of principles on politics and political organisation. In denying the material nature of class and sectional divisions, the emergent 'the third way' was now an ideological solvent for tribal loyalties. Linked with the transition from localised kinship to Libyan citizenship, the theory is essentially programmatic.[9]

Qadhafi's first written explanation of the theory appeared in the *Green Book, Part 1: The Solution to the Problem of Democracy,* extracts of which were published in the official newspaper, *al-Fajr al-Jadid,* towards the end of 1975. In *Part 1,* which was printed in complete form in 1976, Qadhafi provided a model of political organisation radically different from the earlier Nasserist model transposed from Egypt. Dealing in terms which seem simplistic to outsiders, yet relevant to the experience of the majority of Libyans, he renounces forms of representative democracy in favour of collective democracy, which he calls 'the authority of the people'. *Part 1*'s central tenent is that 'all representation is fraud'. To this day, the slogan 'no representation in lieu of the people' taken straight from *Part 1,* is emblazoned on walls and billboards across Libya. Stating his reasons for this repudiation, Qadhafi claims: 'The masses . . . are completely isolated from the representative and he, in turn, is totally separated from them. For immediately after winning their votes he usurps their sovereignty and acts instead of them.'[10]

Paradoxically, Qadhafi's major objection to representative democracy is its partially unrepresentative nature. Elections, in the Libyan context, can split a polling district along tribal lines and produce a result which, in the perception of a minority kin group, deprives them of representation. The competition for votes, among candidates patronised by different tribal units, promotes internal disintegration, undermining the 'nation-building' policies of the country's revolutionary leadership. In Libya, tribal sheikhs can use – and indeed have used – elections to mobilise support for the nominee of their choice, not necessarily themselves, but an individual whom they believe capable of acting on behalf of the tribal élite's interests; they even draw on the votes of traditionally client groups, if they are needed to win a majority in the poll. Political parties, which in the Libyan experience have developed tribal constituencies of support, are treated by Qadhafi in the same way. In his words,

> The party system is the modern tribal and sectarian system. The society governed by one party is exactly like that which is governed by one tribe or one sect. The party, as stated above, represents the outlook of a certain group of people, or the interests of one group of the society, or one belief or one locality.[11]

According to reliable sources, the People's Committees established in 1973 did have a marginal effect in reducing tribalism. In 1977, Dr John Mason, an American anthropologist who had carried out fieldwork in Libya between 1968 and 1970, revisited the oases of Aujela and observed the changes that had occurred since his departure in 1970. He reported that the committee structure had proved notably popular with the younger generation and successful in breaking down the traditional hierarchy of the employer, or *mudir*, and the sheikh. 'Almost all,' concludes Mason, 'are very enthusiastic about the new system and the many positive changes it has brought about.'[12]

The process appears to have been extremely uneven, however, and degrees of success varied. Other sources, notably Fathaly and Palmer, indicate that the People's Committee remained open to abuse by the traditional leaderships. They tell of committee meetings effectively dominated by the tribal elders, and businessmen who are able to influence proceedings either through patronage or the threat of withdrawing patronage. Say Fathaly and Palmer:

> A number of elections resulted in the re-emergence of traditional tribal and business leaders, a class of individuals Colonel Qadhafi had declared to be parasites and ineligible to hold public office. Such elections, with considerable embarrassment to the regime, had to be voided and re-scheduled.[13]

To prevent the domination of the sheikhs and capitalists, the *Green Book, Part 1*, supplemented by organisational guidelines, prescribed an important transformation of the country's existing political structure: the bureaucratic and hierarchical ASU was abandoned. The ASU's Basic Units, renamed Basic People's Congresses (BPCs), became the fundamental form of political organisation, but unlike the ASU's units, the Congresses did not operate a system of closed membership, but were open to the local population. The People's Committees, previously formally autonomous from the structure of the ASU, remained People's Committees responsible for administration, but were elected by the various sub-districts of the BPC. For each people's administrative committee the residents of each sub-district were entitled to elect two members who served for a specified period of three years. The people's committees selected their own chairperson, but day-to-day supervision of their work was entrusted to the 40, or so, members of the executive committee, whose three-member secretariat, like the secretariat of the Congress itself, was elected annually by the meeting of the full BPC. On average, each BPC had 16 of these people's committees, generally for the following areas of administration:[14]

Agriculture	Housing
Building	Municipality
Education	Planning
Electricity	Post and Telecommunications
Employment	Transport
Finance	Water
Justice	Youth Affairs
Health	

By devising a system in which each sub-district selected two members of a People's Committee, Qadhafi hoped to stop a tribe in the majority from excluding a tribe in the minority. Previously, following the ossification of the committees, initially formed in 1973, the tribal leadership had been able to assert control over the local administration. In Libya, like other societies where the predominant form of social organisation is tribal, kinship relations were an important factor in securing promotion within local government. Those who held senior posts were patrons to other members of their family and kin group; merit was frequently a secondary factor. Those from the minority tribes with talent and skills could be subject to exclusion.

A further tier of political organisation came in the form of Municipal People's Congresses (MPCs). Grouping together several urban-based BPCs, these were converted from the former *muhafadha* units of the ASU. The MPCs met annually and elected their secretariats, which were entitled to attend the GPC, but which differed from Basic People's Congresses in that they neither elected people's committees, nor an executive committee to supervise the people's committees of the local BPCs.

Although it is not clear from Diagram 7.1, the nature of the relationships between the different tiers is not meant to be hierarchical. According to the *Green Book*, the BPCs are sovereign institutions and not subordinate to a central authority. In theory, the General People's Congress is not a legislature, but an assembly comprising the three-member secretariats of the BPCs; the executive committee of the people's committees (*al-lajna al-qiyadiya*); and the secretariats of the various occupational and professional organisations. This assembly meets annually to vote on resolutions already decided by the BPCs. Accordingly, the General People's Congress is not intended to determine the country's policy; that is the function of the BPCs, which convene annually to elect their secretariats, and the secretariats of the executive committees, and to receive reports and discuss an agenda of

The relationship between the BPC's and the centralised structure of political organisation was complex. In the *Green Book*, Qadhafi provides the following diagram:

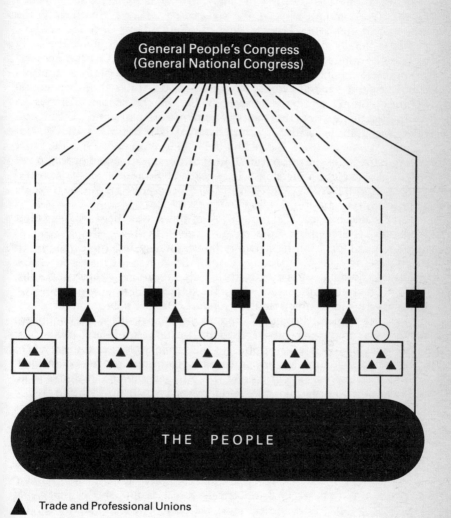

▲ Trade and Professional Unions

☐ Basic People's Congress

■ People's Committees

topical political items to be put before the GPC. A function of the chairperson of the BPC is to convey the consensus view of this annual meeting to the General People's Congress. On this occasion a list of resolutions is decided upon by a simple majority vote.

National administration corresponded with the pattern of local administration. 'The government administration is abolished and replaced by peoples' committees', says the *Green Book, Part 1*. Specifically, the government ministries become peoples' committees; their secretariats, elected annually by the General Peoples' Congress, conduct the daily business of administration. The cabinet is replaced by a General Peoples' Committee, comprised of the secretariats of the peoples' committees chosen by the General Peoples' Congress. The secretariat of the General Peoples' Committee, elected annually by the General Peoples' Congress, is the highest office within the country's administrative structure. The highest office within the legislative structure is that of the secretariat of the General Peoples' Congress itself. Elected by the Congress annually, like the other secretariats, it has the responsibility for the organisation and procedure of the annual congress meetings. The posts of Secretary of the General Peoples' Committee and Secretary of the General Peoples' Congress are the most important in the whole congress system.

First moves towards the application of this system began shortly after Qadhafi's 1 September anniversary speech in 1975. Responding to Qadhafi's call for a transition to popular democracy, his political following in the country began to convert the ASU's Basic Units into BPCs. Confronted with a population traditionally subordinate to tribal sheikhs, and bureaucratic time-servers within the state apparatus, the process took many months to complete and consolidate. Despite the formal inauguration of the General People's Congress in January 1976, the committee system was only partially and haphazardly established. When the Congresses met in late 1975, prior to the January Congress, the levels of effective participation varied enormously from one district to another. Before the congress system was sufficiently generalised, Qadhafi's aides were required to issue guidelines and intervene personally in the formation of individual congresses, where bureaucratic and traditional leaders attempted to exclude popular participation.

In January 1976, the congress system was not ready to receive the transfer of administrative powers, either at district or national level. The final phase of securing the system, the crucial elections of people's committees, commenced when the BPCs convened for their annual meetings in November 1976, elected their secretariats, the secretariats of the basic peoples' committees and held sub-district elections for the 16 Peoples' Committees. Four months later a similar transfer occurred at national level, accompanied by extensive symbolism and celebration. At a 970-member GPC, meeting in the southern city of Sebha on 2 March 1977, Qadhafi, with Fidel Castro at his side, delivered his famous 'Declaration on the Authority of the People'. Henceforth, the Libyan

Arab Republic had expired along with its flag; Libya was renamed the Socialist People's Libyan Arab Jamahiriyah and the flag became a cloth of green.[15]

The leadership hailed the event as of momentous historical significance. As the Declaration, evocatively delivered to the Congress by Qadhafi, maintained:

> The Libyan people, having regained through the revolution their present and future destiny, beseeching the help of God and His Holy Book, as the everlasting source of guidance and the law of society, issue the declaration announcing the establishment of the authority of the people and announce to the people of the world the dawn of the era of the masses.[16]

Jalloud, who gave the keynote address at the Congress, claimed that the Libyan al-Fateh Revolution was the first in history that had not ended in the betrayal of the 'people'. 'For the first time in history,' he declared, 'the leadership precedes the people to express and realise their aspirations by insisting on the necessity of establishing people's power and this is the highest standard of self-confidence.'[17]

In theory, following the Sebha Declaration, all political control was vested in 187 Basic People's Congresses and 47 Municipal People's Congresses. In practice, the existing political leadership continued to exercise varying degrees of power and influence. Whilst the RCC was formally abolished, Qadhafi and his four colleagues retained important positions within the state apparatus: Qadhafi was himself Supreme Commander-in-Chief of the Libyan Arab Armed Forces; Abu Bakr Younis Jaber was Commander-in-Chief of the Armed Forces; Mustafa Kharoubi was Chief of Staff; Khweildi Hamidi was Commander of the Police; and Jalloud, whilst holding no formal office, was a key figure in the conduct of foreign policy and trade negotiations. In fact, neither the police nor the armed forces are mentioned in the *Green Book*; despite the creation of the Congress system, known as the *jamahiri* system, their established structures remained intact.

Several other factors also constrained the imputed sovereignty of the BPCs. First is the control of the agenda distributed to the BPCs and the composition of the list of resolutions for the GPC, by the secretariat of the GPC. Second is the dependency of the local people's administrative committees on centrally-controlled resources, including, most importantly, oil revenues. Last of all, since the GPC is convened annually, except in the case of extraordinary circumstances, the GPC's secretariats inevitably acquire wide-ranging power of interpretation and postponement. The secretariats may not have been in a position to determine the overarching policy, but they had the ability to decide tactics.

Notes

1. F. Waddams, 1980, p. 304.
2. Never admitted by Qadhafi, this has become evident in testimonies from Meheshi and his supporters.
3. John K. Cooley, *Libyan Sandstorm: The Complete Account of Qaddafi's Revolution* (Sidgwick & Jackson, London, 1982) p. 167.
4. This episode receives comment in 'The Struggle For Libya', in *Arabia: Islamic World Review*, July 1984; and John Wright, 1982, pp. 188–9.
5. *Arabia: Islamic World Review* (July 1984).
6. *Arab Dawn* (February 1976).
7. Instances of independent working-class opposition to Libyan capitalists were nonetheless rare; the central conflict was between the state and the merchant capitalists, but Qadhafi's faction could rely on a base of support among the working class, as well as elements of the petit-bourgeoisie, urban and rural.
8. The contents of this appear to have been published subsequently in Chackerian, Fathaly and Palmer, *Political Development and Bureaucracy in Libya* 1977; see also comments by Naomi Sakr, 'Libya's One Man Revolution', in *Gazelle Review*, no. 9 (1981).
9. The practical relevance of the theory to tribal society is explored by John Davis, 'Libya's Tribes under Qadhafi's Rule', *Times Higher Education Supplement* (27 September 1982). Davis argues: '*The Green Book* is a practical document, born of frustration, attempting to circumvent the inertia of conventional administration. Read it as a treatise (one proposing that after the thesis of parliamentary democracy and the antithesis of proletarian dictatorship there must be some Green resolution) and it appears often ludicrous. Read it as a practical document and it makes some sense.'
10. *The Green Book*, p. 8.
11. Ibid., p. 15.
12. John Mason, 'Island of the Blest: Islam in a Libyan Oasis Community', *Papers in International Studies, Africa Series,* No. 31 (Ohio University, Center for International Studies, Africa Programme, Athens, Ohio, 1977) p. 142–4.
13. Omar Fathaly and Monte Palmer, 'The Transformation of Mass Political Institutions in Revolutionary Libya: Structural Solutions to a Behavioural Problem', paper presented on the conference, *Economic and Social Development of Libya,* School of Oriental and African Studies, London, 1981. In addition, Fathaly and Palmer note: 'In many instances, the same class of less sophisticated Libyans that had dominated the ASU emerged as the dominant force in the popular committees. They were generally unqualified for their position and often were abrasive in their handling or mishandling of local affairs.'
14. An incomplete description of the structure of the people's congresses and people's committees can be found in John Davis, 'Qaddafi's Theory and Practice of Non-representative Government in *Government and Opposition*, vol. 17, no. 1 (Winter 1982).
15. *Arab Dawn* (April 1977).
16. Quoted from Frederick Muscat, *September One: A Story of Revolution* (Link Books, Malta, 1981) p. 51.
17. *Arab Dawn* (April 1977).

8 The Islamic Revolution

God's Natural Law

If the *Green Book, Part 1* contained the constitution for the Libyan Jamahiriya, then the publication of the *Green Book, Part 2* early in 1978 provided its economic basis. Boldly entitled *The Solution to the Economic Problem*, this latest instalment of Qadhafi's political guidebook flatly stated that wage-labour was fundamentally incompatible with the goals of the Revolution. The sale of labour was equated with slavery, since it denied the worker any right to the produce of his labour. 'Wage workers are a type of slave, however improved their wages may be,' concluded Qadhafi, pinpointing the wage system as the source of the economic problem that is the subject of his essay. 'The ultimate solution,' he declares, 'is to abolish the wage system, emancipate man from the emergence of class forms of government and man-made laws.'[1]

In place of wage work, Qadhafi proposes a system in which the workers in an enterprise control production collectively in the form of partnerships. 'Man in the new society,' he says, 'works for himself to guarantee his material needs, or works for a socialist corporation in whose production he is a partner or performs a public service to the society which provides his material needs.'[2] Indeed, for Qadhafi, a socialist society is synonymous with a society in which those needs, as such, are liberated from the ownership of others and become the rightful possession of the citizen, either as an individual or as an equal member of a collective. Says Qadhafi:

> The purpose of the socialist society is the happiness of man, which can only be realised through material and spiritual freedom. Attainment of such freedom depends on the extent of man's ownership of his needs; ownership that is personal and sacredly guaranteed, i.e., your needs must neither be owned by somebody else, nor subject to plunder by any part of society.[3]

Predictably, the publication of such a provocative and controversial argument created quite a stir. If Qadhafi had previously shown himself dismissive of communism, he now appeared to be moving towards a Marxist view of economic relationships. That, at least, was the conclusion of Libyan employers and property-owners, to whom the contents of the book were unmistakably directed. And certainly many of the concepts used in this second, 6,000-word essay did seem to be culled from various Marxist texts. Qadhafi's definition of economic exploitation, as stated in the *Green Book*, bears a striking resemblance to Marx's concept of surplus value appropriation. A worker, writes Qadhafi, 'works to get his wages. Since his wages aren't enough to satisfy his needs, he will either search for another master and sell his work at a better price or he will be obliged to continue the same work in order to survive.'[4] Simultaneous with upholding an idealist view of the historical process, he also appears ambiguously to have adopted some elements of the materialist dialectic. For example, Qadhafi argues that:

> [T]he overturning of contemporary societies, to change them from being societies of wage workers is inevitable as the dialectical result of the contradictory economic theses prevailing in the world today, and is the inevitable dialectical result of the injustice to relations based on the wage-system, which have not been solved.[5]

Like Marx, Qadhafi asserts that capitalist ownership has become a significant brake on the expansion of the forces of production. He comments: 'Work for wages fails to solve the problem of increasing and developing production. Work either in the form of services or production, is continually deteriorating because it rests on the shoulders of wage workers?[6] Not that Marxism would appear to be the only political source influencing Qadhafi's thought on the economy and society. Writing in the *New Statesman* in September 1978, N.C. Niblock portrayed Qadhafi's system in *Part 2* as a 'random mixture of anarchism, populism, Marxism and Islam'.

Qadhafi, however, was not undergoing a transition to Marxism. He may have been applying Marxist techniques of analysis to sharpen his arguments, but he denied the historical core of Marxism: the class struggle. For Marx, socialism was achieved through working-class self-emancipation from capitalist rule. His conclusion that the working class created socialism was seminal to his whole intellectual development. For Qadhafi, on the other hand, the struggle of the workers was an obstacle to the realisation of socialism. His socialism was based on the restitution of a natural equilibrium in society that had been destroyed by the advent of wage-slavery under capitalism. As he explains in the *Green Book*:

> Natural law has led to natural socialism based on equality of the economic factors of production, and has almost brought about, among individuals, consumption equal to nature's production. But the exploitation of man by man and the possession by some individuals of more of the general wealth than they need is a manifest departure from natural law and the beginning of distortion and corruption in the life of the human community. It is the beginning of the emergence of the society of exploitation.[7]

Of course, Qadhafi is not the first political leader to seek class peace in the restoration of traditional, pre-capitalist values. Many political leaders, notably in Africa, have appealed to a legendary consensus that supposedly governed society prior to colonisation. Closer examination has shown this romanticisation of these societies to be totally fictional: wages may not have existed, but conflicts arising from the need to obtain an economic surplus certainly did. But, in terms of practical politics, the idea that a period of harmony reigned in pre-colonial societies has been an important factor in generating unification within newly-independent states. It is one that Qadhafi, coming from a genuinely Bedouin background, has not been loathe to use in building support for the Jamahiriya. As with other Arab philosophers, he often invokes the Bedouin ideal of society, in which property was held in common and wage-labour virtually unknown. Indeed, those who received wages were abusively referred to as vagabonds foreigners, outcasts, the rootless. To nomadic society, with its emphasis on communal ownership the notion that members of society should sell their labour to others was alien and abhorrent. Not surprisingly, these values and traditions were bound to infiltrate Qadhafi's philosophy in the *Green Book*. Qadhafi himself has admitted:

> Bedouin society made me discover the natural laws, natural relationships, life in its true nature and what suffering was like before life knew oppression and exploitation. This had enabled me to discover the truths that I have presented and explained in the *Green Book*. It gave me a chance which has never been given to anybody else in my position. I have known and lived life in its very primitive stages. Because of that early life, a very simple life, I have lived life in its various stages right up to this modern age of imperialism when life became very complicated, very abnormal and unnatural.[8]

Only a superficial analysis of the *Green Book* could conclude that Qadhafi parodies Marx's historical schema. Whilst Marx saw class struggle as the motor of history, Qadhafi contends that class struggle, and the emergence of different class forms of rule, is a dangerous deviation from natural law. For example, on capitalism he remarks: 'The capitalist system in its absolute form – the system that is today practised in the United States – is a corrupt and shabby system. It constitutes a danger to the destiny of the American people by putting their fate in the hands of a few tycoons who grow greedier the richer they become.'[9] In other words, for Qadhafi capitalism is a harmful aberration, an exception from the rule, not a system of class rule which creates the conditions for socialism. He acknowledges technological achievement, but concludes that it is the product of scientific endeavour and breakthrough. He believes that the essence of natural law, upon which he constructs his socialism, is unaltered by the growth in the economic forces of production. The *Green Book, Part 2* stresses: 'The essential natural factors of production are basically stable despite their development. The essential stability of the factors of production makes the natural rule sound. It is inevitable, after the failure of all previous historical attempts, which disregard natural law, to return to it in order, finally, to solve the economic problem.'[10]

For Qadhafi, wages have upset the natural balance upon which production rests, removing the worker's right to a share in what he has produced. Their abolition, he postulates, will restore the equilibrium in society. Like the utopian socialists before him, he believes that the road to a socialist society lies through persuasion and example. He perceives that the mere establishment of a Jamahiriya, of a system based on natural law, will ensure universal adoption. During an interview with Dara Jankovic, editor of the Yugoslav newspaper *Zaghreb*,[11] Qadhafi was asked: 'Do you believe that other countries of the world will accept the Third Universal Theory?' He replied: 'In so far as the theory solves Man's problems, it will be responded to. This depends on it being understood. The world's understanding of this theory depends on Libya's activity and we are still at the beginning of our revolutionary programme.' 'What, in your view, should you do in order that the world may understand you?', added Jankovic. 'We should be an example to be followed, and I believe that Libya now represents a unique model as far as governing is concerned,' Qadhafi retorted. In other words, Qadhafi sees the main form of activity linked with the creation of socialism, as that of propaganda, rather than social struggle.

Such a world outlook owes far less to Marx or Rousseau than to the Koranic concept of God's harmony and natural order prevailing in the universe. Qadhafi's thesis on natural law corresponds with the Koranic proposition that God created the heavens and set the constellation of human relations. For example, the Koran states:

> We created man and taught him articulate speech. The sun and the moon pursue their ordered course. The plants and the trees bow down in adoration. He raised the heaven on high and set the balance of all things, that you might not transgress it. Give just weight and full measure.'[12]

Qadhafi's 'socialism based on natural law' is a political elaboration intended to conform with such a Divine concept of Islam; the natural laws he espouses are laws ordained by God, and therefore eternal and immutable. At a conference on Euro-Arab relations in Tripoli in May 1973, he expounded the relation between the Third Universal Theory and Islam in these terms:

> Humanity must utter a cry of indignation to the governments of the world, for them to return to their senses and to their Creator. God had made us his successors on earth in order to do good, but the manufacture of atomic bombs and bacteriological weapons and the threats to occupy forcibly the natural resources of other peoples can only be the makings of the Devil. This grave state of affairs has led us to make available to peoples everywhere the Third Universal Theory. *This theory is not a human invention, nor is it some kind of new philosophy; it is based solely on the truth.* Philosophical theories are subject to constant

change by revocation or refutation, but God's law is that the truth is immortal and unalterable.[13]

Qadhafi argues that the Third Universal Theory is part of, if not the beginning, of a process of Islamic 'renewal'. The justification for this claim lies with the theory's reassertion of natural law; the theory is a corrective to historical deflections from the Divine concept. At the Paris Symposium in 1973, in a debate with Professor Jacques Berque a former member of the French Communist Party, Qadhafi commented:

Renewal as used by Mr. Berque means that at this point we have discovered the essential factors of our history and how they have been misused; so we want to renew them on original terms. The origins of our history is the result of the reactions between nationalism and religion. We ought to revive those factors and channel them in the right direction to achieve the noble human purposes on earth. That is our philosophy as far as origin and renewal are concerned.[14]

Qadhafi sees this process of Islamic renewal in the context of Arab renewal. Whilst not limiting Islam exclusively to the Arabs, he maintains that the Arabs must be exclusively Islamic. Thus, he had called on the Maronites of Lebanon and other Christian Arab minorities to undergo conversion to Islam. In August 1980, he told the Beirut-based daily *as-Safir:* 'Arab christians should convert to Islam because they represent a European spirit in a body which is Arab.'[15] Assuming religious affiliation and national identity to be inseparable, he contends that Islam and Arabism are inseparable. Qadhafi argues: 'just as Judaism and Zionism are united in Israel, so too are Islam and Arabism one and indivisible.' Since Islam began with the Arabs, he assumes that it can be renewed only by the Arabs. Therefore, the resurgence of Arab nationalism, which for him culminates in the Jamahiriya, provides the conditions for the renewal of Islam.

In addition to the renewal aspect there is a dual element of innovation in Qadhafi's treatment of Islam. This is most obvious with regard to his position on wages and property. Whilst the *Green Book* stipulates the need to abolish wages and private ownership of the means of production, there are no such strictures either within the Koran, or the traditions of Prophet Mohammed. Maxime Rodinson, who has studied this field in depth, agrees that 'the Koran has nothing against private property, since it lays down the rules for inheritance, for example. It even advises that inequalities be not challenged, contenting itself with denouncing the habitual impieties of rich men, stressing the uselessness of wealth in the face of God's judgement and the temptation to neglect religion that wealth brings.'[16] Indeed, Qadhafi himself, discussing Islam and the concept of freedom in 1976, claimed that it was 'the duty of Islam to lend legitimacy to ownership.' But when he came to write the second part of the *Green Book* in 1977 he had clearly arrived at the conclusion that wages, the hiring of labour, as well as the wider ownership of land and the means of production, consitituted a violation of God's natural law. He stressed that it was through the interrelationship of both innovation and renewal, that it became possible to restore the *umma* to its original context, following the *hijra* in 622 AD.

Qadhafi Invokes *Ijtihad*

Since there was no precedent within Islam for the abolition of private property and wages, the second part of the *Green Book* provoked consternation and outrage. The *ulema*, who had hitherto been generally supportive of his policies, broke with his regime. Leading members of the clergy stated that the *Green Book* flouted the *sunna*, which was indeed a serious charge capable of arousing internal opposition. The *sunna*, meaning 'beaten path', was formed from the sayings and practices of the Prophet Mohammed as compiled after his death in the *Hadith*, the traditions established by the 'four rightly guided caliphs'–Abu Bakr, Omar, Osman and Ali–who succeeded Mohammed, as well as the codifications of the Manafite school in Turkey, Shafism in the Arabian Gulf, Malikism in North Africa and Hanbali in Arabia. Around 900 AD a consensus had been established on what constituted the *sharia* law. Nowhere in the *sunna* did there appear justification for the *Green Book*'s stipulations on private property. As a result, Qadhafi was accused by members of the *ulema* of moving towards Marxism. At mosques in Tripoli he was accused of holding heretical views which contradicted the *Hadith* and abandoned the *ijma* (or consensus) established in 900 AD. The *Green Book* was openly declared by several leaders of the clergy as incompatible with Islam.

In their defence of private property the urban *ulema* were motivated by more than questions of Koranic interpretation. The social basis of the urban *ulema* was the commercial sector. Not only were many clerics related to merchant families, the *ulema* were bound to merchant capitalism by a complex economic relationship. The clergy's prime source of income was the *waqf*, or religious endowment which they received from trading families. The social prestige of individual clergy derived from the level of endowments and benevolence, in regard to their mosques, shown by wealthy traders. Dependent for their maintenance on the commercial sector, the urban *ulema* did not constitute an autonomous force in society, as had the Sanussi Order previously. The urban clerics were largely integrated with the commercial sector and, following Qadhafi's attack on private property in the *Green Book*, articulated the interests of the merchant class.

Qadhafi's response to their criticism of the *Green Book* was blunt and forceful. Speaking at a Tripoli mosque in February 1978, prior to the introduction of the new land ownership laws, he warned the *ulema* against forming an alliance with the propertied classes and fomenting opposition to his policies. He argued that the *Green Book* was compatible with Islam because it was based on the Divine concept of Islam within the Koran. In

May, when their opposition had failed to subside, he went further and denounced the *ulema* for 'propagating heretical stories elaborated over the course of centuries of decadence.'[17] They were, he said, 'conducting a reactionary campaign against the progressive, egalitarian, socialist concepts of the regime'.[18] When the *ulema* finally submitted he indicted them for 'remembering Islam' only after the new property laws had been introduced. Determined that they should no longer pose a threat, on 21 May he dramatically declared an 'Islamic Revolution' and called on the masses to 'seize the mosques'.[19] The mosques, he maintained, had to be reclaimed from mediaeval *fiqh* specialists who issue statements of religious opinion, and 'had introduced foreign and non-Islamic ideas into *fiqh*'.[20] The people, he claimed, were better qualified to interpret Islam than were the *ulema*.

In July 1978 he accelerated the pace of the Islamic Revolution. In a theological debate on 3 July he emphatically refuted allegations that the *Green Book* was incompatible with Islam. He agreed that it conflicted with the *sunna*, but maintained that the *Green Book* was based firmly on the Koran, which had, in his opinion, been corrupted by incompetent *fuqaha* (Islamic scholars). The *sunna* should not be seen as necessarily pertaining to religion, he claimed, being on the same level of codification as Roman Law or the Napoleonic Code. Declaring that the Koran was the one valid authority, he justified the Third Universal Theory on the grounds that he was applying *ijtihad*–the exercise of independent judgement in relation to the Koran. He stressed that the theory was 'the realisation of the divine precepts in spite of the hostility of the ignorant, the spiteful, the bigots and the reactionary enemies of Islam'.[21] In opposition to the traditional role of the *ulema*, he contended that every citizen should henceforward have the right to *ijtihad*. Thus, he negated the special dispensation enjoyed by the *fuqaha* in determining the correctness of political goals.

By invoking *ijtihad*, Qadhafi was able to achieve social reforms that the *ulema* would have declared in violation of the *sunna*. On the same basis, he could even introduce changes in the *sunna* itself. For example, at Id al-Adha–the feast of sacrifice–in November 1978, he used *ijtihad* to announce that the calendar required changing so that it commenced from Mohammed's death in 632 AD instead of the *hijra* – the flight to Medina – in 622 AD. (The subsequent adoption of the principle has meant that dates in Libya are ten years behind the rest of the Muslim world.) He has also invoked *ijtihad* to deny that the *hajj*, or pilgrimage, is an essential pillar of Islam and to effect changes in the payment of the *zakat*, or charitable tax. In addition, the dispensation provided by *ijtihad* has allowed Qadhafi to place a different interpretation on the *sharia* law. He has, for instance, argued that the penalty for theft, the amputation of a hand or foot, has a symbolical rather than literal intention. According to his judgement, the 'severing of the hand' refers to the removal of sources of temptation. Laws in 1973 and 1974, as well as others since, have effectively integrated the *sharia* into a secular legal system which appears to have derived much of its inspiration from the West.

Falsely labelled a fundamentalist, Quadhafi is, in fact, essentially a modernist in terms of Islamic thought. He is not another Mahdi al-Sanussi, rising out of the Libyan desert to create a theocratic empire in the Sahara; he rejects the closed ritual and mysticism of the Sanussi Order and all Sufi sects. In the sense that he has subordinated religion to the political system, he has much more in common with Ataturk's secularisation of the state than fundamentalist efforts at Islamicisation of the state. In contradiction to current belief in the Islamic Republic of Iran, Qadhafi strongly disagrees that *ijtihad* should be confined to a senior strata of the *ulema*, the *mujtahids*, who alone are deemed qualified to pronounce on matters of faith. Qadhafi's thought, whatever his idiosyncratic interpretation of Islam, is rooted within the tradition of the Arab philosopher Jamal al-Din al-Afghani, and his disciple, the Egyptian nationalist Mohammed Abdu, who argued that the Islamic world could defend itself against imperialism only if it assimilated Western science and technology in conjunction with Islamic practice. Like them, he believes that the Islamic concepts are the key to reforming a society whose backwardness has made it vulnerable to foreign penetration.[22]

Notes

1. *The Green Book* p. 47.
2. Ibid., p. 55.
3. Ibid., p. 65.
4. Ibid., p. 59.
5. Ibid., p. 65.
6. Ibid., p. 57.
7. Ibid., p. 47.
8. Enahoro 'Heart to Heart with Qadhafi', *New African* (Feb. 1983) pp. 37–46.
9. M. Qadhafi, *The Battle for Destiny*.
10. *The Green Book*, p. 49.
11. M. Qadhafi, *The Battle for Destiny*.
12. *The Koran* (Penguin Books, Harmondsworth, 1981).
13. M. Qadhafi, *The Battle for Destiny*.
14. Ibid.
15. Ibid.
16. Maxime Rodinson *Islam and Capitalism* (Penguin, London, 1974) p. 14.
17. Edward Mortimer, *Faith and Power. The Politics of Islam* (Faber and Faber, London, 1982) p. 281.
18. Ibid.
19. Ibid.
20. *Arabia: World Islamic Review* (July 1984).
21. For discussion of this point, see Mortimer, *Faith and Power,* and J.A. Allen *Libya: The Experience of Oil*.
22. M. Qadhafi, *The Battle for Destiny*.

9 Protagonist of Rejectionism

The Arab Capitulation

The backdrop to the 1975–76 political crisis in Libya was a massive swing to the right in the Arab world. Behind this development, which propelled successive Arab regimes to capitulation, and acceptance of United States' patronage, was an important change in the economic balance of forces in the region. The huge surpluses that accrued to the Gulf oil producers generated a trend towards economic liberalisation throughout the area, but particularly in those countries which were not major oil producers. As a general feature of the period, internal pressures mounted for a relaxation of state economic control, so that investment funds could be attracted from the Gulf. The Egyptian *infittah* policy epitomises the response of Middle East regimes to the assertion of Arab economic power after 1973. The Egyptian disengagement from the conflict with Israel was intended to make Egypt economically stable. One other reflection of the trend was the Saudi-sponsored Syrian intervention in the Lebanese civil war, mounted in 1976 to contain the rise of Lebanese revolutionary forces and the Palestinian resistance, then on the point of victory over the rightist state and the Phalangist militia, the Kataeb.

Significantly, Libya was one of the few countries in the region in which this trend to the right was not prevalent. In contrast, the internal pressures in Libya resulted in moves against private ownership of capital; in political terms, the isolation was becoming acute. As Qadhafi emerged from the crisis of 1975, his main hope that the trend to the right and capitulation could be resisted lay with the Palestinian and Lebanese revolutionary movements, and their success in withstanding the Syrian intervention.

Libya had become a leading benefactor of Palestinian organisations long before the conflict erupted. After the catastrophe of the 'Black September' 1970 fighting in Jordan, when the Palestinian resistance found itself under attack by the Jordanian regime, Libya supplied funds and arms for the resistance to re-establish itself in southern Lebanon, where the 1969 Cairo Agreement permitted Palestinians to launch military operations against Israel. By the same token, Libya also contributed to those Lebanese organisations, most obviously the Nasserites, who were allied with the

Palestinian forces. When fighting broke out between Kamal Jumblatt's Lebanese National Movement (LNM),—which included the Nasserites and the Druze Patriotic Socialist Party—and the Kataeb of Bashir Gemayel, the Libyans kept up supplies during the 20 months of civil war. After the Palestinians were drawn into the fighting on the side of the LNM, Tripoli offered a small contingent of troops for the Arab Deterrent Force, which was being assembled by the Arab League to intervene in the Lebanon. But when the Syrians, under the cover of the Deterrent Force, turned on the Lebanese Nationalist and Palestinian forces, Libya withdrew and channelled weapons for the nationalist and Palestinian forces through the Lebanese port of Sidon. In addition, soon after the Syrian actions started on 31 May 1976, Jalloud spent ten days in Damascus or Lebanon, and over a month altogether, working assiduously, but ultimately in vain, to halt the fighting. On 11 June, when it finally became clear that the Syrians had no intention of letting up, Qadhafi accused the Syrian regime of President Hafez al-Assad of 'national treason'.

Qadhafi's objective was to maintain intact the Palestinian resistance and, therefore, the viability of the armed struggle against Israel. 'The Palestinian resistance is above all other considerations,' he declared. 'If the Palestinian resistance is crushed, the Palestinian question will be over.'[1] Indeed, earning the respect of Palestinian organisations, the Libyan leadership was the only one openly to challenge the Syrian actions. The Syrian government, which had failed to adhere to the ceasefire Jalloud had tried to negotiate, was accused of complicity in the Phalangists' slaughter of Palestinians, including the residents of Tel al-Zaatar refugee camp. In a letter to Arab heads of state, Qadhafi requested the recall of Arab ambassadors from Damascus in protest, whilst at the meeting of Arab foreign ministers in Cairo, which followed the breakdown of the ceasefire, the under-secretary of the Libyan Foreign Ministry, Abu Zayed Durdah, proclaimed that history was witnessing 'a crime against the Palestinian revolution.'[2] The Syrian Foreign Ministry spokesman in turn blamed the Libyan government, through its supply of arms to the resistance forces, for the continuation of the fighting. Nevertheless, the final outcome of the conflict was not a complete disaster from the Libyan standpoint. The Syrians achieved their objective of establishing control, but the resistance forces were permitted to operate within a buffer zone, soon to be known as Fatehland, between the Syrian position south of the Beirut-Damascus highway and the Israeli border. After the 1976 clash with Syria, the Libyan priority was to build up the Palestinian and Lebanese forces in this area, so that the confrontation with Israel, although contained, would remain a significant factor in the region's politics.

Through its actions in defence of the Palestinian forces in Lebanon, the Libyan state tried to take on the role of guarantor of the Palestinian revolution. Libya's ability to fulfil this responsibility, however, was circumscribed because the overall balance of forces in the region continued to move against it. In particular, the cold war between Libya and Egypt showed no sign of abating. In 1975 the Libyan authorities became suspicious that Meheshi's *coup* bid had received Sadat's backing. Following the seizure of Arab oil ministers in Vienna in December 1975, the Egyptian government had officially alleged that the operation was mounted by Libya, although the Libyan Oil Minister was one of those taken hostage. The granting of political asylum to Meheshi and Houni was another factor which contributed to the deterioration in relations. On 7 May Qadhafi formally warned Kuwait, Saudi Arabia and the UAE that aid donations to Egypt would constitute an act of hostility towards the Libyan Arab Republic. Convinced that Sadat was deeply involved in efforts to destablise Libya, on 19 May 1976, Jalloud publicly declared that Egypt was preparing to invade Libya.

Most Arab states chose to remain neutral in this conflict. The notable exception was the Sudan. The same internal pressures for a shift to the right existed here, but were much more pronounced than anywhere other than Egypt. Following the successful counter-*coup* of 1971, Numeiri began to seek *rapprochement* with Saudi Arabia. In 1973 he adopted an 'Islamic constitution' which counterposed Qadhafi's modernist interpretation with conservative injunctions favoured by elements within the Sudanese *ulema*. Such internal changes led to a thaw in relations with Riyadh, which had previously criticised and mistrusted Numeiri because of his coalition with the Sudanese Communist Party. The revolution in Ethiopia in 1974 accelerated the process. Numeiri increasingly shifted towards the Cairo-Riyadh axis. His strategy, based on the twin objectives of guaranteeing technical aid from Egypt and financial aid from Saudi Arabia, put him on a course of confrontation with Libya. It became in Numeiri's interest to promote friction with Libya as a way of gaining the backing of both Egypt and Saudi Arabia, as well as that of the wider western world.

The break between Khartoum and Tripoli was precipitated by an abortive *coup d'état* in the Sudan. On 26 July 1976, units from the Sudanese army tried to seize power on behalf of the opposition Sudanese National Front. They took over a number of public buildings in the capital and the provinces, but failed to rally sufficient support to overthrow the President. Although the *coup* attempt was the work of internal forces, Numeiri blamed Libya. His government alleged that the revolt had been planned and directed from Libya, and carried out by 'mercenaries' trained at Kufra. Complaints were lodged with the Arab League and the UN Security Council, whilst all trade and diplomatic links with Libya were cut. The Sudan went on to sign a mutual defence pact with Egypt almost immediately after the incident. Then in August, Meheshi and Houni were extended Numeiri's hospitality in Khartoum, from where they were allowed to broadcast speeches calling for an uprising in Libya against Qadhafi.[3] Numeiri, in his own public statements, claimed that Libya was working with the Soviet Union to oust him.

Re-alignments

The incident was important for the changes it wrought in Libyan foreign policy. The Sudanese re-alignment with Saudi Arabia and Egypt, consummated by the mutual defence pact, effectively put the United States in a strategically dominant position in the region. The prospect that the West would use the US penetration of Egypt and the Sudan to conduct a proxy conflict with Libya could not be dismissed as long as Qadhafi retained his opposition to the existence of the Israeli state and to other United States' interests in the Middle East; in other words, as long as Qadhafi maintained his opposition to an American-framed solution for the region. The implications were such that Libya had no option but to alter its regional strategy. Its response to the events in Egypt and the Sudan was to develop a counterweight to the western influence with alliances with those states which did not have a pro-Washington orientation, including those backed by the Soviet Union. By the following year, as this redirection of policy took effect, Libya had in practice become strategically–though not politically–aligned with the Soviet Union itself.

Although the new policy line had general application, it was initiated in the Horn of Africa. Since the overthrow of the Emperor Haile Selassie in September 1974, the Libyan authorities had started to fraternise with the provisional military government in Addis Ababa. After the Emperor's overthrow, Libya became the first country to send a diplomatic mission to Ethiopia. The major obstacle to agreement was the secessionist war in Eritrea. On several occasions the Libyan Foreign Ministry called on the provisional military government, or DERG, to compromise with the Eritrean movements. In December 1974 an Ethiopian delegation was despatched to Tripoli for talks with Jalloud. They were told of Libya's commitment 'to helping revolutionaries wherever they are, especially Africa', but advised to resolve the conflict with the Eritrean movement. When the Ethiopians refused to alter their position, the Libyan daily *al-Fajr al-Jadid*, on 3 February 1975, printed a commentary highly critical of the DERG's inflexibility. The paper declared:

> Now that the imperialist powers are withdrawing from the continent it is not acceptable that African brothers fight one another. The Ethiopian revolution can prove its liberal credentials only by seeking a fair solution to the Eritrean problem. The situation in Eritrea is one created by imperialism and its agents, including the deposed Emperor. The Eritreans are part of the African revolution. The victory of the Eritrean rebels will be a gain for all Africans and the freedom of Ethiopia itself will not be realised until the Eritreans enjoy freedom.[4]

Such a commentary would not have been published did it not reflect the official position on the conflict, which continued to be pro-Eritrean despite the dialogue that developed with Addis Ababa.

Indeed, the official position, reflected in *al-Fajr al-Jadid*, characterised Libyan policy right up to the rupture in relations with the Sudan in July

1976. The threat of combined Egyptian-Sudanese hostilities after the conclusion of the two countries' mutual defence pact was such that the Libyan authorities decided that closer strategic links with Ethiopia, which was not then fully backed by the Soviet Union, must take precedence over support for the Eritrean liberation movements. Relations with Somalia, where the trend to the right was also evident, became an inevitable casualty of the shift. Libya and Ethiopia, together with South Yemen, were among the states experiencing a reverse process to that which had gathered momentum in Egypt and the Sudan. The main problem from the Libyan point of view was that these allies, compared to its former allies, Egypt and the Sudan, were essentially peripheral in terms of the region as a whole.

The most obvious manifestation of the switch in orientation was the evolution of dialogue with the Soviet Union itself. In December 1976, Qadhafi had visited the Soviet Union for the first time. The visit, not entirely a personal initiative, followed the passage of a motion at the Basic People's Congress in November calling for closer ties with the Soviet Union. The most obvious feature of Qadhafi's talks in Moscow was the wide poitical gap which continued to separate Libya from the Soviet Union and Eastern Europe, but discussions with Leonid Brezhnev and Alexei Kosygin did put Libyan relations with the Soviet Union on a much more stable basis than those with the United States. Much closer links were established in this period with non-aligned Yugoslavia. In August 1977, Qadhafi flew to Belgrade and secured Tito's support for the Arab rejectionist stance against Sadat's negotiations with Israel. In general, much of the shrillness that had marked Libya's relations with Eastern Europe began to disappear.

This change had important consequences for the Islamic orientation of Libyan foreign policy. In implementing the shift in alliances, Qadhafi had clearly deviated from the practice of siding in a conflict with perceived Muslim interests. Libyan pan-Islam was dead in deed, if not in word. The change did not, however, necessarily imply complete renunciation of Muslim causes. Qadhafi had never abstained on anti-imperialist questions within Muslim states, and he continued to support those Muslim struggles which, in his opinion, had an anti-imperialist content. Ideologically, Qadhafi seemed most compatible with the Muslim President of Pakistan, Zulfikar Ali Bhutto, with whom he enjoyed an extremely good personal rapport, which was cemented at the Lahore Islamic summit conference in February 1974 and lasted until the Pakistani leader's removal from power in July 1977. As their relationship developed, Libyan-Pakistani co-operation grew to encompass military assistance, the publication of Islamic literature, and joint exchanges of information with regard to nuclear research. Under Bhutto's leadership the Pakistani treasury secured vital financial subventions from Libya, and Qadhafi was awarded a series of honours from the Muslim state, including the naming of the stadium in Lahore after him. Bhutto's overthrow by General Zia al-Huq, subsequent trial and execution, damaged Libyan relations with Pakistan. Zia rejected Qadhafi's entreaties on Bhutto's behalf and shifted towards closer links with Saudi Arabia and the Gulf. The alliance, which had existed since 1971, was dissolved and, in 1978, Qadhafi declared support for the revolutionary authorities in Afghanistan and began to foster closer ties with India.

There was one anomaly in the general pattern of developments affecting Libyan foreign policy. It was again peripheral to the immediate focus on the Middle East, and concerned Libya's relations with pro-western Morocco. King Hassan's decision in 1974 to escalate Morocco's claims to the Spanish colony of Western Sahara was strongly supported by the Libyan authorities. Following his decision, diplomatic contacts between both governments increased and culminated in a meeting in Malta in January 1975, when it was agreed to resume full diplomatic relations.[5] When Hassan launched his 350,000-strong Green March to reclaim the territory in October 1975, Qadhafi backed him on the grounds that his action was anti-colonialist. The March was praised for being a popular and nationalist initiative, but once the Moroccan army was deployed in combat against the local liberation movement, the Popular Front for the Liberation of Saqiet al-Hamra and Rio de Oro (Polisario Front), Qadhafi began to have second thoughts. The Libyans had previously backed the Front, which they had helped to establish in 1973, although they withheld formal recognition from the organisation. When Hassan began to receive support from the United States and France for what had become a war of annexation, Qadhafi sided with Algeria in the conflict and re-supplied the Polisario Front with arms, transported along the so-called 'Qadhafi trail' through southern Algeria.

The Egyptian leadership took advantage of the strained relations between Libya and Morocco. Following the resumption of Libyan support for the Polisario Front, President Sadat began to develop close links with King Hassan. His motives in this were not explicitly anti-Libyan: his primary intention was to secure an axis with Morocco, the only country in the Arab world with established diplomatic channels to the Israelis. By providing Egyptian backing for the King against Algeria and Libya, Sadat gained a means of conducting secret diplomacy with the Israeli government. Hassan undertook an intermediary role between the Israeli Foreign Minister Moshe Dayan and the Egyptian government. In September 1977 the Israeli Foreign Minister was invited to Morocco, and the King agreed to sponsor a series of initial contacts, either in Fez or Rabat, between Dayan himself and an Egyptian Deputy Premier, Hassan Tuhami.

Border Conflict

Before these preliminary contacts in Morocco took place, Sadat launched a brief, but unprecedented, border war against Libya. This limited conflict, which broke out in July, has received two basic explanations. Firstly, as Mohammed Heikal has claimed in *Autumn of Fury*:

It was hinted that the Israelis had news of a plot against Sadat but they would only give details about it directly to an Egyptian official. So the Director of Military Intelligence was sent directly to Morocco, where he met the head of Israeli Intelligence (Mossad) who produced an implausible story about a conspiracy to assassinate Sadat being hatched by Ghadaffi.

Secondly, there is the official version given by Sadat himself. He claimed that Libya was amassing troops and arms from the Soviet Union for an invasion of his country.

Neither explanation is plausible. In the first place, the Israelis quite probably concocted the story of a Libyan conspiracy in order to draw Sadat into direct negotiations; in the second instance, despite the Libyan military build-up, the Libyan armed forces were never in a strong enough position to mount an invasion of Egypt, which had a vastly superior army. A more satisfactory explanation comes from Sadat's wish to curb Libyan propaganda attacks and support for Egyptian opposition groups, before he entered into more open talks with the government of Menachem Begin.

After border skirmishes in the oasis area of Musaid on 16 July, Egyptian planes bombed the villages of Barada and Sidi Amr. The Libyans claimed to have brought down two planes over Barada and one over Sidi Amr. On 22 July the fighting escalated when the Egyptians commenced heavy bombing of the Libyan air base at al-Adem and Egyptian paratroopers assaulted Q'asr Jidda. The following day, further Egyptian air raids were reported against Barada, Jarabub, Q'asr Jidda, Musaid, and the key towns of Tobruk and Kufra. Whilst the Libyans claimed to have eliminated eight planes, the Egyptians only admitted the loss of one, from which an Egyptian pilot, Major Abdul Hamid Effat, was captured. For two more days artillery duels continued along the frontier. Then, on 25 July, Sadat called a truce, which the Libyan authorities never endorsed. According to most commentators, Egyptian losses were extremely high for such a small-scale conflict – certainly much higher than the 29 Libyan dead admitted by Jalloud. Even those in the West hostile to Qadhafi conceded that the Libyan armed forces had performed well. Whilst Yasser Arafat had interceded on 20 July to negotiate a ceasefire, the consensus has been that it was the Egyptian losses, in addition to an Algerian threat to intervene on Libya's behalf, which caused Sadat to retreat. The Egyptians have ever since desisted from trying again.

In retrospect, the brief border war was a deliberate move precursory of Sadat's fatal offer of peace to Israel. The objective of the conflict, whatever the pretext, was the humiliation of the policy of armed struggle and confrontation with Zionism, which Libya represented and from which Sadat had deviated. The Libyan leadership knew the trajectory of Sadat's politics on the national question and were the first to come out openly in opposition to it. Sadat was, therefore, forced into an ambitious attempt to discredit Libya. Subsequent events were to show that his reckless border war had failed to achieve that goal.

Steadfastness and Confrontation

On 9 November 1977, President Anwar Sadat addressed the opening session of the Egyptian parliament in Cairo. What he had to say was political dynamite. Sadat, in a keynote speech, told the assembled Egyptian deputies that he was 'ready to go to the ends of the earth, and to the Knesset itself', in the interests of bringing peace to the Middle East. Few of those present, either among the state deputies or the observers, took him at his word. It was assumed that he was speaking figuratively. But Sadat was indeed in earnest. He ordered the official newspapers to give added prominence to the passage in his speech carrying his offer to 'go to the ends of the earth'.[6] Before long, the Cairo airwaves were humming with the message, as Sadat had intended, that Egypt was prepared to come to terms with Israel in direct negotiations. Featured on American television, Sadat did not retreat when pinned down. He merely confirmed that he was ready to visit Jerusalem and talk with the Israeli leadership.

He had reached a decision to make this diplomatic gambit after visiting President Nicolai Ceaucescu of Romania. The Romanian head of state, the Eastern European leader with the best diplomatic representation in Israel, advised Sadat that the new Israeli Premier Menachem Begin was a man who, like General de Gaulle with regard to Algeria, could compromise, precisely because he was an authoritative hardliner. Prior to that, in September 1977, King Hassan of Morocco had arranged a meeting between Begin's Foreign Minister Moshe Dayan, and an Egyptian Deputy Prime Minister, Hassan Tuhami. At those meetings, in Fez and Rabat, it had become clear that the Israelis preferred secret negotiations, at least initially. On reflection, Sadat decided otherwise. The situation in Egypt required that he demonstrate that he was firmly in command of the country's direction. In January 1977 riots had erupted throughout the country in the wake of price increases on basic commodities, including bread. When the War Minister General Gamassi had declared that the loyalty of the army would be in question if the price increases were not revoked, a plane had been ordered to stand by in order to evacuate the President and his family to Iran. The crisis, which subsided when the price rises were rescinded, left Sadat in urgent need of boosting confidence, particularly the confidence of international capital, in his regime. What better way was there to generate such support than a regional settlement?

To a fanfare of camera shutters, Sadat arrived in Jerusalem on 19 November 1977. The ranks of the Arab states were now decisively and openly broken, but Israeli and American hopes that other rulers would follow Sadat's example were short-lived. Even if Sadat himself wanted a regional, rather than a bilateral, settlement, he made the fatal error of taking a unilateral decision without consultation with the other Arab states. The one man in the Middle East who knew his intentions in advance of his 9 November speech to the Egyptian parliament was the Shah of Iran, whom he had visited on 31 October, to confer on the proposal that had emerged from his meeting with Ceaucescu in Romania. Returning from Teheran he had stopped in Riyadh to pay his respects to his chief Arab ally, but had apparently only admitted that he was being pressed by the United States for direct negotiations. When the day of Sadat's journey to Jerusalem finally came, King Khaled, who had succeeded Feisal in 1974, prayed that his plane would crash. Sadat had exceeded the terms of his alliance with the Saudis, and although the axis continued to exist in the sense that there was a general convergence of interests in the Arab world, political coordination was finished.

On the eve of his visit to Jerusalem he had flown to Damascus, but had failed to placate the Syrian government, which was suspicious that such an independent initiative would undermine the prospect for regional negotiations. In addition, Sadat's relations with the PLO snapped. Yasser Arafat, present in person when Sadat delivered his historic 9 November address, walked out of the Egyptian parliament after Sadat's offer of peace with Israel, and was never seen in the country again during Sadat's lifetime. His hopes of taking part in a regional peace conference in which the PLO would represent the Palestinian people were dealt a shattering blow by the mission to Jerusalem. The PLO leadership, like the Syrian government, was forced to back-pedal on the issue of compromise with Israel. On 22 November, after agonised discussions, Arafat joined President Hafez al-Assad in Damascus to issue a joint statement, expressing 'their outright condemnation of his [Sadat's] visit and their readiness to apply all their resources to the elimination of its consequences'. The statement then called on the Egyptian people and army to 'resist this treason to the Arab nation'.[7] Sadat retaliated with the formal closure of the PLO office in Cairo and the Voice of Palestine radio facilities in Egypt.

Steadfastness and Confrontation Front
Now that Sadat had provoked a hostile or adverse response throughout the Arab world, the Libyans no longer felt alone in their opposition to his capitulatory policies. Sadat's counter-productive unilateralism, which had even antagonised his potential allies in the Arab world, provided the Libyan leadership with the opportunity to mobilise the Arab states against his regime. Tripoli sprung into life with a flurry of diplomatic activity. Libyan emissaries were despatched to Arab capitals with invitations for an Arab conference in Tripoli, called for 12 December, to co-ordinate the Arab response to Sadat's initiative. The more pro-Western, conservative Arab states, including Saudi Arabia, declined. Algeria, Iraq, the PLO, South Yemen and Syria accepted. The result was the formation of the Steadfastness and Confrontation Front (SCF), whose grandiose appellation was derived from the Libyan emphasis on 'confrontation' and the Syrian preference for steadfastness, implying a defensive stand rather than an offensive one. The regime of President Assad, it seemed, did not want to jeopardise the diplomatic option with an overly 'rejectionist' stance. The Syrian government was, in fact, widely considered, notably by the Iraqis, to

be sympathetic to a settlement with Israel. Nevertheless, the Syrian regime did, in the circumstances created by Sadat's visit, join with Libya, Iraq, the PLO, Algeria and South Yemen in freezing diplomatic relations with Egypt, and in forming a military pact linking all five, with special provision for the supply fo. weapons to the resistance forces in Lebanon.

The Front was at its most effective in the process of ostracising Sadat. The waverers in the Arab world – Morocco, Jordan, Tunisia – were impelled to abandon the Egyptian leader. Libya had set the pace on the day Sadat flew to Jerusalem, when the General People's Congress had met in emergency session to pass a resolution banning from Libyan territory any plane or ship arriving from, or departing to, Egypt. Following the SCF summit, all Arab states were called on to implement similar sanctions. The Front's members demanded Egypt's expulsion from the Arab League and refused to attend future meetings until the League's headquarters had been removed from Cairo. Arab states which had not attended the meeting could not but realise that it was a political liability to remain attached to Sadat's Egypt. Perceiving the importance of swinging the waverers against Sadat, Qadhafi had done his utmost at the conference to ensure that a united bloc emerged. During the summit he had presided over a reconciliation between the 'rejectionist' and the 'non-rejectionist' Palestinian groups, mediating personally between Arafat and George Habash. He had also buried Libya's differences with Syria and, in the interests of maximum unity, had agreed to a communiqué which did not explicitly rule out the existence of an Israeli state. What problems did arise at the summit were not of Libya's making.

Problems, of course, there were. The whole conference was over-shadowed and disrupted by a bitter row between Syria and Iraq. The clash was largely the product of inter-Baathist rivalry, with the Syrian and Iraqi regimes representing different wings of the Arab Baath Party, but the Iraqi delegation, headed by Taher Ramadan from the Iraqi Revolutionary Command Council, compounded the ideological disagreement by accusing the Syrian government of capitulationism and refused to sign the final communiqué unless it included a specific statement of opposition to UN resolution 242. The insinuation was that Syria, by not taking a stand against this resolution which called for an Israeli withdrawal from territories occupied in 1967, recognised Israel within its 1948 borders. Qadhafi, who was resolutely opposed to recognition of Israel, sided with Syria – for the simple reason that it was the one Arab frontline state attending the conference – whilst exerting strenuous efforts to reconcile Iraq, whose participation would add weight and credibility to the Front. On 1 January, 1978, a Libyan delegation, headed by the Foreign Liaison Secretary Dr Ali Treiki, arrived in Damascus for exploratory talks aimed at healing the rift, which had crippled the effectiveness of the Front. The delegation then flew to Baghdad on 3 January, joining Algerian President Houari Boumedienne and PFLP leader George Habash, in a collective petition to the Iraqi leadership. The Iraqi regime, however, riposted that it was incumbent on Syria to change its position. The situation stayed deadlocked and Iraq did not participate in the work of the Front.

Militarily, the SCF by itself posed no real threat to the state of Israel. Nor could it provide an adequate defence of its own members. On 14 March 1978, some 25,000 Israeli troops rolled into southern Lebanon in a move to drive out the PLO forces from the border area adjacent to Israel. Apparently triggered by an al-Fateh commando operation on 11 March, in which Palestinian fighters led by woman commando Dalal Maghrabi struck inside Israel, the invasion in fact resulted from Sadat's break from the Arab confrontation states. His decision to disengage Egypt from the conflict with Israel released Zionist forces to concentrate on the eradication of the Palestinian forces in Lebanon. Despite the mutual defence pact which bound SCF members, the Israeli invasion did not encounter military counter-action by the armed forces of the Arab states. Syrian troops, though within close proximity of the Israeli advance, failed to support the Palestinian forces. Consequently, the war fought by the PLO was very much a symbolic show of resistance. On 21 March, Arafat signalled to the UNIFIL force in Lebanon that he recognised the unilateral ceasefire declared by the Israelis the day before and would suspend attacks on their forces in southern Lebanon. The PLO, not for the first time, had to bear the brunt of the attack by Israel's military machine alone.

Dismayed as he was by the Syrian failure to support the PLO, Qadhafi did not accept that the SCF was finished. He called for the strengthening of the Front through the unification of its member states, claiming that the common political commitment of the member states, at least at the level of nationalist opposition to Israel, created a new basis for viable mergers. In June 1978 he took the opportunity to visit Algiers. Calculating that the Algerians sought Arab political support in their dispute with Morocco over the Western Sahara, Qadhafi for the second time proposed the unification of the two countries. Addressing the Algerian assembly on 3 June, he lectured the deputies on the urgency of unity. 'Even if the Arab countries become free and independent and even if they become popular and socialist, as in Algeria and Libya, in reality they are still mere scraps of paper in a world ruled by giants, in a world which recognises force, in a world which rejects the rights of man and denies the weak their place in the sun,'[8] he declared. In other words, he was pointing out that Algerian independence was an illusion. Specifying the dangers posed by the French military interventions in Africa, such as those in Mauritania and Zaïre in 1978, he argued that if the FLN valued political independence, it must accept unification with Libya. He suggested this could take the form of a joint confederation with Tunisia, but the FLN leadership, rejecting his arguments, turned down the offer because it would loosen their direct political control.

The Syrian Factor

The prospects for unification with Syria were even less propitious. The government in Damascus had abandoned the PLO to fight Israel alone in March 1978, and had refused to impose sanctions against Egypt right up to the beginning of the Camp David negotiations between Egypt, Israel and the United States in the latter part of the year. There seemed little chance that the regime of President Hafez al-Assad would compromise its position with a unification agreement with Libya, the strongest advocate of rejectionism. Fortunately for Qadhafi, however, the changing political fortunes in the region, particularly after the 1978 invasion of Lebanon, were pushing the Syrian leadership down the road to confrontation. Damascus was forced to escalate the conflict with Israel in order to re-open the possibility of a regional peace conference, or a negotiated settlement which would restore Syrian control to the Golan Heights. The Syrian regime had no option but to counter Israeli ascendancy in the region by asserting its own claim to be a regional superpower, otherwise its interests would be excluded from a regional solution that involved concessions to Egypt and Jordan.

To assert Syrian power *vis-à-vis* Israel Hafez al-Assad required allies. His first attempt to gain them focused on Iraq. Prior to the Baghdad Arab summit in late 1978, he arrived in the Iraqi capital in a dramatic bid to reconcile his Baathist detractors. Following the initiative, there occurred a brief thaw in which proposals for the unification of the two Baathist-ruled countries were revived. The pause in the inter-Baathist conflict, however, was brief; following the takeover of Saddam Hussein in July 1979, the ideological rift widened again. Soon after his accession, the new Iraqi President implicated Damascus in a conspiracy to overthrow both him and his regime. By the following year, the problems facing al-Assad had been exacerbated. Internally, there was a growing revolt by members of the Muslim Brotherhood, which led to a rapid deterioration in relations with Jordan, from where the Brotherhood were receiving supplies and clandestine support. For several weeks in 1980 Syria and Jordan hovered on the brink of hostilities. Then, in August 1980, as unrest within Syria simmered, oil supplies from Iran, interrupted by the outbreak of the Gulf War in the summer of 1979, began to run down. According to one report, the major refinery at Homs was that month nearly empty. Whilst alternative sources could have been purchased from the Gulf, Assad wanted to avoid undue dependence on states supporting the Iraqi war effort. Instead, Assad turned westwards for allies, and telephoned Qadhafi for consultations on the crisis. The Libyans agreed to help out but evidently wanted the Syrian government to commit itself to unity with Libya in return. Days later, when Qadhafi called for unity with Syria during his anniversary-of-the-Revolution speech, Assad was compelled to respond positively. Flying to Tripoli on 8 September, he signed an agreement on union within two days of talks with Qadhafi.[9]

The union document contained a number of important clauses. It bound both states to the creation of a unified political structure, a unitary identity and international representation, and a single political leadership. The

Syrian regime was committed to introducing a system of popular committees and congresses, identical to the *jamahiri* system in Libya, with one overall General National Congress, embracing the committees in both countries. Both sides agreed to meet within a month to plan the implementation of the scheme, but it was not until December that a joint committee was formed, with the responsibility for achieving this. Kharoubi and Jadallah Azouz Talhi comprised its Libyan members, and Dr Abdul Rauf al-Qassim and Ahmed Iskander the Syrian members.[10] Following a second visit to Libya by President al-Assad on 15 December, the Libyan newsagency, JANA, announced the formulation of a joint draft plan for the framework of the unitary state and its institutions, whilst taking into account the 'historical differences' in both countries. In the meantime, until the process of unification was complete, it was decided that a joint revolutionary command would be established to preside over the transition period.

Six years later none of the key provisions of the union agreement between Libya and Syria have been fulfilled. Assad has remained cautious about implementing the clauses of the treaty; the Syrian objective has been to strengthen its strategic position through the unification treaty, without arousing internal opposition from sections of the Baath Party to institutional changes proposed under the terms of the agreement. What unity does exist between Syria and Libya is most evident on foreign policy issues. For example, both Tripoli and Damascus united in opposition to the Fahd plan unveiled on 7 August 1981, which gave implicit recognition to the state of Israel in advance of negotiations. The two states were instrumental in convening a meeting of the SCF foreign ministers in Aden, South Yemen, on 13 November, when a resolution was passed committing members of the Front, including the PLO, to work for the plan's rejection. The effect of the Aden resolution was to tie the PLO Chairman Yasser Arafat to the Syrian-Libyan position, when he had seemed sympathetic to the plan. Syria and Libya were thus able, at the 1981 Arab League summit, to thwart the Fahd plan which would have depended on acceptance by the PLO.

As soon as the Syrian regime had agreed to the union, Qadhafi pressed South Yemen to join. He received a positive, but conditional, answer from President Ali Nasser Mohammed. The South Yemeni leader told Qadhafi, on 25 September 1980, that he hoped the union would become possible once the negotiations for the unification of North and South Yemen, then in progress, had been successfully completed. The South Yemeni government had consistently maintained that the unification of the Yemen was an essential prerequisite to wider Arab unification. Therein, however, lay the rub. By November 1980 it had become clear that Saudi Arabia, to protect the influence it enjoyed in North Yemen, had successfully frustrated the process of Yemeni unification. According to the London-based *Daily Telegraph*, on 26 November a rebellion had broken out in the Jebel Raymah district of North Yemen. The paper pointed out that the tribesmen of this area 'usually carry out the quiet instructions from Saudi Arabia, which keeps them supplied with arms and money.' The aim of the revolt was the scrapping of the unification agreement between both Yemens, which was soon achieved when the government of North Yemen decided to postpone the merger in order to subdue the rebellion.

Following the union agreement with Syria, Qadhafi also decided to renew his appeal for unity with Algeria. Speaking to the GPC on 5 January 1982, he revealed: 'I have submitted to Algeria, Libya and Syria for the establishment of unity among these countries. Let the Algerian people, the Libyan people and the Syrian people decide.' The 'people's institutions' in all three countries, he declared, should 'meet and adopt a single decision.'[11] In view of Algeria's past rejection, a third call on the FLN leadership appeared futile, but Qadhafi surmised that the Algerian leader, President Chadli Benjedid, who had replaced Boumedienne on his death late in 1978, would welcome the strengthening support of the Libyan-Syrian alliance. At the end of January he took his plan to Algiers for talks with Benjedid, following the visit there in December 1981 of President Assad. The Algerian leadership for once relented. From the talks between Qadhafi and Benjedid there emerged a compromise formula, in which the Algerian leadership agreed to hold regular government-to-government meetings. Algeria, however, was not bound to introduce the *jamahiri* system or inaugurate institutional changes. The agreement was always in question, and when the Israelis invaded Lebanon in June 1982, there had been only one joint meeting of the Algerian Council of Ministers and the Libyan General People's Committee. Due to the political divisions that arose during the war in Lebanon, no further meetings of that kind have been held, and the whole agreement has gone into abeyance.

Qadhafi Challenges Arafat

The invasion of Lebanon that Menachem Begin launched on 6 June 1982 marked the end of an important chapter in the history of the Middle East. The Israelis mobilised some 120,000 troops, including 80,000 regulars, in an onslaught, ironically codenamed 'Operation Peace for Galilee', designed to destroy the PLO infrastructure in Lebanon. Pitted against heavily mechanised ground forces, naval forces and an aerial blitzkrieg were at most 20,000 fighters from the Joint Forces of the PLO and the Lebanese nationalist organisations. JF units were soon driven back from the South into the Syrian-held Beqaa Valley, or into Beirut, where their headquarters units were based. There, bottled up in the western half of the city, some 4,000 JF fighters, together with 4,500 troops from the Syrian army, heroically withstood an Israeli siege of 67 days, during which time the city was relentlessly pounded by Israeli artillery and bombarded from the air, and food, water and medical supplies were cut off. During that period, the leaders of all the Palestinian organisations, except the Syrian-backed *Saiqa* and the Iraqi-backed Arab Liberation Front, were present in Beirut. Finally, through indirect negotiations with United States' special envoy Philip Habib, and on condition that Palestinian civilians in the camps remained protected by international forces, Yasser Arafat agreed to evacuate Beirut. The first contingent of Palestinian fighters set sail on 21 August, bound for Cyprus and then destinations throughout the Arab world, still carrying their hand-held weapons to show that they had defied defeat. On 30 August, Arafat himself departed from the city for Greece, given a last salute by Lebanese President Elias Sarkis, Prime Minister Chafiq Wazzan, and Lebanese National Movement leader Walid Jumblatt, and escorted by the French navy.

The Israeli invasion had important consequences for the SCF. The four member states were revealed to be just as incapable of halting a large-scale Israeli offensive as they had been of stopping the smaller one in 1978. True, the Syrians did engage the Israeli forces, but only in defence of their own positions in the vicinity of the main Beirut-Damascus highway. Viewing the situation in February 1983, the PLO's Khalil Wazir (Abu Jihad) complained that 'Syria decided to confine the battle to Beirut and participate with the forces it had there if the enemy decided to confine it there too.' The Algerians, possessing the next largest army of the alliance, sent no troops to reinforce the PLO; the Libyans and South Yemenis despatched small units, but these remained behind the Syrian lines in the Beqaa, and were intended more as a gesture of solidarity with the Syrians than with the PLO itself. The nearest the Libyans got to the fighting was Chatoura on the Beirut-Damascus highway. Facing the constant threat of American and Egyptian aggression (described in detail in Chapter 10), Qadhafi decided that the priority was the defence of the Libyan homeland. No one appeared more embarrassed at this failure to fight alongside the PLO than he himself, but in extenuation he told a meeting of Libyan officers on 14 June 1982, one week after the fighting had commenced, that it was impossible to carry out any military action against Israel for 'geographical reasons'.[12] He stressed that had it not been for this factor, he would have ordered troops to the front. Yet if this was a veiled allegation that Syria had discouraged Libya from sending forces, then Qadhafi certainly did not press the point. For strategic reasons he did not want to damage the alliance with Syria; nor did he want to create circumstances in which the war could turn into a regional conflict. In common with all the confrontation states, Libya did not want to be drawn into supporting the PLO by military means.

Qadhafi was, in effect, reduced to posturing. When the invasion had started in early June, he had initially called for the admission of Iran to the SCF. On 12 June Jalloud arrived in Teheran and plans were announced – which have never come to fruition – for the formation of a joint Islamic army. At the height of the siege of Beirut, Tripoli radio broadcast a message from Qadhafi to Arab heads of state, calling for the 'Arabisation' of the resistance in Lebanon. He demanded the immediate transportation to Lebanon of 10 divisions and aircraft, and submitted a breakdown of the units each country was designated to supply: two divisions from Syria; one division each from Morocco, Algeria, Libya, Saudi Arabia and Sudan; two brigades from Jordan; and one brigade each from Kuwait, the UAE and North and South Yemen.[13] To command this pan-Arab army he presented himself. When he received the negative replies that he must have anticipated, he tried to shame Arab leaders with charges of treachery and capitulation. Addressing a meeting of the Islamic Call Society, Qadhafi launched a vehement attack on Saudi Arabia for its failure to implement an Arab oil embargo on the West. He declared:

> We challenge these rulers to stop the oil supply to the USA and to withdraw their credits from US and Zionist banks, and to sever their diplomatic relations with the USA. We challenge them to send a military division to participate in the eviction of the Zionist enemy, as put in the Libyan-Arab proposal.[14]

The Saudis and the Gulf rulers were not the only ones that Qadhafi accused of betrayal of the Arab nation. When the PLO leadership started to consider a negotiated way out of the siege of Beirut, he bitterly crossed swords with PLO Chairman Yasser Arafat. On 3 July, he transmitted a message to Arafat saying, 'It is disgraceful and unacceptable at any price, whether in Beirut or in Lebanon as a whole, that the enemy can negotiate our destiny.' Rather than accept evacuation on negotiated terms he urged the Palestinian resistance to commit suicide. 'Your suicide will immortalise the cause of Palestine for future generations', he declared. 'Your blood is the fuel of the revolution that has become inevitable from the Ocean to the Gulf.'[15] Arafat's reply was sharp and reproachful: 'I say that these steadfast fighters, waging the longest Arab-Israeli war ever, expected that at least Arab planes might be sent up to cover their skies, to protect their children and families. They expected that Arab forces, and how many they are, would break this siege upon them in this forward trench of the Arab nation.'[16] Poignantly, he added: 'I must remind you Brother Muammar, of our numerous discussions which, had they led to action on our agreements, the enemy would not have dared to do what he has.' Although Qadhafi was later to claim that the Sabra and Chatila massacres vindicated his point about negotiations, it remains difficult to see how an even greater conflagration could have been avoided if the Palestinian forces had stayed, deprived as they were of Arab reinforcements.

Fez Plan

Qadhafi and Arafat were now set on a collision course. At the heart of their dispute was the whole question of a negotiated Palestinian settlement, which Qadhafi emphatically rejected. As Arafat sailed from Beirut to Athens, President Reagan announced his 'fresh start' proposals for the Middle East, calling for the establishment of a Palestinian homeland in association with Jordan. The initial response of the PLO leadership, anxious for some diplomatic headway after the evacuation, was noticeably responsive. On 2 September, Farouq Qaddoumi, head of the PLO's political department, described the plan as containing 'positive elements'. The following day, Arafat himself declared, 'we do not reject Reagan's proposals, nor do we criticise them.' Days later, at the Arab summit conference, convened for the second consecutive year in Fez, the proposals received the sympathetic response from Arab governments for which Reagan had hoped. The assembled Arab leaders, including Yasser Arafat and Syrian President Hafez al-Assad, agreed to a response which met the Reagan plan half-way. The synthesis that resulted, known as the Fez plan, was based on an elaboration of the previous year's Fahd plan, demanding the withdrawal of Israel from all territories occupied since 1967, but with an amendment inserted specifying 'the Palestinian people's right to self-determination and the exercise of its imprescriptible and inalienable national rights under the leadership of the Palestinian Liberation Organisation, its sole and legitimate representative.' In addition, it became clear at the summit that Arafat had aligned himself with Fahd and had started a policy of rapprochement with King Hussein of Jordan. The Libyans, objecting to the previous year's Fahd plan, refused to attend a summit which would discuss the same sort of negotiated formula.

The discernible trend towards compromise shown by the PLO leadership alarmed Qadhafi. His immediate concern in the aftermath of the Beirut evacuation was that the PLO should stay within the confrontation camp, that being the orbit of Libya and Syria. Were the PLO to enter into negotiations with the United States, directly or through an intermediary, the legitimacy of Libya's own position would be dangerously undermined. Qadhafi, therefore, resolved to challenge Arafat from within the PLO, preferably before the Palestine National Council met in February to decide the question. On 13 February he arranged a meeting in Tripoli with the leaders of the Popular Front for the Liberation of Palestine (PFLP), the Democratic Front for the Liberation of Palestine (DFLP), the Popular Front for the Liberation of Palestine–General Command (PFLP-GC), the Palestinian Popular Struggle Front (PPSF) and Saiqa, at which a communiqué endorsed by all five organisations was formulated, condemning the Reagan plan and calling on the PLO leadership to state its opposition.[17] Days later, however, Qadhafi's position was undercut when the PFLP and the DFLP suspended their objections in the interests of Palestinian unity. Henceforth, both organisations differentiated themselves from the others which had agreed the Tripoli communiqué by the formation of a 'democratic unity platform'. In fact, earlier, at a closed-door meeting of the al-Fateh Revolutionary Council in Aden on 27 January, a split had opened in the ranks of Arafat's own al-Fateh organisation on the precise issue of negotiations on the basis of the Reagan plan. Colonel Said Abu Musa, one of the commanders who had led the defence of West Beirut, attacked Arafat for his sympathetic response to the Reagan plan, arguing that Arafat was leading the Palestinian movement down 'the road to capitulation'.[18]

Rebellion

Abu Musa was not alone in his criticisms. Arafat's tactics had angered an important constituency within al-Fateh known as the 'Colonel's group', of which Abu Musa was an unsophisticated but respected spokesman. This group saw Arafat's decision to leave Beirut for Tunisia rather than Damascus as a crucial mistake, bound to irritate President Assad, upon whom the future of the armed resistance, however limited, now more than ever depended. Adding to their disaffection was the commitment Arafat had unilaterally given, as Commander of the Palestinian forces, not to re-launch operations against Israel from Lebanese territory. The assassination of Saad Sayel, the architect of the defence of West Beirut, near Baalbek some time in September 1982, was interpreted as a sign that Arafat was prepared to get tough with those who disagreed with his decision. Arafat was suspected by members of the 'Colonel's group' of using a militia based at Chatoura to eliminate Sayel and other commanders who rejected the concessions he was making in the interests of diplomacy. Until Abu Musa spoke up at the Aden meeting, the most prominent exponent of their case was Nimr Saleh (Abu Saleh), a member of the Fateh Central Committee. Saleh had disagreed with Arafat's choice of Tunisia instead of Syria, and had himself gone to Damascus and issued statements strongly critical of the leadership's line. On 21 January 1983 he had even accused Arafat of 'violating the resolutions of the Palestinian institutions'. The Fateh Central Committee, meeting in Kuwait shortly afterwards, had responded by suspending him from all posts in the organisation and refusing him admission to the meeting in Aden. Yet, in the light of subsequent developments, Saleh's cooperation would have been pivotal to settling the differences that had arisen.

Arafat had it within his means to contain the dispute. He could have availed himself of the opportunity provided by the PNC, when it convened in Algiers, to have placated at least some of his critics. He did not. Instead, he inflamed the situation by persisting in a course of action that was palpably unacceptable to the Libyans and the Syrians, and to cadres within the ranks of his own organisation. What he did was commence talks with King Hussein, hoping to find a formula which would provide the Jordanian monarch with a mandate to represent the Palestinians in talks with the Reagan administration. Whilst he pursued this strategy, he started a crackdown on his detractors in al-Fateh, most obviously the 'Colonel's group' and the cadres in the Beqaa Valley. In April, he appointed to key military posts commanders known for their personal loyalty to him, rather than their military experience and popularity within the ranks of the resistance. These included Abdul Hajim, former commander of the southern Beqaa front, and Hajj Ismail, former southern commander based in Sidon. Their appointments only increased the discontent within the organisation; Hajj Ismail was accused of having fled from the fighting in the south as the Israelis advanced. Rather than acquiesce to their authority, which seemed to signal an impending purge, Abu Musa and Samir Quayk led a mutiny. The banner of revolt was raised in the name of 'The New Revolutionary Movement of al-Fateh'.

Support for the rebellion came from Libya and Syria. The two countries saw in the split a mechanism for exerting their own influences over the direction of the PLO. Arafat appears to have recognised this threat to his position only belatedly. His priority was his negotiations with King Hussein. He expected opposition to his initiative to mount within the movement, but evidently had no idea of how widespread it would become. As the rebellion within Fateh gathered momentum, he was finally forced to abort his talks with King Hussein and deal with the crisis. On 13 May, he travelled to Damascus in a late attempt to resolve the crisis. Almost immediately he left for the Beqaa, but refused to concede the rebels' demands. Neither Hajj Ismail nor Abdul Hajim was dismissed, but both had their commands brought under the control of the PLO Chief of Staff, Abdul Mutasim. On 21 May, the Fateh Central Committee met in Damascus, without either Nimr Saleh or Samir Quayk, and withdrew the commands of Abu Musa and other rebel officers. Arafat, in an effort to appease President Assad, then agreed to form a joint commission to inquire into the differences between the PLO leadership and the Syrian regime. Arafat hoped this device would give him time to re-assert his authority within the PLO, but his efforts to re-establish control in the Beqaa were pre-empted by the Syrians. On 28 May, operating with the connivance of the Syrian army, the rebels took over military depots along the Beirut-Damascus highway. When Arafat tried to intercede he was prevented from travelling to the Beqaa by the Syrian authorities. Arafat responded by accusing the Syrian government of interfering in the internal affairs of his organisation, but his attacks on President Assad merely became a pretext for his deportation from Syria. His expulsion in late June provoked an immediate conflict between the rebels and the Arafat loyalists in the Beqaa. But when a ceasefire was declared on 4 July, the rebel movement was clearly gaining the upper hand.

The suppression of the revolt within Fateh had now become a priority for Arafat. In preparation for a show-down, he ordered loyalist forces to assemble in the northern Lebanese city of Tripoli. Crossing by boat from Cyprus, he arrived there to take command on 23 September, having strengthened his hand by gaining the backing of Algeria and South Yemen in his conflict with Syria. Within the proximity of Tripoli itself he strengthened his position through an alliance with the locally-based Islamic Unity Movement. He had, in addition, the benefit of the abstention in the conflict of both the PFLP and the DFLP. Yet, ranged against him within the PLO were the New Revolutionary Movement, the PFLP-GC, Saiqa and the PPSF. Backing them were Syria and Libya.

A delegation from the New Revolutionary Movement, headed by Abu Saleh, had visited Libya in August 1983.[19] During talks with Abu Bakr Younis Jaber, an agreement was concluded under which the Libyans would supply the rebel movement with arms and funds. The other Palestinian organisations supporting the movement against Arafat received similar commitments; for example, Ahmed Jibril's PFLP-GC was supplied with tanks via Libya. Even with such equipment, however, the anti-Arafat forces faced stiff opposition from the Fateh loyalists and their allies. During outbreaks of fighting between both sides in October, it seemed that Arafat was on the point of gaining the superior position. To avert that possibility, the Syrians and Libyans moved decisively to support the rebel movement. The Syrians are believed to have deployed one-and-a-half divisions, and six battalions of the Syrian-controlled Palestine Liberation Army, besides the forces of the various Palestinian fronts, to turn the conflict in their favour. Despite the pressure for restraint exerted by Saudi Arabia and the Gulf states, the Syrian regime showed every intention of forcing Arafat's surrender.

Throughout November and December the noose tightened around his enclave in northern Lebanon. The Palestinian refugee camp at Nahr al-Barid, outside Tripoli, Lebanon, was stormed by Syrian-supported Palestinian forces on 3 November, and much of al-Badawi camp fell on 15 November. The anti-Arafat forces called for the PLO Chairman's surrender, but finally had to accept his negotiated evacuation from the port of Tripoli. Both Arab and international opinion had become sympathetic to Arafat, and the Syrians were placed in the embarrassing position of fighting Arafat at the same time that the Israeli navy was bombarding his positions in Tripoli city. Arafat finally departed from Tripoli in late December, having lost the military battle for control of the movement in Lebanon, but having won a political victory against the government in Damascus.

Whilst tactically siding with the Syrians in the intra-PLO war, the Libyans nevertheless had a number of reservations about Syrian objectives. Qadhafi had no wish to see the Syrian regime extend its tutelage over the PLO; he had, after all, opposed the Syrian action in 1976 to curb the PLO presence in Lebanon. Beyond that, he disagreed with Hafez al-Assad on the fundamentals of the conflict with Zionism. Assad was not an explicitly rejectionist leader; on the contrary, he had accepted the principle of a state of Israel reduced to its 1948 borders, and had endorsed the Fez plan, albeit with reluctance. The Syrian position was based on a negotiated regional settlement.

Qadhafi, on the other hand, was explicitly and incontrovertibly a rejectionist. He was opposed to the Syrian objective of a regional peace conference, but was prepared to conclude a strategic alliance with Damascus so long as Assad maintained a stance of confrontation. When Arafat, after the evacuation of Beirut, showed signs of abandoning confrontation, Qadhafi was willing to co-operate with the Syrians in support of the Fateh rebellion; indeed, the first indications were that Libya was more involved in the initial stages of the rebellion than Syria. Following Arafat's visit to Egypt on 22 December 1983, such backing became even stronger. The Libyans called on the Palestinian people to rise up and overthrow 'Arafat and his clique' from the leadership of the PLO. Arafat was accused of joining the Camp David process, of following in the footsteps of Sadat, and of violating the Arab boycott of Egypt.

Since the formation of the alliance between Arafat and the Egyptians, consummated by Arafat's talks with President Mubarak in December, the Libyans have concentrated on building up the Palestinian 'confrontation movement'. The nucleus for this movement has come from the 'Palestine Alliance' consisting of the PFLP-GC, the PPSF, Saiqa and the New Revolutionary Movement of al-Fateh. Leaders of the Alliance made a dramatic debut at the General People's Congress in February 1984. Speeches critical of Arafat's policy line were given by Ahmed Jibril, leader of the PFLP-GC, and Abu Khaled al-Umla, a leftist intellectual who was emerging as the most influential strategist in the New Revolutionary Movement. A year later, following participation in the fighting in the Shouf mountains in Lebanon, these organisations formed in Tripoli a new Joint Forces Command under the leadership of Abu Khaled al-Umla. Syria and Libya in addition exerted strong pressures on Palestinian organisations to join the new movement, so that Arafat's monopoly in the PLO could be challenged. Some measure of success was achieved in April 1985 when a Salvation Front, linking the four Alliance organisations and the PFLP, was formed on a platform of defending the PLO's independence and right to sole representation of the Palestinian people.

It remains doubtful whether the new Front can pose a serious challenge to the Arafat line within the PLO. The future credibility of the Front depends on the success of confrontation tactics, which Arafat has virtually abandoned. Such tactics are inevitably constrained by the Syrian government. The regime of Hafez al-Assad, which came to power arguing that there should be no independent Palestinian confrontation, shows no intention of permitting the Salvation Front forces to sustain an armed struggle with the Israelis beyond a few symbolic gestures. Although the Palestinian organisations believe they can benefit from Syria's currently ambiguous stance, Damascus can–and has–effectively contained them within the Beqaa area. At one stage in the Shouf war between the Druze and the Phalangists in September 1983 the Syrians, having decided to de-escalate the conflict for their own reasons, unceremoniously pulled back from the Shouf Palestinian forces co-operating with the Druze militia. The organisations hope that Qadhafi can exert some restraining pressure on Damascus on their behalf, but this seems unrealistic, for the Libyans, whilst suppliers of oil to Syria, are not in a great position of political influence. Subject to Syrian-applied constraints on their activity, it has been difficult for such Palestinian groups to assert themselves within the PLO. The Front has posed no threat to Arafat's control of the movement as yet. At the PNC meeting in Amman in November 1984 Arafat obtained the mandate he sought for negotiations with the United States through King Hussein. The Front, without the strength of support to stop him, stayed away from the session.

185

In one sense, the Libyan alliance with Syria on the Palestine question makes sense, however. The future of the conflict with Zionism is most likely to depend on the outcome of the conflict in Lebanon, in which the Syrians are the strongest factor. Supporting Syria in the regional power struggle with Israel in Lebanon therefore coincides, in the current period, with the objectives of Palestinian liberation. In the longer term, if the Syrians achieve some sort of regional settlement of their dispute with the United States, the strategy will doubtless change. Qadhafi himself links the liberation of Palestine to social and political transformations in the wider Arab world. That is why Libyan support for Palestinian organisations has gone in tandem with support for opposition forces in Arab States.

Notes

1 *Arab Dawn* (August 1976).

2. Ibid.

3. J. Cooley, *Libyan Sandstorm: The Complete Account of Qaddafi's Revolution* (Sidgwick & Jackson, London, 1982): p. 119.

4. In *Arab Dawn* (March 1975).

5. *Arab Dawn* (February 1975).

6. For an account, see M. Heikal, *Autumn of Fury: The Assassination of Sadat*, (Corgi, London, 1984).

7. In Helena Cobban, *The Palestinian Liberation Organisation* (Cambridge University Press, Cambridge, 1984).

8. *Arab Dawn* (July 1978).

9. *Jamahiriya Review* (October 1980).

10. *Jamahiriya Review* (January 1981).

11. Ibid.

12. BBC Summary of World Broadcasts ME (16 June 1982).

13. Ibid.

14. BBC Summary of World Broadcasts ME (20 July 1982).

15. *Newsline* (6 July 1982).

16. Ibid.

17. H. Cobban, *The Palestinian Liberation Organisation*.

18. Rashid Khalidi, *MERIP Reports* No. 119 (November-December 1983).

19. *JIR*.

10 Revolutionary Mobilisations

The Revolutionary Committee Movement

The upheavals of 1978 coincided with the growth of revolutionary committees. These were essentially groups of cadres, ideologically committed to the Third Universal Theory, which emerged in Libya towards the end of 1977. Their formation, following the Sebha declaration, proceeded from a call from Muammar Qadhafi for the establishment of 'revolutionary committees in all places'. Some student-based revolutionary committees had, in fact, been established in the universities since the student revolution of 1976, but they were not systematically organised, nor were their responsibilities defined within the political structure. In contrast, committees set up after the Sebha declaration were formed within the BPCs and assigned the task of encouraging participation and guiding the congresses according to the precepts of the *Green Book*. Qadhafi, who assumed the leadership of the movement, disclaimed powers of coercion, and stressed that the committees had responsibilities separate from those of the administration.

A number of factors prompted Qadhafi's call for the establishment of revolutionary committees. By far the most important of these was the fact that the system of direct democracy had begun to falter within months of its inception. The popular response to the creation of the congresses was passive; lack of attendance and abstentionism threatened the congress system. In the absence of mass pressure from below, there was no challenge to the inertia and immobility of the state bureaucracy. Tribal leaders took advantage of the congresses to promote their own sectional interests; in specific instances, congresses became forums to denounce the *Green Book* and condemn the policies of Qadhafi. Instead of the system providing an alternative to the traditional leaderships, the congresses were becoming vehicles for their interests. The problem of integrating the population within the political process remained. Such a transition from local tribal affiliations to a nationalist allegiance to the Libyan revolution required, in Qadhafi's analysis, the intervention of political cadres.

Two important social characteristics distinguish the revolutionary committees. First, a notable feature of their composition is the age of their members; most committee members come from the younger post-revolutionary generation and have no direct experience of the monarchist, or Idrisi, period. They are products of the 'baby boom' of the 1960s which meant that, by the mid 1970s, half the population was under the age of 30. Second, whilst many cadres are students of schools, colleges, or universities, the movement does have a class basis among the lower strata of society: the background of the majority of committee members is not the private commercial sector, but the working class within administration and government services, or to a lesser extent, the wider service sector and manufacturing industry. The leaders of revolutionary committees tend to be graduates from the lower strata of urban society who occupy professional posts.

Cadres for the revolutionary committees were selected according to a rigid procedure. Following Qadhafi's speech urging their formation, intelligence reports on the best and most dependable activists within the BPCs and the student congresses, usually produced by members of the security services and Qadhafi aides, were filed with Qadhafi's office at al-Azizya barracks. Those approved – in general, past participants in *Green Book* seminars and training camps – were then encouraged to form a committee within their local BPC, collecting names from an inaugural meeting held to announce the committee's formation. These names were then fed back to al-Azizya barracks, where they were vetted against intelligence reports on known oppositionists. Those endorsed – the 'core' members – were then obliged to undergo ideological training at specially convened training camps. Here members learned methods of agitation and propaganda; they also received a basic military training, learning how to use firearms, and underwent intelligence training, which included instruction in how to gather information about their locality and work-place, and particulars about those persons with politically hostile and reactionary attitudes. Finally, they were sent back to recruit and build the committee within their BPC. New recruits, however, unless they too underwent the same training, were exempted from deliberations within the committee. Only 'core' members, acting as the link with Qadhafi's office, bore responsibility for the actions of the committee.[1]

Once formed, the committees inexorably acquired stronger powers. Within the BPCs, the committees themselves tended to fill the vacuum created by passivity and the low level of attendance. Soon the committees arrogated to themselves certain administrative functions, in order that the traditional leaders should not dominate and manipulate the system. As the congresses initiated the selection procedure for new officers in February 1978, the revolutionary committee movement assumed responsibility for 'absolute revolutionary supervision of people's power'.[2] Their role, in other words, was to prevent political opponents and traditional tribal forces asserting their interests within the BPCs. One year later they were exercising even greater control. The General People's Congress in March 1979, passed a resolution defining the committees' formal responsibilities.

They were given the right to supervise selection procedure within the BPCs, nominate and veto candidates who did not meet with their approval, and empowered to reconvene meetings and selection procedures. Their powers, successively increased, by the end of 1979 included the right to arrest and detain, to hold revolutionary tribunals, and administer what is described as 'revolutionary justice'. During the course of that year, the movement did in fact make a decisive shift from motivating to enforcing, becoming vested with major security and police powers.

Qadhafi himself had abandoned formal responsibility within the administration during the course of 1978, and increasingly devoted his energies to building up the committee movement. In relation to the change, he has explained:

> I lead the revolution. My mission is to instigate the masses to practice authority. Authority, or power, is in the hands of the masses, through the people's congresses and the people's committees. I lead the movement of the Revolutionary Committees wherever there are revolutionary committees. Whether they are inside Libya or even abroad in the rest of the Arab world, I still preside over or lead this revolutionary movement of committees whose task is to realise the age of the era of the masses, in which the authority of the masses is achieved all over the world, so that we can do away with government, regularise political parties, classes, in order that peace, freedom and happiness would be achieved.[3]

By the beginning of the 1980s, the revolutionary committee movement was a powerful and centralised force. Operating from headquarters in Tripoli, called the Mathuba, or Lion's Den, the committee movement published and distributed a regular newspaper, *al-Zahaf al-Akhdar*, organised rallies and demonstrations, convened seminars and summer training camps, in addition to their other duties connected with the BPCs. The movement's structure was extensive and its influence pervasive. Committees had been formed in schools, offices and factories, though the most important in terms of their power are those within the armed forces, the universities and the municipal people's congresses. Committee members, like Communist Party members in Eastern Europe, have in fact become a privileged tier of society. They enjoy immunity from arrest by the normal security services and benefit from foreign travel. Such is their dominant position within the political structure that Qadhafi has been concerned to ensure their subordination. Accordingly, no structural links are permitted between one committee and another. The effective command structure is vertical and centralised. Qadhafi personally supervises committee activities, sometimes calling committee meetings *en masse*, sometimes inspecting their work on visits to various localities. The Mathuba, or committee headquarters in Tripoli, constitutes a subdivision of his office at al-Azizya barracks.

The movement has thus become a key–if not the main–mechanism through which Qadhafi exercises political control of Libya. Revolutionary committee members in the armed forces have standing orders to reject orders they find incongruous with their military duties and to arrest officers they suspect of conspiracy. The effective leaders of the movement, and therefore of Libya, are some 40 to 50 senior members, chiefly 'the speakers' of the most powerful committees, who meet with Qadhafi on a regular, often weekly basis, to decide the movement's programme of activities. Specific political initiatives are instigated by Qadhafi convening a meeting of speakers from relevant areas of application. If there is an outburst of protest within the universities, for example, he will call together speakers from the university committees and determine the response. Similarly, the formation of revolutionary committees outside Libya, usually where there are concentrations of Libyan students attending foreign educational establishments, has provided him with a mechanism of intervention outside Libya.

The rise of the movement has posed an obvious challenge to the dominant position of the military bureaucracy within the Libyan state. One anecdote illustrates the point well. When, in 1980, the committees commenced a series of televised trials connected with 'economic crimes', Jalloud accused them of exceeding their terms of reference and demanded that their leaders come to his office to be reprimanded. The committees responded by summoning him to *their* office, arresting his brother-in-law on charges of corruption, as well as other relatives and several high-ranking military officers and their relatives. The political crisis that erupted, as tensions mounted on both sides, was only defused by Qadhafi's personal intervention.[4] It was not, however, the last occasion on which he had to countermand committee leaders who had overstepped the mark. In early 1982 he criticised some committee members for trying to build their own power-base and 'behaving arrogantly towards the masses'. Qadhafi has always been careful not to precipitate a direct confrontation between the committees and the leaders of the military establishment. As additional protection, he himself retains a separate network within the armed forces, based on family ties.

The significance of the movement is that it has helped Qadhafi transform political relationships within Libya. The committees, through the suppression of pre-revolutionary political relationships, have integrated the population in a new system of national political affiliation. They have increased participation within the *jamahiri* institutions and become a motor for mass mobilisation. During the political crises of 1978 and 1979, such mobilisations, instigated by the committees, played an essential part in defeating the opposition. Increasingly, however, there is an undeniable trend towards the committees themselves becoming a substitute for mass mobilisation. The danger, as Qadhafi is aware, is that the movement may begin to separate from the mass of the population. If that were to happen, the bond between the political system and the population in general would be weakened. For that reason, Qadhafi is constantly reminding the movement's cadres that they must remain among 'the masses' and 'entrench the revolution within the masses'.

The Overthrow of the Capitalist Class

The formation of the Revolutionary Committee Movement was preceded by the intensification of the struggle between the leadership and the Libyan capitalist class. Speaking in Tripoli, on the anniversary of the al-Fateh Revolution in 1978, Qadhafi entrusted the movement with the expropriation of industrial capitalists and the establishment of workers' committees, called 'producers' partnerships'. 'This is', declared Qadhafi, 'the vital duty of the revolutionary committees; to destroy exploitation, profit, gold and money, of masters and slaves, the oppressive society, until Libyan men and women, from the mosques to the people's congresses, to the cemetery, become equal.'[5] He insisted that the owners of industrial enterprises become 'like all other workers', and stressed that 'the organisation of the struggle for this, throughout the world, should be the revolutionary committees, which should operate secretly or publicly according to circumstances.'[6]

The 'Producers' Revolution'

What followed has become known as the 'producers' revolution'. The revolutionary committees, heeding Qadhafi's call, mounted a 'march on the factories'. The owners of industrial enterprises were dismissed and workplace 'vocational congresses', with powers of managerial control, established in their place. Full compensation and financial indemnity were granted. By the beginning of 1979 private sector ownership had virtually been eliminated from the productive sector of the economy. Shortly after Qadhafi's speech, 29 enterprises were taken over; between 29 September and 1 October 1978 a further 22 were transformed; and on 5 October, nine more followed.[7] Thereafter, the 'revolution' continued on a more sporadic basis until most of the country's manufacturing and service industries, including those owned by the state, had been reconstituted on the basis of 'producers' partnerships'.

This offensive against private capital was not totally unexpected. The 'march on the factories' was the culmination of a campaign Qadhafi had waged all year, beginning with the BPCs' discussions prior to the General People's Congress, when he had raised the issue of a transition from wage-labour to worker-partnerships. The second part of the *Green Book*, published in early 1978, had provided the arguments for the transformation; wage-labour, the purchase of labour power by capitalists, was declared a violation of 'natural law'. Then, in March of that year, the GPC had voted overwhelmingly to raise the minimum wage and introduce partnerships in industry. Finally, in a speech he delivered on 1 May 1978, Qadhafi had affirmed that 'the revolution should be carried on and your march should continue until the workers take over the management completely in all the institutions in which they work.'[8] He elaborated:

> The workers of the Libyan Jamahiriya have to accomplish this objective so that Libya can achieve self-sufficiency and bridle the tongues which spread rumours

and anti-propaganda against Libyan workers to hinder the process of self-achievement. You should not leave a gap in your revolution so to as give an excuse to the enemies of the workers. I am sure that you will never give them the chance if you start organising yourself, as of today, in presenting a magnificent example to the oppressed workers of the Arab world.[9]

Following the earlier measures against the commercial bourgeoisie, Qadhafi and his colleagues had evidently decided to proceed with the expropriation of the country's small productive, or industrial bourgeoisie. Two principal factors encouraged them to come to this conclusion: the first was the rising political opposition of the Libyan capitalist class; the second was the gradual withdrawal of the capitalist class from cooperation with the state in the programme of industrialisation. Whilst in 1962 the private sector had invested three times as much in industry as the public sector, by 1977 it invested about one-sixth of the total. By 1978 it was estimated that the private sector accounted for no more than 20 per cent of industrial production. In 1972, private sector industrial investment was estimated at LD79.4 million, compared with state investment of LD208.5 million; by 1975, at the end of the Three-Year Intermediate Plan, it had risen in absolute terms to LD220.6 million, but was completely outstripped by state investment of LD834.1 milion.[10] By 1976 production in some private enterprises, notably fruit-preserving and canning, had dropped to 3 per cent of their 1975 levels.[11]

The decision to oust the private sector from industry probably had its origins in the on-going conflict between the state and the merchants. Since 1975 the industrialists had been increasingly disaffected with the state monopoly of foreign trade, and their dissent was demonstrated in a marked contraction of industrial imports. Meanwhile, the state planning authorities had begun to formulate the first Transformation Plan. When published, this emphasised the continued growth in infrastructure, particularly transport and communications, but also outlined a substantial expansion in the country's light industrial capacity. Notably, under the plan the town of Tajoura, 20km east of Tripoli, became the proposed site for vehicle assembly. Subsequently, in 1978, Massey-Ferguson opened a tractor plant in Tajoura, followed in 1981 by a truck and bus assembly plant, built in conjunction with Fiat. The Plan provided no real role for the domestic private sector, and the grants and subsidies to private industrialists were cut back.

The producers' partnership, instituted within industry, was a form of workers' cooperative. What, in fact, occurred after the expropriation of the capitalists was not the assumption of direct state control, but a process of cooperativisation. Within each workplace, vocational congresses embracing the whole workforce were established and were vested with control of production. The functions of management, previously the responsibility of owners' nominees, were entrusted to a people's committee, chosen by members of the vocational people's congress, usually from among their

Table 10.1   Economic and Social Transformation Plan 1976–80

Sector	LDm	per cent
Agriculture and agrarian reform	445.3	6.2
Integrated agricultural developments	781.3	10.9
Industry and mineral resources	1,089.7	15.2
Oil & gas	648.2	9.0
Electricity	543.6	7.6
Transport & communications	632.1	8.8
Education	470.4	6.6
Health	171.4	2.4
Manpower	41.8	0.6
Social security	43.2	0.6
Housing	794.2	11.1
Economy	32.7	0.5
Sports, information & culture	91.3	1.3
Municipalities	552.7	7.7
Planning	56.7	0.8
Reserve	325.3	4.5
Nutrition & sea wealth	41.4	0.6
Marine transport	373.5	5.2
Security services	35.0	0.5
Total	*7,170.0*	*100.0*

Note: Figures may not tally correctly through rounding.
Source: Ministry of Planning, 1976.

workmates, but sometimes with outside specialists, accountants and technicians, co-opted. Like the Yugoslavian model of worker cooperatives, the partnerships provide a degree of workers' control over production. They nevertheless operate under enormous constraints imposed by the bureaucracy, the planners, and the administrators charged with implementation of the overall development plan, and suffer from competition for inputs and resources controlled centrally. The institution of such partnerships in effect brought industry within the framework of the jamahiri system, so that individual commercial and industrial units were subordinated to political priorities.

The benefits of the transformation were realised in a number of ways. First of all, it was hoped that workers, being in control of the production process within their various productive units, would have a direct incentive to raise productivity. The more the individual worker produced, the more his share of production, or its monetary equivalent increased; Qadhafi, in

Part 2 of the *Green Book*, stresses the relationship between partnerships and productivity. He explains:

> Whoever works for himself is certainly devoted to his productive work because his incentive to production lies in his dependence on his private work to satisfy his material needs. Also, whoever works in a socialist corporation is a partner in its production. He is, undoubtedly, devoted to his productive work because the impetus for devotion to production is that he gets a satisfaction of his needs through production. But whoever works for a wage has no incentive to work.[12]

For the leadership, there were other benefits, too. Whilst the partnerships retained administrative and managerial control of their enterprises, their effective incorporation within the jamahiri system permitted the state much greater control over the distribution of resources. Eradicating the individual capitalists' domination of the labour market enabled the reorganisation of the workforce. The acute shortages of labour, which afflicted key sections of production, including both agriculture and industry, could only be overcome by a re-distribution of the country's limited supplies of manpower. The creation of producers'

Table 10.2   Migrant Workers, 1975 and 1980

	1975		1980	
Sending Country	*No*	*%*	*No*	*%*
Egypt	229,500	69.1	225,000	43.4
Jordan & Palestine	14,150	4.3	30,000	5.8
Syria	13,150	3.9	30,000	5.8
Lebanon	5,700	1.7	5,700	1.1
Sudan	7,000	2.1	21,000	4.1
Maghreb	41,000	12.3	65,600	12.7
Somalia	—	—	5,000	1.0
(All Arab)	(310,350)	(91.4)	(382,300)	(73.9)
Pakistan	4,500	1.4	25,000	4.8
India	500	0.2	17,000	3.3
Other Asian	500	0.2	10,000	1.9
(All Asian)	(5,500)	(1.8)	(52,000)	(10.0)
OECD & Europe	7,000	2.0	30,000	5.8
African & other	500	0.2	2,200	0.4
Turkey	9,000	2.6	52,000	9.9
Total	*332,350*	*100.0*	*518,500*	*100.0*

Source: S. Birks and C. Sinclair, 'Libya: Problems of a *Rentier* State', in Lawless R. and A. Findlay (eds.) *North Africa: Contemporary Politics and Economic Development* (Croom Helm, London, 1984).

partnerships was, therefore, linked with the objective of economic diversification.

Whilst it is inaccurate to describe the introduction of 'partnerships' as a 'cosmetic' reform, the producers' revolution was, however, a limited process. Partnerships were confined to Libyan workers, mostly in manufacturing and service industries. They were deliberately excluded from the oil industry, and their formation was kept separate from the large foreign workforce, whether free migrants or contract migrants. In the context of the Libyan economy, both are important omissions: oil is the principal source of the state's wealth and, to an enormous extent, growth relies on the labour of foreign workers. Between 1975 and 1980, the migrant labour force increased from 332,350 to 518,500.[13] At the same time, the Libyan workforce rose from 454,400 to 532,000.[14] In other words, the migrant workforce grew to virtual parity with the indigenous workforce. Moreover, in some sectors of the economy, notably in construction, the proportion of migrants was higher than 50 per cent. Libya was, therefore, acutely dependent on the wage-labour of non-nationals, who remained employees rather than equal partners.

Beyond the formation of 'partnerships' in the productive sector, further measures against the bourgeoisie, particularly its commercial sector, followed in the years 1980-81. As the merchants and industrialists shifted their assets into bank deposits, if not into cash, the authorities responded with a change in bank-notes. A date was set for the conversion of all old dinars at the banks; yet the banks were instructed to permit the withdrawal of no more than 100 dinars.[15] Any amount drawn in excess was placed in a frozen account and could only be used for specific purposes. Various attempts to circumvent the regulations, which had been in prospect since 1979, were dealt with under a law on 'economic crimes' introduced in 1981. Many merchants and traders had, in advance of the bank-note change, begun to convert their wealth into foreign currency holdings, or illicitly to transfer their monies abroad. Holdings in Libya had become vulnerable. If discovered, those who had tried to circumvent the regulations were placed on trial.

Even more radical was the introduction of partnerships within the distributive sector of the economy. All commercial enterprises, except individual or family proprietorships, were closed down and replaced by state-sponsored distributive organisations, controlled by workplace people's economic committees, according to the principles of 'partnership'. Entailed in the transformation was the closure of numerous privately-owned wholesale and retail outlets, including the *souks*, or markets, and the gradual introduction of 'people's supermarkets'. Following a programme approved by the GPC in Jaunary 1981, the People's Committee for Economy, meeting on 14 March, set a time-table for the phasing out of retail outlets: all textile, shoe and household appliance shops were required to withdraw from trading by 28 March; butchers by 30 April; and grocers by 31 December. Distribution was taken over by a newly-formed General

Marketing Company, which supplied the newly-constructed 'people's supermarkets', the most famous of which was the Tuesday Market, opened in 1981 by Qadhafi and Yasser Arafat.[16] Many of the items on sale in these outlets were heavily subsidised.

Opposition to the transformation of the commercial sector was widespread and manifested in instances of economic sabotage. In fact, the small traders, who had generally backed Qadhafi's leadership, joined the disaffection of the commercial bourgeoisie; Qadhafi thereby lost an important element of his domestic support. Again, as in 1978, the focus of the resistance of the merchants and traders was the mosque; *imams* were reported to have encouraged the boycott of the 'people's markets' and declared the take overs a violation of 'Koranic principles'. Initially compelled to delay the reforms, the revolutionary committees responded with a crackdown on the commercial resistance, and dozens of market traders were arrested and detained. Several *imams* were dismissed and, on rare occasions, mosques closed.[17] Sheikh Mohammed al-Bishti, a leading member of the *ulema*, was imprisoned and some of the more outspoken merchants, charged with illegal trading or corruption, were subjected to televised trials.

The Women's Movement

A campaign to involve women in the political process started concomitantly with the producers' revolution. Precipitating the campaign was a plea from Qadhafi for the creation of an agitational women's organisation that would aim to combat the social restrictions that excluded women from political and economic activity. Speaking at the same anniversary rally that had inaugurated 'the march on the factories', he pronounced that the time had come to emancipate the one section of society that was 'not yet free'.[18] Stated the Libyan leader: 'I declare that women are still enslaved and tied by serious social chains, and still suffer injustice because, unfortunately, until now there is no revolutionary tool capable of mobilising women for the revolution of their liberation.'[19] In fact, hand-picked women cadres had already been designated to form the nucleus of such an organisation. Following his speech, these announced the establishment of the Revolutionary Women's Formation, committed to combating the obstructions to political and economic activity for Libyan women.

There was no doubt that the organisation faced a daunting task. Libya had been one of the countries in the Arab world where women suffered most from social repression. Well into the 1970s, the majority of Libyan women continued to live as they had done under the Sanussis. They rarely left the home unless accompanied by their husband or a male relative, and the majority would appear on these occasions draped from head to foot in layers of cloth, with a veil that traditionally permitted sight for just one eye.

It was considered shameful for women to behave otherwise. Men even did the shopping so that women had no call to leave the house. Sold by her father to the highest bidder, a woman was treated as the personal property of the male and enjoyed no real legal rights within marriage. Adultery on the part of a woman was punishable by death. As a large family was a man's best guarantee of economic support in old age, the woman's role was predominantly that of childbearing. A poor man, in particular, would have to spend years saving up for the brideprice. Unable to afford other wives, he ruled the one he possessed with a rod of iron. The whole range of social pressures and customs stressed by local notables and the clergy, forced women to resign themselves to servitude and obedience.

The General Women's Federation
It is undeniable that Qadhafi has shown himself to be sensitive to these aspects of women's repression. In 1975 he sponsored the creation of the Libyan General Women's Federation, whose objective, as far as he saw it, was to alleviate the worst features of social repression. By 1979, the Federation was reported to have some twenty local branches. Their main work consisted in providing Libyan women with educational services and household assistance. The branches organised courses to help women overcome illiteracy, and helped girls enter school and university. They held classes in hygiene and baby-care, trained women in sewing, embroidery and pattern-making, and ran nurseries and kindergartens to relieve some of the burden on women at home. Due to the social conditions prevailing in Libya at that time, the Federation attracted only a small minority of women to its ranks, but its ambitions were spelt out in 1979 by Lutfia al-Gabayli, editor of the associated magazine *al-Beit* (The Home). Interviewed by the journalist Vittoria Alliata, she explained:

> Our first aims should be to create healthy families with progressive children. They should be brought up with the conviction that society can be just and honest. And this does not mean frustrating our individuality or giving up our own freedom to work and create. There is plenty of time for everything, as long as we respect the natural rhythms of life and do not abandon all for the sake of a career.[20]

The Federation has been aided by a number of social reforms, authorised by Qadhafi to increase the social and welfare provision for women. Health centres for mothers and children have been established to assist women from the time of conception until the child reaches the age of six. The facilities these centres offer extend to family planning, medical care prior to and during pregnancy, birth and lactation; advice on health and hygiene; baby-care and child education. The People's Committee for Health has also started a programme to supply towns with institutions called Social Care and Enlightenment Centres, which are more specialised in social work and community health. Staffed by Libyan social workers, the centres run courses in 'social education', conduct studies of local problems and intervene in domestic situations. Thirdly, day nurseries have been set up to enable Libyan women to seek work outside the home. In Tripoli there has been inaugurated a Centre for the Protection of Women, which is devoted to the rehabilitation of women such as divorcees, widows and family outcasts, who have no means of support besides crime and prostitution.

Deprived of education in Sanussi Libya, in the period of Qadhafi's leadership Libyan women have witnessed a proliferation of educational opportunities. Education is now free, and compulsory for all Libyans. The People's Committee for Education, like the pre-1977 Ministry of Education, is bound not to discriminate on the grounds of sex when granting stipends to university students. Special departments for women's literacy have been created within academic institutions, rural development centres and at Centres for Social Care and Enlightenment. Three Social Service institutes, one each for Tripoli, Benghazi and Sebha, provide technically qualified graduates with courses in the techniques of social work. At a special women's teacher training centre, 2,500 women enrol annually for a two-year training. Since 1969, the number of females within education has risen steadily throughout the system, most conspicuously at primary level, but progressively at the secondary and university levels.

In addition, the overall social position of Libyan women has been strengthened. Law No. 58, promulgated in 1970, affirmed the equal status of the sexes and wage parity for male and female workers in the same occupation. Law No. 172, decreed by the RCC in 1972, secured for Libyan women what it described as 'human rights'. The law stipulates that no marriage can be entered into, nor legalised by the authorities, unless the bride is at least 16 years old and the bridegroom 18. It also became compulsory that the bride, bridegroom and the legal guardians all consent to the marriage. If the guardians objected to the bride's choice of husband, she had recourse to a court, empowered to adjudicate and authorise the marriage against the guardians' wishes. Likewise, on petition, the court could also set the terms for divorce, with or without the consent of the legal guardians. Further legislation in 1973 extended social security provision to certain categories of women: widows, the infirm, divorcees over 40, the aged, and mothers of illegitimate children (where the father was unknown) became entitled to pensions. For the first time, the right to bear children was granted to women in employment. Women who had completed six months' employment were entitled to 50 days' maternity leave, daily cash benefits, and an extension of 30 days if the delivery was affected by complications. Women who had not completed six months' full-time employment were eligible for certain annual leave provisions.

In spite of these provisions, the numbers of women who have joined the workforce remain small. An educated minority of women from the urban middle classes has undoubtedly taken advantage of the new conditions, but the vast majority has not responded to official encouragement. In 1976, women in Libya comprised 48 per cent of the population; yet, 94.8 per cent of women of working age were not employed in work outside the home.

Just 35,385 women, out of a female working population of 680,415, were in paid employment. Admittedly, the General Women's Federation has some very able and gifted members such as Zahrah al-Felah, who became head of the Federation in 1977 and was one of the first women to participate in the proceedings of the GPC, or Nasahet Gritti, of the journal *al-Beit*, who speaks fluent English, French and Italian (as well as Arabic), drives a car and smokes in public (traditionally, not even adult men smoked in front of their elders).[21] But the advances achieved individually by these women and their like are exceptions rather than the rule. Older women, weighed down by years of social repression, are often the most resistant to social reform.

The Federation encountered persistent opposition to the changes arising from the preponderance of backward social relationships. Social obligations and dependence were such that families could successfully circumvent the marriage laws. To quote from the article by Vittoria Alliata:

> A Libyan girl may marry abroad, wear the latest fashions and dance until dawn, but when it comes to her future, the career of her choice will often be that of her grandmother. She will sell herself to the highest bidder, the man who can afford 10 to 20 pounds of gold jewellery and the traditional wedding costume of hand-woven silk with gold, who can offer her a luxurious home, and pay for a marriage ceremony, complete with orchestras, lasting for a week.[22]

The Revolutionary Women's Formation

It was because of the evident failure of the gradualist and educationalist approach of the Federation that Qadhafi came, in 1979, to launch the Revolutionary Women's Formation. This organisation, which began to crytallise in 1978 from some 30 *ad hoc* women's revolutionary groups, was a movement of women cadres, initially 300-strong, which would integrate the female population into the jamahiri system. The suppression of social backwardness, or at least the outward manifestations of discrimination, which preceded its inauguration, undoubtedly improved conditions for women, but the work of the Formation was hampered by political contradictions.

The third part of the *Green Book*, published in the summer of 1979 and expounding Qadhafi's views on social relations, is fundamentally ambiguous on the question of women. Explaining his conception of human relationships, Qadhafi affirms the family division of labour, emphasising a woman's role in reproduction; in other words, motherhood. Says Qadhafi:

> The flourishing society is that in which the individual grows naturally within the family and the family itself flourishes within society. The individual is linked to the larger family of mankind like a leaf to the branch of a tree. They have no value or life if separated. The same is the case for the individual if he is separated from the family, i.e., the individual without a family has no value or social life. If human society reached the stage where men existed without a family, it would become a society of tramps, without roots, like artificial plants.[23]

The *Green Book* asserts women's political and economic equality with men, but denies them complete social parity. On the one hand, Qadhafi stresses that it is a 'self-evident' fact that women and men are equal as human beings'; he states that 'work should be provided by the society to all able members–men and women–who need work.' On the other hand, he confirms that a woman's basic human role is one of domestic labour and child-bearing. He declares: 'Nothing else would be appropriate for man's nature, and would suit his dignity, except natural motherhood (i.e., the child is raised by his mother) in a family where the true principles of motherhood, fatherhood and brotherhood prevail.'[24] Natural law is invoked to show that a woman who avoids maternity is behaving irrationally. He argues:

> The mother who abandons her maternity contradicts her natural role in life. She must be provided with her rights and conditions which are appropriate, non-coercive and non-oppressive. Thus she can carry out her natural role under natural conditions. Anything else is a self-contradictory situation. If the woman is forced to abandon her role as regards conception and maternity, she falls victim to coercion and dictatorship.[25]

Women's repression is especially marked by the lack of reproductive rights. Libyan women have few means of exercising control over their fertility: there is no legal abortion or contraception in Libya, although both are available on the black market.[26] Traditional, male-orientated social pressures determine a high birth rate. A large family is one way of gaining long-term security and a man's prestige is commonly attached to the number of children he can father. The extended Bedouin family is Qadhafi's own model: accordingly, he placed the family at the hub of social relationships, and reproduction at the centre of the family. Women who reject the 'normality' of their child-bearing role are themselves regarded as abnormal in terms of Arab social norms. 'The woman who rejects marriage, pregnancy and motherhood, etc., because of work', concludes Qadhafi, 'abandons her natural role.'[27]

Reinforcing the social emphasis on motherhood is the political imperative to expanding the Libyan population so that the country can become self-sufficient in labour. The modernisation of social relations, which Qadhafi has tried to achieve through the development of the Women's Federation and the Revolutionary Women's Formation, is linked to the reorganisation of labour in a post-feudal society. The various social reforms, including the provision of social welfare for women, are intended to reduce the burden of reproduction placed on women; ensuring that women have access to clinics and health centres is beneficial for the growth of a healthy working population. The objective has been to increase the domestic productivity of women. For instance, in 1978, Qadhafi proposed the closure of bread shops and bakeries, important employers of male labour. Arguing that these enterprises constituted an unnecessary waste of labour, he argued that women should bake bread at home.

Women in Libya are not being encouraged to take on paid employment at the expense of child-bearing. On the contrary, Libyan women are being encouraged to engage in productive work *in addition* to child-bearing. This is the reason for some of the most favourable maternity conditions anywhere in the world. Yet, even within the workforce, there does still seem to operate a division of labour between men and women. The jobs to which women appear to be directed are those which are not likely to place constraints on their 'motherhood' roles. Qadhafi himself stresses that women should not enter jobs for which he deems them unsuited. 'Driving woman to do a man' work is unjust aggression against the femininity for which she is naturally provided for a natural purpose essential to life,'[28] he declares. 'If a woman carries out a man's work, she will be transformed into a man, abandoning her role and her beauty. A woman has full rights to live without being forced to change into a man and give up her femininity.'[29]

Notes

1. Details of the recruitment of the revolutionary committees can be found in Omar Fathaly and Monte Palmer, 'The Transformation of Mass Institutions', in G.H. Joffe and K.S. McLachlan (eds.) *The Social and Economic Development of Libya* (Menas Socio-Economic Studies, London, 1982).

2. Ibid.

3. P. Enahoro, 'Heart to Heart with Qadhafi', *Africa Now*, February 1983 pp. 37-46.

4. This incident is relayed by O. Fathaly and M. Palmer, 'The Transformation of Mass Instructions', 1981.

5. *Arab Dawn* (October 1978).

6. Ibid.

7. Ibid. Whilst the 'revolution' was essentially supervised by the committees, there were examples of an independent response from workers, notably in the service industries. At the same time, it is clear that the direction and contours of the revolution were set by the committees. In many plants where congresses were established, workers appeared to lack administrative and managerial skills, a factor which helped to generate a degree of confusion.

8. Qadhafi, Muamar, 'Democracy in Industry', text of an address delivered to a rally on International Workers' Day, 1 May 1978, *Arab Dawn Essays* (Arab Dawn, London, 1978)

9. Ibid.

10. For more information on planned and actual growth rates in Libyan industry, see Maja, Naur. 'The Industrialisation Model of the Socialist People's Libyan Arab Jamahiriya', a paper presented at the conference *Economic and Social Development of Libya,* SOAS, London, 1981: and Yusuf, Sayigh. *'The Economics of the Arab World: Development Since 1945* (St. Martins Press, New York, 1978). Figures here are from Naur.

11. S. Birks and C. Sinclair 'Libya: Problems of a Rentier State', in Lawless and Findley (eds.) *North Africa: Contemporary Politics and Economic Development* (Croom Helm/St. Martins, London, 1984) p. 264.

12. *Green Book,* p. 57.

13. Birks and Sinclair, 'Libya: Problems of a Rentier State'. p. 271.

14. Ibid., p. 266.

15. J. Davis, *Principle and Practice of Government in Qadhafi's Libya*, p. 71. Shows how the change in bank-notes was anticipated and circumvented; also, emphasises how measures are applied unevenly throughout Libya.

16. 'Merchants profiteering: an era comes to an end', *Arab Dawn* (May 1981).

17. For example, the mosque at Jughbub, the former site of the Sanussi Order's headquarters, was shut down following hostile preaching.

18. *Arab Dawn* (October 1978).

19. Ibid.

20. Vittoria Alliata, 'Open forum for women's issues', *Arab Dawn* (June 1979); first published in *The Middle East* (February, 1979).

21. Ibid.

22. Ibid.

23. *The Green Book*, p. 80.

24. Ibid., p. 95.

25. Ibid., p. 98.

26. Qadhafi comments: 'There is a deliberate intervention against conception which is the alternative to human life. In addition to that, there is a partial deliberate intervention against conception, as well as against breast-feeding. All these are links in a chain of actions against natural life' (*The Green Book*, p. 95).

27. Ibid., p. 103.

28. Ibid., p. 104.

29. Ibid.

11   The Conflict in Chad

Seeds of Discord

Under Qadhafi's leadership Libya has become deeply entangled in the affairs of its Southern African neighbour, Chad. In fact, the level of Libyan involvement in Chad has generally exceeded that in any other country. Libya has been an active participant in Chad's domestic upheavals since 1971 and has kept a military presence in the country since 1973. Despite the deployment of military units in Uganda in 1979, and the despatch of small contingents to Egypt in 1973 and Lebanon in 1982, it is only in Chad that Libyan troops have undertaken a decisive and prolonged military intervention. It is also only in Chad that the Libyan leadership has directly challenged the interests of a major power, namely France. The situation in Chad has always provided a central, and strategically important, focus in the conduct of Libyan foreign policy.

There are two conventional explanations for Libya's prolonged interest in Chad. The first concerns periodic but unconfirmed reports about Chad's potential mineral wealth, including possible deposits of uranium in the Tibesti mountains and oil in the northern desert areas; it is implied that Libya has increasingly asserted control in northern Chad to exploit these resources. The second explanation is more fanciful; it is claimed that Qadhafi has inflated designs on the whole of the north African region, and is trying to build up some kind of Saharan empire, similar to the zone of Sanussi trading influence in the last century.

Neither explanation provides an adequate understanding of Libya's motives. Characteristically, Libyan activity in Chad is opportunist and haphazard. There has never been any masterplan, just a series of responses to internal conditions in Chad. Chad's lack of centralised authority, due to strong regional and ethnic forces, has allowed Tripoli to promote its own interests. Of these, the most important has become control of the Aouzou Strip, a 40,000 square mile border zone. Under the 1935 unratified Franco-Italian Treaty, the Strip was assigned to Libya, but following the Second World War the French colonial authorities tried to integrate the zone within Chad. When France withdrew from the Fezzan in 1954 the monarchy effectively acknowledged the annexation with the conclusion of the 1955 Franco-Italian Treaty. Qadhafi, aiming to eradicate this legacy of colonialism, has utilised the conflict in Chad to restore Libyan sovereignty.

The border imposed by the French delineated no ethnic or religious divisions. Strong commercial, as well as both ethnic and religious, kinship tied together the inhabitants of northern Chad and southern Libya. Within the area of the Aouzou Strip the most populous ethnic group were the Tebu, 45,000 of whom were spread out over a wide expanse of territory, from Kufra in the north to the shores of Lake Chad in the south. Largely a nomadic people, their encampments were found over an area of 2,000 miles, but the vast majority was concentrated in the northern Ennedi area, especially that part encompassed by the Aouzou Strip.

The Tebu, converted to Islam by Ould Suleyman Sanussi in the late 19th century, were, nevertheless, not of Arab origin. Ethnically, the Tebu were black Caucasians and, despite their conversion to Islam, still retained much of their previous animist heritage and independent system of tribal authority. Divided primarily between northern Tedas and southern Dazas, and subdivided again in a clan structure, the Tebu all recognised the overall headship of a *Derde*, or judge, chosen from among notables of the Tomagra clan. Despite French colonial efforts to contain them within the colonial boundaries of Chad, the Tebu continued to migrate between Chad and Libya. Herding, the most widespread form of economic activity, was supplemented by trading with Libyan-based merchants. The Tebu, like the Sanussi tribes of Cyrenaica, had thrived from the caravan route that had once crossed the desert between West Africa and Sebha and Kufra in Libya, to the north.

These routes were the source of long-standing historical connections between the two countries. Just as the Tebu clans had migrated north, so had nomadic Arab tribes penetrated south from Libya and west from Darfur in the Sudan. The result was that, over a period of many centuries, Arab settlements had been established in Chad, and a series of Arab sultanates formed, especially in the northern and central areas south of the Tebesti range. Having extensively intermarried with the local, Equatorial African tribes, at the time of independence in 1960 the ethnic Arab population was estimated at 400,000,[1] the vast majority of whom were locally-born. Particular concentrations of Arabs could be found in the sultanates of Kanem-Bournou, Baguirmi and, most importantly, Ouaddai.[2] Nevertheless, many of the Arab population continued to owe forms of allegiance, political and religious, to the former lands–Libya and the Sudan. As Richard Adloff and Virginia Thompson note, in *Conflict in Chad,* published in 1981: 'Some Arabs retain close ties with their ancestors' homeland, as in the case of the Sanussi Fezzanese, who emigrated to Chad first to escape the Ottoman and then the Turkish conquerors of Tripolitania. As recently as the 1950s, the governor of the Fezzan reportedly owned animals and had vassals in Kanem.' Proof that these allegiances still counted after the take-over in 1969 is the fact that the Sanussi royalists made Chad the base of their planned 1972 operation to overthrow Qadhafi.[3]

Eight decades of French colonial control in Chad had, by 1960, failed to dissolve the various affiliations that united the northern peoples with their kinsfolk in Libya and the Sudan. The lines drawn on the map masked the artificiality of an entity called into being to serve French strategic interests. France had declared sovereignty over a broad expanse of territory, embracing heterogeneous groups of peoples, purely to consolidate its hold on equatorial West Africa. Chad, north and south, was – as it remains – a tribally structured society, composed of some 192 different ethnic groups. The French colonial authorities, preferring to rule through collaboration with local leaderships, such as the sultans in the centre and north and the tribal chieftaincies in the south, made no attempt to integrate the population within a unified national state; in other words, to create a Chadian nation. The French did, however, build the infrastructure of a Chadian state. With the exception of Abeche, all the towns in Chad began as French military outposts, and including the capital, Fort Lamy (later called Ndjamena), which evolved around a garrison established on the site of a Kikoto fishing village. The borders were also tinkered with, both in the north and the west, for security reasons. The objective was to bring the Tebesti mountains into the framework of Chad and, therefore, reduce cross-border migration by the Tebu, who proved to be the most independent and resistant to the colonial authorities of all the ethnic groups in Chad.

The French colonial authorities had no economic interests in Chad *per se*. Development was undertaken to defray the costs of colonial administration. The primary beneficiaries were the Sara people – at 1,300,000 strong, the most populous minority in the country. Located in five southern colonial prefectures of Mayo-Kebbi, Moyen-Chari, Logone Occidental, Logone Orientale and Tandjile, the Saras were in possession of the best arable land. Into these fertile areas the French introduced crops intended for export, above all cotton, which was found to be peculiarly suited to the local soil and climatic conditions. Plantations, called *cordes des chefs*, were worked by Sara farmers, organised and assigned export quotas for crop yields through the established system of tribal authority. In order to maintain a stable supply of labour for the plantations, the French eventually eradicated the slave trade which persisted well into the 20th century. Exported through outlets in the Camerouns and French Congo (and, to a lesser extent, British-colonial Nigeria) cotton production had risen to 28,000 tons in 1946 and was the main domestic source of revenue.[4] Such production rates became in themselves incentives for further investment by the metropolitan government, particularly after the Second World War, when hydraulic works, locust control and mechanisation were sponsored.

As a result, the Saras began their rise to political ascendancy. The *cordes des chefs* policy enhanced the power of the Sara chieftaincies *vis-à-vis* the Arab sultanates. The collaboration between the Sara chiefs and the colonial authorities in Njdamena became the main underpinning of the

Chadian state. Both accrued a surplus from the cotton production of the Sara farmers and co-operated to ensure the continuation of the system. Whilst the colonial authorities levied a head tax, the highest in French Equatorial Africa, on the individual farmer, the chiefs were, from the 1920s, permitted to retain a proportion of the crop for their own use. So much did the chiefs appropriate, however, that local rebellions broke out in the Ligone Occidental and Orientale areas. Much to the relief of the southern farmers, the French finally repealed the *cordes des chefs* policy in 1955, primarily because the practice of tributes had become fundamentally restrictive to the development of cotton production.

The subsequent decline of the chiefs coincided with the rise of the farmers and agricultural traders, whose interests were represented by the formation of the Parti Progressiste Tchadien (PPT). Founded by a black administrator from the French Antilles, Gabriel Lisette, this organisation was very similar to the model of the Parti Démocratique de la Côte d'Ivoire (PDCI) of Felix Houphouet-Boigny; that is to say, the party sought political independence, but remained nevertheless openly collaborationist towards metropolitan France. Although defeated in the 1952 elections to the territorial assembly, Lisette fought back and led the party to victory in 1957, following the aboltion of the *cordes des chefs* policy and the political assertion of the farmers that accompanied it. In 1957 Lisette became Chad's first Prime Minister and seemed destined to lead the country to independence, formally scheduled for 1960.

A power struggle within the PPT prevented that from happening. In May 1959, on the eve of independence, Lisette was ousted from within his party by a self-made Sara trader and protestant, François Tombalbaye, who had gradually extended his influence throughout the party during the 1950s.[5] In August, whilst Lisette was at a conference in Israel, Tombalbaye sent him a letter telling him not to return. Tombalbaye's action was subsequently endorsed by the Sara-dominated national assembly, accepted by the French, and he became in rapid succession head of government and head of state. His appointment symbolised a switch from the pan-francophone policies pursued by Lisette to policies of Chadian 'nation-building'. But since Tombalbaye's concept of a Chadian nation was essentially associated with the southern Saras, the consequence was the disaffection of the Arab and Tebu north, where the Parti National Africain (PNA) was formed by the Arab sultans and notables to rival the Sara PPT.

Essential to Tombalbaye's process of 'nation-building' was the centralisation of power in the hands of the presidency and the Sara-dominated bureaucracy, under his authority. Tombalbaye set out to create a one-party state and, in 1962, two other parties were banned: the PNA reluctantly accepted a merger with the PPT to form the Union pour le Progrès du Tchad (UPT). Those who opposed Tombalbaye, such as the Minister for National Education, Toura Gaba, were purged. In February 1962 the national assembly was dissolved, and it was announced that, in the forthcoming elections, the party with the majority of votes would assume control of all offices. Inevitably, this meant the UPT, which in 1964 became the official party of a declared one-party state. Henceforth, the assembly served as little more than a rubber stamp for Tombalbaye's highly personalised style of rule. Effective power was exercised through the UPT and its institutions, such as the Women's Auxiliary led by Kalthouma Guebang, and the party-controlled youth and labour organisations, whose leaders almost all came from the Sara-south.

Tombalbaye's monopoly of political power soon gave rise to resistance from the peoples of the north. This opposition was never cohesive, reflecting the fragmented tribal character of the area, but it proved resilient and enjoyed a degree of constancy. During the 1950s, an organisation named the Association des Enfants du Tchad was formed in Cairo, from which the Front de Libération du Tchad (FLT) split in 1964, chiefly along ethnic lines. Both organisations wanted to establish an Islamic Republic, but only the FLT, whose membership was virtually restricted to Ouaddians, was committed to armed struggle. Backed by the Muslim Brotherhood in Egypt and the Sudan, the organisation launched small-scale military raids against French and Chadian forces from bases in the Sudan. Much more significant than either group, however, was the Union Nationale Tchadienne (UNT). Inaugurated on the eve of the 1958 elections to the national assembly, and led by Arab and Muslim intellectuals, the organisation aimed to challenge French sponsored Sara domination. This the UNT duly did following Tombalbaye's crackdown on political opponents in 1962–63, beginning underground activity in preparation for an uprising in central and northern Chad, parts of which, especially the Borkou-Ennedi-Tebesti (BET) region, remained under French military administration in the period after independence, as they had done for much of the century.

The long-intended revolt became possible once the French had departed in January 1965. Tombalbaye's imposition of a southern military regime in place of the withdrawn French forces fomented popular unrest. In Mangalme, an isolated part of central Chad, peasants rioted against tax collectors. Ignited by this incident, rebellion spread rapidly eastwards through central Chad to Guera, Batha, Salamat and Ouaddai–an area inhabited by some 500,000 people. Marauding bands of rebels roamed the countryside, ambushing military patrols, attacking scattered military and administrative outposts, killing government collaborators and stealing their cattle. About the same time, in the northern Tebu areas, the southern military occupation also caused discontent. Relations between Tombalbaye and the Tebu *Derde*, already strained on account of Tombalbaye's refusal to appoint the son of the *Derde*, Goukouni Ouaddai, to a government post, deteriorated. In protest against the southern military occupation, the *Derde* uprooted himself from his headquarters in Bardai and, together with one thousand of his clansmen, exiled himself in Libya. There he stayed, the guest of King Idris, whilst the Tebu clans joined the rebellion against Tombalbaye.

In 1966 the revolt, which was of an erratic and diffuse nature, took on a broader political dimension. At a conference held in the Sudanese town of Nyala on 22 June 1966, the UNT, the FLT and other northern oppositionists formed a common front, the Front de Libération Nationale du Tchad, better known as Frolinat. The political programme agreed at the conference committed the new organisation to a struggle for liberation from Sara control, and the creation of a state in which sectarian privileges were abolished. The FLT group soon broke away, largely for sectarian reasons of the kind that Frolinat had been created to overcome, but the Front and the Nyala platform soon became the main poles of attraction for the northern opponents of Tombalbaye. If there was one man responsible for that success, it was Ibrahim Abatcha.

A former member of the UNT, Abatcha and his lieutenants, Djabalo Othman and Mohammed Ali Taher, led a peripatetic life, touring the world in search of support for a war of liberation. In Cairo he recruited followers from university students based there, and six of these accompanied him on a visit to North Korea, where all received six months' training in protracted guerilla warfare.[6] Returning to Chad via the Sudan in October 1965, Abatcha and his six 'Koreans', as they were nicknamed, were instrumental in promoting the revolt that began in Mangalme that year. Following the conference at Nyala, they created Frolinat's First Liberation Army. Touring Arab villages in eastern-central Chad, the Liberation army put into practice the political methods learned in Korea, inaugurating popular councils on which Liberation Army commanders and political organisers were equally represented. The First Liberation Army even made sorties into southern Chad, setting fire to cotton plantations and sabotaging communications.

Abatcha's death in combat in eastern-central Chad in 1968 robbed the Frolinat of its most formidable military leader and respected political exponent. The armed struggle, however, continued with Abatcha's lieutenants in the First Liberation Army. Mohammed Ali Taher spread Frolinat's operations into the Tebu areas, picking up support for the organisation in the Borkou, Ennedi and Tibesti (BET) region to the north. Following agitation by Taher, in March 1968 the Tebu Nomad Guard in Aouzou mutinied and slaughtered their southern officers. Tombalbaye, witnessing the revolt grow in intensity, responded by invoking the 1960 mutual defence treaty with France. The subsequent intervention in the north by the French forces soon restored the situation, forcing the surrender of the Tebu Nomad Guard in August. No sooner had French forces withdrawn in November, however, than the Tebu rose again . By late 1969, when Qadhafi toppled the Sanussi regime in Libya, Tombalbaye had lost control of all BET settlements except Faya-Largeau, Fada, Bardai and Ounianga-Kebir. The situation in the north was so out of hand, in fact, that the French decided to concentrate on putting down the revolt in the more strategically significant region of central Chad. Without any intervention on the part of Libyan forces, the whole of the Aouzou Strip had been liberated from Chadian government control.

Support For Frolinat

Libya was being sucked into involvement in Chad long before the Free Officer take-over in 1969. In 1966, Frolinat established an office in Sebha and began recruiting from Chadian students studying at the Islamic University at al-Beida.[7] Idris, however reluctantly, was compelled to show some sympathy towards his co-religionists among the Tebu and Arabs of Chad. The result was limited material aid for the insurgents, but no official recognition, no supplies of weapons. The latter came from Egypt and the Sudan, and sometimes Algeria, but not from Libya. Idris did not want to be drawn into the conflict further than was necessary, and strove at all times to maintain correct relations with the Chadian government. During the last few months of his reign, he made himself unpopular with the Frolinat leaders by his decision to sign with Tombalbaye's regime a series of cooperation agreements, which covered improved communications, the maintenance of Islamic institutions in Chad, and the status of Chadian workers in Libya.[8] The contentious issue of the border appears not to have been raised.

Qadhafi's support for Frolinat was discernibly stronger, but no less ambivalent. Whilst the new Libyan regime extended arms and funds, Qadhafi distanced himself from the line of confrontation put forward by Abatcha and his successors. Libya acted to promote within Frolinat the leadership of a more conservative figure, Abba Siddik, who was similarly favoured by King Idris. The son of a Chadian father and Central African mother, Siddik was one of the few Muslim founding members of the PPT. Between 1957 and 1959, he had served as Lisette's Education Minister, resigning after Tombalbaye's seizure of power. Joining Frolinat in 1967, Siddik emphasised a political solution based on national reconciliation rather than a war of liberation. As Frolinat's roving ambassador, he argued for a series of changes involving the withdrawal of foreign forces, fiscal and agrarian reform, parity of the French and Arabic languages, and the elimination of racial and religious discrimination. Siddik was, therefore, the ideal leadership candidate for the Libyan authorities who had no interest in promoting a sectarian or separatist solution that could become just as much a problem for them as for Tombalbaye. Qadhafi was in particular opposed to the creation of an independent Tebu entity that would resist Libyan claims to the Aouzou Strip, which he had begun to assert. He preferred a negotiated settlement that would recognise a Libyan sphere of interest in the north.

Qadhafi hoped to construct a unified liberation movement around Siddik, through which he could exercise influence in the Chadian conflict. The ethnically fragmented character of Frolinat, never a homogeneous organisation, made this extremely difficult to achieve. Frolinat's military forces even evolved along ethnic lines: there was the Arab-dominated First Liberation Army, which drew its support from the Arab population of central Chad; then there formed a Second Liberation Army, otherwise named the Forces des Armées du Nord (FAN), composed of Tebu from both the Tebesti mountains and the BET plains, which itself divided much along tribal lines. Siddik, the Libyan candidate, only had the allegiance of the First Liberation Army. Support from the Liberation Army, and its strongholds in eastern-central Chad, ensured his elevation to the post of General Secretary at the Third Consolidation Congress, held at Futra in August 1971, but his appointment without election was challenged by the Tebu leadership of the Second Liberation Army. Siddik's attempt at a conference of the military forces in Sebha that month to press ahead despite criticism only resulted in exacerbating the split. Backing Siddik, Libya responded by clapping in jail the leader of FAN, the *Derde*'s son, Goukouni Ouaddai. Such interference, however, merely widened the breach. During October 1972, following the release of Goukouni, FAN was reorganised independently at a conference in Gamour as the Conseil de Commandant des Forces des Armées du Nord (CCFAN), under the leadership of Hissene Habre, a member of the Anakaza clan of the Bourkou Tebu, who had supplanted Goukouni during his detention, and was to prove the most implacable of Qadhafi's Chadian opponents.

Libya's overt support for Siddik had meanwhile had its effect on relations with Tombalbaye. In August 1971, after the Third Consolidation Congress at Kufra, the Chadian President accused Qadhafi of subversion, and broke diplomatic ties. Qadhafi's swift repsonse was to grant Frolinat official recognition, and provide Siddik with office and radio facilities.[9] Tombalbaye's rejoinder, which came at a press conference on 8 September, was an announcement that he would give similar facilities to those forces seeking Qadhafi's overthrow. Indeed, the 1972 Abdullah Sanussi plan to invade Libya from Chad indicated that his offer was serious; Sanussi officials were known to have visited Chad in their preparations for the conspiracy. Tensions were in fact escalated by both sides, but inasmuch as direct conflict served the purpose of neither Qadhafi nor Tombalbaye, the intention was to coax a political accommodation. Soon both sides pulled back from the brink. Qadhafi, negotiating for French Mirage jets, proposed mediation. Tombalbaye, wanting security rather than instability on his northern border, was favourably disposed. With Hamami Diori, President of Nigeria, acting as an intermediary acceptable to both sides, talks finally commenced early in 1972.

What transpired was a remarkable period of collaboration between Libya and Chad. A communiqué issued in Niamey on 12 April 1972, stating that both countries agreed to resume diplomatic relations, presaged the quick withdrawal of the Frolinat leadership from Tripoli to Algiers. The move reduced Tombalbaye's objections to an agreement, but Qadhafi held out until Chad had severed all its links with Israel, including the services of Israeli military advisers. Only when that was accomplished, during November 1972, did a settlement become possible. A formal treaty, recognising the principle of a Chadian-Libyan 'zone of solidarity', was finally signed on 23 December during a state visit Tombalbaye paid to

Libya.[10] Whilst the precise boundaries of that zone were undefined, there was no doubt that it was the Aouzou Strip that was intended. Tombalbaye could not go beyond this concession because he did not possess the constitutional authority to cede Chadian territory, although it is widely acknowledged that he did in private concur with Libyan control of the Strip. In 1973 Libyan troops moved into the area under cover of the treaty, and they have remained in occupation ever since. In exchange, the Libyans completely renounced their support for Frolinat and extended to Chad's government development credit worth 23 billion CFA francs.[11] Repaying Tombalbaye's visit in March 1974, Qadhafi announced the formation of a joint bank to provide the country with investment funds, lessening Chadian dependence on France – or so Qadhafi hoped.

Tombalbaye's downfall in 1975 brought an end to this unusual period of cooperation. Ousted on 13 April 1975 by leaders of the Chadian armed forces, predominantly southerners, Tombalbaye was succeeded by a military junta called the Conseil Supérieur Militaire, committed, with French backing, to the goal of an internal rather than external settlement. The head of the junta, General Felix Malloum, a southerner, had no intention of endorsing the Libyan take-over of the Aouzou Strip. A number of overtures from Tripoli, including a visit to Ndjamena by Libyan Foreign Secretary Dr Ali Treiki, failed to persuade him otherwise. As the Tebu and Arab leaders were showing opposition to the Libyan take-over, Malloum's strategy was to seek a compromise with those amongst them amenable to a negotiated solution. Both Siddik and Habre greeted his assumption of power with some optimism, and showed willingness to accept negotiations. The clash between Habre's fighters and Libyan troops in northern Chad in June 1976 indicated that Malloum was on his way to achieving some form of internal settlement without Libyan involvement.

Qadhafi hoped that Malloum, like Tombalbaye, could be brought to terms. Aiming to demonstrate that Libya could not be excluded from influence in Chad he commenced a policy of rapprochement with CCFAN, the Tebu dominated section of Frolinat. In doing so, he was fortunate to be able to exploit a rift between Habre and Goukouni, respectively leader and deputy leader of CCFAN, over the incident of the Claustre kidnappings. Goukouni and Habre disagreed on the release of several hostages seized by CCFAN forces in northern Chad, notably Madame Françoise Claustre, a French archaeologist, Pierre Claustre, her husband, captured trying to secure his wife's freedom, Dr Steaman a German missionary, and a technician of the French Mission of Administrative Reform.

Goukouni took the more conciliatory approach of arguing that CCFAN should accept a Libyan offer of mediation with France, but Habre refused to deal with Libya whilst it was in possession of the Aouzou Strip. The ordeal, which in the case of Madame Claustre lasted for three years, was only ended when Goukouni toppled Habre at a meeting of CCFAN forces in Yebbi-Bou on 18 October 1976, and paved the way for Libyan mediation. The hostages were finally handed over to the UN Secretary-

General by Qadhafi at a ceremony in Tripoli on 29 January 1977. Goukouni and Qadhafi had by that time agreed to put their past differences behind them.

Goukouni, despite his evident reservations about Qadhafi's erratic policy, now became the chief beneficiary of Libyan support. His forces, suitably reorganised and strengthened by new Libyan supplies, launched an offensive against Malloum's government, calling the military administration 'retrogressive and dictatorial.' Sweeping through Borkou-Ennedi-Tibesti he swiftly re-captured Bardai (which had been captured by government forces) driving Malloum's army out of Zouar and Ouri, taking prisoner some 350 southerners, and finally he establishing himself as the effective leader of Frolinat. The remnants of the First Liberation Army abandoned Siddik, regrouped as the Volcan Army under the command of Ahmed Acyl, the most pro-Libyan of the Chadian rebel leaders, and at a meeting in Karangua in August 1977, formed the Conseil Provisoire de la Révolution. The way was thus prepared for a merger with Goukouni with the formal expulsion of Siddik, accused, in a conciliatory gesture, of discriminating against Tebu fighters during his tenure as General Secretary.[12] Habre was similarly ousted from CCFAN as Goukouni strengthened his overall authority within the organisation.

Both deposed leaders soon became subject to Malloum's appeals for an internal solution. Siddik, persuaded to talk, met with Malloum's representatives in Geneva and Khartoum. He eventually agreed to co-operate in December 1977 at a meeting chaired by President Bongo of Gabon, on condition that he was made Vice-President, that all political prisoners were released, and the armed forces purged of officers who had engaged Frolinat forces in combat. The talks were broken off as being totally unacceptable to Malloum, and Habre became the focus of the government's hopes. He proved much less demanding than Siddik. Based at Fada with several hundred of his clansmen, Habre was ready to make an alliance with Malloum against the Libyans, whom he blamed for his overthrow. An agreement between his forces – which retained the name FAN – and the government was signed in Khartoum on 5 February 1978, committing Malloum to an amnesty for political prisoners, the formation of a government of national unity' within two months, the election of a constituent assembly and the reorganisation of the armed forces, but *not* the removal of officers who had fought Frolinat, a condition which Malloum could not have met. In the circumstances, the deal was an important victory for Malloum's strategy; he had neutralised a major guerrilla leader and secured the frontier with the Sudan, Habre's main political backer.

Nevertheless, Malloum was forced by Goukouni's victories in northern Chad to accept negotiations with Libya. Like Tombalbaye before him, he found that the internal settlement depended on an external agreement. He therefore accepted a Libyan invitation to an all-party conference on Chad convened in Sebha on 24 February 1978. The result of this meeting was an agreement to call a ceasefire for 10 April, signed by the three heads of state concerned–Qadhafi, Malloum and Diori of Niger. Goukouni, under duress from Libya, approved the pact for Frolinat. In exchange for the pressure that the Libyans had evidently exerted on Goukouni, Malloum climbed down on the question of the Aouzou Strip, and soon withdrew official complaints about Libya that his government had lodged with the UN. A subsequent re-convened meeting of the various parties in Sebha concluded with nominal recognition of Frolinat.[13] But whilst this was a political face-saver for Qadhafi, who had pledged full support for Goukouni, there was no hiding the fact that the real effect of the Sebha agreements was to isolate Frolinat.

Goukouni, however, was not without some independent means to influence the situation and rid himself of the debilitating Sebha accords. Five days after the 10 April ceasefire deadline, he launched an all-out offensive against Malloum. Pressing southwards, in May Frolinat was within striking distance of the capital. The failure of Malloum to honour his commitment, agreed at Sebha, to renounce all military treaties with France prior to the ceasefire provided Goukouni with the pretext to revive the conflict. A third Libyan-sponsored peace conference, planned for Tripoli in June, never took place. The Libyans, just as much as Malloum, were dismayed with Goukouni's action. The turn of events, however, soon compelled them to come down on the side of Frolinat.

What forced Qadhafi back behind Frolinat was French military intervention. Faced with the rout of the regular army, a predominantly conscript force of 3,000 southerners, Malloum invoked the Defence Pact with France. The French seized the opportunity to re-establish their waning influence in Chad; strikes by French airforce Jaguar bombers, flying sorties against Frolinat forces advancing down the road from Abeche to Ndjamena, rapidly brought the offensive to a halt. Defeated in a key battle at Ati, site of a French army garrison, the Volcan Army of Ahmed Acyl fled, leaving quantities of Libyan-supplied weaponry on the battlefield. With the retreat of the Volcan Army, recriminations with Frolinat resurfaced along ethnic Tebu and Arab lines: Goukouni and Acyl split, and Frolinat once again succumbed to internal power struggles. Adding to the process of disintegration was the advent of the Third Liberation Army, led by Abu Bakr Abdul Rahman. Backed by Nigeria, and based in the Nigerian border region, the formation of this new force indicated a growing Nigerian interest in the Chadian conflict. Even among the Saras there arose new divisions; riots against Malloum's junta broke out in the areas of Lere and Pala, Mousoro and Mongo, undermining Malloum's ability to exploit the fragmentation within Frolinat.

There was one chief beneficiary of the turmoil that engulfed Chad: Hissene Habre. Enjoying the backing of the Egyptian and Sudanese governments, largely because of his anti-Libyan stance, Habre had built up a capable military force in eastern Chad, yet had abstained from the fighting between Goukouni and Malloum. Always the opportunist, Habre waited until Goukouni's military threat had receded before committing himself to the CSM. Once he had done so, however, he moved swiftly to fill the political vacuum in Chad. Appointed Premier in the government of national unity proposed under the Khartoum agreement concluded between Malloum and Habre shortly after the latter's overthrow by Goukouni, there was no hiding the fact that the real effect of the Sebha consolidating his internal position, by placing his own supporters in key administrative posts. By 1979, having prised out many pro-Malloum officials, he was challenging the CSM's overall power. Evidence that he was syphoning off arms from the national arsenal for FAN, as well as conniving with French military officials, created daily suspicions that he was planning a military *coup*, and generated unrest within the Sara peoples. In opposition to the Malloum-Habre alliance, a Sara opposition movement was formed in the south under the leadership of Wadel Abdul Kader Kamougue.

Events soon demonstrated that Sara fears were justified. On 12 February 1979, FAN tried to stage a *coup d'état*. After two days of fighting, FAN units had seized the African quarter of Ndjamena and gained control of the radio station; sections of the regular army joined the flight southwards by much of the Sara population of Ndjamena. Most resistance came from gendarmes loyal to Kamougue's organisation, but a total Habre victory was only avoided by the surprise intervention of Goukouni. Having recovered from his defeats of the previous year, Goukouni launched his regrouped forces southwards. Safe passage was granted by the French military commanders at Mousoro and Ati. His timely arrival in the capital deprived Habre of the victory that had seemed to be within his grasp. The stalemate that resulted was only broken by Nigerian mediation: a conference was convened at Kano in March 1979, and attended by all the major participants, broke the deadlock with an agreement imposed on the parties by Libya and Nigeria. Under the terms of the agreement, which was signed by Habre, Goukouni, Abdul Rahman and Malloum, all the parties to the conflict were bound to the establishment of a new constitution, the release of prisoners, impartiality of radio broadcasts, the demilitarisation of Ndjamena, acceptance of an external control commission, and the creation of a provisional government pending elections.

The composition of such a government proved the most contentious issue. The first Kano conference in March 1979 failed to resolve the distribution of government posts. Bargaining at a second Kano conference in April finally produced a government under Mahamout Choua Lol, a member of the Nigerian-backed Third Liberation Army, but his appointment was clearly no more than a stop-gap solution. Lol was never more than a figurehead, whose position depended entirely on power-broking between Habre and Goukouni. Both leaders divided the posts between themselves: Goukouni became Interior Minister and Habre became Defence Minister. The Sara General Djogo was appointed Vice-President and Commander-in-Chief of the armed forces, but Kamougue and the Nigerian favourite, Abdul Rahman, and the Libyan favourite, Ahmed Acyl, were excluded from office. So incensed with this display of independence was the Nigerian President, General Ironsi that he abruptly pulled out Nigerian troops monitoring the ceasefire in Ndjamena and closed the road to Chad. Feeling equally betrayed, Libya responded by strengthening Acyl's Volcan Army. United in their opposition to the Habre-Goukouni regime, all six of Chad's neighbours met in Lagos between 26-27 May and set a 25 June deadline for the incorporation of 'other elements' into the government, which they claimed was too narrowly based to carry out the Kano accords.[14]

In some respects that assessment was correct. The Goukouni-Habre regime did face a number of challenges from those parties they had excluded from participation in the government. In May, Habre's FAN forces, despatched to crush a southern rebellion in Mayo-Kebbi, were defeated by fighters loyal to Kamougue. On 2 June, a Front d'Action Commune Provisoir was formed as an alternative administration by all the opposition organisations under the auspices of Libya and Nigeria. Through this Front d'Action, Libya extended its support to Kamougue's group and Acyl's forces, which soon afterwards advanced into the BET and took Salamat. At the same time, the Third Liberation Army, from bases in the Nigerian border area, launched an unsuccessful attack on Ndjamena. By the end of July, the Lol government had collapsed, as both the Nigerians and Libyans intended it should, making way for a new conciliation conference in Lagos.

The settlement that emerged from the Lagos conference bore the imprint of both Libya and Nigeria. For the first time, all the parties to the conflict were present at the same negotiating table. Although under obvious pressure from the conference-backers, much greater agreement prevailed among the various factions than before. The biggest single cause was the defeat of a FAN expeditionary force sent into southern Chad to put down Kamougue's rebellion. The setback suffered by Habre's forces in fighting with those of Kamougue meant that Habre's position in the negotiations at Lagos was weakened; the southern Saras refused to accept the re-imposition of a regime controlled by Habre. Goukouni's star, on the other hand, was in the ascendant. He was preferred by the southerners, and had the backing of Kamougue against Habre. He had also increased his prestige by a string of minor victories over Libyan forces, when they had advanced into the BET behind Acyl and the Front d'Action. Due to the change in the balance of forces, the Lagos meeting awarded Goukouni the presidency of a newly proposed interim administration until elections were held. The other posts in the administration, called the Government of Unity and National Transition (GUNT) were distributed among the clients of Chad's neighbours. Several Libyan candidates received portfolios: Ahmed Acyl became Foreign Minister, Abba Said became Interior Minister, Abba Siddik (back in favour) Minister of Higher Education and Adem Dama Minister of Public Works. In addition, at the insistence of the conference-backers, an eighteen-month time limit was placed on the provisional government, whilst supervision of GUNT's mandate was entrusted to the OAU. After a decade of entanglement in Chad, Qadhafi had at last obtained the kind of agreement he wanted. Given the internal divisiveness of Chadian society, however, could it survive?

Direct Intervention

In practice, the Government of Unity and National Transition (GUNT) constituted the government of Chad for just under two years. The administration, whose existence was always tenuous, was finally overthrown on 7 June 1982, when FAN forces under the command of the country's erstwhile Defence Minister, Hissene Habre, stormed Ndjamena and decisively established control. Ethnic tension undoubtedly contributed to this victory, but the chief contributory factor was the support for Habre which came from outside sources, particularly the Reagan administration, which saw Habre's army as a surrogate force in the US conflict with Libya. The CIA itself has since admitted in a closed briefing that its operations played a significant part in ousting GUNT. The Washington-based correspondent Jeremy Campbell, reporting in the London *Standard* on 28 June 1983, wrote that 'Leaders of the central African republic of Chad were toppled by a rebel army covertly supported by the CIA, while the US publically committed itself to end the fighting.' Quoting from secret testimonies, Campbell disclosed that the CIA was supporting Habre with arms and training to the tune of ten million dollars.[15]

Habre, who was re-appointed Defence Minister under the Lagos accords, had broken with GUNT in early 1980. Joining him were two Sudanese-backed Ministers, Hadjero Sanussi and Mohammed Saleh.[16] By the time at which they defected, the cabinet had met only once, no political reforms had been achieved, and there had been no progress towards the integration of the various armies. Nor had the OAU honoured its obligation to provide a military force to uphold the government's mandate. Habre, whose intransigence in government helped to create the deadlock, decided that the moment was propitious to challenge Goukouni for power. On 12 January 1980 FAN struck at Goukouni's forces in Ouaddai and captured the town of Am Dam. A showdown between Goukouni, the Tebu mountain leader and Habre, the plains Tebu leader, one backed by Libya, the other by the Sudan, was imminent. Sporadic fighting erupted around Ndjamena, where contingents of five Chadian factional armies were based. Whilst such clashes in the capital continued during February and March, Habre's main group of forces in the area around Ouaddai prepared for an offensive. On 16 March they commenced their advance towards Ndjamena, but were halted by Goukouni's forces at Bokoro and Mongo, to the north of the city. On 1 April Kamougue's forces from the south tried to drive

FAN from the capital, but were repulsed with heavy losses at the bridge over the river Chari.[17]

Four ceasefires came into effect and four ceasefires broke down. A fifth attempt by President Eyedema of Togo, crossing the river Chari in a dug-out in early April to negotiate between the factions, fared no better. After its collapse into renewed fighting on 9 April, the GUNT cabinet met and decided to dismiss Habre, Mohammed Saleh and Hedjero Sanussi, none of whom were present. Rejecting further ceasefire initiatives, Goukouni declared that the conflict would be resolved militarily. However, he lacked the same sort of military assistance Habre was receiving from Egypt and Sudan. By June, Habre's fortunes were evidently on the rise. He was even secure enough to tour the West to obtain political support, claiming in his visits to European capitals that FAN was in control of Oum Hadjer, Ounianga-Kebir and Faya-Largeau.[18]

GUNT lasted as long as it did simply because of Libyan military intervention, the factor that saved the administration from certain disaster in the closing months of 1980. Faced with Habre's seemingly inexorable march through the Tebu strongholds in the BET, Goukouni, grew so desperate that he resorted to Libya for assistance. The fall of Faya-Largeau on 9 June, cutting his lines of communication with Bardai, was the last straw. Despite opposition from Kamougue, he travelled to Tripoli and, following talks with the Foreign Liaison Bureau, signed a Treaty of Friendship with Libya.[19] Soon afterwards, Goukouni invoked the Treaty's clause on military cooperation. The Libyan armed forces responded that September by mounting a military operation to rescue GUNT from its predicament. Libyan troops were first deployed in October and moved quickly into the offensive. By November, they had driven FAN from Faya-Largeau and other areas of northern Chad. Habre's troops had no answer to the bombing runs of the Libyan air force. The FAN contingent in Ndjamena was ultimately vanquished in December, but further and protracted engagements continued in the eastern part of the country, notably in the area around Abeche. During these clashes, Libyan armed forces suffered some serious losses, mainly from skirmishes, but were mobilised in such numbers that this could not affect the final outcome. At the peak of the fighting, an unprecedented 14,000 troops were involved in operations – 7,000 regulars and 7,000 members of the Islamic Legion.

Some 2,000 remnants of Habre's erstwhile 4,000-strong army took refuge in western Sudan. This did not deter the Islamic Legion from launching a series of cross-border 'hot pursuit' raids on their scattered guerrilla camps in Darfur province, from where they mounted minor attacks on Libyan patrols and outposts in the area near Abeche. The Libyans finally called a halt to such operations after President Sadat had threatened that 'if one Libyan soldier enters Sudan, Egypt will act with its own forces'. Speaking in Tripoli in March 1981, Qadhafi responded: 'We have no wish to send out troops beyond Chad. We are bringing all confrontations to an end, including the one with Sadat's army.' By that time a local rebellion had erupted in Darfur province over the appointment of a non-Darfuri governor in al-Fasher. Thus, Habre's battered army gained a reprieve, but one that was to cost Libya dearly.

Libyan Motives

The motives behind the Libyan intervention in Chad are often misconstrued. Although a proposal for a merger between the two countries was tentatively put forward, there was no implication that Libya intended to absorb the country within the Jamahiriya. As with Tombalbaye, the essential objective was to sustain a government in Ndjamena that would accommodate Libya's strategic interests, primarily the Aouzou Strip.[20] How that was arranged was, as far as the Libyans were concerned, open to negotiation. Qadhafi was aware that any attempt to enforce a solution could drag Libya into a war of attrition, carrying with it hazardous domestic repercussions. The military operation was conceived as an emergency and temporary measure, to prevent a regime hostile to Libyan interests taking over in Ndjamena. The Libyans were committed to withdrawing once the OAU had assembled the mandate force it had initially pledged. When assurances to this effect were prised from the organisation at the Nairobi summit in 1981, the Libyans agreed to pull out. Libya was in exchange nominated to host the 1982 OAU summit conference. One of the main obstacles to the provision of an African peace-keeping force, lack of OAU funds, was overcome when the Mitterrand government in France extended some assistance.[21] Libyan troops commenced their departure on 2 November 1981, their tasks deemed completed. Officially welcomed back in Libya on 28 November, they were accorded a victory parade through the streets of Sebha, where Qadhafi, flanked by Yasser Arafat and Polisario General Secretary Mohammed Abdul Aziz, took the salute.[22]

An additional factor prompting the withdrawal was the animosity that had developed between Goukouni and his Libyan rescuers. Once GUNT's position had been secured by Libyan military action, Goukouni entered into increasing collaboration with the Mitterrand administration. He came under gradual pressure from the Elysée and from francophone states in West Africa to revoke the mandate for the Libyan military presence and turn towards France for protection. Goukouni, who had his own objections to the Libyan hold on the Tebu-populated Aouzou Strip, was inclined to accept such advice, and colluded with the French government to bring about a Libyan withdrawal.[23] When the arrangements for an OAU force were completed, he complied and revoked the mandate. The Libyans, lured by a French decision to lift an arms embargo put in place by President Giscard d'Estaing, duly departed. Goukouni, who had been promised French military and financial assistance to reconstruct Chad, trusted his fate to a force raised from states that had very little interest in his political survival.

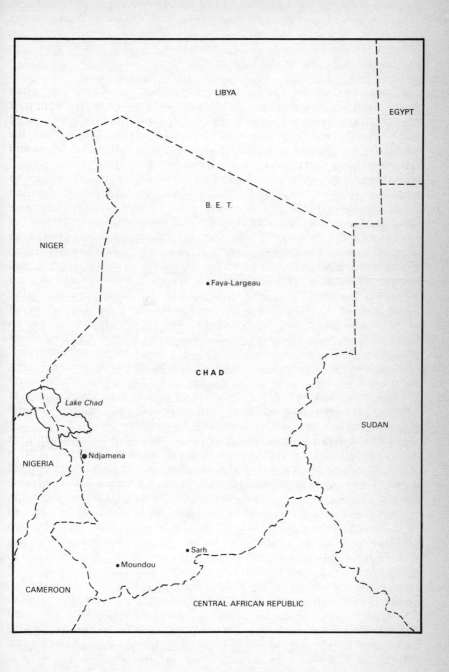

Events soon proved that this trust in the OAU was greatly misplaced. Habre, though down, was not out. His army, rebuilt by the CIA in the Sudan, rose again like a phoenix from the ashes.[24] When the Libyan withdrawal took effect in November, FAN units moved openly back into the area around Abeche. By early 1982, they were re-established across Ouaddai and poised for a major push down the road from Abeche to Ndjamena. Against their advance, the OAU forces took no counter-action. When Goukouni's forces were defeated on 5 June, at the battle of Massaguet, some fifty miles north of the capital, the President himself was unable to rally the OAU forces to the defence of the city. Routed at Massaguet, his own units retreated northwards in the direction of their Tebesti homeland. Thirty-six hours later–on 7 June–Habre's fighters entered the capital unopposed by OAU forces, which maintained a stance of strict neutrality.[25] Goukouni, crossing the river Chari to the Camerouns, eventually fled to Libya.

On this occasion, however, the Libyan authorities decided not to intervene. Goukouni's earlier switch of allegiance was clearly an influence on their decision, but domestic considerations also seemed to rule out a second military intervention in Chad. According to Qadhafi, some 300 Libyan soldiers were killed in the 1980–81 offensive against Habre, though taking the Islamic Legion into account, the figure was probably much higher. A further offensive would most likely prove even more costly in terms of casualties. Libya, due to host the 1982 OAU summit, wanted to secure wider African backing to re-impose the Lagos accords.

Goukouni's status as the OAU-recognised Head of State of Chad was essential if the Lagos settlement was to be restored. The GUNT President was therefore given passage to Bardai, and supplied with radio and diplomatic facilities. Ahmed Acyl, the pro-Libyan Foreign Minister, was believed to be on the point of joining him when, on 19 July, he was killed in the southern town of Lai,[26] reportedly having been felled by an aeroplane propeller. Camerouns radio, releasing news of his death, maintained that the circumstances were not mysterious. It was indeed, unusual, however, that his successor, Sheikh Ben Omar, should entertain the idea of talks with Habre. These had commenced between Habre and the southern leader, Vice-President Kamougue; Ben Omar, as the new leader of the Volcan forces, was invited to participate. The south was not yet firmly under FAN control and Habre, playing on Kamougue's earlier opposition to Libyan intervention, hoped he would acquiesce in his take-over. The negotiations, no more than preliminary contacts, were broken off some time in August, by which time it had become clear that there was no prospect of reconciliation. Kamougue, whilst retaining a large degree of autonomy, continued to align himself with GUNT and the Lagos accords, and had, by the end of the year, begun to mend his fences with Libya.

Qadhafi aimed to have the 1982 OAU summit in Tripoli re-endorse GUNT as the legitimate government of Chad. He was encouraged in this view by the fact that Libya, as the host country, was in a position to influence invitations and the agenda. His judgement could not have been more wrong. Libya's attempts to convene the OAU summit in Tripoli proved disastrous: on two occasions, in August and again in November, Libya failed to obtain the two-thirds quorum necessary for the summit. The first was aborted because of a boycott over the Polisario (Chad was not represented); the second foundered on who should assume Chad's seat at the conference–Goukouni or Habre's Foreign Minister, Idris Miskine. Over a third of the African countries refused to attend unless the seat was allocated to Miskine; they even rejected Qadhafi's compromise offer that the seat be kept vacant. The controversy that resulted split the continent between the pro-Western states and the nationalist regimes. Habre suddenly found himself acclaimed by the pro-Western camp because of his deep antagonism towards Qadhafi. At the Vittel summit of francophone states in 1983 Mitterrand, who had previously pledged French support for GUNT, obligingly demonstrated French support for Habre.

Nevertheless, Qadhafi continued to cast about for some sort of diplomatic settlement based on the principles of the Lagos accords. In April 1983 he embarked on a tour of West Africa to sound out support for the agreement. He visited Nigeria, Benin and Upper Volta–all with governments that could be considered broadly sympathetic–and elicited favourable responses in each case. Most importantly, President Shehu Shagari of Nigeria signed a communiqué which committed both countries to 'reconciliation among the Chadian brothers as a foundation for a lasting peace in the country'.[27] Qadhafi is believed to have approached President Eyedema of Togo next in the hope that he would agree to resume the role of intermediary. Habre would have none of it. His defiance was indicated by a number of skirmishes that took place between FAN and Nigerian troops over a disputed border on Kinasura Island on Lake Chad between 18 April and the end of May.[28] As for Libya, Habre lodged complaints about the Libyan presence in the Aouzou Strip with both the UN Security Council and the OAU Secretariat. Emboldened by the financial and military assistance that he was receiving from the Reagan administration, Habre was in no mood for compromise.

Qadhafi fell back on the strategy of military pressure that he had successfully applied against both Tombalbaye and Malloum. Goukouni's forces, strengthened by Libyan supplies, had already begun to launch minor operations within the BET. In December 1982, they drove FAN out of Goura. Brimming with confidence, Goukouni declared in a statement on 24 March: 'When we return to Ndjamena we will be able to address ourselves fully to the construction of a progressive and revolutionary society, in order to pull our people out of misery, ignorance and exploitation.'[29] In April FAN claimed Ounianga-Kebir. Following the collapse of Qadhafi's diplomatic initiative, these operations were dramatically escalated. Habre's army suffered heavy casualties in engagements in the region of Dourbali, 150 miles to the east of the capital, as well as in attempts to retake Goura. Speaking at Cotonou in the Ivory

Coast, an adviser to Habre, Dr Facho Balam, admitted that the regime had endured 'a very serious defeat at Goura.'[30] He disclosed that out of a force of 1,700 men, FAN had lost 394 men, of whom 142 had been killed, and 252 taken prisoner. The see-saw of Chadian political fortunes was swinging back in Goukouni's favour.

Keeping Habre in power, however, became a vital test of the Reagan administration's commitment to help friendly pro-Western leaders in trouble. To sustain his regime the United States strove to mobilise Western support. The device used was a propaganda campaign alleging that the Libyans were mounting an invasion of Chad. Towards the end of May 1983, the Egyptian and Sudanese regimes, evidently collaborating with Habre and the United States, charged that Libya was poised for a major military thrust into Chad. On 1 June the State Department deliberately tried to give credence to these claims with a statement that the United States was 'seriously concerned about an upsurge of Libyan military action in northern Chad.' Some limited logistical involvement there was, but of a Libyan offensive, there was no evidence. Nevertheless, the assertions of Libyan military action continued, reaching fever pitch in August 1983, as Goukouni's forces, albeit equipped with Libyan-supplied Soviet-made tanks, assembled for an assault on the key crossroads town of Faya-Largeau.[31] As the Reagan administration constructed an air-bridge to supply Habre with arms and advisers, Libyan units joined the battle for Faya-Largeau in an attempt to pre-empt external military intervention on Habre's behalf.

Zaire had already agreed to send Habre 760 reinforcements, and France was coming under strenuous American pressure to resume its former military role in Chad.[32] The Reagan administration created a crisis of West African confidence out of the issue of Habre's defence in order to induce French military intervention. Clearly irritated by the Reagan administration's tactics, the French Foreign Minister Claude Cheysson angrily riposted: 'We do not submit to American desires. We have no reason to act only with the Americans or systematically with the Americans.' But submit France did. Faced with the prospect of francophone states, such as Zaire, Senegal and the Ivory Coast, turning to the United States for military aid, France yielded to the intense pressure.[33] As the fall of Faya-Largeau became imminent, Mitterrand responded with the deployment of French paratroopers stationed in the Central African Republic. An initial force of 65 paratroopers arrived on 10 August, on the eve of Goukouni's seizure of the key northern town, and within the weeks that followed larger units were added, bringing the total force up to some 3,000 men. The operation appeared timed so that France would not be obliged to participate in the defence of Faya-Largeau (which was subsequently renamed Faya-Abatcha, after the founder of Frolinat).

The immediate consequence of the French operation was a political and military impasse. The French government resisted demands for a counter-offensive and the expeditionary force, equipped with no more than light armoured cars, adopted a purely defensive role. French forward positions were established at Salal and Abeche, demarcating a line which effectively divided the country between Goukouni and Habre. Soon the areas north of this line were absorbed by Goukouni's forces, whilst in the south and central areas, Habre strengthened his positions and regrouped his forces, now bolstered by American instructors and Israeli-trained Zairean commandos. The Reagan administration showed obvious dissatisfaction with the French *de facto* partition of Chad, but France could not be provoked into a more aggressive role. Interviewed by the French Middle East and Africa specialist Eric Rouleau in *Le Monde* on 25 August, Mitterrand stressed that French troops 'cannot be considered an auxiliary force, subject to a strategy in whose determination they have no part.' Moreover, according to Rouleau, Mitterand did not want to become associated with American efforts to 'overthrow the regime of Colonel Qadhafi, towards whom he harbours neither hostility nor resentment.' The same week, the French Defence Minister, Charles Hernu, travelled to Chad and bluntly refused to loan Habre French forces for a counter-attack. Instead, Paris opted for a diplomatic settlement of the conflict and, in open defiance of Washington, contemplated direct negotiations with Libya.

Qadhafi seized the opportunity created by the French disagreement with the United States. Sensing Mitterrand's unease, he offered France a political settlement of the conflict. Paris, although ostensibly dismissive, responded positively. Within days of the French military deployment, Mitterrand had despatched his personal attorney and advisor, Roland Dumas, to Tripoli for exploratory talks.[34] As a result of these contacts, the French and Libyans reached an informal agreement to promote conciliation among the Chadian factions. That September, the Libyan representative to the UN, Dr Ali Treiki, flew to the Republic of the Congo and, whilst attending celebrations to mark the 20th anniversary of the Congolese Revolution, raised the question of an OAU-sponsored diplomatic initiative with, amongst other African leaders, OAU Chairman Mengistu Haile Mariam of Ethiopia, and President Jean-Baptiste Agaza of Burundi, host to the 1984 conference of francophone states.[35] Mengistu, learning of the diplomatic breakthrough with France, undertook to convene an OAU-sponsored meeting of the various Chadian factions, similar in model to that which had produced the Lagos accords in 1979. The conference was scheduled to begin in Addis Ababa, the headquarters of the OAU, on 9 January, 1984.

Five days after the elapse of that date, Mengistu finally cancelled the conference because of Habre's steadfast refusal to attend. Reading a statement on 13 January, Mengistu announced that 'marginal and protocol' issues had prevented the summit from convening.[36] This was a reference to the official welcome extended to Goukouni Ouaddai when he arrived in Addis Ababa on 8 January, which Habre invoked as a pretext for boycotting the meeting. Claiming that only he was entitled to such an official ceremony, Habre had instead sent his Interior Minister, Taher

Guinassou. Since Guinassou could only defer to Habre in Ndjamena, the conference became futile. Despite putting considerable pressure on Habre to attend, the Mitterrand administration could not deliver Habre to the negotiating table, nor extract concessions from him. On the eve of the OAU-sponsored meeting, he flouted the French by sending an envoy to Cairo, and announced that he intended to set out on a tour of former French West Africa.

The Quai d'Orsay at most secured the cooperation of Habre's Foreign Minister, Idris Miskine, who participated in the preparations for the conference. Backed by France, Miskine was an important figure in his own right and could have emerged from the meeting pivotal to any agreement. His sudden death the day prior to the planned summit averted that threat to Habre. Miskine was believed to have been engaged in a major quarrel with Habre over the conference. Ndjamena radio announced that Miskine had died of an acute attack of malaria, although journalists who attended a press conference with him the previous day reported that he was in good health. The circumstances surrounding his death have remained a mystery.[37]

Confronted with Habre's patent intransigence, Mitterrand became impatient to disentangle France from Chad. His resolve was strengthened by a series of clashes with Goukouni's forces in the aftermath of the aborted conference. Two Jaguar bombers were lost from an operation that in any case was costing the Elysée £300,000 per day; pressures, both financial and public, favoured a withdrawal. To facilitate such a disengagement, Mitterrand decided to go over the head of Habre and seek a settlement directly with Qadhafi. This was what the Libyans themselves were hoping for in the period after the conference failure. Assisted by Moroccan intermediaries, a series of contacts commenced, culminating in a formal agreement concluded on 16 September 1984, in which both countries undertook to withdraw their forces, 'simultaneously and concomitantly', between 25 September and 10 November 1984.

American allegations that the Libyans had not honoured their part of the bargain were probably designed to sabotage the agreement, but these were generally discounted by the French Ministry of Defence. The Ministry dubbed as 'fantasy' a report in the French daily, *Libération,* that there were still 3,000 Libyan troops in Chad after the deadline. According to the *Daily Telegraph* on 22 November: 'The Ministry insisted that the information had come from American sources and was considered exaggerated by the French General Staff.' On 7 January 1985, Charles Hernu stated that about 1,500 Libyan troops were in Chad in violation of the agreement. The indication was that these were remaining to counterbalance the American and Zairean military presence in support of Habre.

The agreement with France represented a major diplomatic achievement for Qadhafi. Most importantly, the French did not insist on a withdrawal of Libyan forces from the Aouzou Strip. France, the former colonial power, had in effect tacitly accepted the extension of Libyan sovereignty to the Aouzou Strip. There was, in addition, an informal agreement that the area north of the 16th parallel constituted a sphere of Libyan influence. Qadhafi, meeting with Mitterrand on the island of Crete in November 1984 to review the process of disengagement, also raised a number of areas for future cooperation. According to *Newsweek* of 24 December 1984, the meeting increased the possibility of 'French willingness to resume arms sales to Kaddafi once all Libyan troops have left Chad.' After a fourteen-year-long power struggle with France over Chad, Qadhafi had obtained a settlement which recognised Libyan interests.

Notes

1. Richard Adloff and Virginia Thompson *Conflict in Chad* (Hurst, California, 1981) p. 4.
2. Ibid., p. 3.
3. See J.K. Cooley, *Libyan Sandstorm*, pp. 98–99.
4. Adloff & Thompson, *Conflict in Chad,* p. 14.
5. Ronald Segal. *African Profiles* (Penguin, London, 1963); provides biography of Tombalbaye.
6. *Conflict in Chad,* p. 51.
7. Ibid., p. 55.
8. Ibid.
9. *Le Monde* (19 September, 1971).
10. *Conflict in Chad,* p. 124.
11. Ibid., p. 123.
12. *Jeune Afrique* (16 December, 1977).
13. *Conflict in Chad,* p. 74.
14. *West Africa* (4 June 1979).
15. Quoted in *Jamahirya Review* (July 1983).
16. *Conflict in Chad.*
17. Ibid.
18. Ibid.
19. Cooley, *Libyan Sandstorm*, p. 205.
20. *African Research Bulletin,* pp. 5966–67.
21. France also supplied Oueddei with some limited military aid. See Anthony Sylvester 'Chad: Exit Habre the Soldier, Enter Habre the Statesman': in *New African* (September 1982) p. 29.
22. See *Jamahiriya Review* (December 1981).
23. Anthony Sylvester, 'Chad: Exit Habre the Solider, enter Habre the Statesman': in *New African* (September 1982) p. 29.
24. For account, see Jon Swain, 'The Shepherd, The Outlaw, The Ruler, The Legend', *Sunday Times* 13 June 1982).
25. Sylvester, 'Chad: Exit Habre the Soldier, enter Habre the Statesman' in *New African* p. 29.
26. BBC Summary of World Broadcasts, 13 August 1982.
27. Jamahiriya International Report (JIR), vol. 2, no. 1 (14 May 1983).
28. *Economist* (25 June 1983).
29. JIR, vol. 1, no. 25 (15 April 1983).
30. Ibid., quoting Bardai Radio.

31. See *Guardian* (24 June 1983).

32. JIR, vol. 2, no. 6 (8 July 1983).

33.. The Reagan administration had already begun to supply Habre from bases in Egypt, the Sudan and Zaire without informing France.

34. *International Herald Tribune* (18 August 1983); original source, Reuters newsagency.

35. JIR, vol. 2, no. 9 (2 September 1983).

36. See *Jamahiriya Review* (February 1984).

37. Radio Bardai (10 January 1984) suggested that Miskine's death was the result of a 'power struggle' in Ndjamena.

12 The Struggle For Libya

Reagan's 'Squeeze' Strategy[1]

During the 1977–81 Carter administration, the Tripoli authorities tried on several occasions to woo the United States away from its negative stance towards Libya. That these moves coincided with Carter's nursing of the Camp David negotiations appears paradoxical, but Qadhafi was inclined to view the overall shift in American foreign policy under Carter as a positive development in terms of what could realistically be expected from Washington. Besides, there was always a certain logic in fostering improved links with the United States: North America was a substantial oil market for Libya, and an important supplier of technology. Beyond that, there was one event in particular which created the impression that Carter could be open to Libyan lobbying.

Late in 1977, Carter received reports of a Libyan-backed plan to assassinate the American ambassador in Cairo, Herman Eilts, though where the report originated from remains obscure. Carter responded by addressing a personal plea to Qadhafi to do what he could to stop the operation. Qadhafi, who had not anticipated the personal intervention of the American President, replied to the effect that the report of the plan was a fabrication. Certainly, whether or not a conspiracy against Eilts was intended, no assassination attempt transpired. What was significant was that Qadhafi was left with the feeling that Carter was more accessible than his predecessors had been.

Libya reacted to Carter's personal contact with overtures to the United States for a new era of cooperation. In March 1978, the Foreign Liaison Bureau embarked on a series of 'people-to-people' visits, which it hoped would generate a climate more favourable to Libya. The Bureau was particularly anxious to smooth a passage for the granting of export licences for Boeing 727s, withheld by the administration on grounds that they had military potential. The focus of the Bureau's efforts was President Carter's brother, Billy, whose opinions the Libyan authorities believed would carry weight with the administration.

Billy, an unsophisticated real-estate dealer from Atlanta, Georgia, was approached in July 1978 by a convoluted route, which culminated in contact being established by the former Libyan ambassador to Italy, Jibril Shalouf, who had spent some weeks cultivating Billy's business partners.[2] Billy was extended – and accepted – an invitation to visit Libya, having been told that the visit could prove lucrative for his own business ventures. Accompanied by seven Georgian colleagues, he arrived in Tripoli in late September, and attended the Libyan-American People's Dialogue. After his return to the United States, his links with Libya continued to develop. In January 1979, he played host to a troupe of Libyan dancers in Georgia and helped set up the now defunct Libyan Arab Friendship Society. The same month, by coincidence, the US Department of Commerce relented and issued export licences for the Boeing 727s.

The decision probably had more to do with Boeing Corporation pressure than with Billy Carter, however, for there is only one instance on record when President Carter sought out his brother's Libyan connections.[3] In November 1979, the White House asked the Libyan authorities, through Billy, to intercede with the Iranian government to secure the release of the American embassy hostages in Teheran. Tripoli, which was not in a position of influence with Teheran, tried and failed.

Relations between Libya and the United States were on the decline towards the end of the Carter administration. The turning point was the sacking and burning of the United States embassy in Tripoli on 2 December 1979, an incident provoked by the administration's decision to freeze Iranian assets. On 7 May 1980, after the failure of Libya's mediation with Teheran, the State Department retaliated with the expulsion of several members of the Libyan People's Bureau in Washington D.C., on the pretext that they had been persecuting dissident students. In August that year, in by far the most aggressive move yet, plans were unveiled to conduct Sixth Fleet exercises in the Gulf of Sirte, which Libya has claimed as sovereign waters since 1973. In September, when the exercises commenced, Carter ordered the Fleet to stay outside the zone claimed by Libya, but American air activity around Libya's border discernibly increased. The American-owned, Paris-based *International Herald Tribune* reported that a US air force C-135 electronic surveillance plane 'flying at the edge of Libyan airspace', escorted by an F-14 fighter squadron, was intercepted by Libyan jets twice in one week. In addition, according to this report, additional Navy F-14s were scrambled from the deck of the aircraft carrier, *John F. Kennedy*, though an actual clash with Libyan forces was averted. The task force, on that occasion, was under orders to avoid a conflict, which Carter feared could exacerbate the hostage crisis he was already facing.

Following Ronald Reagan's take-over at the White House in January 1981, relations deteriorated even further. The circumstances in which Reagan was elected pointed the future course of developments. The holding of the US hostages in Teheran, which had dragged on month after month in 1980, involved each day the humiliation of United States power. The helicopter rescue mission, which crashed to disaster in the Salt desert, made the American military complex look both incompetent and impotent. The fall of the Shah's regime was itself a major defeat which seriously affected the balance of forces in the region. At the other side of the world, in Nicaragua, a second American client ruler, Anastasio Samoza, had been overthrown in a popular uprising. In addition to the pyrotechnics in Tripoli, the US embassy at Islamabad in Pakistan was gutted by fire, whilst in Afghanistan a revolutionary take-over of power had occurred in Kabul, followed by the mass intervention of Soviet troops.

During Carter's last days at the White House, he had reacted to these events with a tougher foreign policy line, declaring the Carter doctrine of US military security in the Gulf region, and launching the Rapid Deployment Force (RDF), but he had already lost the confidence of important sections of the American capitalist class. The 'liberal' foreign policy establishment, such as the Trilateral Commission of which Carter was himself a protégé, had lost influence. In the ascendant was right-wing chauvinism and militarism, which provided the ground-swell of support for the election victory of Ronald Reagan – a man who claimed he would reassert the global authority of the United States.

Backing Reagan was an alignment of conservative business-financed institutions, as well as powerful sections of the Zionist movement. In 1972, the year George MacGovern was nominated the Democrats' presidential contender, Eugene Rostow, one of the foremost supporters of the Vietnam war in the Johnson administration, had founded the Committee for a Democratic Majority.[4] In the wake of Carter's election, the organisation, which was dedicated to winning the militaristic argument, dissolved into a broader-based, but more wide-ranging Committee on the Present Danger (CPD). *Commentary*, a journal published by the American-Jewish Committee, and edited by CPD member Norman Podhoretz, became the Committee's effective mouthpiece. In 1977, both Rostow and Podhoretz collaborated to form the Jewish Institute for National Security Affairs, a vehicle for mobilising the Zionist movement in the United States behind the CPD. A similar organisation in some ways was the Centre for Strategic and International Studies at Georgetown University in Washington. Among its many luminaries were (and possibly still are) the right-wing strategist Edward Luttwak, who holds dual British and Israeli citizenship; Robert Neuman, a US ambassador to Saudi Arabia; Michael Ledeen, an outspoken opponent of Libya; Ann Armstrong and Henry Kissinger.[5] Reagan's victory over Carter in 1980 was also a triumph for the politics of these people and their policies, which included the re-establishment of US hegemony over the Third World.

A campaign against Soviet-sponsored terrorism was launched within weeks of Reagan's inauguration ceremony. Libya – regardless of whether the accusation was appropriate or not – was spotlighted as 'a base for Soviet subversion'. The administration afforded Qadhafi the title of 'the most dangerous man in the world',[6] and, as part of a psychological war, rumours were spread about assassination attempts against Qadhafi.

Furthermore, in March 1981, the Sixth Fleet commenced new maneouvres off shore from Libya, this time within the Gulf of Sirte. For four days, from 10 March, two aircraft carriers, ten other vessels and several squadrons of carrier-borne F-14 fighters conducted exercises. The Libyans, anticipating some kind of provocation, avoided reacting in haste. The next move on Washington's part was the encirclement of Libya. On 8 July 1981, the Assistant Secretary of State for African Affairs, Chester Crocker, told Congress that the administration would supply arms to African opponents of Libya 'to help those who see the problem as we see it.'[7] The Pentagon went on to announce that it was prepared to sell Tunisia 54 M-60 tanks, of the kind used by the Israeli armoured corps. So anxious was the administration to place a stranglehold on Libya that the Deputy Defence Secretary, Frank Carlucci, even visited Algeria – a country which did not necessarily see problems the way Washington did – and raised the possibility of selling C-130 transport aircraft to the Algerian air force.[8]

A number of factors explain why Libya became a priority target for the United States so soon after Reagan's takeover in Washington. One of these was the country's economic significance. A plan to invade Libya and seize the oilfields was hastily formulated during the Arab oil embargo of 1973. In January 1974, *New York Times* correspondent Drew Middleton reported that Washington strategists, working on the basis of improved logistics, preferred the take-over of oilfields in Libya rather than of those in the Gulf. Demonstrating the United States' capability to achieve this goal, especially after the rescue mission in Iran, was an aspect of Reagan's re-assertion of American power.

Much more pertinent was the fact that the administration wanted to eliminate Arab nationalism and the threat it posed to the relationship between Israel and Egypt. Qadhafi epitomised Arab nationalism at its most radical and militant. Under his leadership, Libya had armed and trained liberation movements and rebel groups fighting American-backed regimes from El Salvador to the Philippines, and was a leading supplier of the Palestinian resistance. Following the overthrow of the Shah of Iran and Samoza of Nicaragua, such actions spread alarm among clients of the United States. Attacking Libya, then, was linked with proving that the Reagan administration, unlike that of Carter, would no longer abandon unpopular pro-American regimes.

The collision finally came in August.[9] A giant battle formation from the Sixth Fleet, led by the nuclear-powered aircraft carrier *Nimitz*, sailed into the Gulf of Sirte to conduct further exercises specifically authorised by the White House. On 19 August, the Libyans responded by sending up two SU-22 bombers to monitor movements. Without warning, both planes were attacked and shot down by F-14s from the carrier *Nimitz*'s Black Ace squadron. Subsequent American claims that the action was pre-emptive are belied by the Pentagon's own admissions that the Libyan pilots had received no orders, transmitted by radio, to open fire on the American planes or fleet. Had the Libyans wanted to engage the Americans, they would more likely have despatched MIG or Mirage fighters. All the evidence to emerge since has pointed to deliberate American provocation. Before the incident occurred, the Pentagon warned that the exercises would be held in a 3,200-square-mile zone. The Libyans appear to have acted when the F-14s exceeded this range. That much was revealed during a press conference aboard the *Nimitz* on 24 August, when Vice-Admiral Rowden admitted that the clash had occurred outside the designated area. Adding to his words, Rear Admiral James E. Service said: 'About the closest we came was about 25 miles to their coast.'[10] Previously, the American command had insisted that the incident arose some 60 miles out, within the declared zone.

During this period, the Reagan administration was actively trying to secure Egyptian participation in a conflict with Libya. Sadat himself was agreeable, but some strong opposition was voiced by senior commanders and government members to further episodes like the 1977 border conflict. The deaths of Defence Minister General Ahmed Bedawi, together with the commander and the chief of staff of the western military zone, in a mysterious helicopter crash at the Siwa Oases on 2 March 1981, undoubtedly improved Sadat's internal position, for those killed reportedly opposed the President's designs.[11] They were replaced by military officers known to be more pliable, and the incident was followed by the introduction of martial law along the border, and the deployment of 200,000 troops, constituting six infantry, six armoured and three airborne brigades.[12]

In July, French intelligence sources were quoted as saying that an Israeli General Staff working group had been seconded to the Egyptian President to produce a plan for the invasion of Libya.[13] The American presence in the Gulf of Sirte was intended to embolden Sadat, indicating that the Reagan administration, unlike that of Carter, would support Egypt in a war with Libya. Sadat's assassination in October 1981, however, meant that the American scheming never came to fruition. Sadat's successor, Hosni Mubarak, inherited an internal crisis and required time to establish his own position and authority. In the emergency after Sadat's death, contingents from the armed forces were re-deployed throughout Egypt, with an airborne unit dropped on the town of Asyut.

As the Egyptian crisis persisted, Reagan introduced another element in his 'squeeze' strategy. On 10 March 1982, he declared an embargo on the import of crude oil from Libya and the export of United States technology to Libya. The pretext for this embargo was the White House claim that Libyan 'hit squads' were at large in the United States on a mission to assassinate Reagan himself. No evidence was brought forward to substantiate the allegation, and the FBI has since admitted that an investigation revealed no trace of such a Libyan-backed group.[14] Once the boycott was in force, however, one reason or another was invoked for not lifting it. As the United States purchased 35 per cent of Libya's crude oil, and was thereby the largest customer, the move was evidently designed to paralyse the Libyan economy. Already in 1981, pressure was being steadily applied on American oil companies to bring home their US personnel, culminating in a Presidential order instructing Americans to leave. Eventually, some 3,000 did, although half were later to return.[15] Pressures were also exerted on US oil companies to withdraw from Libya, and two 'majors' – Exxon and Mobil – did finally do so.

The prospects of military confrontation rose again in February 1983, when President Reagan over-reacted – or took advantage of one of President Numeiri's habitual claims to have unearthed a Libyan conspiracy against himself – with a massive show of strength directed against Libya.[16] The speed of the military build-up was surprising, and gave the impression that an actual invasion might be imminent. First, the Pentagon suddenly ordered four AWAC surveillance aircraft from the United States to Cairo West airfield, from where they could conduct reconnaissance missions over Libyan territory. Next, the powerful *Nimitz* and its supporting battlegroup steered a course from the eastern Mediterranean to the Gulf of Sirte. All the pointers indicated that the administration was poised to unleash a bloody sequel to the clash of the previous year.[17] Then, the Americans backed off almost as quickly as they had begun. The de-escalation stemmed from the Egyptian government's reluctance to become embroiled on the United States' behalf. One senior Egyptian official, quoted in the *Times* on 21 February, fulminated angrily: 'We are furious. The Americans are trying to implicate us in things that do not involve us.' Indeed, the Egyptian Defence Minister, Field Marshal Abdul Halim Abu Ghazala, speaking at a routine meeting of the Egyptian-American Military Commission in Cairo, commented: 'I cannot see any sign of crisis, or of Libyan aggression against the Sudan.'[18] Beyond the arrest of a few Sudanese oppositionists alleged to be supported by Tripoli, Numeiri never did furnish any proof that there was a Libyan threat to his regime. The Reagan administration, however, seemed unconcerned about the veracity of Numeiri's claims as long as they provided a pretext for encircling Libya.

Almost an exact replay of the same incident occurred in August 1983, the *casus belli* this time occasioned by Hissene Habre's accusations that Libya had mounted an invasion of Chad. An American aircraft carrier, the USS *Eisenhower*, was sent towards Libyan-claimed waters and surveillance aircraft put on operational duties, only to see once again the Egyptian government decline the invitation to mobilise against Libya.[19] Lastly, in March 1984, a Sudanese claim that the Libyan air force had attempted to bomb the Omdurman radio station brought the AWACs back for a fourth occasion. For once, the Egyptians somewhat relented and, under their 1975 defence pact with the Sudan, despatched troops to reinforce Numeiri's forces. But Egyptian President Mubarak would do no more than fortify his Sudanese ally, and showed every intention of wishing to avert a clash with Libya.[20]

On balance, it is plausible that the Libyan air force was responsible for the raid on the radio station. There was certainly a cause in that the station broadcast anti-Qadhafi propaganda, on behalf of both the Sudanese government and the Libyan opposition. The evidence is by no means conclusive, however (Edward Mortimer of the *Times*[21] has suggested that Numeiri himself may have authorised the bombing), but it remains the most likely theory. More sinister is the evidence that Qadhafi was being deliberately enticed into a conflict with the Sudan. According to the *Observer*'s Middle East correspondent, Patrick Seale, there was never any Libyan plan, as Reagan maintained, but an attempt to lure Libyan forces into the Sudan, thereby obliging the Egyptians, under the terms of the 1975 mutual defence pact, to engage them. 'Qadhafi prudently ignored the bait offered him,' concluded Seale in his 13 March column. It would seem that the premature disclosure of the *Nimitz*'s movements and the despatch of the AWACs, both of which were reported in the American press, alerted Qadhafi to the scheme. Desperate attempts to hush up the details of the conspiracy failed, and the administration emerged worse for the experience.

During the past few years, the CIA and other intelligence agencies have spread ever more bizarre rumours about events in Libya. Since Reagan came to power in 1981 there have been, to my knowledge, reports of at least two attempted *coups* and three assassination bids on Qadhafi or Jalloud, with regard to which no factual basis has been offered. Journalists who track down the sources of these stories inevitably come up against 'intelligence sources' or 'diplomatic sources', but rarely carry out independent verification. The most spectacular hoax yet was a rumour that Qadhafi's plane had been shot down on its return from Moscow in May 1981, the Libyan leader only surviving because the Soviet Union, learning of the plot somehow, advised him to change planes. More recently, even the British Foreign Office has become involved in such rumours: on 16 November 1982, the *Guardian, Daily Mail* and *Daily Telegraph* each carried reports of a foiled *coup*, based on a briefing given by the Foreign Office to diplomatic correspondents the previous afternoon. The reports said that 100 Libyan officers had been arrested for planning to shoot Qadhafi when his plane touched down at Tripoli after a visit to China. Yet, rigorous checking with the air-lines revealed that the airport was not closed and that there was no sign of abnormal activity. Neither Amnesty International nor foreign news services knew of any wave of detentions; in fact, the Reuters' correspondent in Tripoli had not even heard the rumour, and the agency did not bother to cover the story.

Nevertheless, misinformation has provided much of the justification for the diplomatic ostracism of Libya. The United States abruptly severed relations with Libya on 6 May 1981, and the entire staff of the People's Bureau in Washington was expelled, on grounds of 'provocations and misconduct'. Further diplomatic sanctions, this time against the Libyan mission to the United Nations in New York, were imposed in 1983, limiting the hours that the Libyan ambassador to the UN could spend at his weekend retreat. What exactly constituted the 'misconduct' was unspecified, but it is probable that the surveillance and harassment of dissidents of which the People's Bureaux were accused did not exceed that carried out by diplomatic missions friendly to the United States – say South Korea, for example. Contrary to the general impression created, it was Libyan students rather than Libyan dissidents who were the primary targets of harassment in the United States. Approximately 3,000 Libyan students were registered on courses in the United States at the time when diplomatic links were broken, and as the climate of tension increased, there were many attacks against Libyan students. They also became subjected to a number of official restrictions and, in March 1983,[22] a ban was imposed on Libyan students attending courses related to nuclear science and aviation, affecting some 500 Libyan students.

Short of all-out war, the Reagan administration had, by 1984, tightened the squeeze on Libya as far as possible. Towards the end of 1984, the State Department was considering a ban on the import of goods from Libya chiefly refined products; as these do not in any case count significantly such a ban would be unlikely to do much economic harm.[23] There does exist a blueprint for the invasion of Libya, which has been discussed within the administration, but it yet again depends on collaboration with the Egyptians, and so far the required level of cooperation has not been forthcoming from the Mubarak regime. An important reason for that is the employment of some 200,000 Egyptian workers in Libya. Following the bungled operation against former Libyan Prime Minister Abdul Hamid Bakoush in November 1984, the prospect of hostilities did appear to come closer. Tension rose when Mubarak summoned a meeting with his military commanders and the Cairo-Alexandria highway was closed – a move normally associated with troop movements. Mubarak, however, emerged from this state of deliberation only to put a damper on speculation. His Interior Minister, Ahmed Rushdie, ordered a prompt end to the anti Qadhafi campaign in the official media.[24]

Libya's Military Build-Up

Even with American logistical and aerial support, the Egyptian armed forces would not find an invasion of Libya easy to accomplish. Since the acquisition of the first Mirage fighters from France, Libya has assembled a formidable arsenal. Whilst not as strong as Egypt in military terms, Libya has developed sufficient armed power to deter Cairo from a more adventurous policy of confrontation. The 1977 conflict revealed that the Egyptian armed forces, despite their vast numerical superiority, suffered from serious weaknesses. The mobility of the Libyan forces, enhanced by their use of the Brazilian-made Cascavel armoured car, was much greater than that of the Egyptians.[25] Sophisticated electronic weaponry would be required to put Libyan radar and missile installations out of action, but there would be no guarantee that the Libyan forces could not muster the capability to retaliate with devastating effect – such as bombing the Aswan Dam, or striking at nuclear installations in southern Europe – as Qadhafi has threatened Libya will do in the event of war.

For over a decade, Libya has steadily accumulated arms from the Soviet Union. The relationship of buyer and supplier was established in 1974. In April of that year, Staff Major Jalloud flew to Paris where he conducted some preliminary talks with visiting Soviet Premier Podgorny. As a result of these, he secured an invitation to visit the Soviet Union, which he took up in June. Following negotiations with the Soviet leadership, he returned to Libya with a deal that amounted to the single largest purchase of arms by any one country: an arms package worth a staggering $12 billion. Since that contract – the first of many – Soviet Antanov AN22s have regularly delivered consignments of arms from bases around the Black Sea, or from depots in South Yemen, or prior to the Gulf War, from Iraq, whilst Soviet and East European ships have unloaded cargoes of weapons at Tripoli and Zuwara in the east of Libya, and at Derna and Tokra in the west.[26] By the late 1970s, NATO sources estimated that the Libyan army had been delivered 2,000 assorted T-54, T-55 and T-62 tanks;[27] more recently, there have been reports that the Soviet Union has supplied Libya with tanks of the T-72 type, ahead of its general introduction within the Warsaw Pact. With Soviet equipment the Libyan navy has grown from practically nothing to being, next to the Egyptian navy, probably the largest in the Arab world. In 1981 Libya was said to be operating three Foxtrot-class submarines – the al-Fateh, the al-Badr and the al-Ahad – and three amphibious landing craft of the Polnochury class.[28] The military arsenal includes SAM missile systems of various grades, and warplanes of various types, with several squadrons of MIG-21s and MIG-23s, two squadrons of Tupolev TU-21 bombers and some Tupolev TU-22 supersonic bombers.[29]

The Soviet Union is not, however, the only supplier. Besides the Soviet Union itself, other Warsaw Pact members have participated in the build-up of the Libyan armed forces. The East German Office for Industrial Technical Trade in Pankow has sold Libya the Klashnikov AK-47 assault rifle, the RPG rocket-propelled grenade-launcher, and other items of infantry hardware; so, too, has the Czechoslovakian equivalent, Omnipol.[30] According to American sources, which are not always the most reliable, Eastern Europe has also been the source for helicopters, minesweepers, missile boats, and a range of sophisticated optical, infra-red, and fire-control systems – indeed much of the gadgetry necessary for carrying out electronic warfare. In addition, there are reports that Warsaw Pact equipment, including Soviet, has been transferred from Syria to Libya under the military arrangements of the Steadfastness and Confrontation Front.[31] Allegedly, 500 T-62 tanks were delivered this way in 1978 and, since the act of union between the two countries in 1981, the volume is believed to have grown. American sources claim that military shipments from Syria to Libya, following the union, have included 130 aircraft, SAM missiles, SCUD missiles and artillery pieces equipped with anti-tank guns.[32]

This arms-purchasing relationship with the Warsaw Pact countries did not develop out of a political preference. The change initially occurred because Libya wanted to reduce its dependence on its previous leading supplier, France. The subsequent decision of President Giscard d'Estaing to impose an arms embargo on Libya, following the dispute over Chad, vindicated this switch. On the same basis, Qadhafi is equally determined that Libya should not be reduced to over-dependence on the Soviet Union. The Libyan military authorities have concluded separate arrangements to secure spare parts for Soviet equipment from India, which manufactures MIG fighters under licence, North Korea and Yugoslavia.[33] Libya has also become a patron to the newly-emerging arms industries in the Third World, Brazil being a chief beneficiary. Besides the Cascavel armoured cars, Brazil has sold Libya 200 EE-11 Urutu armoured patrol cars, and Libya is in the market for further Brazilian equipment, including the Tucano jet.[34] Pakistan under President Bhutto was another important source of military assistance for Libya. When Sadat withdrew Egyptian military advisers, Bhutto despatched six hundred Pakistanis, together with 30 air force instructors, to replace the Egyptian personnel.[35]

The same policy of diversification has meant that Libya has striven to retain access to current Western weapons technology. From those Western European states that can be persuaded to sell, Libya has bought. Prior to Giscard d'Estaing's arms embargo, arms purchases from France were at a peak: French exports to Libya included some 200 AMX-30 tanks, self-propelled Howitzers, 38 Mirage F-1 fighters and Crotale air defence missiles, most of which had been delivered by the time President Mitterrand lifted the ban on arms sales in 1981.[36] Italy, despite membership of the military wing of the NATO alliance, has conducted a discreet trade with Libya, selling to the Libyan navy OTOMAT missiles, Wadi-class corvettes, and has fitted out ten French Combattante-11 missile boats supplied to Libya by the Mitterrand administration.[37] The Italian authorities have also supplied to Libya American-designed Chinook CH-47C helicopters, made under licence in Italy, and (reputedly) 75 West German Leopard 1 battle tanks – the main NATO battle tank. Libyan arms-buyers have, in addition, bought from the Western European arms market a variety of smaller weaponry and have, through Syria, successfully obtained NATO's HOT and MILAN anti-tank guided missile systems, originally purchased from the Euromissile agency in Paris.[38] Both are deemed superior to the US TOW and Dragon systems in service with the Egyptian armed forces. Qadhafi has shown a deft hand in circumventing Western arms bans, playing off one rival supplier against another.

Reports that Libya is trying to assemble a nuclear bomb by similar diverse methods have been circulating in the West for almost as long as Qadhafi's leadership itself. According to Mohammed Heikal, Jalloud flew to Peking in 1970 and offered the Chinese government one billion dollars for a nuclear bomb. Ever since then, alarmist reports have been circulating in the West about the danger of Libya gaining the nuclear option. These reports tend to exaggerate Libya's actual endeavours and obscure the motives behind the search for nuclear weapons.[39] Libya does have nuclear ambitions, both civil and military, but the objective of the bomb must be seen in the context of breaking the Israeli monopoly on nuclear weaponry in the Middle East. Even so, Libya has not been very successful in achieving this goal. Libya's main hopes depended on cooperation with Pakistan. Whilst Bhutto was in power, Libya assisted financially with the purchase of uranium yellowcake from Nigeria for the Pakistani research centre located at Islamabad. The overthrow of Bhutto by Zia al Haq, however, soon put paid to the relationship. More recently, there has been speculation that the West German company OTRAG, expelled from Zaire in 1979, has relocated its satellite-launching facilities in the Fezzan and is assisting, in return, with the development of the Libyan nuclear programme. So much rumour surrounds OTRAG's supposed activities in Libya that it remains virtually impossible to extract the full facts.[40] What is known is that Libya is proceeding with a civil nuclear programme, and has established its own nuclear research centre. A small research reactor, supplied by the Soviet Union, has been constructed at Tajjura, but more significant would seem the nuclear power station being constructed in the Fezzan by the West German company, KWU.

At present, Libya remains a conventional military power. The arms build-up, although substantial, conceals many weaknesses which undermine the country's military capability. The most obvious deficiency is the shortage of technical skills required by some modern, chiefly electronic, weaponry.[41] Although conscription and population growth have raised military strength from one soldier to every 124km in 1970, to one soldier to every 38km in 1985, in a combat situation the Libyan armed forces would be greatly overstretched. One-third of the regular Libyan army could go into battle in tanks and the remainder could ride in armoured personnel carriers. To overcome shortages, therefore, especially in technical areas, Libya has imported foreign military forces. In the past, Egypt provided many key technicians; more recently, instructors have come from Eastern Europe and other pro-socialist states. Reportedly, one squadron of MIGs[42] is flown by North Koreans, whilst Palestinians and other Arab nationals have been recruited on an individual basis to pilot other aircraft. There does, however, remain a limit to the numbers Libya can employ; financially, they are a drain on foreign exchange, and politically, they could become a source of antagonism to the local population.

This dilemma is likely to persist. The Libyan armed forces, constrained by a small population, would be outnumbered in a confrontation with Egypt or any other potential aggressor. Libya has a total regular military strength of, at most, 60,000,[43] compared to Egypt's 400,000-strong army, or the 250,000 troops at the disposal of the United States Central Command (formerly the Rapid Deployment Force).

The Armed People

Qadhafi has responded to the problems facing Libya's conventional armed forces by developing a non-conventional military strategy. Since the time of the Sebha declaration of 1977, if not before, he has been committed to the concept of the 'armed people'. By the turn of the decade, plans were advanced for the creation of a militia 50,000 strong, but first the clash in the Gulf of Sirte, then the war in Lebanon, impelled him towards the goal of total mobilisation. Speaking on the anniversary of the revolution on 1 September 1982, he affirmed:

> We are working day and night to train people to carry arms. But we are not engaging in armed propaganda. There are traditional methods which have become obsolete. Nor are we simply training them to use rifles and machine guns. We are training them to handle tanks, missiles, aircraft and submarines. The people themselves will be armed.

He claimed that the survival of the revolution was at stake on this one issue. 'You must give up luxuries and turn them into weapons,' he declared.[44]

The conflict in Lebanon altered Qadhafi's perception of the Arab struggle with Israel. The blows which the Israeli military machine struck at the PLO convinced him that Libya's regular armed forces were appallingly unsuited to the nature of the external challenge. He contended that the Palestinian military should not have accepted the premise of an orthodox military structure, that of a military wing separate from the civilian population – a development which had indeed begun to erode the position of Palestinian forces in Lebanon. The policy of the armed people, not to be equated with the formation of a militia, was in contrast based on the abolition of the distinction between the armed forces and the civilian population. The basic principle was laid down in the Sebha declaration, point four of which reads: 'Defence of the homeland is the responsibility of every male and female citizen. Through general military training the people shall be trained and armed.'[45] Addressing a rally on the anniversary of the declaration in 1978, he added:

> Wealth, power and arms should be in the hands of the people. When we have an armed people and when military training becomes general for all Libyans and arms are distributed to everyone, then we shall not have soldiers whose specific job would be defending people.[46]

Qadhafi believed that only a comprehensive form of military mobilisation could deter an aggressor. Faced with an armed population, he argued, an invading power could not rely on the defeat of the regular armed forces to bring the conflict to an end. It would be obliged to sustain an occupation against a protracted war of resistance that would defy a military solution. Explaining the concept in a 1983 edition of *al-Zahaf al-Akhdar,* Qadhafi expounded:

Such an army cannot be defeated, for when the armed people exists, either the whole people succumbs or it triumphs. But it is impossible for the whole people to disappear. Conventional armies are, however, based on a defeatist idea because when an army surrenders or its striking force is destroyed or when it loses a battle, the whole country surrenders and falls to the enemy. This is a peculiar situation. But when the people as a whole are involved in the battle, the situation is different. Why should we then make victory dependent on a group which, when it is defeated, causes the defeat of the whole country too?[47]

There is perhaps one other factor which also influenced Qadhafi. In August 1980, Libyan troops stationed at Tobruk mutinied. The full details of the affair remain shrouded in secrecy, but it would appear that the commander of the Eastern Military Sector, Captain Idris ash-Shuheibi, embarked on an uprising against Qadhafi.[48] He appears to have gained the backing of some officers within the zone, but before the revolt could spread from Tobruk, where it had started, revolutionary committee units, including some flown in from Tripoli, mounted a counter-attack and put it down. Local residents interviewed by journalists attested to the sound of extensive gunfire. Speaking at a rally on 28 March, Qadhafi disclosed that regular troops had been removed from bases in the Eastern Sector, and their barracks converted into a school, presumably for the military training of the local population.[49] Trained units of the armed people, as yet largely a militia formation, took over duties from regular forces. The army was purged of malcontented officers. More importantly, Qadhafi began to question the bases of accountability in the armed forces. In a live American television interview in May, he hinted that the regular armed forces were no longer trustworthy.[50]

Even by 1983 the cause for alarm had not entirely faded. The 1 April edition of *al-Zahaf al-Akhdar* was headlined 'Military Corruption', and alleged that the Libyan military 'is dominated by corrupt and ignorant men whose sole preoccupation lies in thinking how to import their urgently needed contraband.' The article cited the case of military personnel in Tobruk 'engaged in smuggling', and stressed that there was nepotism throughout the services. It concluded: 'The reactionaries within the army are as great a threat as the regimes of Batista and Franco to the Cuban and Spanish peoples and the juntas in Chile and Guatemala today. The corrupt men within the army are following directly in the footsteps of military men in other countries.' The same edition carried the report of a speech in which Qadhafi emphasised that 'the solution lies in the emergence of the armed people and the disappearance of the regular army.'

Nevertheless, the transition from regular armed forces to the armed people is fraught with dangers. In Algeria, in 1965, Ben Bella's decision to form a militia became the prime factor instigating the take-over by the army under Houari Boumedienne. How much greater then the challenge being posed to the regular armed forces by Qadhafi, with his plans to abolish a separate military structure? Whilst Qadhafi's own position was stronger than Ben Bella's, the period of transition still required careful handling. His practice, in the event, was to put his own trusted lieutenants in the armed forces in control of the change, whilst he himself assumed overall supervision. The precarious circumstances of the period – the battle of Sirte, the economic boycott, the invasion of Lebanon, the civil war in Chad – required that the leadership, Qadhafi and the other four Free Officer leaders, display resolve and unity.

Symbolic of that unity was the participation, on 4 September 1982, of all the senior military commanders in the military graduation ceremony at Tripoli's Libyan Air Defence College. Qadhafi attended the passing out parade flanked by Brigadier Abu Bakr Younis Jaber, General Commander-in-Chief of the Libyan Armed Forces, Bridgadier Mustafa Kharubi, Chief of Staff, and the chiefs of staff of the army, navy and air force.[51] The following day he was present at a similar ceremony – this time at the Air Defence College in Misrata – together with President Ali Nasser Mohammed of South Yemen, Staff Major Jalloud, Brigadier Abu Bakr Younis Jaber, the chiefs of staff of the various services, as well as members of the diplomatic corps. Qadhafi, who handed out certificates to the top ten graduates, told cadets that their passing out brought the goal of the armed people closer.[52] The same day, in the company of senior officers, he reviewed a plant for the maintenance of missiles, radar and other electronic equipment operated by the Libyan air force.

By the close of the year, the military authorities were claiming that the demobilisation of the regular armed forces had begun. On 14 December JANA issued a statement announcing that 'tens of thousands' of Libyan servicemen had been demobilised as part of a process that 'affirmed Libya's positive march towards the abolition of the regular military establishment, and its replacement by the armed people, so that self-defence will become the direct responsibility of the people.[53] The troops involved were not specified, but it seems that the more specialised units were unaffected by the change. The bulk of those demobilised were undoubtedly conscripts from the regular army, demobilised after Libya had pulled out of Chad, and probably constituted only a fraction of the 'tens of thousands' claimed officially. Until this day, the transition has not fully embraced the services, though it remains Qadhafi's avowed intention that the policy will leave no stone unturned.

Titular responsibility for achieving the armed mobilisation of the civilian population was assigned to Major Khweildi Hamidi. Hamidi, who had previously controlled the security services as Interior Minister, was appointed Commander of Urban Militarisation. His first initiative, in this respect, was the organisation of students into units of the armed people. Addressing a joint meeting of the Basic People's Congresses and student congresses in Misrata on 12 August 1982, he pointed to the examples of Algeria and Vietnam as two countries where an armed people had defeated superior military forces. He explained that the armed people policy was 'an integrated plan aimed at the military training of the combatants capable of forming a stiff fighting unit.'[54] Then, on 14 August, he reviewed students undertaking tank and vehicle training, and secondary school students commencing logistics classes, before on 19 August inspecting students at Tarhuna performing live ammunition drill.

That those in education should lead the way was a theme underlined by Qadhafi in his 1982 1 September anniversary speech. Referring to Libya's 30,000 teachers, he said that these too must mobilise militarily within schools. 'Every man and woman teacher has to become an officer and train students how to fight', he insisted. Next, in April and May 1983, he accelerated the process with a call for the extension of the *jamahari* system throughout educational institutions, made on the occasion of the 13th anniversary of the British military evacuation, at Gamal Abdul Nasser Airbase near Tobruk. In the ensuing weeks, prompted by this speech, there transpired sporadic take-overs of educational institutions by staff and pupils, their formal transformation into 'barracks', and the inauguration of military training as part of the curricula.

Back in 1977 the Ali Wraith secondary school in Tripoli had been the first to pioneer such courses, but throughout 1983 the process became generalised. In May 1983, JANA reported that 'self-management' had been established at the Higher Technical Institute at Brak, the Yusuf al-Thram secondary school (barracks) in Benghazi, the March 10th secondary school (barracks) for women teachers in Tripoli, the Gamal Abdul Nasser secondary school (barracks) in al-Marj, the Qasr Bin Ashir secondary school (barracks) in Tripoli, the Qadisiyeh secondary school (barracks) for women teachers in Kufra, the Misrata Institute for Social Services, and the Omar Mukhtar boys school in Benghazi.

For Qadhafi total mobilisation meant no exceptions. He was insistent that the armed people should not consist only of armed men, but involved the mass participation of women. Towards this end, a Women's Military Academy was opened in Tripoli in 1978, and the first batch of women graduates passed out on 30 August 1981. In a speech delivered on the occasion, Qadhafi told women military students that their training marked 'the beginning of the end of the era of harems and slavery and the beginning of women's liberation in the Arab nation.'[57] Addressing the Women's Revolutionary Formation in Benghazi on 12 February 1981, he warned: 'If this nation wants to win, then each one of us, we must all, men and women, fight in the trenches, do weapons training, and fight our enemy.'[58] In April that year, women students from Hawary women teachers' institute in Benghazi conducted rocket handling exercises in a display attended by Hamidi, whilst Qadhafi, in a speech on 8 May 1982 encouraged all women to enlist for military training. Just as the Israelis had 'mobilised both men and women to confront the Arab nation,' he told them, 'so the Arab people had to mobilise men and women to resist.'[59]

No aspect of the policy provoked more controversy and internal opposition than this. Qadhafi's efforts to integrate women into the process of militarisation carried very little favour in a society riddled with

241

backward and perverse attitudes towards women. Husbands restrained their wives from participation, and authoritarian fathers prevented their daughters from taking up military training. Qadhafi's response was to launch the revolutionary committee movement on a campaign to win the argument, but resistance to the policy of women's militarisation was so widespread that Qadhafi was involved in a losing battle, even within the BPC, where he could usually rely on the revolutionary committees to push policy through. It soon became impossible to contain the opposition, which burst into the open at the General People's Congress in February 1983. Losing the vote at the conference, Qadhafi appeared to give way, and in his speech he acknowledged that the decision was a democratic one, even though he disagreed with it.[60]

For the next year Qadhafi agitated for the acceptance of women's military service. He was not discouraged by the fact that the BPCs continued to register opposition to the scheme. On 27 June 1983 he made a point of attending the annual graduation ceremony at Tripoli Women's Military College, and took the opportunity to challenge his detractors within the BPCs. Addressing the women cadets, he declared: 'As of now we shall not accept that any one may harm the dignity and pride of a woman who answers the call and joins a military college, a military secondary school, or a military barracks.'[61] He stressed that Libya 'could not accommodate trivial and frivolous people who obstruct the militarisation of our resources and debilitate our fighting spirit. We shall crush all such threats, since we cannot accept the reversal or squandering of our achievements.' He argued: 'Negative attitudes must be overcome, so that women can enter military colleges and contribute to the build-up of a military defence for the Jamahiriya.' Due notice was given that the leadership would not tolerate future attempts to prevent women's military service and training. That September, the first class of women pilots passed out from Metiega Air Force College near Tripoli, a facility open to both sexes, for flight training in MIG 25s.

As the BPCs commenced their preliminary discussions prior to the General People's Congress in March 1984, Qadhafi escalated his campaign to reverse the decision of the previous year. On 22 January he backed a women's take-over of the Women's Military College in Tripoli, when women students and staff assumed responsibility for the administration of the establishment. Visiting the College, Qadhafi described the women's action as 'an historic leap which placed women on the same level as men.' He stressed: 'History will record your initiative and the attitude of parents to it. This action shows your patriotism.' A declaration issued by the women called for the full inauguration of women's militarisation, not just of volunteers in specialised colleges, but of comprehensive participation 'in all military colleges.' The official news agency JANA, reporting on the response to the establishment of women's self-management at the college, claimed on 30 January that 'hundreds of women are applying to enrol for military service.'[62]

Yet, when the question did come before the GPC in March, Qadhafi was once again defeated. What had started has a minor defeat had become a crisis of his authority as Leader of the Revolution. This time, unlike the previous year, he refused the outcome. Days afterwards, in a speech on the anniversary of the Sebha declaration, he registered his defiance, declaring:

> The call that seeks to paralyse half the Libyan people and keep them away from military training and the carrying of arms is a call made on the prompting of America and Israel and the reactionaries. He who opposes the training and emancipation of women is an agent of imperialism, whether he likes it or not or whether he knows it or not. He is an agent and a fifth columnist, and the one who paves the ground before the enemy of our land. On this occasion, the door for volunteering will be wide open before Libyan men and women to train for the people's liberation war and for fighting on all fronts of the Arab nation in the battle of Arab nationalism.[63]

Even before the GPC had concluded its sessions, the Revolutionary Women's Formation had begun to instigate protests against the decision across the country. Demonstrations by women were reported outside military facilities in al-Beida, Ul al-Aramb, Ajdabiyeh, Aujala, Ajkhara, Sabratha, al-Azziziya and the oases of Jaod as statements were issued demanding the recall of the BPCs in emergency session to 'abrogate all articles that minimise the capability of Libyan women to exercise their rights.'[64] In fact, the BPCs were not recalled in the way that the women demanded. Finally, the crisis was resolved by Qadhafi himself invoking his prerogative in revolutionary affairs to revoke the decision of the Congress. Announcing his move on 12 March, he told women volunteers attending training courses at Yarmath Taha Camp that henceforth military training for women would be compulsory. Stressing that he was responding to the 'popular will', which had not prevailed at the Congress because of the assertiveness of 'reactionary forces', he stated that 'general military training is compulsory for women in the Jamahiriya', and added that 'military training will resume at girls' educational institutes.'[65] The policy of the armed people was secured at last, but at the cost of undermining the credibility of the jamahiri system of direct democracy.

The Libyan Opposition

Besides the manifestation of opposition within the country, Qadhafi was also troubled by the growth of an externally-based Libyan opposition movement. In deciding to overturn the vote of the BPC in March 1984, his major concern was that the two should not combine. Just such a convergence of opposition was what the Reagan administration was hoping to achieve. The 'squeeze' stratagem was intended to climax in the installation of an opposition provisional government-in-exile in a Libyan town, from where it could call for outside military assistance. The policy is in fact remarkably similar to that employed against the Sandinistas in Nicaragua, but in a much less advanced phase of development. That the Americans are working towards this objective explains why Qadhafi has been so relentless in his attempts to eliminate the external opposition, to the extent that he has harmed relations with several European countries, including Britain. The alternatives for Qadhafi are very limited. Every cluster of exiles represents a potential threat, a prospective government-in-exile that can win external aid for the overthrow of the Jamahiriya.

Exiled political opponents of Qadhafi have always existed. In the initial, post-monarchic period, the opposition was confined to pro-monarchist families and a handful of discredited politicians. It was only after his relations with Egypt deteriorated that an actual opposition *movement* began to crystallise. Sadat responded to the clash over policies with Qadhafi by dropping his objections to the presence of exiled political opponents, and Cairo increasingly became the sanctuary for Libyan dissidents. After the royalists, the next to arrive were officials and members of political parties purged during the cultural revolution. Then, in 1976, former RCC members Omar Meheshi and Abdul Mounim al-Houni were granted political asylum in Egypt, and permitted to organise the first proper opposition group, the Libyan National Rally. In May 1976, Meheshi had begun to broadcast from Cairo on behalf of this organisation.[66] The group was conspicuous, however, by its lack of support. It was treated by Sadat as a useful but expendable pawn in his power struggle with Qadhafi, and the activities of the group always remained within the range of Egyptian control.

Nevertheless, there is no doubt that Qadhafi was irritated by the activities of Meheshi's group. He at first asked the former Tunisian Foreign Minister Mohammed Masmoudi to intercede with Meheshi, persuading him that a reconciliation was possible if he returned to Libya. Failing that, Qadhafi appears to have resorted to efforts to eliminate Meheshi.[67] In March 1976, the Egyptian security service announced that seven men had been arrested in connection with an operation to assassinate Meheshi and Houni. The authorities in Tripoli denied the charges, but they had an obvious interest in having the two former members of the RCC silenced. Interviewed in *al-Ahram* that same month, Meheshi had called Qadhafi a 'despot' and 'psychopath'. After his arrival in Cairo, moreover, he had started working towards the creation of a government-in-exile. In August 1976 he had visited President Numeiri in the Sudan with a view to gaining facilities for such a government. There was also evidence that the French intelligence service, Service du documentation extérieure et de coutre-espionnage, was assisting Meheshi and Houni. French President Giscard d'Estaing asked SDECE, to find ways of undermining Qadhafi, and assisting Meheshi and Houni was one of them. SDECE operatives were reported to have liaised with Meheshi's organisation for a period.[68]

But nuisance that he was, Meheshi's challenge to Qadhafi turned out to be no serious threat. As time wore on, he was exposed as little more than a one-man band. His partner, the ailing Houni, deserted political activity and, in 1981, Meheshi himself suffered a mental breakdown and entered a hospital in Kuwait.[69] Since then he has disappeared completely, triggering speculation that he was induced to return to Libya, or was abducted by Libyan security officials.[70]

Members of the Libyan National Rally merged with those of another unsuccessful exile initiative, Faisal Massoudi's Libyan Democratic Front, to become the Libyan Democratic National Rally. Formed in 1980, this organisation is headed by Dr Suleyman Mughrabi, the first Prime Minister after the overthrow of the monarchy, who defected in 1977 and was granted political asylum in Britain. With no coherent political programme, nor cadres, however, and just an irregular publication called *Saut Libya*, the group appears to have faded even more quickly than Meheshi's. Beyond disseminating rumours about Libya, the organisation is largely impotent.

Another former politician who emerged to form his own opposition organisation was Abdul Hamid Bakhoush. A prime minister under the monarchy, Bakhoush escaped to Cairo in 1977, and three years later founded the Libyan Liberation Organisation, initially not much more than a one-man band. In 1982 Bakhoush joined forces with Bashir al-Rabti, formerly Chairman of the Federal Umma Council of Libya, Egypt and Syria, who had fled Libya in 1981. Without much support, the group has produced only one issue of its publication, *al-Tahrir*, and that was to announce its formation. Even other exiles agree that Bakhoush is ineffectual and entirely dependent upon the Egyptian authorities, with whom he enjoys limited cooperation. The group's position is unclear on the issue of restoration of the monarchy, but it is firmly committed to the re-introduction of private capitalist relations. An arms dealer by profession, Bakhoush has a dubious reputation among those who would normally be the most sympathetic to his cause.

Two further right-wing groups to have appeared are the Libyan National Movement and the Libyan Constitutional Union. The LNM is pro-Iraqi Baathist in orientation, and is the Baghdad regime's alternative to the various groups supported by the Egyptians. Founded in the Iraqi capital in 1979, the organisation is led by Imran Boures, its General Secretary, and Suleyman Fares, both men with no prior record of political activity. Due to Iraqi backing, the group enjoys some material advantages over other groups, including facilities to produce a programme on Iraqi radio, publish a magazine, *Saut at-Talia* (Voice of the Vanguard), and manufacture propaganda cassettes called *Saut at-Talia al-Masmoun*, but it seems to have only limited success in smuggling its propaganda into Libya.[71] Moreover, Baathism no longer has the same support among intellectuals that it had in the years of the monarchy.

The Libyan Constitutional Union is one of the smallest of the political sects opposed to Qadhafi. Based in Manchester, where it was probably formed in 1981, the group is led by Mohammed Ibn Ghalboun, his brother, and a circle of friends. One of these, Ali Saeed, was interviewed on television in Britain during the siege of St. James' Square. Outside Britain the group, which is pro-monarchist, has no known adherents, even among members or the royal family. Its success in the media is not matched by its success in the exile community.

Far more serious for Qadhafi than the threat posed by these minor groups is the growth of an opposition movement composed of students studying abroad. Following the bitter fights between pro- and anti-Qadhafi students in Libyan universities in 1976, right-wing students abroad established the General Union of Libyan Students. The rapid expansion of this organisation since that time has resulted in the development of perhaps the largest of all the opposition movements. The organisation now claims that it has affiliated branches in Britain, the United States, Germany, Italy, Greece, Egypt and Morocco (though this has recently gone underground because of the union with Libya). However, beyond the publication of a magazine, *Shuhada Abril* ('April Martyrs' – an allusion to the students hanged in April 1976), the union has little in the way of centralised coordination. Local branches, such as that in Britain, have mobilised supporters for demonstrations, but there is no evidence that the union has infiltrated and built cells in Libya on the scale that it claims. Libyan security services carry out rigorous surveillance of students based abroad.

The main form of internal opposition has come from Islamic fundamentalism which began to grow in strength after the 1978 Islamic Revolution, in response to Qadhafi's interpretation of Islam. The Muslim Brotherhood, subject to a crackdown in 1973, has since experienced something of a revival. Equally significant has been the rise of new groups, some of which organise from abroad. For example, in 1979 the Islamic Association of Libya was formed to spread propaganda of a religious hue against Qadhafi, either through the publication of its magazine, *The Muslim*, or through conferences in Europe or the United States. Another group, committed to armed struggle against Qadhafi, is the Revolutionary Council of the Prophet of God. This is a clandestine organisation, possibly linked with another group, which made its debut in 1979 with the announcement, issued from Cairo, that it intended to carry out a sentence of death on Qadhafi for 'mishandling the country's funds through buying obsolete and defective equipment from the Soviet Union.'[72]

By 1980, the opposition had grown to the extent that it was making Qadhafi so uneasy he decided to strike back. The Revolutionary Committee Movement summoned to a conference at Gar Younis University in Benghazi in February of that year, was authorised to accomplish the 'physical liquidation' of political opponents. The result was the formation of what the Western media has termed 'hit squads'. These were sometimes groups of committee members, sometimes hired professional assassins, paid to eliminate key Libyan opposition figures. They commenced their operations in April 1980, following Qadhafi's 'final warning' for opponents to return to Libya or be executed abroad. When the campaign was called off in June, 10 political opponents had been eliminated. In London in April journalist Mohammed Mustafa Ramadan and lawyer Mahmoud Nafiq were killed; in Italy five businessmen were similarly disposed of; and single assassinations occurred in Athens, Beirut and Bonn.[73]

Simultaneously, the committees instigated a campaign against internal opposition. Several waves of arrests were reported during 1980, coupled with allegations that some oppositionists had died or vanished. In February it was claimed that the founder of the Arab Baath Party in Libya, Amer al-Tahir Dighais, had been killed in custody.[74] In November it was reported that Sheikh Mohammed al-Bishti, the imam of the Qasr Mosque, had disappeared.[75] According to the General Union of Libyan Students, a total of 16 students in Libya had been imprisoned and four killed. Also in 1980 there were televised a series of trials of those charged with so-called 'economic crimes', such as embezzlement, bribery, hoarding and fraud.

Opposition sources have argued that the crackdown on the opposition was provoked by an attack on Qadhafi's life. There is no evidence to substantiate this charge, however plausible. True or not, Qadhafi certainly acted on the assumption that the liquidation of a few opponents would discourage the growth of opposition, particularly within the emigré population, which had, by 1981, risen in number to 50,000, 15,000 of whom resided in the United States.[76] His worst fear was that the emigrés, over whom he had no direct control, would increasingly fall under the influence of the exiled opposition groups. The assassination squads were intended as a deterrent to those thinking of joining the ranks of the opposition.

Subsequent events, however, were to prove that Qadhafi had failed to stem the tide of defections. During 1980 Mansour Kekhia, Libya's long-standing ambassador to the UN, defected and went underground. More significant, however, was the defection during this period of Mohammed Yusef Migharief, Libya's ambassador to India. Of the same generation as Qadhafi, Migharief had taught economics and mathematics at Benghazi University before he was appointed to head the state comptroller's commission in 1973. Posted to Delhi in 1977, he assiduously built up a circle of similarly disaffected officials, including a former military officer-turned-diplomat called Ahmed Ahwas. Joining Migharief in exile in Cairo in February 1981, Ahwas had previously served as an officer in the Engineering Corps, and had reputedly taught Qadhafi at Gar Younis military college, before serving on the diplomatic staff of several embassies, finally becoming the Chargé d'Affaire in Guinea. The National Front for the Salvation of Libya, (NFSL) of which both men were the prime instigators, was formally launched on 7 October 1981, probably in Khartoum, on a platform of combined armed and political struggle against Qadhafi. It soon became established as the most prominent, and recognised, of all the opposition organisations.

Behind the National Front for the Salvation of Libya (NFSL) were a number of important emigré businessmen, landowners and merchants whose property in Libya had been progressively expropriated by the revolutionary leadership. The Front was their instrument for regaining power and, therefore, their property. In June 1984, *Arabia*, revealed: 'The Front is financed by Libyan businessmen who run important companies – both in Europe and in the Middle East. It is said that during the Front's congress in 1982, one Libyan alone contributed £1.5 million.'[77] Leading members of the organisation include Mohammed Drak, a former minister, Abdul Saif Majid Nasser, the former royalist governor of Sebha, Abdussalam Ali Aila, a former diplomat, and Abdulaziz Omar Shennib, once a staff colonel in the royal army.

Within the leadership of the Front there was a division of responsibilities between Migharief and Ahwas. Migharief, the General Secretary, supervised the political and propaganda work, namely the establishment of contacts with sympathetic governments, the despatch of delegations to conferences abroad, and the publication of *al-Inqah*, the Front's official magazine. Ahwas, the professional soldier, headed the Front's military wing, the Salvation Corps. The decision to establish the headquarters in the Sudan was influenced by the need to carry out both forms of activity. Location in Egypt, as demonstrated by the experiences of other opposition groups, implied working under a series of rigorous constraints imposed by the regime's security services. The regime of President Numeiri of the Sudan, on the other hand, was prepared to let the Front exercise a greater degree of political independence, to the extent of permitting the Front to conduct military training on Sudanese territory. The Front was Numeiri's answer to Libya's support for Sudanese opposition groups.

To the Reagan administration, searching for a Libyan political alternative to Qadhafi, the National Front was a godsend. Even if there were no actual CIA involvement in the creation of the organisation, it clearly dovetailed with American purposes. The administration has since tried to promote the Front as an equivalent of the 'Contra' NDR in Nicaragua, that is, an organisation that could be used to destabilise Libya through economic sabotage and military intervention. As hostility towards the United States is popular in Libya, Migharief has done his best to distance the Front from the United States. He has publicly warned the United States not to interfere in Libyan affairs, and has stressed that the Front does not want – nor does it receive – aid from the United States. Evidence that the CIA has been the source of much aid and finance, however, would appear to belie this overt posturing. Sudanese government officials have admitted that arms from the United States have been passed on to the Front on a third-party basis from Sudanese supplies.

The Salvation Corps commenced a military offensive in early 1984. The first known instance of armed action was an attack on a Libyan army base at al-Walya on the Tunisian border.[78] Soon afterwards, the Front claimed to have mounted an assault on the al-Abyar military base on the Egyptian border. During the same period there also occurred a number of assassinations, or attempted killings, of Libyan officials abroad. On 21

January 1984, Libya's chief representative in Rome, Omar al-Taggazy, was gunned down as he left his home for the Libyan People's Bureau.[79] The attack was claimed by a group calling itself the Volcano. Qadhafi himself accused al-Fateh, perhaps hoping to embarrass Arafat over the Front's efforts to make contact with Arafat's organisation, but Libya has never yet officially made a practice of admitting raids by the National Front. The fact that the Front itself is given to exaggeration makes it difficult to ascertain the realities of the situation. It is virtually impossible to gauge the level of the Front's support within Libya.

A sign that the National Front was beginning to have some impact within Libya may be perceived in Qadhafi's reaction to the defeat of his motion calling for women's militarisation. Speaking in his Sebha anniversary address on 2 March, Qadhafi lashed out bitterly with these words:

> I am now convinced that there is a reactionary force in the popular congresses, and in no sense must it exercise authority over the popular masses. It must be purged. It must be liquidated so that authority remains in the hands of the masses, who are the only ones to have an interest in the revolution. The task of the revolutionary committees is that they should get ready to settle accounts with the remnants of the royalist society – the reactionary class – who constitute a danger to the freedom of the masses.[80]

Within days of his declaration, the Libyan People's Bureaux in London and Athens were taken over by the Revolutionary Student Force, namely the Revolutionary Committees based in the universities of those countries. The move was in line with a General People's Congress decision to authorise a shake-up of the Foreign Liaison Bureau and diplomatic service, in which the Foreign Liaison Secretary, Abdul ati-Obeidi, a leading *factotum*, was replaced by Dr Ali Treiki, a former Foreign Liaison Secretary and ambassador to the UN. Obeidi in many ways became a scapegoat for the defections of professional diplomats. (Qadhafi had already signalled that such a move was imminent in a speech at Gamal Abdul Nasser Airbase in March 1983,[81] when he called for popular committees to handle diplomatic relations instead of professional diplomats.) The take-over of the People's Bureau in St. James' Square, London, was intended to achieve just that: the People's Bureau Secretary in London, a career diplomat named Adem Kuwiri, was dimissed and succeeded by a student-dominated people's committee, the spokesman for which was a press attaché and revolutionary committee member, Dr Omar Sodani.[82]

Almost immediately there began a campaign against opposition figures in Britain. In Manchester, there were bomb attacks on members of the Libyan Constitutional Union, and in London blasts followed against Marina's newsagency in Bayswater and the Blue Angel Restaurant off Regent's Street, a known meeting place for Libyan emigrés. Anglo-Libyan relations deteriorated, but even this damage was exceeded when gunfire, directed at a General Union of Libyan Students' demonstration on 17 April, issued from the first floor of the London office of the People's Bureau, wounding several protesters and killing a woman police officer, WPC Yvonne Fletcher. In extenuation, the Libyans could–and did–cite provocation; their spokesman, Sodani, was arrested outside the Bureau for arguing with the police about the demonstration, but by any standards the over-reaction was out of all proportion to the incident. Tripoli's persistent reiteration that the shooting had been done in self-defence never carried much conviction, and ultimately the Libyan refusal to negotiate sensibly cost them diplomatic links that they would have preferred to have maintained. All the bureau staff were expelled, and Libya currently has just one diplomat based in London, Mr Musa Musallem.

Just as the Bureau episode drew to a close in London, the Libyan opposition struck, for the first time, in the heart of Tripoli. On 8 May 1984 an unspecified number of gunmen, perhaps eight, tried to storm Bab al-Azziziya Barracks and shoot Qadhafi. Failing to achieve that objective, they took refuge in a block of flats in Tripoli. Fighting with members of the security services and the revolutionary committees continued for five hours, until all the participants in the raid were slain. Although the Libyan authorities claimed that the operation was the responsibility of the Muslim Brotherhood, the attack seemed to be synchronised with a National Front Salvation Corps assault, mounted the same day, on the eastern town of Ghariyan,[83] The plan, if there was one, seemed aimed at paralysing the leadership through the assassination of Qadhafi, whilst the Salvation Corps seized a town and appealed for an uprising. If that was the design, it was certainly ambitious, and the Front paid a heavy price for such adventurous tactics. Not only was Qadhafi shown to be in a strong position, but during the attack Ghariyan, Ahwas and the Salvation Corps were routed and killed.[84]

Qadhafi appears to be justified in alleging Western complicity in the operations. Within days of the attacks, Migharief flew to Washington for talks with senior members of the State Department. But whilst he put the case for increased American support, the indication since the upsurge of military action in the first quarter of 1984 is that the Front's challenge has begun to fade. The initiative has been handed back to Qadhafi. The weeks after the raids saw the revolutionary committees round up and detain several hundred suspected opposition sympathizers, in a move to smash any kind of base the opposition groups had established in Libya. By June 1984, Qadhafi was boasting of his triumph over the National Front. On 11 June, he told a rally marking the 14th anniversary of the evacuation of the American bases that, instead of commemorating just one victory on this occasion, there was cause to celebrate 'two victories.'[85]

Notes

1. See Louis Eaks, *From El Salvador to the Libyan Jamahiriya. A Radical Review of American Policy Under the Reagan Administration* (Third World Reports, The Main Event Ltd., London, 1981).

2. 'Inquiry Into the Matter of Billy Carter and Libya', Subcommittee to Investigate Individuals Representing the Interests of Foreign Governments (US Senate, 2 October 1980)

3. In May 1979 the State Department vetoed the export of 747s ordered by Libyan Arab Airlines, on the grounds that they had 'potential significant military application'.

4. Third World Reports *'From El Salvador to the Libyan Jamahiriya. A Radical Review of American Policy Under the Reagan Aministration'* (The Main Event Ltd., London, 1981) p. 65.

5. Ibid.

6. See 'The Most Dangerous Man in the World', *Newsweek* (20 July 1981).

7. *Emirates News*, UPI report (10 July 1981).

8. *Newsweek* (20 July 1981).

9. For a Libyan account, see *Jamahiriya Review* (September 1981).

10. In *Jamahiriya Review* (September 1981) p. 11.

11. Third World Reports, *From El Salvador to the Libyan Jamahiriya. A Radical Review of American Policy Under the Reagan Administration'* (The Main Event Ltd., London, 1981) p. 63.

12. Ibid., p. 62.

13. 'Oil Embargo: Washington Forced to Act Alone in Bid to Destablise Libya', in *Jamahiriya Review* (April 1982).

14. See Abdullah Kerim, 'Jamahiriya Breaks Wall of Isolation', in *Jamahiriya Review* (August 1982). Includes FBI dismissal of 'hit squad' claim.

15. See *Newsweek* (20 July 1981) and J.K. Cooley, *Libyan Sandstorm* (1982) p. 269.

16. J.K. Cooley, *Libyan Sandstorm*.

17. See my 'Reagan Climbs down from Clash with Libya', in Jamahiriya International Report, vol. 1, no. 22 (4 March 1983).

18. Ibid., (quoted from *Times* of 21 February 1983).

19. *Guardian* (4 August 1983); and *International Herald Tribune* (4 August 1983).

20. *Guardian* (20 March 1984); and *Guardian* (21 March 1984) for Egyptian response.

21. 'Suspicion Grows that Khartoum Launched Raid on its Own People', in *Times* (21 March 1984).

22. For an account of US authorities' harassment of Libyan students, read 'US Economic Blockade Fails', in *JIR*, vol. 12, no. 9 (2 September 1983).

23. For question of further sanctions, see 'What Can Be Done About Kaddafi', *Newsweek* (3 December 1984).

24. Ian Mather, 'Egypt Turns Down the Heat on its Feud With Libya', *Observer*, 2 December 1984).

25. Cooley, *Libyan Sandstorm*, p. 250.

26. Cooley, *Libyan Sandstorm* p. 248.

27. Estimates from Stockholm International Peace Research (SIPRI) yearbook, 1980 (London, 1980).

28. Cooley, *Libyan Sandstorm*, pp. 250-51.

29. See *Defence and Foreign Affairs Handbook* (Copley and Associates, South Africa, 1980).

30. Cooley, *Libyan Sandstorm*, p. 249.

31. And vice-versa; see SIPRI yearbook, 1980, Appendix 3A, p. 158.

32. Cooley, *Libyan Sandstorm*, p. 249; fails to specify what American sources he used.

33. Cooley, ibid., p. 248.

34. Personal correspondence.

35. *Military Review*, No. 11 (Fort Leavenworth, Kansas, November 1979).

36. SIPRI yearbook, 1982, pp. 222–3.

37. Ibid.

38. Cooley, *Libyan Sandstorm*, p. 250.

39. For example, BBC Panorama, 16 June 1980.

40. Cooley, (*Libyan Sandstorm*, p. 235) grossly exaggerates OTRAG's activities in Libya.

41. J. Wright, *Libya: A Modern History*, p. 201.

42. *Defence and Foreign Affairs Handbook*, p. 335, and Wright, *Libya: A Modern History*. This North Korean squadron was reported to be based at Bomba.

43. Estimates vary according to sources. This is my own evaluation based on a number of sources, including *Jane's Defence Weekly*.

44. In *JIR* vol. 1, no. 10 (17 September 1982).

45. Text of Declaration from F. Muscat, *September One* (Adam Publishers, Malta, 1981).

46. *Arab Dawn* (April 1978).

47. *Al-Zahaf al-Akhdar* (English edition Vol. 4 No. 2. (23 April 1983) p. 1.

48. 'The Struggle for Libya', *Arabic Islamic World Review,* (July 1984).

49 In Tripoli Home Service, (28 March 1981): Summary of World Broadcasts ME/6687/A/1, Qadhafi declared: '. . .we now announce the evacuation of regular troops from these military positions and, as you see, the camps which were in Tobruk region have been turned into education centres, schools, institutes and university colleges . . . But, brothers, we should not put much trust in reaction that has sold itself to the devil.'

50. 'MacNeil-Lehrer Report', US National Public Broadcasting Network, (7 May 1981).

51. *Jamahiriya Review* (October 1982).

52. Ibid.

53. *JIR,* vol. 1, no. 17 (24 December 1982).

54. *Jamahiriya Review* (September 1982).

55. *JIR* (17 September 1982).

56. Building the Jamahiri System', *Jamahiriya Review* (June 1983).

57. *Jamahiriya Review* (October 1981).

58. *Jamahiriya Review* (March 1981).

59. *Jamahiriya Review* (June 1983).

60. *JIR,* vol. 1, no. 22 (4 March 1983).

61. *JIR,* vol. 2, no. 5 (8 July 1983).

62. *JIR,* vol. 2, no. 21 (18 February 1984).

63. *JIR,* vol. 2, no. 23 (17 March 1984).

64. Ibid.

65. *JIR,* vol. 2, no. 24 (21 March 1984).

66. Wright, *Libya: A Modern History*, p. 188.
67. Cooley, *Libyan Sandstorm*, p. 167.
68. Ibid., p. 192.
69. Ibid., p. 168.
70. *Arabia* (July 1984).
71. Ibid.
72. BBC Summary of World Broadcasts, ME/6011/A/1.
73. *Arabia* (July 1984).
74. Amnesty International (in correspondence with the author, 1984).
75. *Arabia* (July 1984).
76. BBC Summary of World Broadcasts, ME/6391/A/1.
77. *Arabia* (July 1984).
78. Salvation Corps communiqué.
79. See 'Attack on Bureau Member will not affect Libya's Stand', *JIR*, vol. 2, no. 20 (4 February 1983).
80. *JIR*, vol. 2, no. 23 (17 March 1984).
81. *JIR*, vol. 2, no. 1 (14 May 1983) for details of speech.
82. *JIR*, vol. 2, no. 22 (3 March 1984).
83. *Arabia* (July 1984).
84. Ibid.
85. JIR, vol. 2, (June 1984).

13 Reckoning with Isolation

The Foreign Relations Crisis

The growth of the Libyan opposition movement demonstrates more clearly than any other factor the political isolation that encroached on Libya at the beginning of the 1980s. When Menachem Begin launched the invasion of Lebanon in June 1982, Libya was enveloped by hostilities and ostracised by neighbouring states. To the east, Libya faced overtly belligerent states in Egypt and the Sudan. To the south, Hissene Habre had just taken power in Chad and was reviving his challenge to the Libyan hold on the Aouzou Strip. To the west, relations with Algeria and Tunisia were more stable, but there was still a powerful legacy of mistrust and mutual suspicion. In January 1980, the Tunisian government had virtually accused Libya of instigating an uprising in the southern town of Gafsa. The charge followed a long period of strained relations, in which Libya had supported Tunisian opposition groups who had hoped to start a popular rebellion in the Gafsa area, which had a history of unrest. The same year, there arose a dispute with Malta over off-shore drilling rights in the Mediterranean; both countries had agreed in 1976 to submit the issue to the International Court of Justice in the Hague, but the Maltese Prime Minister Dom Mintoff had invited the US oil company, Texaco, to carry out tests before the verdict was reached. He responded to Libyan gestures of anger with the expulsion of Libyan advisers in August 1980, as well as the conclusion of a defence pact with Italy. Qadhafi seemed unable to contain the tension mounting around Libya's borders.

Beyond the various crises that encircled the Jamahiriya, there developed a strong disagreement with Saudi Arabia. Much of the friction came from the decision of Saudi Arabia to massively increase oil production. The oil glut that resulted made it difficult for those countries with lower levels of production to sell their oil on the world market without price cutting. The Libyans were also offended by certain specific political actions. The most important of these was the Saudi move towards military collaboration with the United States. Riyadh's decision in October 1980 to provide facilities for United States AWAC surveillance aircraft, operated and commanded by American personnel, provoked strident condemnations from Qadhafi. At the height of the pilgrimage season he questioned the Saudi right to custody of the Holy Places of Islam whilst American forces were present on sovereign Saudi territory. He declared that the pilgrimage to Mecca could no longer constitute a sacred duty for Muslims because the deployment of the AWACs defiled the sanctity of the Holy Places.[1] The subsequent decision of the Saudi government to purchase the AWACs the following year, on terms Qadhafi considered humiliating (such as the ban on their use against Israel) brought equally forthright denunciations.[2] During the siege of Beirut, Qadhafi unceremoniously described Crown Prince Fahd, who guided Saudi policy abroad, 'the pig of the Peninsula.'

Foreign Policy Goals

To understand the crisis in Libyan foreign relations, it is helpful to review the goals of Libyan foreign policy. Libya's external relations have been guided by two objectives. Firstly, Libya has an ideological commitment to anti-imperialist causes, most obviously the Arab nationalist struggle for the liberation of Palestine. Libya has supported financially, and sometimes materially, movements considered politically sympathetic from the Philippines to El Salvador. Secondly, Libya tries to maintain stable diplomatic relations with most states (the exceptions being Israel and South Africa) regardless of their political hue. This approach is necessary because Libya relies on foreign trade, particularly the export of oil. The crisis in the country's foreign relations has emerged because of many of those states with which Libya aims to conduct normal trading relations are also states which purchase Libyan oil. During the early 1970s, the Libyan international trading position was such that it was possible for both goals to co-exist without serious political ramifications, but in conditions of a world oil glut it has become increasingly difficult to maintain support for anti-imperialist movements at the same time as retaining normal trade and diplomatic links.

Towards the end of 1981, Qadhafi showed signs of recognising the threat that isolation posed. Several events appear to have awakened him to the danger. Firstly, in August there transpired the dogfight with US planes in the Gulf of Sirte. Then, in October Mohammed Migharief and Ahmed Ahwas founded the National Front for the Salvation of Libya. In Chad, Egypt and the Sudan were building up Habre's forces for a new offensive against Goukouni Oueddei, and Egyptian troops were massing along the frontier with Libya. Qadhafi's reaction was to strengthen his strategic position with the conclusion of a mutual defence treaty, called the Red Sea Pact, with Ethiopia and South Yemen, which was signed in Aden on the same day as the Sirte incident.[3]

Yet, as a response to the American aggression, and the escalation of tension with Egypt and the Sudan, the Red Sea Pact appeared so inadequate that it emphasized the weakness of Libya's position. The circumstances in which either of the two countries could honour their obligation to assist Libya in a military confrontation were exceedingly remote. In fact, the prospects for Libya receiving any direct military support, even from its partners in the SCF, were bleak. The Syrians had their own commitments and, in the 1977 clash with Egypt, the Libyans felt badly let down by the failure of Algeria to come to their aid. Since the death of Houari Boumedienne in December 1978, the hopes of greater Algerian backing had wilted rather than grown.

Qadhafi believed that it was possible to deter military challenges through a policy of internal militarisation and arms build-up. In the end, he only realised the pressing need to combat the country's political isolation when the Reagan administration raised the spectre of an oil embargo. For a country that was the third largest supplier to the United States this could become a grave development. Libya could survive by shifting the volume of exports to Europe, but it would be placed in a catastrophic position if the United States won over its European allies to the idea of an embargo. If Western Europe complied with an oil boycott, Libyan foreign exchange earnings would virtually dry up within months. The chances that eighty per cent of Libyan oil exports could be transferred to Eastern Europe and the Third World, were not promising. Unable to shift the balance of its trade, Libya would be forced back on reserves that would dwindle to next to nothing within two years. Whilst that was clearly an eventuality the leadership was determined to avoid, it was openly acknowledged that the crisis could not be resolved through a policy of retrenchment. The leadership had to go out and strengthen trade ties with Western Europe, if necessary by fostering improved political links.

Fortunately for the Libyans, when the American Secretary of State, Alexander Haig, pushed the case for a Western oil embargo of Libya at a NATO meeting in Brussels in December 1981, he was rebuffed. The states of Western Europe did not want to participate in an American scheme that could do unnecessary harm to their economic interests. West Germany, for example, depended on Libya as its third largest oil supplier, whilst companies throughout the continent were deeply involved in various development projects. The Libyan authorities immediately resolved to strengthen trade ties with Western Europe, seeing in them the best form of insurance against the kind of blackmail Washington was planning. It was no accident that in February 1981 a high level British trade mission visited Libya, consisting of representatives from GEC, Laings, Wimpeys, Pauling Systems and WS Atkins, led by an Under Secretary at the Department of Trade, Ray Williams. The State Department in Washington responded by threatening to blacklist those European companies which conducted trade with Libya. When Aer Lingus announced that it intended to sell Boeings to Libya, the State Department warned that it would ban the air-line from purchasing American-made equipment if the deal went ahead. On that occasion, Aer Lingus backed down, but the Irish government, because of its trade surplus with Libya, refused to be bludgeoned into line. The pressures exerted by the Americans were patently unsuccessful.

Qadhafi, in the meantime, was planning a much more politically-orientated initiative. He was trying to solicit invitations for an official trip to Europe. Initially rebuffed by the Italian government, a request was accepted by the independently-minded Austrian Chancellor, Bruno Kreisky. Qadhafi's plane touched down in Vienna on 10 March; the same day, Washington retaliated by formally declaring a unilateral official embargo on oil imports from Libya and a ban on the sale of technology to Libya. Despite the blow, Qadhafi proceeded to exploit the opportunity to embarrass Washington. At a press conference on 12 March he proposed that Kreisky should act as an intermediary between Libya and Europe because 'what he says about us in Western Europe will carry even greater weight than what we ourselves say.'[4] The issue of the day in Europe was the Reagan administration's decision to deploy Cruise missiles, and Qadhafi warmed to the theme well, professing: 'I personally support the new peace movement in Europe which opposes the deployment of medium-range nuclear missiles. It seems that the US nuclear hell is being transferred to Europe in the form of military bases, nuclear missiles and warships.' Pinpointing the United States as the common adversary, he added: 'We, the Arabs and Europeans, are not prepared to die instead of the American people.'[5]

By expressing support for the European peace movement, Qadhafi hoped to present himself as a peacemaker and Reagan a war-monger. Prior to his departure from Vienna, he conducted a well-publicised meeting with members of the Green Movement, including Roland Vogt MEP, and Professor Alfred Mechterscheimer. 'I consider this meeting a very good starting point for future encounters. We can't discuss everything at once, but we will hopefully achieve our aims together,' he told them.[6] Further to the point, during 1983 a group of Libyan women students paid a visit to Greenham Common women's peace camp, and in Bonn, on 22 October, Libyan students joined a peace movement march, handing out leaflets condemning 'the United States military presence and installation of weapons of destruction aimed at imposing its hegemony on people by force.[7] Part of the interest stemmed from genuine fears about the decision to locate Cruise missiles at Comiso in Sicily. The Libyans felt they had as much to fear from their deployment as did the Soviet Union. In their own limited way, and for their own interests, they were pursuing a 'de-coupling' strategy in which they sought to capitalise on differences between Europe and the United States.

On the eve of the Israeli invasion of Lebanon, the initiative seemed to be working fairly well. Just prior to the outbreak of hostilities in June, Libya had commenced a new round of trade negotiations. In May, the Italian authorities relented somewhat and permitted entry to a high-level Libyan trade mission led by Jalloud. Talks followed with Italian Premier Giovanni Spadolini, but the high-point of the visit came on 22 May, when Jalloud was granted an audience with Pope John-Paul II.[8]

Less symbolic, though of more political significance, was a visit to

France undertaken on 1 June by the Libyan Foreign Liaison Secretary Abdul ati-Ubeidi. Discussions with French Foreign Minister Claude Cheysson elicited a promise actively to encourage French companies to trade with Libya. Referring to American pressure for a boycott, Cheysson commented: 'We even took contrary steps, and bolstered our cooperation.'[9] The Mitterrand administration had in fact already lifted the arms embargo imposed by President Giscard d'Estaing and, as long as France failed to comply with American objectives, there seemed little prospect of other European states sticking their necks out. When the war broke out in Lebanon, there was no change of tack.

Once the immediate danger of the boycott had passed, Libya began a more systematic policy to diversify oil marketing. Barter deals, in which oil was exchanged for arms and other technology, became one form of trade with the USSR and other Eastern European states. These deals were dramatically expanded following Jalloud's visit to Moscow during the fighting in Lebanon.[10] The increased vulnerability felt by the Libyan authorities made them anxious to secure much firmer trade and military links with Eastern Europe. Within six months of the Israeli siege of Beirut, Qadhafi had himself conducted three unprecedented tours of Eastern European countries. Firstly, after the 1 September anniversary, he held talks in Czechoslovakia with president Husak and in Poland with General Jaruzelski.[11] Then, in October, he was briefly in Belgrade and Bulgaria.[12] Thirdly, in January 1983, he visited Romania for talks with President Ceaucescu and continued on a second leg to Bulgaria for a longer spell of consultations with President Zhivkov.[13] Comparing these visits with the sheer omission of visits to Eastern Europe in the early part of his leadership (Qadhafi, it will be remembered, first went to Moscow in 1977) the actual shift taking place in Libyan foreign policy becomes apparent. Eastern Europe was assuming a much more important role in Libyan trade and development, and on 18 March 1983 an agreement in principle on a Treaty of Friendship with the Soviet Union was signed in Moscow by Jalloud and Premier Tikhonov. In 1982, the volume of trade between the two countries was estimated at $1.87 million, more than twice the 1981 figure of $770 million.

Another outlet that the Libyan authorities explored was the Far East. Having severed relations with the People's Republic of China in 1979 over Peking's strong support for President Sadat, Libya took the opportunity, after the Egyptian leader's death in October 1981, to commence overtures for a fresh diplomatic start. At a meeting of the International Forum Against Zionism, Racism, Imperialism and Reaction in Tripoli in March 1982, Qadhafi hinted that 'it would be wise to leave the door open for China to join this forum when it decides to break once and for all with the imperialist forces that are opposed to the people at this forum.'[14] China, of course, showed no signs of doing what Qadhafi requested, but such was the pressure of events that, in May, Tripoli welcomed a Chinese envoy, Hua Yong, for trade negotiations. The next move was a mission to Peking in

August 1982 by the Secretary of the General People's Committee, Jadallah Azouz Talhi, when an agreement was concluded for the participation of Chinese state companies in Libyan development projects.[15] Finally, in October of that year, Qadhafi himself was afforded a state visit to Peking, which he used to evoke the notion of Third World solidarity. At a banquet in the Great Hall of the People, he lambasted the United States before Premier Zhao Ziyang and hundreds of guests, and called on Third World countries, including China, to join forces against superpower aggression.[16] The Chinese leadership was not impressed, but did agree to the establishment of a joint trade commission, the one concrete achievement of his visit. (In April 1983 it was reported that Chinese firms had tendered for 21 'major projects'.)

Other sorties into the Far East were made at roughly the same time. Qadhafi himself, on his return from the People's Republic, stopped in Piyongyang for a meeting with Kim Il Sung and other leaders of Democratic Korea. Not that Libya's close ties with North Korea precluded the development of trade links with South Korea. In fact, South Korean firms, including Hyundai Engineering and the Daewoo Corporation, have become involved in heavy construction projects–a factor that was underlined by the arrival in Tripoli in June 1982 of the South Korean Minister of Construction, Jo Chol Chun.[17]

Of more political significance, however, was the mission to the Philippines' government by Jadallah Azouz Talhi and a delegation consisting of the Secretary for Light Industry, Musa Abu Freiwa, and the Secretary for Communications and Marine Transport, Bukhari Salim Hoda.[18] Although concerned with trade, the visit signalled Libya's formal decision to abandon the Moro secessionist movement. No formal renunciation was ever made, but the splintering of the movement into three factions some time in 1981 enabled Libya to rationalise its political stance towards the Marcos government. Faced with an ineffective liberation movement, the Libyan authorities decided to cut their losses and foster trade links with the regime in Manila.

The Rationalisation of Foreign Policy

Libyan foreign policy entered a period of rationalisation. During this period, the leadership reconsidered its external political orientation in the light of Libyan isolation. Prompting the re-appraisal were several factors, but one that stands out in particular is the double failure to convene the 19th annual OAU summit in Libya in 1982. The summit, initially scheduled for August in Tripoli, was from the outset jeopardised by a long-running dispute over the membership of the Saharan Arab Democratic Republic (SADR), the former Spanish colony of Western Sahara declared independent by the Polisario Front. Morocco threatened to boycott the meeting if the Polisario were admitted, and the United States flexed diplomatic muscle to dissuade other pro-Western or aid-dependent states from participating. The Libyan authorities nevertheless went ahead and invited the SADR, since it had previously been agreed to admit them at a meeting in Addis Ababa.

The result was that when the conference was opened in Tripoli on 5 August, Morocco and its supporters–chiefly the francophone states–carried out their threat to boycott the meeting, and only 31 states from the necessary quorum of 34 were represented. The Reagan administration, whose influence had been instrumental in mobilising support for the boycott, positively gloated at its success, which prevented Qadhafi from chairing the OAU and Libya from representing Africa at the UN for the forthcoming year. Qadhafi, however, resolved to try again, and insisted that the summit be re-convened in Libya sometime later in the year. Five states–Libya, Congo, Mali, Tanzania and Zimbabwe–formed a liaison group assigned responsibility for ensuring that a *quarate* summit would take place in Tripoli in November.[19]

This time Libya secured an agreement with the Polisario voluntarily to withdraw from the proceedings 'in the interests of African unity'. With that concession made, Qadhafi hoped that the summit could be convened without objection, and envoys from the liaison committee were despatched to countries involved in the boycott in order to persuade them to change their stance. One emmissary from Libya even arrived in Kinshasa in a bid to placate President Mobutu, despite Zaire's resumption of diplomatic links with Israel. Objections, however, there were. A row erupted over who should represent Chad–Goukouni Oueddei or Habre. Libya would only recognise Goukouni, but the pro-Western camp, effectively the same states which had stayed away from the August meeting, demanded the admission of Habre's Foreign Minister, Idris Miskine. In response, Qadhafi proposed to leave the seat vacant, but that did not prove an acceptable compromise, and so the second, reconvened summit went the way of the first. Once again there were 31 countries in attendance–3 less than the required quorum. In consequence, Kenyan President Daniel Arap Moi remained Chairman of the organisation, and it was decided that the 1983 summit would be convened in Addis Ababa.

In the aftermath of this débâcle, Qadhafi completed the long-impending revision of Libyan foreign policy. He was by now convinced that to overcome Libya's isolation, both in Africa and the Arab world, Libya's immediate sphere of interest, he must come to terms with a number of key states. Throughout 1983 these became the recipients of persistent Libyan conciliatory initiatives and lobbying. Late in April Qadhafi departed on a tour of West Africa that took him to Nigeria, Benin and Upper Volta (now Borkina Faso) in a bid to restore Libyan influence in the area after the OAU fiasco.[20] The purpose of the trip was to secure from Nigeria, the most important state in sub-Saharan Africa, a statement in support of the Libyan position on the Chadian question, and President Shagari did indeed meet him part-way with a communiqué reaffirming Nigerian support for the Lagos accords. When Shagari was overthrown on 31 December 1983, Tripoli was quick to cultivate a working relationship with the new military government of General Mohammed Buhari. In February 1984, Jalloud visited Nigeria and, on his return, claimed in a paean to the new regime: 'We have found the new government in Nigeria to be nationalist, believing in the people, determined to solve their problems and believing that Nigeria must play a positive role in the African continent.'[21] Whatever differences there were, Tripoli continued to regard good relations with Nigeria as essential to its policy in Africa.

More historically significant was the policy change effected in the Arab world. Deciding that the time had come to ease tensions, Qadhafi journeyed through the Middle East in June 1983 on a tour that encompassed Saudi Arabia, Jordan and North Yemen, three of the most conservative states in the region.[22] The theme of his tour was the need for Arab unity, especially in the field of foreign policy. On that score he received only a lukewarm response, but his initiative did result in a limited reconciliation with Saudi Arabia and North Yemen. There even transpired, for a short period, a flurry of diplomatic activity as military missions exchanged visits, and North Yemen agreed to discuss unification. No tangible benefits materialised, but as past differences were set aside relations entered a period of détente. Libya abandoned open criticism of Saudi policies, whilst Riyadh moderated its stance towards Qadhafi. The Libyan authorities seemed to have hoped for more practical cooperation with Saudi Arabia, most obviously in easing their own cash-flow problems. In late September 1983, Jalloud flew to Riyadh for a meeting with King Fahd about issues which Jeddah radio said were of 'mutual interest'.[23] What actually transpired between the two sides went unreported, but Libya does appear to have requested a 'financial contribution' to help pay for a planned pipe-line project that would transport water across the desert. The Saudis evidently declined, though not in a way that left Tripoli feeling insulted.

Better results were forthcoming from a 'historic compromise' that Qadhafi reached with his longest standing Arab foe, King Hassan of Morocco. Bent on neutralising the state which had spearheaded the OAU boycott, as well as instigated other anti-Libyan moves, Qadhafi arranged through a number of intermediaries a visit to Morocco for talks with Hassan.[24] The mission went ahead on 1 July and Qadhafi, calling on Hassan to set aside past differences, implored the Moroccan monarch to accept unification with Libya. To the general amazement, Hassan accepted. The West seemed bewildered, but then Qadhafi was a shrewder judge of Hassan's situation than was Washington. Qadhafi realised that Morocco, in its own way, was just as isolated as Libya, being embroiled in a costly and draining conflict over the Western Sahara. Supplies of western arms could help him stave off defeat, but they were expensive and no guarantee of victory. Friendly relations with Libya, on the other hand, could remove one of the Polisario's most important backers and gain some income to boost the Moroccan economy and pay for the war effort. Required in return was a more sympathetic posture towards Libya, but in the circumstances that was hardly an exorbitant price to pay. Thus, an agreement was born from obvious mutual interests, but it is one that has stuck because both sides have gained something from the bargain.

The next few months witnessed the regular shuttling back and forth of emissaries between Tripoli and Rabat, culminating on 22 January 1984 with the first joint meeting of the Libyan General People's Committee and the Moroccan Cabinet in Rabat.[25] Finally, the details of a treaty of unification were agreed by Qadhafi and Hassan in a meeting at Oujda in August, and submitted to the General People's Congress in Libya and referendums in Morocco, coinciding with the fifteenth anniversary of the al-Fateh Revolution. Endorsement was unanimous in Libya, as expected, whilst in Morocco the treaty was approved by an overwhelming 99.9 per cent from an extremely high turn-out of 97 per cent. The campaign waged by Hassan and other party leaders was obviously an important contributory factor in such massive ratification; another, much more fundamental reason, lay in the fact that 16,000 Moroccan workers were employed in Libya, and the union agreement opened up the possibility of more jobs in Libya for a workforce that was 20 per cent unemployed in Morocco. The explanation given by a young student, interviewed by the *Daily Telegraph*, was typical: 'If the union provides work in Libya, then the people will thank the King.'[26] Forced to borrow heavily to pay for imported food and oil, Hassan doubtless hoped that Libyan aid, in one form or another, could alleviate the full impact of austerity measures which had already sparked off riots in the northern cities early in 1984.

It is ironic that whilst Qadhafi should be enjoying a thaw in his relations with pro-western states, like Saudi Arabia and Morocco, his links with Europe should be once more threatened. Two events in particular raised the spectre of a major deterioration in relations. Firstly, in July, 1983 France intervened in Chad, and Libyan relations with the Mitterrand administration deteriorated. Secondly, in April 1984 Britain severed diplomatic ties with Libya following the shooting incident in St. James's Square. Re-opening the prospects for further isolation, the above developments were seized upon by the Reagan administration as a pretext for again launching its campaign for a comprehensive western trade embargo of Libya.[27] That more cautious voices prevailed in Europe testifies to the fact that the balance of interests within EEC countries still favoured the maintenance of commercial and business ties. Moreover, there were some serious political objections to the scheme. The EEC foreign ministries felt that if Europe did join the embargo, the result would be to force Libya into greater dependence on the Soviet Union and Eastern Europe.

Qadhafi has proved very adept at exploiting those fears. He has hinted that if Libya is pushed into a corner, it will have nowhere to turn but to the Soviet Union. Addressing a mass rally at Tobruk on 28 March to mark the fourteenth anniversary of the evacuation of British troops, Qadhafi declared: 'Let the USA understand that Libya has approximately 3,000 kilometres of coast on the Mediterranean. Libya, to vex the USA, can give the necessary facilities to the superpower which is hostile to the USA.'[28] There remained some doubt as to whether the Soviet Union would take up the offer, if it were made, just as there must have been some reservations about how earnest Qadhafi was in making it, but United States concern about a potential military alliance has remained a constant factor since that time.

Despite disruptions, Qadhafi regarded a balance in relations between Eastern and Western Europe as indispensable to Libya's independence. In the latter half of 1984, having consolidated his position after the 8 May attempt on his life, he strove to restore some sort of equilibrium with moves to appease governments in Western Europe. In September, he welcomed to Tripoli the Greek Prime Minister Andreas Papendreou, one of the more sympathetic European leaders, who had come to power in 1981. During talks with Qadhafi Papendreou agreed to act as a mediator with the French government, in a bid to reach a settlement over Chad, and direct negotiations hosted by the Greek leader eventually took place between Qadhafi and President Mitterrand on the Greek island of Crete. Subsequently, in another instance of cooperation, the Papendreou government undertook to sell Libya arms and help in the establishment of a Libyan arms industry.

A second initiative focused on Spain; on 19 December 1984, Qadhafi arrived in Palma, Majorca, on an unscheduled 'private visit' that included a meeting with the Spanish Prime Minister, Felipe Gonzalez, together with Dr Bruno Kreisky, who had stood down from the Austrian Chancellorship earlier that year, but still remained on friendly terms with Qadhafi.[29] Whilst he was there, Qadhafi raised the question of better relations with Britain. Towards that end he made the placatory gesture of recommending the release of four Britons detained in retaliation for the arrest in Britain of Libyan students charged with various offences connected with the bombings in Manchester and London. Their release, approved by a majority vote of the BPCs, prior to the General People's Congress in February, followed negotiations between Qadhafi and the Archbishop of Canterbury's envoy, Terry Waite. Qadhafi hoped that in exchange Whitehall would upgrade relations, and possibly expel the detained students, but his wishes have so far been frustrated by the Foreign Office. He is, however, likely to persist with such endeavours for the simple reason that economic, if not political, links remain a crucial priority.

Notes

1. See Mortimer, *Faith and Powers the Politics of Islam* (Faber & Faber, London, 1982).

2. *Jamahiriya Review* (November 1982).

3. *Jamahiriya Review* (September 1981).

4. *Jamahiriya Review* (April 1982).

5. Ibid.

6. *Jamahiriya Review* (May 1982).

7. *JIR*, vol. 2, no. 14 (11 November, 1983).

8. *Jamahiriya Review* (June 1982).

9. Ibid.

10. *Jamahiriya Review* (July 1982).

11. *JIR*, vol. 1, no. 11 (7 October 1982).

12. See *JIR*, vol. 1, no. 12 (12 November, 1983). Qadhafi stopped in Bulgaria on his way to China, and in Yugoslavia on his return. Jalloud, meanwhile, went to Hungary.

13. *JIR*, vol. 1, no. 20 (7 February 1983).

14. *Jamahiriya Review* (April 1982).

15. *Jamahiriya Review* (September 1982).

16. *JIR*, vol. 1, no. 13 (29 October 1982).

17. *JIR*, vol. 1, no. 7 (6 August 1982).

18. *JIR*, vol. 1, no. 11 (1 October 1982).

19. *JIR*, vol. 1, no. 16 (10 December 1983).

20. *JIR*, vol. 2, no. 1 (14 May 1983).

21. *JIR*, vol. 2, no. 23 (17 March 1984).

22. *JIR*, vol. 2, no. 5 (8 July 1983).

23. *Jamahiriya Review* (November 1983).

24. *JIR*, vol. 2, no. 5 (July 1983).

25. *Jamahiriya Review* (February 1984).

26. 'Why Moroccans queue for the Libyan lifeline', *Daily Telegraph* (3 September 1984).

27. *Daily Telegraph* (1 May 1984).

28. *JIR*, vol. 1, no. 25 (14 April 1984).

29. *Times* (20 December 1984).

14 The Transitional Society

The State of Autarky

Qadhafi's revolution currently faces a dual crisis. The threat of external aggression has coincided with a prolonged down-turn in the world oil market. Libyan oil exports, which account for 99 per cent of foreign exchange earnings and 53 per cent of GDP, have contracted sharply in the last five years, not as a result of oil reserve depletion, but because of the slump in global demand for crude oil. Figures released by the Petroleum Secretariat in June 1985 put the level of exports at 890,000 b/d, less than half their 1980 total.[1] More recently, following the imposition of the comprehensive US trade ban in February 1986, oil production was raised to 1.1 million b/d. To beat the deadline set by the administration US oil companies dramatically raised their liftings. Since then the Libyan authorities have concentrated on regaining their market share, but in the wake of OPEC's December 1985 decision to increase rather than restrict production, the country's oil revenues have plummeted.[2] The latest projections for 1986 suggest that revenues may be no more than a third of their 1980 peak.

As the country remains excessively dependent on revenues from oil, the deterioration in the terms of trade has been even more pronounced than in the case of some other oil-producing states. Whilst oil income has declined from $22 billion in 1980 to an estimated $10bn in 1985, the trade balance has steadily worsened, cutting the trade surplus from $11.5bn in 1980 to $2.5bn in 1984.[3] Moreover, during the same period, the Libyan current account position has weakened even more dramatically: where in 1980 the country realised a current account surplus of $8.2bn, in 1984 Libya achieved an unprecedented current account deficit of $2,670; and although the deficit has fallen to $1,920 in 1985, the substantial outflow of service and transfer payments means that a current account deficit is likely to be an attendant economic factor for the rest of the decade. According to a 1985 survey by Wharton Econometrics of Washington D.C., Libya would record a current account deficit of around $600 million in 1990.[4]

To finance foreign trade, the Libyan authorities have been increasingly compelled to draw upon their reserves of foreign exchange. As these have dwindled – from $10.4 million in 1980 to $3.7 million in 1985 – the various

Table 14.1   Oil production, revenue and currency reserves, 1980–85

	1980	1981	1982	1983	1984	1985
Oil production ('000b/d)	1,790	1,215	1,115	1,105	990	910[a]
Revenues from oil production (US$'000)	22,000	15,000	14,000	11,500	10,000	10,000[b]
Estimated financial reserves (US$ millions)	10,400	8,700	6,700	4,500	4,100	3,700

Notes: a = Mid-year projected average based on released export figures and domestic consumption.

        b = Mid-year forecast.

Sources: *BP Statistic Review of World Oil Industry;* OPEC; Wood Mackenzie and Company, Edinburgh; *Middle East Economic Digest; Middle East Economic Survey;* OECD.

constraints on capital investment have mounted. In each successive annual development plan since 1980, the amount of expenditure has been reduced: the annual development budget for 1985 is approximately 19 per cent lower than that for 1984, falling from LD2,110m to LD1,700m.[5] Accordingly, economic activity is slowing down, as it has done since 1981. The rate of growth for 1985, projected at 9.4 per cent, in real terms was under 3 per cent, and forecasts for 1986 and 1987 point to a contraction in the country's GDP, of the order of 2–3 per cent. No projected growth rates have yet been published for the period of the 1986–90 Third Five-Year Plan, but the budget allocated to investment is well under half that assigned to the 1981–85 Second Five-Year Plan.

Like other oil-exporting states, amidst the changing conditions of the world oil market, the Libyans have encountered some difficulty in re-adjusting their economic planning. Their former five-year Transformation Plan, 1981–85, which set the annual growth rate at 9.4 per cent, was formulated against the backdrop of the second oil price boom in 1979. Following the interruption of supplies from Iran, caused by strikes and dislocation during the Iranian revolution, spot market prices had risen to over $40 in September 1979; in October, Libya decided to break the OPEC ceiling price of $23.50 per barrel and set prices for its crude at $26.27 per barrel.[6] Two further price increases, both of four dollars, followed in December 1979 and January 1980. Accordingly, the Secretariat of Planning, calculating on the basis of higher income, allocated a total of LD18.5bn for the development budget, far above the investment budgeted in the 1976–80 five-year Transformation Plan.

The Transformation Plan was formally adopted by the annual meeting of the General People's Congress in January 1981. The agricultural sector, with a budget of LD3,100m, was accorded the largest single allocation, but there was clear emphasis on the development of heavy industry, which was allotted LD2,730m. In fact, if the budgets for light and heavy industry are combined, industry received the larger allocation. Over the plan period, industrial output was scheduled to grow at a rate of 21.6 per cent annually, and the contribution to national income of the non-oil sectors to rise from 35 per cent to 53 per cent. Within six months, however, the phenomenon of an excess of supply over demand in the world oil market had produced a major contraction in the country's crude exports. By the third quarter of 1981 crude exports had slumped to about 650,000 b/d from an average of 1.7m b/d in 1980. The sharp diminution of revenue inexorably undermined the development plan and jeopardised financial arrangements.

The scale of the crisis confronting Libya was revealed at the General People's Congress in February 1983. Giving his annual report, the Congress Secretary Mohammed Rajab, declared: '1982 witnessed continued international developments and a deterioration in the oil market, characterised by a continued fall in demand and pressure on prices, which led to a reduction in sales prices set by OPEC.' Libya, he said, 'suffered a reduction in prices of no less than 15 per cent, coupled with a considerable

Table 14.2   Second Social and Economic Transformation Plan, 1981–85

Sector	Allocation (in LD millions)
Agrarian reform & land reclamation	3,100
Heavy industry	2,730
Light industry	1,200
Oil & gas	200
Electricity	2,000
Education	1,000
Information and culture	150
Manpower	150
Health	560
Social security	130
Sports	100
Housing	1,700
Municipalities	1,300
Communications & marine transport	2,100
Economy	500
Planning	80
Reserve for projects	1,500
Total	*18,500*

Note: Libyan dinar 0.41 = £1 as at 22 July 1985.
Source: Compiled by author.

reduction in the volume of exports'. He went on to warn: 'The continued world recession throughout 1983 means that the original figures set for oil revenues will be hard to reach.'[7]

Two factors exacerbated the decline in export earnings. First, the Libyan share of the oil market shrank due to the relatively high price of Libyan crude in relation to the prices charged by other exporters, notably Saudi Arabia. Libyan Zueitina crude was the most expensive crude in the world market, costing as much as $11.5 per barrel more than Saudi Arabia's Arabian Heavy; the normal differential between the two was $2.2 per barrel. In 1981 Libyan crude was, on average, priced $4 higher than the light 'marker' crude of Saudi Arabia, which expanded production from 8.5 million b/d to 10.3 million, creating the beginnings of a glut in the world market. The majors subsequently reduced the size of their liftings and, faced with persistent official resistance to lower prices, two US companies, Exxon and Mobil, finally decided to abandon operations in Libya.[8] It was not until there was a discount of $1.50 off the official marked price of $37.50 per barrel, which was set in December 1981, that the authorities were able to restore some oil company confidence and induce a rise in production. Following the discount, production rose to 1.7 million b/d.

A second temporary blow to the country's export earnings came in the form of the US trade sanctions of March 1982, applying to the export of Libyan crude oil and the import of American technology. As the United States was Libya's biggest trading partner, accounting for 35 per cent of oil exports, the country experienced serious dislocation in oil production and marketing. Trade between the two countries had previously reached a high point: according to figures produced by the US Department of Commerce, Libyan exports to the United States rose from $1.4 million in 1974, to $8,594.7 million in 1980. Between January and September 1981, however, exports to the US slumped to $4,916.9 million, and between January and September 1982 had further dropped to $493.5 million. Total oil exports crashed from 1.2 m b/d on the eve of the embargo to a new low point of 600,000 b/d, prompting a price cut of $10 per barrel on the previous year's price, designed to stimulate export demand.

Shortages of foreign exchange began to emerge as a problem in Autumn 1981, when oil sales first plummeted in conditions of a market glut. Following the March 1982 US embargo, they became acute: the cash-flow situation deteriorated to such an extent that Libya was effectively unable to keep up its foreign payments. For a week in late 1981, the Central Bank of Libya stopped all foreign payments; around the same time, the authorities also secured the facility of a $250 million Euroloan in order to establish a credit rating for the country.[9] However, the sensitive option of foreign borrowing was deferred in favour of counter trade and cutbacks in consumption. For six weeks after the Reagan administration imposed its first sanctions, the authorities maintained a complete ban on the import of consumer goods, including cars.

Trade debts started to accumulate from the second half of 1981. By

October 1982 they had escalated to an estimated $2,000–$3,000m. The usual four-month bureaucratic delay in payment to foreign contractors was extended to about nine months, or in some areas, notably construction, even more. Turkish companies, heavily concentrated in the construction sector, were owed $700 m in 1982; Italian companies, many involved in off-shore oil exploration, were owed $622 million.[10] Towards the end of 1982, currency reserves had fallen to about four months' import cover, and although the cash-flow improved slightly in 1984, trade debts remained a constant feature of economic life. Debts to foreign contractors had risen to $4,000 m in 1985 and, in some cases, payments were four years in arrears.

In the absence of a significant recovery in the oil market, further stringent controls were necessary. In 1984, faced with a spending budget equivalent to $18,000 million and revenues projected at $10,000 million, the General People's Congress took the unprecedented decision of instructing the Central Bank to balance expenditure against revenue on a monthly basis. The Congress also voted to remove subsidies from the service industries, which were duly established along financially autonomous lines. Lastly, in January 1985, the Congress agreed to set up Consumer Guidance Committees, specifically to monitor and reduce local domestic consumption. In fact, the urgent need to save foreign exchange by curbing consumption had been a major theme in Qadhafi's speech to the 1985 Congress. In a televised address, Qadhafi issued this appeal for cutbacks and sacrifice:

If you save large enough sums, you will be increasing the foreign exchange reserve. Libya would thus appear strong in the world because it has large reserves. Afterwards you would be able to build factories, plantations, schools, and you would be making a stride along the road to progress. You would become an advanced state and no longer be underdeveloped. It doesn't mean there is no money . . . No, we want to save so that we can pass through the stage of transformation quickly – in a few years – and build factories and till the land and advance. The matter rests with us, our effort, our will and our awareness. We can make a big jump and be ahead of all the third world countries and become an advanced country in a matter of years.[11]

Food shortages are the most obvious sign of the country's creeping austerity. As the country's foreign exchange reserves have declined, the supply of various foodstuffs has contracted. The shelves at the state supermarket, full when the private retail sector was abolished in 1981, are now frequently empty of essential household goods, including food items. In February 1986, Benghazi's state-run supermarkets contained no baked bread, just flour and yeast; students at Gar Younis University had not received meat from their refectories for many months. For their supplies, local people were turning to the private agricultural markets, permitted since 1982 following criticism of the General Marketing Corporation, voiced at the annual meetings of the BPCs; otherwise, food and other goods

Table 14.3   Annual Decline of Development Budget, 1981–85

	1981	*1982*	*1983*	*1984*	*1985*
		millions of dinars			
Agrarian reform & land reclamation	460	347	295.5	287	225
Heavy industry	500	493	400	375	300
Light industry	200	na	95	85	60
Oil & gas	60	40	30	na	na
Electricity	250	190	200	180	150
Education	180	157	140	120	110
Information & culture	24	20	15	na	na
Manpower	25	na	10	na	na
Health	105	82	70	60	50
Social security	22	15	15	na	na
Sports	23	na	15	na	na
Housing	270	230	200	170	150
Municipalities	220	215	215	180	160
Communications & marine transport	306	355	310	270	225
Economy	200	140	60	na	na
Planning	15	10	12	na	na
Reserve for projects	140	na	287	383	270
Total	*3,000*	*2,600*	*2,370*	*2,110*	*1,700*

Note: Libyan dinar 0.41 = £1 sterling as at 22 July 1985.
Source: Compiled by author.

were being obtained from the country's thriving black market. This has grown tremendously in recent years, and currently provides items such as butter and mutton at double the official, subsidised price.

As yet, there is no reason to assume that the current austerity is a permanent and deepening process. With a population of only 3.4 million Libya is well placed to withstand the depressed conditions of the oil market. Whilst national income has declined in the last five years, figures for 1984 reveal a *per capita* GDP of £5,713, higher than that of many industrial states. On present trends, therefore, the leadership has some room to decrease domestic consumption without inducing discontent. In fact, one unforeseen benefit of the recent unfavourable financial conditions applying to Libya has been a more efficient distribution of resources. Under the impact of foreign exchange shortages, the tendencies to overspending and mismanagement have decreased. Where spending committees once signed up foreign contractors without guaranteeing finance, they now wait for their project allocation and limit expenditure to their agreed budget.[12]

Long-term Prospects

Although the short-term outlook for Libya is gloomy, the long-term prospects are much brighter. New oil discoveries, including major finds of 2.8bn barrels at Sarir and Masalah in December 1984, have extended Libya's life-span as an oil exporter. According to projections made in 1984, Libya has reserves sufficient for 52 years at the current rate of extraction. The decline in revenues, whilst damaging in the short-term, does have limits, and Libya could gain when there is an upturn in the market. Wharton Econometrics of Washington D.C., predicts that oil production will rise from 1.1 million b/d to 1.4 million b/d between 1987–1990, allowing the resumption of economic growth.[13] However, the longer-term post-oil prospects very much depend on Libya's response to present conditions.

The leadership is responding to the decline in oil income with efforts to increase productivity and output in the agricultural and industrial sectors. Falling rates of growth, and forecasts of stagnation in the oil market have emphasised the importance of generating self-sustained growth independent of the oil sector. As budget allocations have contracted, causing delays and cancellations in several areas, Libya has undergone a period of rigorous and necessary investment rationalisation. Resources are being concentrated on a number of priority projects, including the so-called 'industrial fortresses'–heavy industrial complexes–through which Libya hopes to become an autonomous centre of capital accumulation. Although these projects were planned prior to current economic conditions–many of them rolled over from the previous 1976–80 Transformation Plan–they have not been abandoned because of their capacity to diversify the economy away from dependence on crude oil exports. Since the General People's Congress of 1982 there has been a moratorium on the funding of industrial projects, except for work relating to the fortresses, which receive the largest share of actual investment in development budgets.

Industrial Fortresses

There are two types of industrial fortress: those related to downstream oil activity, namely refineries and petro-chemical complexes, planned for diversification *within* the hydrocarbons sector; and those based on the production of other mineral deposits and designed for diversification *away* from the hydrocarbons sector. Examples of the former type include the petro-chemical plants at Mersa Brega and Ras Lanuf, begun respectively in 1977 and 1978, and the major az-Zawiyah Oil Refinery where first-stage production occurred in 1974. Falling within the latter category are the Misrata Iron and Steel Works and the Zuwara Aluminium Smelter, commissioned under the 1981–85 Transformation Plan and the cement plants at Derna, Labdah and Zliten. As the least affected by shortages of foreign exchange, the Misrata Iron and Steel Works, the Zuwara Aluminium Smelter and the Ras Lanuf petro-chemicals complex occupy a position at the top of the industrial hierarchy. Between 1980 and 1985 the country's metallurgical industries, comprised essentially of the Misrata and Zuwara schemes, were projected to grow at a rate of 60 per cent, higher than the rate forecast for other industries. Petro-chemicals, the next in order of importance, was projected to grow at a rate of 38.1 per cent.[14]

Within the hydrocarbons sector particularly, diversification is proceeding well. Since the announcement in June 1985 of the completion of a third-phase extension at the az-Zawiya refinery, following the addition of a second-phase expansion in 1977, the Libyan authorities are claiming almost to have reached self-sufficiency in their refining capacity. The az-Zawiya complex, which supplemented an earlier and smaller refinery at Mersa Brega, now has a refining capacity of approximately 180,000 b/d, and domestic output will be increased further with the completion of the refineries under construction at Misrata and Ras Lanuf. Output from the petro-chemical industry, so far confined to urea, ammonia and methanol, was estimated to rise from LD9.3m in 1980 to LD48.1m in 1985.[15] In 1985, exports of petro-chemicals, primarily urea from the Mersa Brega complex, capable of 1,000 tonnes per day, earnt Libya LD51 million in foreign exchange: in the same year, exports of refined petroleum products were worth approximately LD299.5 million.[16]

By contrast, diversification outside the hydrocarbons sector shows no signs of generating substantial export earnings as yet. Neither the Misrata Steel Works, nor the Zuwara Aluminium Smelter, two prospective sources of post-oil foreign exchange, will come on stream much before the year 2000. If conditions of over-capacity persist in the steel and aluminium markets, income from exports could be negligible. Given the enormous costs involved in both prestige projects – LD4.6 billion in the case of the Misrata project and LD1.25 billion for the Zuwara site – it could, even on the most optimistic assessment, take decades to recover the investment. According to estimates in 1984, output in the country's metallurgical industry remained under LD10 million and output in the chemical industry, distinct from petro-chemicals, less than LD30 million. In fact, outside the hydrocarbons sector output has risen most in the building materials and food processing industries, but consumption is local, not foreign.

Raising the investment/growth ratio outside the hydrocarbons sector becomes urgent with the reduction in foreign exchange earnings from oil. Before the deterioration in the oil market, the chronically low output in sectors other than oil imposed few constraints on capital investment. In fact, the Libyan economy proved generally incapable of absorbing investment allocations. In successive development plans, the actual rate of growth was invariably lower than the projected rate of growth. Since 1968, the rate of plan fulfilment has fallen markedly, and the proportion of the 1981–85 Transformation Plan left unfulfilled is the largest yet. In 1968, actual investment is estimated to have surpassed the target by 2.1 per cent, but by 1973 the rate had fallen to just 28.0 per cent of planned investment; and by 1976 plan fulfilment figures had plunged to 21.6 per cent. Between

1981 and 1985, actual investment ranged from 75–85 per cent less than planned investment.[17]

Of all the economic sectors agriculture has the lowest absorptive capacity. Having exceeded targets in the 1972–75 Three-Year Intermediate Plan, investment in agriculture underwent a major contraction in the second half of the decade. Following the drawdown of groundwater levels, especially in the Jefara Plain region, capital inputs failed to restore sectoral growth. Whilst the 1976–80 Transformation Plan allocated $5,065.5m to agriculture, with a projected rate of growth of 15.8 per cent, the real growth rate was only 3.6 per cent. By the end of the Plan period, agriculture's share of GNP has fallen from 4.8 per cent to 3.5 per cent. In the 1981–85 Transformation Plan the projected growth rate was 7.5 per cent, but by the end of 1985 the sector's percentage of GDP had dropped below 2 per cent.[18]

Shortages of indigenous labour remain the biggest impediment to efficient investment. Economic growth in the 1981–85 Transformation Plan, like its predecessors, has relied extensively on foreign labour, both skilled and unskilled. At the start of 1985, the migrant work force had risen to about 520,000, over a third of the country's total manpower. In the years since the Plan was adopted, however, the considerable disadvantages of a large migrant workforce have begun to outweigh the benefits. As Libyan foreign exchange reserves have declined, the outflows from the economy, in the form of workers' remittances, have become the major debit on the deteriorating trade balance. To cut down the outflow, the Libyan authorities have developed two responses: in 1984 regulations were imposed restricting transfers to half the remittance, subject to an $86 surcharge; and in 1985, towards the end of the five-year plan, the authorities began to contract the supply of migrant labour. In August 1985, a 1982 resolution of the General People's Congress calling for cutbacks in the foreign labour force was finally put into practice. Accordingly, amidst a political furore with neighbouring states, some 45,000 workers, two-thirds of them Egyptian and Tunisian nationals, were repatriated. Key groups of Arab migrants received offers of permanent settlement, and some returnees were prevented, under currency regulations, from transferring their complete savings and property.[19]

In order to reduce the acute dependency on migrant labour the Libyan leadership has, for the past four years, striven with ever more intensity to increase the labour-productivity of the indigenous work force. High labour-productivity was an important theme in Qadhafi speeches to the annual meetings of the BPCs in 1983 and 1984. Following his address at the 1983 General People's Congress, when he criticised 'trivial posts carrying high salaries' in the administration, which were 'unproductive and beyond discipline and accountability',[19] a series of measures was approved, lengthening the working day from 8 to 12 hours, introducing in some enterprises round-the-clock shifts, and a crackdown on rampant absenteeism supervised by revolutionary committees and traffic committees. More recently, the authorities have begun the militarisation of production, bringing in soldiers to supervise output, and appointing what are called 'national cadres', otherwise members of the revolutionary committees, to senior managerial posts in state-run companies.

'Great Man-Made River' Project

Meanwhile, the authorities have started confronting the second major obstruction to economic growth: the inadequate supply of water. To expand the volume of available water and boost agricultural production, the country has embarked on the 'Great Man-made River' project, which at $9 billion overwhelms other schemes in both scale and expense. It is planned that the river, in reality a series of five pipe-lines, will transport 2 million cubic metres of water per annum from 20,000-year-old artesian wells in the southern desert, the site of a water stratum 450 km wide by 150 km long, to the coastal areas where agricultural production is concentrated. Along the way, the line will feed irrigations systems covering a third of a million hectares and allow the replenishment of groundwater resources in the Jebel Akhdar and Jefara Plain. By 1990, it is estimated that water from the 'Great Man-made River' (GMR) will be sufficient to permit production of 80 per cent of the country's cereal needs.[20]

Earlier attempts to utilise the underground water nearer source, in Kufra and Sarir, proved commercially unviable. In 1980, following surveys which indicated that the costs of production could be halved, the Secretariat of Planning switched to a proposal to transport water to the main northern farming areas. According to Dohali Migharief, director of the project's spending committee, the GMR is, in commercial terms, the most feasible option for Libyan agriculture. A cubic metre of GMR water costs an estimated 16 cents, in comparison with desalinated water at $3.75 per cubic metre, and imported water, transported in oil tankers, amounting to $2.80 per cubic metre.[21] Moreover, if hydrogeologists' predictions of replenishment are confirmed, studies confidently conclude that Libya can rely on 50 years' supply.

The first stage of the project, launched on 31 August 1984, is a 400 km pipe-line carrying water from Tazerbu and Sarir to Ajdabiya on the coast. Following its completion in 1989, a second stage for transporting water from aquifers in Fezzan to Tripoli will commence, followed by a third stage which will extend the system from a holding reservoir at Ajdabiya to Sirte, a fourth stage from Ajdabiya to Tobruk, and a fifth stage from Tripoli to Sirte. As it is largely financed by taxes levied on consumer goods, including oil, oil products and cigarettes, the scheme is the only one to have escaped the stringent financial controls placed on investment. Bills from foreign contractors undertaking work on the vast project, most importantly the Dong Ah construction company of South Korea, are settled within 10 days of their receipt.

If the leadership does make headway in resolving the difficulties posed by manpower and water shortages, this does not necessarily imply that the constraints have been removed from self-sustained growth. The Libyan economy remains fundamentally dependent on inputs of foreign expertise and technology. With a continuation of these inputs, Libya can achieve a degree of self-sufficiency in agricultural and industrial production, but in the foreseeable future is unlikely to develop independently as a centre of capital accumulation. The country's economic growth remains based on income from a finite energy resource, subject to the vagaries of the world oil market. Without substantial non-oil resources, Libya has so far proved unable, within the world division of trade, to transform its role which, whether the oil market picks up or not, remains that of an oil producer of declining power.

From State Capitalism to Post-capitalism?

The external antipathy generated by the Libyan revolution in recent years arises from an internal process of social transformation. Since 1969, the country has undergone a transition from emerging capitalist property relations to the progressive abolition of capitalist property relations. The revolution instigated by Qadhafi has passed through four distinct phases of economic change: the first was the development of state capitalism, including, most importantly, the imposition of domestic state control in the oil sector; the second, occurring between 1975 and 1976, was the creation of a state monopoly of foreign trade; the third was the expropriation of industrial, or productive capital, accomplished by the 'producers' revolution' of 1979; and the fourth was the expropriation of large sections of commercial capital, including elements of the traditional petty-bourgeoisie, with the state take-over of the distributive, wholesale and retail sector beginning in 1981. By 1986 private capitalism in Libya seemed to be in the process of being eliminated.

The most recent changes have affected landownership. In November 1985, the leadership decided to proceed with the expropriation of all forms of landownership other than farmer proprietorships in a gesture symbolising the overthrow of the capitalist landowning class. The revolutionary committees attacked the Land Registry in Tripoli and burnt the records of landownership. The landholdings concentrated in the Jefara Plain had been exempted from the earlier programme of agrarian reform because of their ownership by Libyans rather than Italian settlers. Their eventual re-distribution had become imminent, however, following the introduction of regulations on the ownership of second homes and rented property in 1978. The lands had remained in private ownership because of their high agricultural productivity, but the management and abuse of declining groundwater sources encouraged re-distribution. The final expropriation of the landowners preceded a more general re-organisation of agriculture, which began in February 1985 with the creation of 420 'self-sufficiency' farms. Politically and economically, a 10-hectare family farm

275

was perceived as the most desirable unit of agricultural production.[22]

As a consequence of this process of social transformation, antagonisms have been engendered with most states in North Africa and the Middle East. Beyond ideological and foreign policy differences, the various capitalist states of the region perceive a political threat in the wish of the Libyan leadership to 'export' a form of social organisation entailing the overthrow of capitalist interests. Whilst this has not prevented a number of states from entering into strategic foreign policy alliances with Libya – for example, Morocco and Syria – it has undermined Libyan unification initiatives and made Libya a focus of hostility and suspicion in relations with other states. More in response to the vulnerability of the pro-western capitalist states in the region, than the challenge actually posed by Libya, Washington has struggled to put the Qadhafi revolution in 'quarantine'. Conversely, the same internal transition which has brought an adverse reaction from the United States has helped cement much closer ties with the Soviet Union and other transitional societies.

Libya today is a qualitatively different society than it was in the early years of RCC control. In 1974, Ruth First, in her study of the Libyan Revolution, observed:

> There is a large and growing petit-bourgeoisie, which is mostly urban, ranging from small businessmen and shopkeepers, to professionals, intellectuals and students, and a spreading strata of public officials.[23]

Since then, the class composition of Libyan society has changed profoundly. The petit-bourgeoisie remains an important factor, but has, nevertheless, declined in its social significance; the traditional petit-bourgeoisie of small businessmen and shopkeepers has, in particular, faced a series of restrictions impeding its accumulation of wealth and status. It is now technically illegal for them to employ staff, even the most junior assistants, without these becoming equal partners. Most recently, moves have been instituted to curb the increase of public officials, and students and intellectuals, other than those who comply with the *Green Book* ideology, have no major social influence. The commercial bourgeoisie and the small productive bourgeoisie have been eliminated.

Conversely, the working class has grown in size and social importance. Whilst between 1975 and 1980, the population increased at an annual rate of 5.2 per cent, the country's indigenous workforce rose by an annual 3.2 per cent. Taking the higher birthrate into account, the rate of growth of the labour force marginally exceeded the rate of growth of the school-leaving population. Thus the working class was growing at the expense of other sections of society: for instance, independent artisans and small-holders were becoming employed workers.

Unlike Saudi Arabia and the Gulf states, the Libyan leadership has not pursued policies designed to preserve the pre-capitalist social structure of the population. The state has consistently promoted the development of industry and the creation of an industrial workforce. Between 1975 and

Table 14.4 Occupational Distribution of Libyan Workforce, 1975–80

Occupation	1975		1980	
	No.	%	No.	%
Managerial & professional	11,620	2.5	19,940	3.6
Technicians	37,650	8.2	63,710	11.6
Clerical	31,410	6.9	44,650	8.1
Skilled and semi-skilled workers	251,365	55.3	307,160	56.3
Unskilled workers	122,055	26.8	109,740	20.1
Total	*454,100*	*100.0*	*545,200*	*100.0*

Source: Secretariat of Information, Tripoli.

Table 14.5 Distribution of Nationals by Economic Sector, 1973, 1975 and 1980 ('000's)

Economic Sector	1973		1975		1980		Annual rate of growth 1975–80%
	No.	%	No.	%	No.	%	
Agriculture	110.4	25.5	115.5	25.4	130.30	24.5	2.4
Petroleum & gas	8.2	2.0	8.0	1.8	8.6	1.6	1.4
Mining & quarrying			4.1	0.9	5.3	1.0	5.3
Manufacturing	13.3	3.1	19.1	4.2	32.7	6.1	11.3
Electricity, gas, water	8.6	2.0	9.4	2.1	14.1	2.6	8.4
Construction	30.6	7.1	34.6	7.6	42.8	8.0	4.3
Trade, restaurants, hotels	34.2	7.9	40.8	9.0	40.0	7.5	–0.4
Transport, storage, communications	42.1	9.6	47.2	10.4	60.0	11.3	4.9
Finance, insurance, real estate	5.2	1.2	6.1	1.3	7.1	1.3	3.1
Social and personal services	180.1	41.6	169.6	37.3	191.9	36.1	2.5
Total	*432.7*	*100.0*	*454.4*	*100.0*	*532.8*	*100.0*	*3.2*

Source: Based on information in J.S. Birks and C.A. Sinclair, *The Kingdom of Saudi Arabia and the Libyan Arab Jamahiriya: The Key Countries of Employment* (World Employment Programme Research Working Paper, International Labour Office, Geneva, 1979); and J.S. Birks and C.A. Sinclair, *Arab Manpower: The Crisis of Development* (Croom Helm, London, 1980).

1980, the workforce employed in manufacturing industry grew at an annual rate of 11.3 per cent, outstripping the expansion of the indigenous workforce in any other economic sector. In 1985, the Secretariat of Information released figures showing an industrial workforce of 69,000. By the standards of more populous states in the region, this figure is negligible; by Libyan standards, it represents an important shift within society. To the extent that the growth has been retarded, conscription and the spread of administration are to blame. The proliferation of people's committees, which now employ a third of the total workforce, has facilitated the withdrawal of the local population from the productive sectors of the economy, although this has occurred because of social influences and lack of sectoral skills, not because of official policy. Qadhafi has constantly stressed the objective of labour self-sufficiency in every economic sector.

The changing balance of class forces is an indication of the transformation taking place in Libya. Until the 'producers' revolution' of 1979, Libya could accurately and uncontroversially be designated a form of state capitalist society; typically, the period between 1969 and 1979 was a classic period of bourgeois national revolution, in which the state organised the domestic accumulation of capital in conjunction with the private sector. However, in the period following the political crisis of 1976, Qadhafi and his faction within the leadership moved away from this model of state capitalist development; with the publication of the second part of the *Green Book* in 1978, the nominal goal became the creation of a collectively-owned economy, in which planning, production and distribution are supervised by the associated producers themselves. Hence, the introduction of producers' partnerships in manufacturing and service industries. Through the establishment of 'vocational congresses' Libyan workers gained legal control over the means of production and the organisation of their labour-power.

Effectively, in the last decade, Libya has undergone a shift *away* from an essentially capitalist society. Several key features which define the nature of a capitalist society no longer apply in the case of Libya. Firstly, in general, the means of production and distribution do not constitute commodities; to the extent that commodity relations exist, they are confined to self-employed farmers and businessmen. Secondly, in regard to the indigenous population, the wage-form has been progressively eliminated. Notably, the process of change has not simply involved the replacement of private ownership with state ownership; crucially, it has entailed the transformation of the relations of production. Qadhafi is himself conscious of the fact that the mere substitution of state ownership for private ownership does not produce a socialist economy. For example, in a speech to the Arab Conference on Workers' Culture in Tripoli, on 23 December 1983, he observed:

> The development which affects ownership did not solve the issue of the worker's right to the production he yields directly and this is evident in the status of the producers who are still wage-earners despite the alteration of ownership.[24]

Nevertheless, it must be stressed that the transition towards a post-capitalist society is partial and fragile. The system of work-place committees, or vocational congresses, has been deliberately excluded from the two areas of the economy defined as strategic, namely the oil industry and the Great Man-made River project. Moreover, despite the recent expulsions of migrant workers, Libya relies on the foreign labour market to fulfil 25–30 per cent of total labour requirements. In this foreign labour market capitalist relations of production prevail: Libya's foreign workforce is prevented from forming, or joining, work-place committees, and exercises no control over production. In addition, migrant workers are not allowed to organise, publish, or take strike action. Quite often, contract migrants, usually concentrated in the construction industry, are physically segregated from the indigenous population and subjected to the labour discipline of the foreign companies that employ them. For instance, in August 1985, 120 Indian construction workers were deported for taking strike action at the site of a military airfield being built by an agency of the Czechoslovakian government.[26]

The absence of work-place committees from the strategic areas of the economy, which produce the majority of the country's wealth, does not necessarily imply that Libya is ruled by a state capitalist ruling class. Within the Libyan state there are a series of bureaucratic élites who compete for influence and resources, but they do not constitute a social layer which could accurately be described as a 'class'. Nominally, whilst vocational congresses are excluded from the oil sector, control of oil production, and the distribution of the wealth accrued from oil production, lie with the Basic People's Congresses and the General People's Congress. The privileges of the three most important bureaucratic élites within the Libyan state – the leaders of the military, the revolutionary committees and the administrative structure – are derived from their particular forms of labour-power, not ownership of capital. As such, their privileges are located in the sphere of consumption, not ownership. Members of these various élites gain in the way of better housing and medical care, their own supermarkets and easier access to travel visas; but the position they occupy and the benefits the receive do not arise from the ownership of property.

Contemporary Libya is best portrayed as a transitional society, possessing capitalist and post-capitalist characteristics. The state no longer promotes capitalist relations of production within Libya, but has not evolved socialist forms of organisation either. The possibility that the more anti-capitalist trends apparent in recent years will be reversed cannot be dismissed. Two factors could facilitate the restoration of the private capitalist sector. The first is the autonomy of the state in relation to other social forces, including the working class; this is reinforced by the absence of workplace committees in the oil industry and the excessive dependence on foreign labour. Secondly, there remains an important ideological tension between a state which rejects the democratic self-organisation of the working class and, at the same time, renounces forms of private property. In the long-term, officials within the state could form the basis of a renewed private sector; this already seems evident with the growth of the black market. Much depends on the personalities of those who occupy positions within the state, notably Qadhafi himself. Currently, Qadhafi remains an obstacle to the restoration of private ownership.

Notes

1. See J. Bearman, 'Ambitious Counterattacks against Advancing Crisis', *Arabia: Islamic World Review* (October 1985); and J. Bearman, 'Revolution in Recession', *South* (October 1985).

2. Libya, along with Algeria, Iran and Venezuela, has voiced reservations about the OPEC strategy of regaining market shares by higher levels of production. See *MEED* (15–21 February 1986).

3. *Libya: An Economic Report* (The National Westminster Bank, August 1985).

4. *MEED* (21 December 1985).

5. *Libya* (National Westminster Bank, August 1985).

6. P. Terzian, *OPEC: The Inside Story* (Zed Books, London, 1985) p. 271.

7. *Jamahiriya Review* (March 1983). At the 1982 General People's Congress, the Oil Secretary, Abdul Salam Zaager accused 'a number of oil-producing states' of a conspiracy, inferring Saudi Arabia and the smaller Gulf states.

8. Exxon decided to pull out of Libya in 1981; Mobil followed suit in 1982. Both companies were placed under pressure by the Reagan administration to leave, but political factors were of secondary importance. Mobil's President, P. Tavoulareas, cited the fall in profits from Libyan operations. See *Jamahiriya International Report*, vol. 1, no. 4 (25 June 1982).

9. According to Libyan banking sources, the loan was secured in order to establish a credit rating for the country and introduce to the market the newly-inaugurated Libyan Arab Foreign Investment Company (LAFIC). This is the body which handles the state's equity in Fiat, Mario Miraldi and the Tamoil refinery near Cremona, all in Italy. It does not supervise banking investments. See *MEED* (18 December 1981).

10. For an account of Libya's debt burden, see Michael Petrie-Richie, 'Libya – an exporter's nightmare', *MEED* (15 October 1982).

11. BBC Summary of World Broadcasts ME/7842/A/1.

12. BBC SWB ME/7892/A/2.

13. *MEED* (21 December 1985).

14. Alan George, 'Libya', *Arab Industry Review* (1984).

15. Auditing Bureau, Tripoli, Libya.

16. Ibid.

17. Yusuf Sayigh, *The Economics of the Arab World: Development since 1945* (1978) calculates that plan fulfilment in 1968 was 63.2 per cent. A revised and updated assessment can be found in Maja Naur, *The Industrialisation Model of the Socialist People's Libyan Jamahiriya*, paper presented to the 1981 SOAS conference on Economic and Social Development of Libya.

18. J. Bearman, *Arabia* (October, 1985). Claims that Libya expelled foreign workers to hit at the economies of neighbouring states have little foundation. Moves towards the repatriation of migrants had been building up for several

months. More details can be seen in J. Bearman, 'The Exodus from Libya', 1985, private paper.

19. *Jamahiriyah International Report*, vol. 1, no. 22 (4 March 1983).

20. Adotey Bing, 'Harnessing Desert Waters', *Africa* (June 1985).

21. Terisa Turner, 'More Water than the Nile', interview with Dohali Migharief, *Middle East* (April 1986).

22. A. Allan, 1981, *Libya: The Experience of Oil* (Croom Helm / Westview, London, 1981) p. 244. The move towards land distribution in the coastal strip areas only occurred after considerable delay and deliberation. Studies were commissioned for this part of the country much later than elsewhere. Much of the 1981–85 agricultural budget was devoted to land re-distribution rather than capital investment.

23. R. First, *Libya: The Elusive Revolution*, 1974, p. 251.

24. *JIR* (February 1984). Qadhafi's speech to the Arab Conference on Workers' Culture contains some of his most revealing comments about the role of the working class. For instance, calling on workers to overthrow the capitalist system in their country, he declared: 'All forms of material wealth in any society are attributable to workers' effort. Nonetheless, they are the most oppressed section of society because they give away their effort to their employers.' It was the task of revolutionaries, said Qadhafi, to make workers conscious that 'what is called profit' is, in reality, 'the stolen effort of the workers'.

25. Correspondence with Secretariat of Information, Tripoli; further details in Birks, S. and Sinclair, C. *Arab Manpower: The Crisis of Development* (Croom Helm, London, 1980). Chapter on Libya.

26. *MEED* (17 August 1985).

15 The Qadhafi Factor

The role of Muammar Qadhafi is likely to be just as pivotal in the future as it has been in the past. No account of the Libyan revolution could be complete without due appraisal of his importance. Developments in Libya are not simply the product of particular objective conditions; the subjective factor of Qadhafi has vital bearing on the nature of events. Try to diminish that role and it becomes impossible to explain why things happened in the way they did. There was no historical necessity for Libya to have developed along the radical path that it has. Different circumstances present different choices, but there is no reason that the ones adopted should be the only ones open to action. Qadhafi operates within objective conditions, but he also changes them. The pursuit of Arab unity, the instigation of the cultural revolution, the creation of the jamahiriya system, the inauguration of the revolutionary committee movement and the programme of militarisation – on all these issues the subjective factor of Qadhafi's leadership has been decisive. Nothing was inevitable about the policies that have characterised Libyan development. Much has depended on the preferences of one man, and his continuing success in determining policy. Such is Qadhafi's position within the Libyan political system that his sudden removal from the scene, through death or deposition, could precipitate a major breakdown within the power structure and process of decision-making.

In backward countries, the function of leadership is more critical than in advanced states. In advanced states, political decisions are mediated through developed institutions; the legitimacy of the leadership rests on these institutions. In the Third World, a leader cannot derive legitimacy from political institutions inherited from his predecessors because the institutions are not in themselves legitimised. Third World societies are in transition from pre-national political forms to the nation-state structure. The mass of the population retain allegiances to tribal and religious interests, which have a direct intermediary role in their daily lives. The state institutions, lacking in popular endorsement, are usually unstable and bureaucratic. The most enduring institution is that of the armed forces, guardians of the state. In the more backward states, it has become axiomatic that access to power lies through the barrack rooms. No military leader, however, can simply rely on the armed forces to establish his legitimacy. Legitimacy can only be gained through achievements. Without these achievements, such a leader has a tenuous existence, doomed to life in the shadow of past triumphs and events.

These are the conditions confronting Qadhafi. The demands placed on his capabilities are, therefore, far greater than those imposed on the capabilities of leaders in advanced states. He cannot rely on the institutions of state to initiate political action, but must resort to direct intervention. His speeches assume a significance greater than those of political leaders in the more developed world. In a speech, Qadhafi must conciliate, argue and provide hope. Quite often at a rally Qadhafi will respond to questions, and digress from his speech as the occasion demands. Circumstances have made it necessary that Qadhafi, who initially made few public pronouncements or appearances, master communication techniques. Western observers fail to realise that his 'unpredictability' can sometimes be an asset; in the conditions of Libya, a leader must think on his feet, incite or retract according to circumstances that can change equally unpredictably. Faced with disputes in the people's congresses, he goes from one person to another, to cajole, teach, harangue, and offer personal assurances to different interests, such as the farmers, students, womens' groups, or the Islamic Call society. Television and radio are deployed to ensure that his speeches and actions gain the widest coverage. The talents of the Beduoin headman have been transported into the age of the electronic revolution.

Qadhafi's legitimacy rests on a record of revolutionary achievement. His leadership has secured a profound social and political transformation that continues until this day. Libya has been created in fact from a name on the map. His popularity is not purely the result of a more equitable distribution of income. Besides a significant rise in Libyan living standards, there are important political victories to his credit – the monarchy overthrown, the British and American bases ousted, the Italian settlers expelled, a unitary and participatory political system developed, the capitalist class expropriated, and landownership abolished. Such actions, loathed in the ruling circles of the West, can, in a country with a history of national oppression, turn a leader into a popular hero. That is what happened in Egypt with Gamal Abdul Nasser, and what has happened in Libya with Qadhafi. More than anything, the adversity of the West has helped to mobilise internal political support for Qadhafi. His metamorphosis into an anti-hero in the West has elevated his prestige in the eyes of the Libyan masses. Whole sections of Libyan society – peasants downtrodden under the West's client, the Sanussi regime, the urban poor deprived of jobs and houses in a country with abundant oil revenues – gain vicarious pleasure from Qadhafi's assertion of Libyan power and identity. In a country that formerly suffered foreign domination, Qadhafi's anti-imperialism has proved enduringly popular.

Around Qadhafi there has developed something of a personality cult. What this phenomenon is must be clearly understood. For some commentators it is evidently a matter of attributes and proclivities: Qadhafi's sojourns in the desert, the Bedouin tent where he conducts business in Bab al-Azzizya barracks, his austere lifestyle, his preference for a female bodyguard. These are of course aspects of Qadhafi's image, but it is wrong to assume they are simply affectations with no other significance. Qadhafi is, after all, a genuine son of the desert, and there is no reason not to believe that he is most at ease among Bedouin people.

The issue of image, however, misses the purpose of personality cult. Certainly, Qadhafi promotes his image, but the basis of his personality cult is the concept of political infallibility. The assertion that the Third Universal Theory, authored by Qadhafi, provides the ultimate solution to the problems of humanity lies at the heart of the personality cult. The cult therefore derives from an ideological basis, and functions as underpinning to the political system. Through his own personality Qadhafi provides an identity for the state; his frugal lifestyle, the female bodyguard, even the tent in the barracks are symbols of the Jamahiriya. The cult is a reflection of his position at the focal point of political relationships in Libya.

It is because of Qadhafi's location within the political structure that his own foibles and qualities are important. His weaknesses, like his strengths, can affect both internal and external developments. Given to rumination and solitude, Qadhafi can sometimes become inaccessible and reclusive. By temperament he has always been impulsive. Some of his initiatives, including foreign excursions, have been launched on an impromptu basis, following consultation with just a few aides. His visit to Tunisia in January 1982 was arranged at a moment's notice. When Qadhafi instigated the Cultural Revolution in 1973, or the Islamic Revolution in 1978, there was no real prior indication of his intentions. The element of spontaneity can be an important counter to bureaucratic ossification in Third World states, but the shifts and turns pronounced from above have, over a period of time, eroded credibility in the policy being pursued at any time. In all revolutions there is a need for changes of direction, but the emotional volatility of Qadhafi, his restless nature, can generate an atmosphere of uncertainty. Driven by ideals, he apprehends the world in idealist terms, and is not always the most realistic of people, especially with regard to what can be achieved. He is creative, but not practical. He has the ability to embark on initiatives but not to follow them through to completion. His frustration when he encounters political set-backs can boil over into fits of anger. In fact, despite the personality cult, Qadhafi is very much a fallible human being.

He is also a paradox, a man who is both a radical and a conservative. Whilst he has been largely responsible for the break up of traditional political forms and kinship relations, no one in Libya is more committed to the preservation of traditional tribal values and cultural forms than Qadhafi. At the February 1985 General People's Congress, he urged endorsement of a law on public ethics, carrying penalties for those who transgress its code of behaviour.[1] According to Qadhafi, the purpose of the law was 'to alert people to adhere to good manners, so that this in future would become part of our traditional behaviour and so that bad manners would not become our traditional behaviour'. Those convicted of 'acts of violation of honour' would forfeit their membership of the people's congresses and the right to hold office. Qadhafi similarly regards personal appearance as important. When out of uniform, he takes pride in wearing Libyan traditional dress. Unhappy with the ubiquitous western suit, the familiar hallmark of Arab officialdom, he has sponsored the creation of clothes factories which produce Libyan dress. Libyan youth are encouraged not to abandon their Arab heritage; and drugs, like alcohol, remain taboo – the signs of a decadent society. For entertainment Qadhafi promotes the indigenous Libyan folk arts and, in particular, equestrianism. Most sports in fact are sponsored. He himself rides and plays football for recreation. Whilst admiring western technology, Qadhafi eschews western-style commercialism. Libya is one of the few countries in the world where tourism is discouraged.

Earnest in his Muslim faith, Qadhafi's earthly joys are primarily domestic. Qadhafi is a public man who had kept a private life. Divorced from an earlier marriage, in 1970 he married Safia, a professional nurse. Together they have had seven children, six boys and a girl.[2] The family live in simple accommodation in the married quarters of Bab al-Azizya barracks. In the earlier years of the marriage, Safia appears to have had no public role, but latterly she has taken on minor duties and engagements. In March 1981 she accompanied Qadhafi on his visit to Vienna, and in March 1984 she carried a message to Indira Gandhi on her husband's behalf.[3] She also pays private visits abroad, but unlike the wives of many Arab leaders there is no evidence that she is extravagent in her buying habits. Likewise, the Qadhafi children are not sent to private schools abroad, but attend a local state school in Tripoli.

Qadhafi's enemies are always asking how much longer he can survive. It is a question which defies a clear-cut answer. Now aged 44, Qadhafi could go on in his present capacity for another 30 years. He could equally well be gunned down tomorrow. He has already been the target of some six assassination attempts, and has survived at least four planned *coups d'état*. The fact that he has endured indicates that his position is still strong, though there are reports that the strain in recent years, particularly since the growth of the opposition movement, is beginning to take its toll on his health. Following the commando attack on Bab al-Azizya barracks in May 1984, he was reported to be taking a considerable number of sleeping pills, which were affecting his concentration. There is, however, no sign, beyond the threat of assassination, that his leadership is generating mass opposition. Obviously, the growth of unrest cannot be ruled out as economic problems increase, but even an upsurge of opposition would not in itself imply the overthrow of his revolution.

When speculating on Qadhafi's future there is a possibility, often obscured, that should be considered. With the passage of time, Qadhafi could increasingly become just a figure-head leader; his interventions could decline. It is quite plausible that, in conditions of a political crisis, Qadhafi could be ousted from within by the Revolutionary Committee Movement, without being formally removed from his post as leader of the revolution. Mao in China, it should be recalled, survived some serious errors of judgement, lost his control on government, but retained his position as Chairman until death. So monolithic is the Libyan political structure that intervention by the revolutionary committees is the one mechanism that exists to bring about bloodless change at the top.

Another question asked is how will Qadhafi go down in history. Interpretations will, of course, vary. Judged on his own terms, Qadhafi has been astoundingly successful. Consider that, in 1959, whilst a schoolboy in a remote desert town, he pledged himself to bring the Arab nationalist revolution to Libya. He formed his own Nasserist group, infiltrated the army, built up a junior officers' movement and overthrew the monarchy; and he has sustained the revolution for sixteen years in the face of tremendous odds and in confrontation with the strongest military power in the world. That is a staggering achievement, and Qadhafi's successors, when their time comes, will have to live under his shadow for many years.

Notes

1. BBC SWB ME/7842/A/1 (7 January 1985).
2. Vanya Kewley, 'Deserts Teach You to Rely on Yourself', *Sunday Times* (10 February 1985).
3. *Jamahiriya Review* (April 1984).

16 The Bombing of Libya: Reagan's War with Qadhafi

On Tuesday, 15 April 1986, at 2 am Libyan time, aircraft from the United States' Air Force and Navy struck at six main targets in the vicinity of Tripoli and Benghazi. It was the first military intervention launched by the United States since the 1983 invasion of Grenada, and represented a dramatic escalation of the confrontation between the Reagan administration and the Libyan leadership. According to US official figures, a total of 36 people were killed; journalists in the Libyan capital, however, estimated that there were over 100 dead and twice as many wounded.[1] Among the known casualties were members of Qadhafi's own family; his wife Safia, and three of the couple's children suffered pressure shock from the blast of a 2,000lb bomb which hit their accommodation. Seriously injured, the three children were rushed to hospital. Hours later, Qadhafi's sixteen-month-old adopted daughter, Hanna, died from brain damage. Two sons, Saef al-Islam and Khamees, aged three and four, remained in intensive care for several days.[2] Qadhafi, who had taken the precaution of sleeping in an underground office, survived physically unhurt but emotionally shaken.

Justifying the air raid, the Reagan administration linked the operation with the bombing, on 5 April 1986, of La Belle discotheque in West Berlin. The explosion at La Belle killed one American soldier and injured 60 others. The Reagan administration cited Libyan involvement in the attack and, to provide a legal cover for retaliation, claimed self-defence against further acts of terrorism against United States personnel. White House officials stressed that the targets of the raid were only terrorist installations. In a televised address, Reagan himself declared:

> My fellow Americans, at 7 o'clock this evening, Eastern time, air and naval forces of the United States launched a series of strikes against the headquarters, terrorist facilities and military assets that support Muammer Qadhafi's subversive activities.[3]

Contrary to the impression given by American spokesmen, not least by the President himself, the weight of the evidence indicates a powerful military assault on the apparatus of the Libyan state. The targets of the operation did not correspond with the qualification 'terrorist installation' or 'infrastructure';[4] all were key points in Qadhafi's system of command, communications and control. They were: Qadhafi's headquarters and command centre at Bab al-Azizya; his alternative command post, and the base of the Islamic Legion, at the Jamahiriya Barracks outside Benghazi; the headquarters of the Security Service in central Tripoli; Sidi Bilal naval base and academy to the east of Tripoli; and the country's two main airports, Tripoli and Benina, near Benghazi. In addition, there was a series of supplementary strikes against signals and radar installations. White House spokesman Larry Speakes termed the strikes against these secondary targets a 'defense suppression mission'.[5]

There is even evidence to support the view that Qadhafi was himself a target of the operation. Reagan's claim that 'we were not out to kill anybody' is amply contradicted by members of his own staff. It has emerged from sources within the administration that the bombing of Bab al-Azizya Barracks, in the first wave of a two-wave attack, was undertaken in the hope of resulting in Qadhafi's elimination. Even before the administration had received knowledge of Qadhafi's fate, officials of the National Security Council had drafted a statement describing his death as 'fortuitous'.[6] According to one administration advisor, intimately involved in the planning stages of the operation, 'We hoped to get him. But nobody knew his whereabouts'.[7]

Despite the failure to locate Qadhafi, his downfall remained the principle objective of the US action. The bombings were meant to produce tensions within the Libyan armed forces, prompting discontented officers into an attempted *coup d'état*. Hinting that a military uprising was the objective, the US Secretary of State George Shultz, the architect of the raid, told reporters on 17 April, that the targets were selected to leave an 'impression' on the Libyan military hierarchy.[8] Asked if his statement implied that the United States was trying to overthrow the Libyan leader, he replied that a *coup* would be 'all to the good.'[9] Moreover, another un-named source within the administration has disclosed that the action was designed to 'convince senior officers of the folly of Colonel Qadhafi's policy.'[10] The attacks on Qadhafi's system of command and communications were launched primarily to create an opportunity for his officer opponents.

Work on a strategy for overthrowing Qadhafi had been proceeding in Washington for many months. The bombing of Libya was the climax in a sequence of events beginning – paradoxically – with a terrorist incident for which the White House has claimed no Libyan involvement. This was the hijacking of TWA flight 847 to Beirut by Shiite gunmen in June 1985. The incident was one of the rare occasions when the US public was directly exposed to the violence of the Middle East. For 17 days, under the gaze of the international media, 29 Americans were held hostage. The Reagan administration, unable to intervene with any prospect of success, suffered a humiliating blow to its prestige; but more importantly, the TWA hijacking brought into public scrutiny, and started to undermine, the US strategic relationship with Israel.

The principal demand of the hijackers was the release of Shiite prisoners held by Israel. The Israeli authorities, through their refusal to concede, antagonised broad sections of the US public. An ABC poll taken in two samples, one on 17 June and another on 19 June, showed that 54 per cent of Americans felt that Israel had *not* 'done what it should'.[11] Moreover, the poll revealed that 32 per cent believed that the US 'should reduce its ties to Israel in order to lessen acts of terrorism against the US in the Middle East'; by 30 June the figure had risen to 42 per cent.[12] Hijacking Americans had evidently become a potent weapon against the Washington-Tel Aviv axis.

After the TWA hijacking, the Reagan administration resolved to strengthen its position in the Middle East and nullify any gains made by its Arab adversaries. The US conflict with Libya, despite Tripoli's condemnation of 'terrorism against civilians', suddenly found fresh impetus. As Lou Cannon and Bob Woodward of the *Washington Post* reported, from discussions with officials in the administration just three days after the bombing of Libya:

> Sources said it was the TWA hijacking that brought anti-Libyan and anti-terrorist policies together. The secret planning led to a number of military options in which Libya was increasingly singled out as the main target, even though several other nations, notably Syria and Iran, were also considered to be centres of terrorism.

The plans included a CIA covert operation to undermine Colonel Qadhafi and contingency planning with Egypt for a possible US-Egyptian attack on Libya.[13]

Until the TWA incident, US strategy against Libya had been on the back burner for nearly two years. The killing, on 23 October 1983 in Lebanon, of 241 US marines by a suicide truck bomber not only precipitated an American withdrawal from Lebanon, but deterred further US engagement in the region. In the words of one long-standing associate of the American President: 'Reagan took that catastrophe hard even though the invasion of Grenada next week softened some of its impact. It began to change his thinking.'[14] Indeed, following the disaster Reagan was disinclined to endorse plans for a militarily active US role in the region. Briefly, he persisted with a programme of covert action, but in March 1985 cancelled further operations, following damaging evidence of CIA involvement in a plot to assassinate Hezballah leader Hussein Fadlallah, which led to the deaths of 80 Lebanese civilians.[15]

Within the Republican administration there were always those who wished to restore confidence by some kind of a show-down with Arab adversaries of the United States. Perhaps the most important protagonist was George Shultz, an ex-marine profoundly angered by the massacre of marines in Beirut. Following the carnage in Beirut he consistently pressed for the military prosecution of Arab resistance to US designs.[16] Initially rebuffed, he found his position enormously strengthened after the TWA hijacking. On the US right there developed a clamour for reprisals. The incident gave fresh impetus to that coalition of forces – the Zionist lobbies,

West Coast business interests and Republican militarists – who were originally responsible for the earlier confrontation between Libya and the United States. Reagan, sensitive to pressure from these quarters, eventually came round to accepting Shultz's case for a more active military role in the Middle East. In July the shift was symbolised by Reagan's notorious 'misfits and loony-tunes' speech, in which he denounced five so-called 'terrorist states' – Iran, Libya, North Korea, Cuba and Nicaragua.

During the period of American abeyance, Libya's position in the region began to improve. Most importantly, Libya's strategic and political situation was enhanced by the overthrow of President Jaafar Numeiri in April 1985. Sudan's 'spring revolution', bringing to power a Transitional Military Council under General Sowar al-Dahab, removed Qadhafi's most persistent and implacable opponent in the Arab world. The Libyan leadership was quick to take full advantage of the change; Libya became the first state to recognise the new provisional government, and responded to overtures for reconciliation by sending to Khartoum a 40-strong delegation led by Jalloud.[17] There followed, in rapid succession, a series of agreements in which Libya formally ended support for opposition forces in Sudan, including the Sudanese People's Liberation Army of Colonel John Garang, and provided limited material aid for the reconstruction of the Sudanese economy. In exchange, the Sudanese military government expelled from the country Libyan opposition organisations, notably the Salvation Front, which eventually transferred its headquarters to distant Iraq. By June, the time of the TWA hijacking, relations had improved to the extent that both Sudan and Libya had entered into limited forms of military co-operation.[18]

Numeiri's decline and fall accentuated the vulnerability of US allies in the region. Among the Gulf states, the conservative pro-western leaderships began to acquire doubts about the reliability of US protection in the face of Iranian advances in the Gulf war. Two countries, the United Arab Emirates and Oman, symbolically distanced themselves by establishing diplomatic relations with Moscow. Meanwhile, in Egypt, President Hosni Mubarak was also coming under domestic pressure to adopt a more independent and assertive line in foreign policy. Within the region in general there began to emerge a crisis of confidence in United States' willingness to act in defence of its Arab allies.

The outcome of this celebrated 'declaration of war on terrorism' was an immediate escalation of violence in the Middle East. Four incidents in particular had an important bearing on the shaping of US policy towards Libya:

1. On 1 October, the Israelis bombed the PLO headquarters just outside Tunis, killing at least 73 people;
2. Between 7 and 9 October, four members of a Palestine Liberation Front (PLF) faction headed by Abu Abbas held up the Italian cruise liner *Achille Lauro*, and demanded the release of several Palestinian prisoners;

3. On 24 November, a group called Egypt's Revolution hijacked an Egyptair flight to Malta;
4. And on 27 December, members of the Palestinian Revolutionary Brigades, the military wing of al-Fateh Revolutionary Council, led by Abu Nidal, carried out simultaneous attacks on El Al passengers at the terminals of Rome and Vienna airports, in which 15 people, including four attackers, died.

Washington utilised each of these incidents to expand its intervention in the region and prepare public opinion for an ultimate clash with Libya. The Israeli air strike against Tunis provided the administration with a precedent and model of long-range military action. The first US military intervention, based on the exercise of air power, followed during the *Achille Lauro* affair: on 10 October, after the Egyptian government had granted the hijackers free passage out of its territory, US jets intercepted, and forced down the plane carrying them to Sigonella airbase in Sicily. In the case of the subsequent Egyptair hijacking by Egypt's Revolution the administration implied Libyan sponsorship and tried to encourage Egyptian military action against Libya. Finally, in response to the Rome and Vienna attacks, Washington built on claims of Libyan involvement to authorise a new period of heightened confrontation with Libya.

Libya's guilt was largely pre-determined. The Reagan administration failed to provide any tangible evidence of the Libyan state's involvement in either the hijacking of the Egyptair liner, or the Rome and Vienna airport killings. Libyan responsibility was imputed by links with Palestinian rejectionist leaders, in the first instance with Abu Maizer, a member of the PLO Executive, independent of any specific group, but aligned with the Salvation Front; and in the second instance, with Abu Nidal, whose military organisation had limited access to a training ground south of Tripoli. No corroboration was forthcoming.

William Casey's CIA has seemed remarkably unconcerned to publish or release exact information about the nature of Libya's relationships with Palestinian organisations. If the Agency was to do so, it would most probably undermine the case for confrontation with the Libyan leadership. What evidence is available indicates that the Libyan state is unable to control or direct Palestinian organisations. In 1984 a Libyan initiative to group Palestinian and Arab opposition organisations within the framework of a Pan-Arab National Command proved only partially successful. The organisations affiliated to the Command retain a wide degree of autonomy; most organisations remain supplicants of Libyan aid. Whilst occasional trade-offs occur, few Arab organisations associated with Libya could be called puppets. The majority of Palestinian rejectionist organisations are based in the Syrian capital, Damascus, and maintain their military camps in Lebanon's Beqaa Valley.

In building their case against Libya the Reagan administration published, in January 1986, a document entitled 'Libya Under Qadhafi: A Pattern of Aggression'.[19] Listing alleged acts of violence under Qadhafi's leadership, the document, described as a 'State Department study', claimed that the Libyan leader uses terrorism 'as one of the primary instruments of his foreign policy,' but cited not one example of violence against US citizens beyond the 1979 sacking of the US Embassy in Tripoli in the mass protests against President Carter's policy towards Iran. Despite repeated statements about Libyan 'hit squads' in the United States, the study fails to provide one instance of any substance to back up the allegations.

Libya did not become the object of US military aggression because it posed a serious threat to the strategic interests of the Reagan administration. It was chosen because it was the weakest and easiest of US adversaries to attack. Despite huge arms purchases, and a programme of military mobilisation, the country's military capacity remains limited. Due to shortages of manpower and technically qualified personnel, Libya's naval and air strike capabilities are considerably below what the armaments statistics would otherwise suggest. Whilst the Libyan air force has, on paper, 535 military aircraft, it is estimated that only half are currently combat-worthy.[20] The SAM-5s which the Libyan army installed after the 1981 clash in the Gulf of Sirte are of Vietnam war vintage, and have become increasingly ineffective against the electronic systems currently utilised by fighter-bombers. Thus, American military forces are in a position to carry out an operation against Libya without incurring extensive casualties. Libya's defences could be easily overwhelmed and the only way the leadership could retaliate would be through isolated terrorist actions, on foreign soil, which would further assist the US goal of isolating the country.

Two events in the second half of 1985 accentuated the country's vulnerability to foreign aggression. The first was the repatriation of 35,000 migrant workers, the majority from Egypt and Tunisia. In response, President Mubarak accused the Libyan leadership of trying to sabotage the Egyptian economy, and Tunisia broke off diplomatic relations, precipitating border mobilisations by the two sides. The second development was the renewed friction between Libya and France over Chad. Prior to the Franco-African summit conference in Paris in December 1985 the French government had begun to deploy troops south of the 16th parallel, the line separating the forces of Goukouni Ouaddai and Hissene Habre: Libya had reacted by threatening to increase its own military contingent north of the line and, in February 1986, fighting erupted with a new offensive by Goukouni.[21] To halt his advance the French air force bombed an airfield built and used by Libya at Ouedi Doun.[22] Libya in turn struck back with a single Sukoi bomber, which emptied its load on N'jdamena airport. However, the tension eventually subsided with Qadhafi deciding to exercise restraint towards the insurgent Goukouni.[23]

One further factor increasing the country's military exposure was the outbreak of a power struggle within the leadership. In the Autumn, friction had arisen between Qadhafi and several military commanders. At the time, the Revolutionary Committee Movement, with Qadhafi's apparent blessing, was engaged in a campaign to eradicate the privileges enjoyed by Army officers, including special supermarkets, priority housing, access to foreign exchange and exit visas for foreign travel. The Committee also organised a crackdown on the blackmarketeering and smuggling rackets run by military officers. As a result, morale within the officer corps slumped and disaffection began to surface. By August, following the diplomatic strains with Egypt and Tunisia, there were signs that the dissent was beginning to take an organised form. Some units refused to mobilise along the Tunisian border, and Hassan Eskhal, Commander of the Central Military Region, and a cousin of Qadhafi's married to an Egyptian, tried to lead an Egyptian-backed military uprising.[24] However, his bid for power was of short duration and he was killed, reputedly at Bab al-Azizya, having gone there to confront Qadhafi with some kind of ultimatum.

A final theme in the renewed policy of confrontation with Libya was provided by the long-standing desire to disrupt the country's economic ties with Europe. The current Republican administration, influenced by, if not sharing, the concerns of conservative foreign policy 'think-tanks', has consistently sought to prevent Western European states, especially West Germany, from purchasing their supplies of raw materials from areas outside the sphere of United States' global control. Whilst almost an anomaly in the Third World, Libya is just such an example of a strategically important trading partner which operates independently of United States' power. Unlike Mexico and Venezuela, it is not dependent on the United States-centred financial and commercial system: unlike Saudi Arabia and the smaller Gulf states, its territorial integrity and the survival of its political regime are not guaranteed by the exercise of United States' military power.

Libya's strategic ally is the Soviet Union. Whilst there are tensions in the two states' relations, it is Soviet-supplied arms and military technology, whatever their limits, which underwrite the endurance of the Libyan state apparatus. Trade with Libya therefore reduces the dependence of European states on the exercise and dominance of US military force, whilst providing foreign exchange in the form of dollars to a country aligned with the Soviet Union. To the Reagan administration this has become an unacceptable and harmful practice. Were the process to continue, and were other Third World states allied to the Soviet Union to become key trading partners of Western Europe and Japan, the importance of US military power to both NATO countries and Far Eastern states would gradually decline.

It was Western Europe which provided the real battleground in the US conflict with Libya. The Reagan administration utilised the terrorist attacks at Rome and Vienna airports in an attempt to shift Western European states away from trade with Libya. In early January 1986 the Reagan administration began exerting pressure on its allies in Europe to join in a trade embargo against Libya. Their peremptory refusals brought strong criticism from the United States. Reagan's former National Security

Advisor, Robert MacFarlane, described the European rejections of the administration's call for sanctions as 'indefensible', and said it was time to be a 'little bit more firm' in putting the American official view. He added that it was 'a slack time in the oil market and the European countries could 'easily get oil from other sources.'[25]

In the absence of European compliance, the administration's decision to impose a unilateral trade ban, announced on 8 January 1986, was rendered merely symbolic. Before the embargo was implemented, the administration had already used up most of its economic leverage in regard to Libya. Not only had the administration stopped the trade in crude oil and technology in March 1982; in 1985 the ban had been extended to include refined oil products, principally to exclude petrochemicals from the American market.

US oil companies were adequately placed to overcome the more serious aspects of the full trade ban. The five companies – Amerada Hess, Continental, Grace, Marathon and Occidental – were left with the option of using European subsidiaries formally to take over operations and assets in Libya. The presidential order for a withdrawal of US personnel from Libya was more difficult to get round, but Tripoli partially countered the move by doubling the salaries of US oilmen, who were already earning an average of $100,000 per annum. This proved a sufficient incentive to keep many oilmen in Libya, despite the threat of imprisonment and heavy fines in the United States.[26] At the same time, the oil companies were able to replace those who did leave with staff from other countries, including Britain, recruited on an individual basis by such agencies as the UK-based Jawaby Oil Service.[27] Even President Reagan's decision, on 8 January, to freeze Libyan assets in the United States proved to be something of a damp squib; the Libyan authorities had pre-empted the President's move by liquidating most of their assets in the United States, so that by January 1986 there remained no more than an estimated $400 million from total foreign asset holdings of about $27 billion.[28]

To compensate for the weakness of the unilateral trade measures, the administration tried to draw Qadhafi into an armed confrontation, hoping the atmosphere of heightened tension would force the European states into line. Plans for a military operation, code-named 'Prairie Fire', were put into motion. In January 1986 the Sixth Fleet was ordered to begin the first of a series of provocative exercises off the Libyan coast. Altogether, the administration proceeded to hold three sets of manoeuvres, the first in the last week of January, the second in the second week of February, and the third in the third week of March.[29] Qadhafi, facing a loss of prestige in the eyes of his own following, reacted to the third announcement of exercises with a declaration that his country would defend a 'line of death' across the 32nd parallel, which delineates Libyan–claimed territory in the Gulf of Sirte.[30] With the credibility of both sides at stake, the result was a military clash greater in scale than the brush between the Fleet and the Libyan airforce in 1981.

When, on 24 March 1986, US naval aircraft from Sixth Fleet carriers flew across the 'line of death', a Libyan corvette began moving towards the edge of the Gulf. The Sixth Fleet responded by sending up aircraft and attacking the vessel. Soon after, a patrol boat, which came to pick up survivors, was also struck. In retaliation, Qadhafi ordered the firing at the US aircraft of six SAM-5 missiles from Ghurdibiyah missile station near Sirte. The Sixth Fleet hit back with the bombing of the Ghurdibiyah base, and the next day there were sorties against two further Libyan naval vessels and the apparently still functioning radar system of the missile station.[31] There was then a pause in the hostilities, as Qadhafi decided not to risk further forces.

Unable to match the United States with conventional forces, the Libyan leadership allegedly pursued the option of selective attacks on American military targets abroad. The security service in Tripoli is reported to have sent coded instructions to several people's bureaux ordering them to prepare to undertake operations against United States' military targets.[32] One such message was allegedly received by the People's Bureau to East Germany in East Berlin; on receiving it, the security staff at the bureau felt licensed to proceed with a terrorist operation against American servicemen in West Berlin. A bomb duly exploded at La Belle's discotheque, a venue frequented by American servicemen, on 5 April; the blast killed two and injured 204 others.[33] The day before the operation, the bureau in East Berlin had reportedly sent a cable to Tripoli telling the security authorities that they would 'be very happy when you see the headlines tomorrow'.[34] A second message, despatched within minutes of the blast, reportedly said that an operation was 'happening now'.

Through the interception of the coded messages the United States' administration was able to blame the bombing of the La Belle discotheque on the Libyan authorities. Reagan claimed that the cables were 'irrefutable' proof of 'Libyan involvement'.[36] The White House, however, has never clarified the nature of the involvement. In fact, the administration was highly reluctant to publish the full text of the cables. The official reason given for this reticence was national security; journalists were told that the United States did not want to reveal its intelligence sources. Another, perhaps more important, motive was the administration's evident desire to obscure the wording of the cables. At a time when the White House was trying to demonstrate Qadhafi's sponsorship of terrorism, none of the messages provided 'irrefutable' proof of involvement on the part of the Libyan leadership. Sources within the administration, and a West German translation of the cables testify that the Libyan leadership did not authorise the bombing, or specify the target.[37] President Reagan merely inferred the responsibility of the Libyan leadership from evidence his advisors knew to be ambiguous.

Using the pretext of Libyan involvement, the Reagan administration once again began to exert pressure on the Kohl government in Bonn to introduce trade measures against Libya.[38] 'The US has asked West Germany to impose economic and political sanctions on Libya after claiming Libyan involvement in the discotheque bomb attack', reported the *Times* on 9 April. The same day, Bonn responded to the administration's overtures with the expulsion of two Libyan diplomats, but held out against a trade embargo. Washington was left irritated and dissatisfied with the lack of deference shown by a key European ally whose co-operation was essential to the policy of breaking trade ties with Libya. Failure to gain the compliance of the Kohl government, or that of any other European administration, convinced the White House that a further escalation of the military confrontation was required. The bombing of Tripoli and Benghazi followed five days later, Washington's reply to the resistance and obduracy of its allies.

There is no doubt that the operation has produced some tangible gains for the administration. Whilst there is virtually no support for the United States' action among the Libyan population, the raid has weakened Qadhafi's position within Libya. His own following has become increasingly factionalised; divisions relating to both personalities and political direction have surfaced within the Revolutionary Committee Movement.[39] Moreover, the bombing has heightened the friction between the revolutionary committees and the army; the people's militia and the army; and some sections of the revolutionary committees and the people's militia.[40] Following the raid there were reports of in-fighting between revolutionary committee supporters of Jalloud and Qadhafi, arising from Jalloud's assumption of effective control during the hours following the bombing of Bab al-Azizya and Qadhafi's temporary incapacitation.

To restore his authority within the state apparatus Qadhafi has been forced to concede the re-introduction of a broader-based leadership. Two weeks after the bombings, he re-convened the Revolutionary Command Council from its five remaining members – apart from himself, Jalloud, Hamidi, Kharoubi and Younis Jaber.[41] Together the five have become known as the 'historic leadership'. Bound by personal ties and common interests the five generally accept Qadhafi's supreme position, but there are differences over the form of leadership. Jalloud is in favour of a more formal collective leadership with effective collective powers. He is backed by the Soviet Union, through its ambassador to Tripoli, Oleg Peresidkin, and is reputed to have strong support within the administration and oil industry. During a visit to Moscow in late May 1986 the Soviet leadership appeared to endorse Jalloud. However, the option of a broad-based leadership is being resisted by Qadhafi and a number of his close advisors, namely Abdullah Ibrahami, Khalifa Khanaish, Abdul Hafez Massaoud and Said and Ahmed Qadhafadem. To counter Jalloud's ascendancy, the Qadhafi camp seems to be promoting the role of Khweildi al-Hamidi. (As far back as January, Hamidi was handling oil negotiations with Saudi Arabia – a task which normally falls within Jalloud's sphere of responsibility.)[42]

Leaving aside the question of domestic instability, there are a number of respects in which the bombing mission has failed the Reagan administration. Firstly, the ECC countries have not joined the economic boycott of Libya; they have merely responded by trying to placate Washington with cutbacks in Libyan diplomatic representation and the signing of a declaration against terrorism naming Libya as a sponsor. Secondly, West European oil companies, and their East European equivalents, seem poised to take advantage of the US economic withdrawal from Libya. Although US oil companies liquidated their Libyan assets by 30 June 1986, in line with a presidential directive, the Libyan National Oil Company (Linoco) has secured the co-operation of several European firms in maintaining production and overcoming restrictions on the procurement of US-made drilling equipment.[43] There is no guarantee that the difficulties can be surmounted, nor has the source of tension between the Reagan administration and its allied European governments been removed. If Qadhafi survives the current political turmoil and economic dislocation, Washington may soon face the choice of whether or not to escalate the conflict with Qadhafi's Libya.

Notes

1. For an eyewitness account of the destruction and reactions in Libya see Robert Fisk in the *Times*, 15, 16 and 17 April 1986.
2. *Times*, 15 April 1986.
3. *Times*, 16 April 1986.
4. The term 'terrorist infrastructure' was used by White House spokesman Larry Speakes, making the first official disclosure of the United States' military operation. See the *Times*, 15 April 1986.
5. *Times*, 15 April 1986.
6. George Wilson, 'Colonel "Was the Target"'. *Guardian*, 19 April 1986.
7. Wilson *Guardian*, 19 April 1986.
8. Christopher Thomas, 'Shultz Hoping for a Military Coup', *Times*, 19 April 1986.
9. Thomas, *Times*, 19 April 1986.
10. Claudia Wright, 'Reagan Draws the Line of Fire', *South* (May 1986) pp. 19–20.
11. Mohammed Shiraz, 'Buying Back Lives with Expensive Truths', *Arabia: Islamic World Review*, no. 48 (August 1985) pp. 35–6.
12. Shiraz, *Arabia* (August 1985) pp. 35–6.
13. Lou Cannon and Bob Woodward, 'Raid Called Outcome of Long Debate', *International Herald Tribune*, 17 April 1986.
14. Cannon and Woodward, *International Herald Tribune*, 17 April 1986.
15. Ibid.
16. Marcelino Komba, 'Precarious Initiatives', *Africa: The International Business, Economic and Political Magazine,* (June 1985) pp. 28–9.
17. Blaine Harden, *International Herald Tribune*, 17 March 1986 and 28 March 1986.
18. Cannon and Woodward, *International Herald Tribune*, 17 April 1986.
19. See Donald Neff, 'The Shift in US Policy that Threatens Disaster', *Middle East International*, no. 274 (2 May 1986) pp. 3–4.

20. See Richard Halloran, 'Libya's Military Is Weak by Middle East Standards', *International Herald Tribune,* 27 March 1986.

21. Jon Bearman, 'Tripoli Moves To Head Off a Showdown', *South* (February 1986) p. 25.

22. Michael Dobbs, *International Herald Tribune,* 17 February 1986 and 21 February 1986.

23. Michael Dobbs, *International Herald Tribune,* 18 February 1986.

24. See 'Libyan Colonel Dead', *Arabia: Islamic World Review,* vol. 5, no. 53 (January 1986) p. 13; and Andrew Lycett, 'Qadhafi's Great Escape,' *Middle East* (December 1985) p. 13.

25. Alex Brummer, 'US Condemns Allies' Inaction Rebuff', *Guardian,* 6 January 1986.

26. *Guardian,* 3 February 1986.

27. David Hawley, 'Libyan Sanctions–Reagan's Damp Squib', *MEED,* (18–24 January 1986) pp. 6–9.

28. Jon Bearman, 'Qadhafi Rides the US Punch', *South* (February 1986).

29. *International Herald Tribune,* 11 February 1986.

30. *International Herald Tribune,* 17 February 1986.

31. See *International Herald Tribune,* 25 March 1986 and 26 March 1986.

32. Bob Woodward, 'Cables Point to Gadafy Link', *Guardian,* 23 April 1986.

33. John Tagliabue, 'Woman, US Soldier Killed in Bombing at Berlin Nightclub', *International Herald Tribune,* 7 April 1986.

34. Bob Woodward, *Guardian,* 23 April 1986.

35. Ibid.

36. Woodward, *Guardian,* 23 April 1986; see also *Times,* 8 April 1986.

37. Woodward, *Guardian,* 23 April 1986.

38. *Times,* 9 April 1986.

39. Jon Bearman 'Return of the Historic Five', *South* (June 1986) p. 32.

40. One source of tension is Qadhafi's intention to install a contingent from the Revolutionary Committee Movement within the Army, primarily to ensure his security.

41. *Times,* 24 April 1986.

42. See David Hawley, 'OPEC Seeks a New Direction', *MEED* (1–7 February 1986) pp. 30–1.

43. See Michael White, *Guardian,* 25 April 1986.